GREAT LIVES IN BRIEF
A New Series of Biographies

ACCURACY
BREVITY · CLARITY
MULTUM
IN PARVO

HENRY FORD *by Roger Burlingame*

MAHATMA GANDHI *by Vincent Sheean*

ALEXANDRE DUMAS *by André Maurois*

HANS CHRISTIAN ANDERSEN *by Rumer Godden*

CHARLES DARWIN *by Ruth Moore*

JULIUS CÆSAR *by Alfred Duggan*

JAMES J. HILL *by Stewart Holbrook*

ELIZABETH I *by Donald Barr Chidsey*

NAPOLEON III *by Albert Guérard*

GILBERT STUART *by James Thomas Flexner*

These are BORZOI BOOKS
Published by ALFRED A. KNOPF *in New York*

JAMES J. HILL

James J. Hill

A GREAT LIFE IN BRIEF

BY

Stewart H. Holbrook

New York   ALFRED A. KNOPF   1955

L. C. catalog card number: 54–7220

© Stewart H. Holbrook, 1955

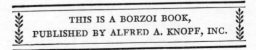

THIS IS A BORZOI BOOK,
PUBLISHED BY ALFRED A. KNOPF, INC.

FIRST EDITION

11417

JAMES J. HILL

I

IT IS SIGNIFICANT of James J. Hill's complex character that of two of the best remembered stories about him, one paints him as hero, the other as villain. Once, in a Dakota blizzard, when a section crew was trying to clear track for a stalled Great Northern passenger train, President Hill of the railroad came out to snatch the shovel from one man and send that bemused working stiff into the president's private car for hot coffee, while he himself shoveled snow as though driven by steam. One after the other, the gandy-dancers were spelled off and drank fine java in unaccustomed elegance while the Great Northern's creator and boss wielded a shovel. *That* was Jim Hill for you. Again, because the mayor of a small Minnesota town objected mildly to all-night switching in his village, Hill swore by God that its people should walk, then had the depot torn down and set up two miles away. That, too, was Jim Hill.

Hill may well have induced more European peasants to settle in the American West than any other man, and most of their daughters praised him for it, even while some of their sons cursed his memory by calling a particularly stubborn and harassing weed by the name of Jim Hill mustard.

That was the way it went with Jim Hill.

He has been termed the Commodore Vanderbilt of the West. It is not a sound analogy. Hill was an original. In his lifetime men called him the Little Giant and the Red River Pirate, and said that he desolated Minnesota, populated the Dakotas, made Montana a state, and stole Puget Sound. Others hailed him as the true prophet of Northern wheat, the friend of the farmer, the curse of homesteaders, the Oregon Bandit, the Empire Builder. He was each and all of those things, a legend while he lived, a legend still in death—and death came during the First World War. The measured critical writing on the man is yet so meager that it seems improbable that a fair estimate of his character will be made.

What he accomplished, however, is not vague. It can be measured in part by the thousands of miles of railroad that he built or acquired, the millions of acres homesteaded at his call, and by the fifty-three millions of dollars he bequeathed to his heirs or to good works. When Hill died, his empire ranged unbroken from the Canadian border to Missouri and Colorado, from the Great Lakes to Puget Sound and Oregon.

One of Hill's appealing qualities, which many think were somewhat limited, was that he was not an emperor whose knowledge of his realm came solely from his agents and captains. When the Great Northern's number-one train whistles for Sauk Center or Fargo

or Wolf Point or Whitefish or Bonners Ferry or
Wenatchee, on its way two thousand miles across the
top of the United States, the echoes scarcely find a
stark butte or a mountain valley that Jim Hill himself
did not know at first hand.

One who has been riding the Hill Lines for many
years is likely to fancy that in them one finds certain
qualities of Jim Hill the man. By this is meant the
land and the climate and the very towns and stations
of this now spectacular, now monotonous, but usually handsome, harsh, desolate, wild, and bitter region. There is forlorn little Malta, an angry sun beating down, baking the false-fronts, roasting the soil,
while dust clouds roll up from behind the Western
Star or the Empire Builder . . . Or Havre at night,
snapping from cold, coyotes howling within sound
of the roundhouse . . . Or the glittering hill that
is Butte at evening, seen from the Northern Pacific's
Limited as she comes out of the high pass of the
Rockies—Butte twinkling with astonishing brilliance
in this high, thin air, while away to the south rises the
gigantic stack that is Anaconda, spewing yellow fumes
and death to vegetation . . . The tumultuous
Kootenai, boiling white over rocks, sea green in the
deeper pools . . . Then the immense lushness of
the Wenatchee orchards . . . Finally, the long
thundering bore straight through the Cascade Range
and emergence into the dripping, fog-ridden silence

of the towering firs, the most somber and melancholy forest on earth; and soon the lights of Puget Sound and the hoarse voices of ships leaving for the Orient.

Sixty years ago Hill hitched all these things together, then went on to tie them to Denver, to Omaha, to Kansas City, St. Louis, and Chicago. They comprised the Hill Lines, Jim Hill's System, and they crossed and threaded and bounded a genuine empire. Offhand it is difficult to think of another American who had quite so much direct influence on quite so large a region.

Most of Hill's country is decidedly northern in climate and character. They have *winter* there, a season that brought out the best in Jim Hill, a winter sort of man whose forebears originated in the Scottish Highlands. Before ever he owned a locomotive, Hill walked across Minnesota on snowshoes; he had driven dog teams to Fort Garry and slept in the open of subarctic Manitoba when it was Prince Rupert's Land. Winter marked him, too. By the time he was forty, his massive shaggy head, his leathery face, his graying beard, and his immense shoulders reminded his friends of a rather grim old lion. What struck you, too, was the man's one good eye. It was as black as night, save that it often seemed to glow from deep in his dark, weathered countenance like a live coal at the bottom of a cinder pit.

Some men come to look the way they do because

conditions and their own bent have forged their personality. Hill was one of these. At fifty, as at seventy, he made men think of some craglike piece of geology, decorated with frosty tamarack, standing above a canyon in the mountains. That was Jim Hill, old Rock of Ages himself, a neolithic legend with a volcanic base.

He was born September 16, 1838, in the hamlet of Rockwood, County of Wellington, in what is now Ontario and was then Upper Canada, the third of four children of James and Anne (Dunbar) Hill. The Hills were stanch Protestants from Armagh, Ireland, whose antecedents were probably among Cromwell's men; the Dunbars originated in Scotland.

It was a custom in the Hill family, as with many another at the time, to name the eldest son for the father; when an earlier son James died, the Hills named their second son James Jerome. Like the others, he was born in the log house his parents had built on their fifty-acre place in the Ontario bush, as the Canadian backwoods was known. In later years Anne Hill often remarked that the happiest day of her life was when the last tree in the clearing which could possibly fall on her house was cut down.

If there was anything that distinguished the Hill-Dunbar home from those of other bush pioneers in the neighborhood, it was the books on a shelf in their

log house: the *Works* of Shakspere, the *Poems* of
Robert Burns, *The Pilgrim's Progress*, a dictionary,
and the Bible. Whether or not these volumes were
the source of it, the one remarkable thing that the community seemed to recall, in later years, of Hill's youth
was that the boy read "everything he could lay hands
on."

The Rockwood settlement would appear to have
been particularly fortunate in that it harbored a number of Quakers, including an old man, John Harris,
late of Cork, Ireland, who taught the district school
where Hill learned to read; and William Wetherald,
an English Quaker with a college education.

In 1848 Wetherald, encouraged by the Hills and
a few other families, opened Rockwood Academy,
a private school in which young James Jerome was
enrolled. Wetherald was apparently a really fine
teacher who chose deliberately what seemed to him
the best things a child should know. He held that
mental discipline, and not mental craftsmanship, was
the ideal. He taught the usual courses of reading, writing, arithmetic, and geography, and also gave his
pupils an excellent grounding in English and Latin,
with a little Greek and the beginnings of geometry.
This educational fare was extraordinary for the time
and place, but more so was the manner in which it
was set before the youngsters. Wetherald was probably one of those rarities called a natural teacher.

Thirty years after his schooldays, James J. Hill, by then one of the giants of the Northwest, begged his old teacher to pay him a visit. The aged Wetherald did so, to Hill's great delight, and the two men continued to correspond until the former's death, the Quaker always signing himself "Thy old friend and teacher."

During the youth's fourth year at Rockwood Academy, James Hill Senior died, and shortly thereafter the widow and children moved to nearby Guelph, where James went to work in a grocery store. He was now head of the family. His pay was four dollars a month. Though his parents had hoped the lad would become a physician, the matter was dropped when young James, playing Indian with other boys, was struck by an arrow that cost him the sight of one eye.

Hill clerked in the little store for four years. Nothing much happened, save that he continued to read a good deal, often under the benign direction of good Schoolmaster Wetherald. Plutarch charmed him. Byron fairly hypnotized him. He also got good strong doses of the life and times of Napoleon, and came to adore the daughter of another emperor, Lalla Rookh, the heroine of Thomas Moore's famous poem. It is more than probable that some of this reading prompted young Hill's first dreamy ambition. He had breathed the wild free air of Byron. He had followed Napoleon up the Nile. He had saturated himself with the romantic melody of Lalla Rookh's journey from Delhi to Cashmere.

So, in 1856, and not yet turned eighteen, young Hill quit the store at Guelph, said good-by to mother, brother, and sisters, and set forth with the idea of going to the Orient, preferably India. His money got him only as far as Syracuse, New York, where he worked for a farmer, earning enough to permit to move on to New York City, then to Philadelphia, in one of which he hoped to ship before the mast. But neither here, nor in Richmond, which he also visited, did "suitable opportunity present itself" for carrying out his original scheme.

He had not yet given up the Orient. Perhaps some port on the Pacific was the proper place to ship. He would go there. He knew the best way to get to the West Coast of the United States. It was by way of one of the trappers' brigades. A schoolmate at Rockwood Academy who came from the Red River of the North had told him about the brigades. They left Fort Garry and St. Paul every spring and headed for the trapping grounds of the Rocky Mountains, even beyond the Rockies, even to the Pacific ports of Portland and San Francisco. That way lay the Orient.

Hill went to Chicago, then on to the Mississippi, and by river steamer to St. Paul, the rising new metropolis that only recently had ceased to call itself Pig's Eye. Here was the center of a sizable trade in furs.

Hill got there in late July 1856, just a week or so too late to join the last brigade of the season, that headed by the redoubtable Major Edwin A. C. Hatch.

Whether or not young Hill was sorely disappointed is not known. The Orient had suddenly receded, and here he was in the unromantic mud of a jerry-built frontier city. In any case, he did not grieve long; Hill could always muster patience when he had to, and this was one of those occasions. Then, too, the sights and sounds of St. Paul, capital of Minnesota Territory, were such as to attract even a more sophisticated youth than this country lad from the Ontario bush.

When Hill arrived there in mid-1856, St. Paul was in its first great boom. The flush times were to continue for a little more than twelve months longer, or until the Panic of Fifty-seven transformed the city, as a local historian described it, into a "place of no money, no values, no property, no business, no banks, or banks with empty vaults; no courage, no hope, notes due, mortgages foreclosed, men heavily in debt, land depreciated from 50 to 75 per cent, and no foundation to build on."

Twelve months of flush times, so it turned out, was all that young Hill needed to get set. And neither then nor later did panics hurt him, anyway. Like his contemporaries, Rockefeller and Carnegie, he welcomed business or money panics. Panics shook the stuffing out of insecure institutions, leaving useful fragments that able hands might pick up and make into something solid.

Twelve months in St. Paul before the debacle of 1857 was time enough. In that brief period Hill's energy put down such firm root in the community that he never again talked of trapping his way West. St. Paul was to be his base of operations for the next six decades.

II

THE LIFE of St. Paul was concentrated in a few blocks of muddy streets that crowded the levee. Here came the river boats from Dubuque, St. Louis, and New Orleans, bringing supplies and trade goods that were sent on by oxcart or dogsled to the trading posts of the Red River of the North, a stream that rose in the Dakota country and flowed into Lake Winnipeg, deep in Rupert's Land.

The town held at least five thousand people in 1856. Five hotels faced the river, and another, the International, was just going up when Jim Hill arrived. Five newspapers could scarcely report the comings and goings, the real-estate deals, the rumors of still greater events, and the work of the legislative assembly.

The imposing Merchants Hotel was like a huge hive. Men were hastening in or dashing out, mostly afoot, though several hacks were doing a good business too. One must hurry here, for no one knew at what hour some big-money man from the East would arrive and wish to buy a full block of business property, or perhaps a hundred acres for subdivision. Almost every other place was a real-estate office, and it might have appeared to a stranger that all of St. Paul, and much of Minnesota Territory, as yet far from surveyed, was for sale by the lot, block, acre, section, and township.

Newsboys ran about shouting the *Daily Free Press*, the *Democrat*, the *Pioneer*, the *Times*, and the *Minnesotan*; and none ever lacked the makings of a "big" story. If need of one was felt, the editor himself sat down and composed praise for the salubrious climate, which obviated all dangers of cholera and smallpox and even cured consumption. That was story enough. A piece of the great western land boom had at last hit the new Northwest, and St. Paul was its center.

"All was bustle," recalled one of the pioneers, T. M. Newson. "Our streets were crowded with strangers; our stages filled with passengers; our hotels overrun with visitors; our real estate men were thick as blackberries . . . and there was a general air of activity in every direction, while ten and sometimes twelve steamboats lay at our levee."

The levee was all noise and action. Bells rang, whistles emitted warnings, paddles churned the black waters, sparks blew out of the tall stacks like roman candles. From somewhere in the night on the river came the moans of other boats, coming up or going down. Under the weird light of the levee torches, even at two in the morning, moved the great wooden-wheeled wagons called Red River carts, coming for freight to tote across the flatlands along the muddy and wickedly erratic stream that flowed north into Canada. Indians, half-breeds, and Frenchmen chattered or grunted and swore at the oxen and horses. Stevedores roamed about, working ship or working saloon, first one then the other. The waterfront dives never closed.

Within twelve hours after young Hill first saw the levee, he had a job as clerk for J. W. Bass & Company, agents for the Dubuque & St. Paul Packet Company's line of river steamboats. It was his duty to check incoming and outgoing freight. He handled the waybills. He kept an eye on the warehouse. He kept the time of the roustabouts; and when need be, in an emergency, he was expected to pitch in and work like any dock-walloper. It was no exalted job.

At about the time when Jim Hill began work on the levee, two other purposeful young men arrived in St. Paul. One was Theodore Hamm, of Baden, Germany, who presently opened a saloon and boarding-house; and, finding the local beer not to his liking, soon opened a brewery. The other was Chauncey W. Griggs, Connecticut Yankee. Griggs and Hill quickly became fast friends.

The boom times continued into 1857, and now instead of twelve, Hill often counted twenty-four steamboats loading or unloading at one and the same time. Crime was booming, too. Proprietor George McKenzie of the Mansion House was robbed and killed, and his body was thrown into the river. A

Robert Johnson was also robbed, clubbed, and dropped into the river, to die later of his injuries. Street holdups became nightly occurrences. And one evening Jim Hill and his friend Charley Coffin of the steamer *War Eagle* were set upon with knives by three toughs. Coffin suffered bad cuts on one arm, and Hill was wounded between the ribs. But Hill knocked the gang leader down and out. The police arrived and arrested the trio. They turned out to be members of a Fourth Street gang called the Chicago Star Cleaners.

Legend has it that during Hill's several years on the levee he was one of the boys, the young men about town who drank deep, gambled some, and had a good time generally. One hopes the legend is nearer the truth than the "authorized" account, which, so far as young Hill's social life is concerned, ranges from the prim to the colorless and makes no mention of a persistent tradition, known even to Hill's descendants, that somewhere there is a photograph of a young and gay James J. Hill, cane in hand, beating the stuffing out of a taxidermist's black bear masterpiece in a St. Paul museum.

Whether or not Hill had an occasional night on the town, it is certain enough that nothing whatever prevented him from tending to business. His employers were soon permitting him to set rates for freight and passengers. He went out after new business, which he seems to have garnered without much trouble, less because of his personality than because he knew all the routes and distances, the times of arrival and departure of boats, stages, and oxcart trains; and he kept up to date with the ever changing transportation schedules. When Bass & Company sold out to another firm, Hill went with the trade. By then he was virtually running the business anyway.

Hill's quick intelligence soon let him know that the Mississippi packet business was a cutthroat enterprise as savage as war between Sioux and Comanche. He rather liked it that way, and thought that it provided a superb education for a young man of energy and talent. It might also, as he suggested, "offer a richly rewarding field." With his apparently innate ability to appraise the events and vagaries of commerce, Hill was elated in 1857 to ship the first export of Minnesota-grown wheat. It had been grown on the Le Sueur prairie, and it went to St. Louis. Hill reflected that only three years before, Minnesota had been importing wheat.

A little later, Hill was even more pleased to transship by river boat the first Minnesota flour to be exported. This had been milled at Minneapolis. Because Hill knew all about the flour market in the eastern United States, which preferred Ohio flour above all else, he advised the Minnesota shippers to use a label that he was glad to suggest. They agreed. Taking a piece of the oil paper used in his manifold book, Hill then and there designed and cut a stencil that was inked on each of the fifty barrels: *Muskingum Mills, Troy, Ohio—The Genuine.*

By this time it must have become apparent to people whose affairs centered at the St. Paul levee that James J. Hill could be described as a mighty smart young man. One is inclined to side with Hill's official biographer when he remarks that his subject did not wait for opportunities—"he made them." Hill noted for example that during the winter, when the river fleet was tied up and often frozen in, the boats suffered damage by ice and by looting. He suggested to the owner of one that Hill move into the cabin for the winter, to sleep there nights and act as a watchman. The deal was made, and the smart young man moved in, taking with him an armful of books which included scientific treatises and a set of Gibbon. By spring, said his friend, Archbishop Ireland, Hill had read and annotated all his books. "He wasted in foolish frolics neither his money nor his time."

Indeed he didn't. He was playing the standard role of a Horatio Alger hero even before the Massachusetts author had invented his Work & Win formula for juvenile literature. He not only did his regular work efficiently, but was pretty good in any emergency. When the firm he was working for took an agency for reapers, and the machines arrived, it was discovered that no one knew how to assemble the complicated parts. Young Hill said he would find out. He knew that a farmer named Cormack "up back of Fort Snelling" was using a similar reaper. Hill drove there, looked the rig over carefully, then returned to the warehouse and proceeded to put the machines together. They worked fine.

Another time, when his firm was anxious to get the steamer *Itasca* to Minneapolis to be unloaded, and the only river pilot available turned up drunk, Hill took the wheel. He had no license, but plenty of confidence. He drove the boat upstream against a strong head wind without trouble until they came to Cheever's Bar, where she started to pile up on the rocks. Hill called for full-steam-ahead and "jumped her," taking her over the obstruction as though she had been an amphibian. The jolts broke several of the *Itasca's* timbers, and she leaked; but she did not stay on the rocks, and Hill got her to Minneapolis, had her unloaded, and took her back to St. Paul without further trouble. Even if the boat called for repairs, Hill's employers must have appreciated the nerve and confidence displayed.

The Civil War caused little change in his life, and though he did try to enlist, his bad eye was considered too great a disability, which goes to show the lack of imagination of the recruiting officers. Hill probably would have made a first-class colonel for the Engineers, or a magnificent quartermaster for a division. His good friend Chauncey Griggs enlisted in the Third Minnesota and came back a colonel and a hero. Hill himself was something of a hero one day in 1864, when he leaped fully clothed into the Mississippi and brought to shore a half-drowned boy and a man who had tried to save the boy, but had gone under too. The local papers reported the incident.

The end of the war found Hill set up for himself as a forwarding agent and general transportation man, with an increasing number of side lines. He had charge of the St. Paul business of the Northwestern Packet Company, giant of the upper river, which had traffic arrangements with the Chicago, Milwaukee & St. Paul Railroad at Prairie du Chien, and with the Illinois Central at Dunleith. He was buying, pressing, and selling hay. He operated a large warehouse. In winter, when time permitted, he struck out on snowshoes to see what was going on across Minnesota, and took pains to inspect the Red River region, the source of so much business through St. Paul. He bought furs, wheat, and wood to cut up and sell for fuel.

Within a year after war's end, Hill became agent for the new and tiny, yet grandiosely named, St. Paul & Pacific Railroad Company, whose doubtful tracks ran from the St. Paul levee to the twin towns of St. Anthony-Minneapolis, ten miles distant. Hill promptly built a new warehouse next to the railroad depot, with its lower floor on a level with both the car tracks and the docks. This eliminated the cost of dray-age from dock to rail and permitted the struggling railroad to handle freight more cheaply than the teams that had been undercutting the St. Paul & Pacific on the haul between St. Anthony-Minneapolis and St. Paul.

Noting that the railroad often had trouble getting fuel, Hill proposed that he supply its hungry locomo-tives. After that, the road never lacked for wood. Hill considered wood a very poor fuel. Coal was what a railroad should have. He had meanwhile made a sur-vey of all available sources of coal, and presently leased deposits in Iowa, which in time grew to twenty-three hundred acres. He brought in a shipment that the St. Paul & Pacific discovered was indeed superior to wood. And now, taking Chauncey Griggs as part-ner, he organized Hill, Griggs & Company. For the next several years this outfit operated a fuel, freighting, merchandising, and warehouse business. It also held what was virtually a monopoly of the coal business in St. Paul and the region roundabout.

In the decade since he had come to St. Paul, Hill had grown to be a man of affairs. It was time to take a wife. During his bachelor days on the waterfront, he and many of his friends had discovered near the levee an excellent boardinghouse in which the star waitress was a charming little black-eyed girl named Mary

Theresa Mehegan, the daughter of Timothy and Mary (McGovern) Mehegan, immigrants from Ireland. Mary was working to help support her widowed mother. She was not only pretty, she was highly intelligent. She took Jim Hill's eye.

The story has it that as Christmas approached one year, Hill proposed to his fellow boarders that they make up a collection to give to Mary as a gift of the season. Hill himself started the purse with a substantial amount, then urged his friends not to be backward. Probably they expected Mary to use the money, after the manner of young women, to buy clothes. But smart Mary invested it in education. She quit her waitress job and took off for Milwaukee, where she entered a convent school. Not long after her return to St. Paul, she and Jim Hill were married "at the bishop's residence of the Cathedral Parish in St. Paul." The day when a devout Catholic daughter married the son of a rigidly Protestant family was August 19, 1867, or approximately one hundred and seventy-seven years after the Battle of the Boyne.

This is perhaps the place to say that the married life of Jim Hill and Mary Mehegan was apparently as ideal as one could wish. "He never," said Mrs. Hill in a well-remembered remark, "brought his business home." Though he seems not to have embraced the Catholic Church as a communicant, Hill first and last made gifts to it amounting to approximately one million dollars, a portion of which went toward the establishment and endowment of a seminary in St. Paul for the education of students preparing for the priesthood. In presenting this handsome gift, Hill said that he did not care what denomination it was as long as a true religious spirit governed it. Then he added a statement that has given pause to more than one working stiff. "Look," said James J. Hill, "look at the millions of foreigners who are pouring into this country and to whom the Roman Catholic church represents the only authority that they either fear or respect. What will be their social view, their political action, their moral status if that single controlling force should be removed?"

Mr. Hill did not answer his question, which was rhetorical anyway; and left his hearers to imagine chaos without further hint from him.

III

THE MAN who has to influence the direction of Hill's life as perhaps no other at this period was also a Canadian, Norman Kittson, born in 1814 at Sorel, Lower Canada. When the eighteen-year-old Hill first saw him, Kittson was in his forties, with long hair and beard, both graying, a face already well weathered from a quarter of a century's exposure to the suns and blizzards of the beaver regions, and bright searching eyes that contrasted somewhat with his correct, if most reserved, manners and a reticence that was marked even in a true Briton, grandson of a soldier who had come over with General Wolfe to drive the French out of Canada. Kittson peers forth from an old photograph like a kindly and somewhat tired patriarch.

As a lad of sixteen, Kittson had entered the employ of the American Fur Company. After ranging over the fur-bearing regions of Lower and Upper Canada, he arrived in Minnesota in the 1830's and started trading on his own account, shipping his furs from St. Paul. By the time Hill arrived there, Kittson held the honored place of an early pioneer. He had already served several terms in the Minnesota legislature as a member from the Pembina district, the region along the border of Canada centering at the trading post of the same name, which was the port of entry. His trading had been profitable. He moved into St. Paul, established an office, built a fine house for his growing family, and in the year Hill was married, was elected mayor of the city. Shortly afterwards he became agent at St. Paul for the venerable Hudson's Bay Company.

To appreciate the factors that were to lead, soon after Kittson's appointment as agent, to an alliance with Jim Hill, it is well to know that this remarkable outfit, less a company than an institution of empire, was just then being sorely tried by swiftly changing conditions and was gradually losing control over its own domain. This was an immense piece of Canada called Prince Rupert's Land. It was a little more than half as large as the United States.

The charter of this corporation was granted in 1670 by Charles II, King of England, to his cousin Prince Rupert and seventeen other noblemen and gentlemen under style of "The Governor and Company of Adventurers of England trading into Hudson's bay." The limits of the lands granted were expansive though vague, and were finally defined as including all territory watered by streams flowing into Hudson Bay. Besides the complete lordship and entire legislative, judicial, and executive power within these limits, the corporation also received the right to "the whole and entire trade and traffic to and from all havens, bays, creeks, rivers, lakes and seas into which they shall find

entrance or passage by water or land out of the territories, limits or places aforesaid." The company was
expected to maintain warships, armies, and forts, and
to carry on warfare against all non-Christians. These,
as one understands the matter, included Indians.

The early success of this corporation had been great.
Its profits had been truly immense. Then came the
wars between England and the United States, to remove forever that portion of the corporation's empire
south of the 49th parallel. Even worse, one of the
company's own directors, a Scottish nobleman named
Lord Selkirk, virtually forced the company to sell him
116,000 square miles, a tract about twice the size of
England and Wales combined.

The humane Selkirk wanted this as land on which
to settle evicted crofters of the Highlands, victims of
the new craze for raising sheep, which called for
more grazing land. They were sent over by way of
Hudson Bay, then made a frightful trek by land over
the trappers' routes to Lake Winnipeg, and south in
the Red River Valley. Here they came, wrote Bruce
Hutchison, men and women, "plodding through the
rotten snow, babies on their backs, a kilted piper leading them."

But farming and trapping could not exist side by
side. Quarrels quickly arose with the half-breed
trappers, and twenty-odd of the settlers fell at the
Massacre of Seven Oaks. New settlers were sent over,

the pipers still playing, to found the settlement of
Kildonan, later a part of Winnipeg, and they stayed.[1]
But independent trappers and opposition traders of
the North-West Fur Company, all of whom were
considered virtual poachers by the Hudson's Bay people, continued to infiltrate its domain. In 1821 the
opposition outfit was taken over by the older concern,
which again enjoyed a monopoly. In 1859, however,
the Hudson's Bay license expired, and the region was
open to all. Ten years later, when the Dominion of
Canada was being formed, the government purchased
from the ancient company its still huge empire. This
relieved the company of its governmental functions,
but left it intact as a commercial enterprise.

Determined in spite of all to hold its place of dominance as the first trading and trapping concern in
North America, the Hudson's Bay men sought to
open the shortest and quickest route into and out of
the region. This was obviously by way of the Red
River and St. Paul. Advised by, and acting through,
their shrewd agent in St. Paul, who was Norman
Kittson, the corporation bought the *Anson Northrup*,
an old Mississippi River steamer, pulled her to pieces,
toted the parts across Minnesota, assembled them

---

[1] Lord Selkirk paid for his generosity and idealism. "One of
the most generous and disinterested men in the history of colonization," remarks the *Encyclopædia Britannica*, "he fell a vic-
tim to the predatory selfishness of his rivals. He died at Pau in
1820, broken-hearted."

there, probably near present-day Fargo, on the Red River, and called the result *The Pioneer*. Plying between Fort Ambercrombie in Minnesota and their chief post at Fort Garry, in what was soon to be Manitoba, the *Pioneer* was so successful that a year later another boat was added.

Now, before becoming agent for the Hudson's Bay Company, Kittson had acted for the independent trappers and traders, and he did not let them down. For a few years he acted for both the company and the independents. Nobody was quite satisfied with the arrangement, and in 1866 Kittson suggested to Jim Hill that he might do well if he could find a way to transport the independents and their supplies between Minnesota and Dakota points and the Manitoba trapping and farming regions.

Hill was already the most successful forwarding agent in St. Paul, and now he turned some of his attention to the business of the Canadian independents. By heroic efforts, the St. Paul & Pacific railroad, with which Hill had been closely affiliated, had pushed its rails north and west from Minneapolis to St. Cloud; from there a stage and freighting line carried passengers and goods to Fort Ambercrombie or some other landing on the Red River, where they were put aboard one of the Hudson's Bay Company steamers for the downriver run to Fort Garry. Hill had first call on the railroad, and his route by rail and team

to the Red River was infinitely quicker than the ox-
carts which, to the number of six hundred, were still
creaking their rutty way across Minnesota.

Hill found the business as profitable as it was interesting. He was ready to take any pains to please a
customer, and he liked to recall filling an order for a
Selkirk clergyman who wanted "two cases gin, one
case sugar, two tuning forks, and one copy each of the
works of Tennyson and Longfellow." Another Red
River customer wrote to ask Hill about getting a loan
from a bank; said he had some mink skins as security.
Hill replied, telling the man to send on his mink skins
and to draw on Hill for a thousand dollars cash. This
was the sort of "accommodation" that made friends
and money too.

Hill was no man to leave transportation on the Red
River in the hands of a monopoly. He moved crews
of men to Fort Ambercrombie and set one gang to
building flatboats, another to getting out oak and
plank for a steamboat. Before any of Hill's craft were
ready to take the water, the region of Fort Garry and
the Selkirk settlements exploded in what history calls
the Red River Rebellion. Led by Louis Riel, a brilliant, vain, and flighty French-Indian, the half-breeds
or Metis were encouraged by American imperialists in
Minnesota and by the anti-British Fenians in the
United States and Canada to attack and capture the
Hudson's Bay Company post of Fort Garry. They

then raised a flag bearing the French fleur-de-lis and the shamrock, the latter in honor of Irish-American Fenians, a few of whom took part in the uprising. Riel was very polite and theatrical. He made speeches and saluted the ladies; but he made the terrible mistake of executing a prisoner, Thomas Scott, an Ontario Orangeman, who thereupon became and has remained Canada's favorite martyr.

It is probable that both Hill and Kittson knew pretty well, through the latter's connection with the Hudson's Bay Company, what was going on in the lower Red River country. They wanted to know more. In mid-March 1870 Jim Hill set out from St. Paul to see for himself. By then comparative order had been established at Fort Garry and a sort of peace made through the efforts of Riel himself and of Donald A. Smith, sent by the government of the newly established Dominion of Canada as special commissioner to the Northwest Territories, the grab-bag name chosen to designate the vast region that reached from approximately Lake Superior to the Rockies and the isolated Province of British Columbia.

Though this trip was only one of many that Hill made into the lower Red River country, special significance is attached to it because of an event along the way. The way was difficult enough, for winds swept untrammeled across the flatlands, piling snow into mountainous drifts. From some point along the

St. Paul & Pacific, Hill and a driver set out for Breckenridge on the Red River. Hill never forgot this trip. Day turned night. Night became chaos. Twice when they failed to reach a way-station, Hill and driver slept in the snow. At Breckenridge, Hill bought a team of dogs and sledge and struck north alone.

The dogsled trip wasn't quite so bad as the stage. One night he holed up in a deserted sod hut. A second night he simply unhitched the animals, then huddled with them beneath the snow. He crossed the Canadian border, heading into the teeth of a gale coming down from Hudson Bay. Here on the last lap to Fort Garry, Hill and his dogsled met a party coming from the Fort. In it was Commissioner Donald A. Smith, soon to be Lord Strathcona. He told Hill that the Rebellion had been put down and that he was going to Ottawa to make his report to the Dominion government. We shall meet Smith again. It is worth mentioning here that in later life both men often recalled their meeting in a hut on the windblown prairie of Manitoba. They had liked each other from the first.

During the next year and more, Hill spent a good part of his time in the Red River Valley. He was preparing his campaign against the Hudson's Bay Company's transportation monopoly of the river; and in the spring of 1871 the bustling town of Winnipeg, which had outgrown its original name of Fort Garry, was astonished to see a brand-new and strange boat at its levee. This was the steamship *Selkirk* of James J. Hill, who let it be known that he proposed to conduct a freight and passenger service between Breckenridge, Minnesota, and Winnipeg.

The *Selkirk* apparently came as no less a surprise to the people of Winnipeg than to the head man of the Hudson's Bay Company itself, the same Donald A. Smith who had been sent by the government to settle the Rebellion. Along with this opposition steamboat, Jim Hill had another surprise in store. Let Beckles Willson, biographer of Lord Strathcona, relate how these matters appeared to Donald Smith:

"The only steamer navigating the waters of the Red River had been the *International*, belonging to the Hudson's Bay Company, which carried only the Company's goods. But suddenly an American steamer, the *Selkirk*, appears, heavily freighted with merchandise for the province. This circumstance alone would not have contributed to the complete breakdown of the oxcart system; but it appeared that, according to American law, all goods passing through American territory intended for Canada were required to be duly bonded in the United States customs. This law had been practically a dead letter so far as the Red River carts were concerned, but the promoter of the new steamship enterprise had found means to induce the American government to enforce it. The result was that, having himself taken the precaution of entering bonds, and as neither the cart brigades nor the Hudson's Bay Company's steamer *International* had complied with the law, the new-comer for a brief space enjoyed a handsome and lucrative monopoly. It is interesting to recall that the tariff levied from St. Paul to Winnipeg was sixteen shillings sterling per one hundred pounds. Moreover, it was payable in cash, whereas the freight by carts had been payable half in cash, half in kind, a practice which considerably lessened the actual freight charges.

"When Mr. Smith heard of this proceeding he was for a moment non-plussed. But with his surprise was mingled considerable admiration for the shrewdness displayed by his trade antagonist in this exploit. 'He must be a very able man,' he said."

Hill was indeed "an able man," and so was Donald Smith. In response to Hill's coup in the matter of a forgotten customs law, Smith acted with such celerity as to rouse Hill's admiration. What Smith did was to transfer immediately the Bay Company's *International* to its agent in St. Paul, who was Norman Kittson and an American citizen. Kittson bonded the boat, and the Bay Company announced that it was now ready to accept freight for all comers.

Rate and speed wars began at once. Hill doubled his efforts to get and hold new business. Newspapers apparently were subsidized by both Hill and the Bay

Company. Levee runners of persuasive powers were engaged. Hill himself went often to Winnipeg to fan the old flames of local hatred against the Hudson's Bay people.

Meanwhile, new troubles broke out along the river. The Fenian brotherhood of Irish-Americans, which had failed to bring promised aid to Louis Riel, was now prepared to attack Canada in numbers, capture the seats of government and commerce, and bring the Dominion under Fenian rule. Canada was to be held hostage until Great Britain freed Ireland. It was as simple as that. The campaign called for simultaneous attacks by columns entering Canada from Vermont, western New York, and Minnesota. The downtrodden French-Canadians, the enslaved Metis, and all really decent Anglo-Canadians would rise and help the invaders to establish freedom.

Such was the wild plan. The attack from Vermont was met at the border by Canadian militia, who started shooting, and the invading column was repulsed with a few dead and many wounded. The freedom army approaching from New York ran head-on into militia and well-armed farmers. There were more shooting and several casualties. Jim Hill himself, who was an eyewitness, left a clearly written and humorous account of the Fenian attack on Manitoba. This was on October 5, 1871:

"This morning at 7 o'clock a band of thirty Fenians

under Generals Curley, O'Neill, Donnelly, and O'Donahue, composed of about twenty of the hardest looking roughs and ten Pembina loafers, made an attack on the Hudson's Bay post at North Pembina, which was occupied by one of the Company officers and his clerk, and captured without resistance being offered. They at once set about clothing their half-naked squad of roughs and loading up a wagon with provisions.

"Either the plunder had too much attraction for them or they thought they would rest on their freshly-gained laurels, for they remained in the post until 11 o'clock, when they were surprised by Colonel Wheaton (United States Army) and twenty-three men from Fort Pembina coming down the road in an army ambulance and a four-mule wagon. Colonel Wheaton unloaded his men and deployed them as skirmishers and advanced upon the fort at double quick. As soon as the Fenian leaders saw the United States troops coming over the Canadian boundary they at once dropped everything and fled. And such a flight! Some on foot and some on Indian ponies, with the wagon-load of provisions all scattering to the woody banks of the Red River."

In about twenty minutes, wrote Hill, Wheaton and his soldiers returned with Generals O'Neill, Donnelly, and Curley in the ambulance, and ten Fenians on foot. They had thrown away their arms and tried to hide in the bushes. General O'Donoghue (whom Hill called O'Donohue) and the others made good their escape. Wheaton took charge of the stores and weapons. These consisted of a few sacks of flour, two hundred United States breechloading rifles, a case of sabers, a few old carbines, and fourteen thousand rounds of cartridges. Loading these into the mule-team wagon and marching the prisoners under guard, Colonel Wheaton took the remains of the raid back to Fort Pembina.

At about five o'clock that day, Hill reported, "a French half-breed rode through Pembina to the United States fort on a gallop, taking news of the capture of General O'Donohue. It seems that the general got hungry or dry and went into a half-breed's house and was there taken prisoner by the breeds, but not until he had made them pledge him that they would not deliver him to any but the United States authorities." He was presently brought to the fort. The Fenian raid from Minnesota was at an end.

General O'Donoghue was released after a few hours on the ground that the Americans had no actual evidence that he had committed a crime. A few days later the other Fenians were freed on a similar convenient excuse—whatever they had done had occurred outside United States jurisdiction. "As usual," comments Joseph Kinsey Howard in his study of Louis Riel, "American judges were unwilling to punish American citizens for the innocent pastime of armed invasion of neighboring countries."

It behooved a man who had set up competition to the Hudson's Bay Company to observe his business closely in the field, so Jim Hill spent much of his time at this period in the Red River Valley. On foot, horse-back, river boat, or snowshoes, he rode and walked the country between Breckenridge and Winnipeg. Observant as always, he was struck by the deepest, darkest loam he had ever seen, which showed in the deep ruts. He ranged all of the short rivers that flowed into the Red from east and west. Once, on the Tongue River, Hill's half-breed companion dislocated an arm. To set it, Hill "cut a box elder stick about five inches in diameter, with a crotch in one end. I took my under-clothes and bound them in a roll and put it under the man's arm and got him under the cart with a stick between his legs. I put the fork against this, cut a notch in the end and let the rope twist through the notch and back to the wheel. Then I got a stick out of the cart, and took a twist on the rope so that the same power that hauled his arm ahead pressed through the crotch on the notches and pushed the end of the stick down tight."

This was going to be Spartan treatment. "I took care to sit across him," Hill said. "I had his head under the cart. I felt reasonably certain that there would come a time when it would be necessary for me to keep him in that position. I gave him a stick to hold, then tied it to his wrist. When I got a good strain on him he began to yell, but I kept going until I felt the bone had been pressed into place. I got him out from under. He found that the joint was back. Through the night he was a little delirious, and he tried to have me take two of the best horses and said he would take the worst one and try to make the trip back to his home."

Hill had been successful as a surgeon, and now the poor half-breed, freed of his terrible pain, wanted to thank God and His saints for the deliverance. With him he had a little prayer book in French, and though he could not read, he thought it would do if Hill read the offices and he repeated them. So, Hill turned priest, though not a thorough one. "I went through the services," he said, "taking a line or two at the top, one in the middle, another at the bottom. I got through the entire prayer book, I think, in less than twenty minutes. He [the half-breed] felt that he had done the biggest day's work in his life."

While seeing virtually every mile of the land on both sides of the Red, Hill continued to run his steam-boat to some purpose. He cut freight and passenger rates below those of the Hudson's Bay Company's boat. He continued to meet and talk with Winnipeg merchants, with trappers and traders, with everyone who might have need to travel or ship by the river.

It is probable that neither Kittson nor Donald Smith had believed that Hill would become such powerful competition; he was actually taking business that the old company had enjoyed for years.

So, on another trip from Montreal to Winnipeg, Donald Smith stopped at St. Paul for discussion with Kittson, and then with Hill. The outcome was a coalition, though it did not appear so. What the public saw was that Hill sold his steamboat, flatboats, other equipment, and entire business to Kittson, who then formed the Red River Transportation Company. Kittson was the ostensible owner and manager, Hill a secret partner. Out of this line he was to make the foundation of his fortune.

With the appearance of this new outfit, rates on the Red River went up and stayed there. During its first season, the Red River Transportation Company returned a net profit of 80 per cent. Whether or not Kittson was content with this rich source of income isn't on record. Hill at least was not content. His close association with the St. Paul & Pacific Railroad had brought him to the belief that rail lines rather than steamboats would dominate traffic in the Northwest. He knew well enough that the St. Paul & Pacific was jerry-built and jerry-managed. It was undependable even with good luck. Yet sometime in 1872 he remarked of it: "The line could make money if there was somebody to manage it."

There was another road in Minnesota, too, the
Northern Pacific, which had been chartered to build
west from the shore of Lake Superior to Puget Sound.
This was to be a transcontinental after the style of
the Union Pacific, complete with land grant. By
1873 this road had laid track from Duluth westward
to the Red River by way of Brainerd. Meanwhile,
the St. Paul & Pacific had extended its original ten
miles between Minneapolis and St. Paul by one line
to Sauk Rapids on the Mississippi and another to
Breckenridge on the Red River. And by 1873, too,
the Northern Pacific had, through dizzy financial and
legal methods, obtained control of stock in a portion of
the St. Paul & Pacific, which portion was thereupon
separately organized as the First Division Company.

The exact relations of these three entities need not
be gone into exhaustively. Sufficient to know that the
trickery was devised and put through for the sole benefit of the Northern Pacific, giving that line access to
St. Paul and to the Red River Valley.

In 1873 came the country-wide panic that took
its name from the year. It was set off by the failure
in Philadelphia of Jay Cooke, the most eminent banking man in the United States. Cooke had set out to
raise one hundred million dollars to finance completion of the Northern Pacific. He failed to do so. His
banking concern failed, and along with the failure
came a crash of institutions of such magnitude that

the event and the day went into history as the greatest
disaster up to that time.

Within forty-eight hours railroad construction
ceased not only on the Northern Pacific, but on roads
in California, Texas, Iowa, and Maine. In the nation's capital angry crowds surged around the First
National Bank, demanding their cash or the hides
of the bank's officials. Sawmills ground to a halt in
Michigan. Blast furnaces along the Monongahela were
banked. All over the country, thousands stood in line
to stare numbly at the grimly closed doors of empty
banks and trust companies. The whole great bubble
of expansion and inflation was coming down in water.

Jim Hill watched the almost complete demoraliza-
tion with considerable interest while both the Northern Pacific and the St. Paul & Pacific went bankrupt. He was particularly pleased to note that after
the latter road defaulted on its bonds, the subsequent
foreclosure sale extinguished the right of the Northern
Pacific to those tricky shares in the smaller line on
which it had relied for entry to St. Paul. This was
apparently the moment Jim Hill had been waiting for.

IV

UNTIL James J. Hill and his associates laid sure and steady hands on the St. Paul & Pacific Railroad, it had known a currently fantastic present and an increasingly tragic past, but never anything that could be described as a future. Its founders, indeed, had not considered it a railroad at all, but a machine for making money. The prevailing business-promotion ethics of the period were of the widest latitude, and promoters also enjoyed the occasional helpful activities of legislators. These factors operated in the case of the road that Hill had been watching with interest.

It began in 1854 as the Minnesota & Northwestern Railroad, which obtained a charter and land grant from Congress, said to have been secured by fraud and bribery. In any case, a select committee of the House scotched the charter, and the grant was canceled. Three years later Congress approved a large land grant to Minnesota for the benefit of the same crowd, now in the guise of the Minnesota & Pacific Railroad. The eminent Russell Sage was one of the moving spirits, and in his talented hands the new company received some five million acres and built less than ten miles of undependable track. Yet, the state legislature was urged to award it as bonus a few million dollars in state bonds. These were sold, and the cash apparently disappeared into the pockets of the promoters. More money was obtained by selling stock to farmers, merchants, and small-time speculators.

The Minnesota & Pacific went into insolvency. Then, in order to prevent defrauded creditors from recovering, Sage and his crew induced the Minnesota legislature to pass an act by which the bankrupt outfit was reorganized into two parts, one called the St. Paul & Pacific, the other The First Division of the St. Paul & Pacific. This act had the happy effect of relieving the two new corporations of the debts of the old company, though it did not affect their land grant and franchise rights. Having now made it impossible for creditors to trouble them, Sage and associates lobbied an act through Congress (in 1865) by which the grant was increased to ten sections for each mile of the railroad. Next the promoters mortgaged the railroad and its land grants to a group of Dutch capitalists, who were given to understand that the future of the St. Paul & Pacific was the way to immense fortune.

The Dutch put $13,380,000 into the company, $8 million of which was siphoned off by various devices, such as phony construction jobs, and the road again went into the hands of a receiver, a man named Jesse P. Farley who has been described as without

education and devoid of "experience worth mentioning in railroad matters." Yet he was far from a fool,
and his eye was keen to the main chance. His business
ethics appear to have been about average for the period, which is to say that they were plastic.

The physical properties of this pathetic railroad
were in keeping with its financial status. It could run
trains, after a fashion, from St. Paul to Sauk Rapids, or
76 miles; and from Minneapolis to Breckenridge, or
207 miles. There was also the brief beginning of a
branch at Brainerd. And there were snatches of un-
connected track north and south of Glyndon. The St.
Paul & Pacific tracks were something to see—and to
ride over. A civil engineer in its employ told Jim Hill
that there were fifteen distinct patterns of iron in use,
most of it purchased in small lots at various times. Ties,
bridge materials, and other property were scattered
all along the right of way, and often even along track
already laid. Nobody seemed to know who owned
them, and many a tie and timber went to improve the
fence or barn or house of some settler.

The rolling stock consisted of a few well-worn locomotives and a collection of well-battered passenger
and freight cars. The schedule of trains was beyond
knowing; trains came and went according to the
weather, the business of the moment, and the whims
of officials, road-masters, construction crews, and even
section gangs. Over the far portion of the Red River

section of the road, where traffic was lighter than light, all trains quit running in December, and operation was not resumed until May.

This was the outfit that Jim Hill had said could make money if it had a manager. Hill repeated this statement to his good friend and business associate Norman Kittson. He had a notion, he said, that the poor Dutchmen who had put nearly $14 million into the line, only to see the money dissipated and the company go into receivership, could be bought off for a comparative trifle. Yet Hill knew that the trifle was more money than he and Kittson could raise from their own resources.

Both Hill and Kittson were familiar with what was going on in new Manitoba. Their Red River Transportation steamboats had in 1874 moved a colony of five hundred Icelanders to Winnipeg, and during 1875–6 the same boats, crowded to the rails every trip, had moved no less than six thousand German-speaking Mennonites to settle on the Manitoba prairies west of Winnipeg. This country was in a boom. So were western Minnesota and the northern portion of Dakota Territory. Through it all ran the Red River.

Hill and Kittson were also familiar with the new and immense project just getting under way in the Dominion of Canada. This was the privately owned, but government-sponsored Canadian Pacific Railway

Company. There were several reasons why Canada wanted a coast-to-coast railroad. The United States had recently purchased Alaska, and there was a good deal of talk, in and out of the press, that the aggressive Yankees might snap up British Columbia next. This province, isolated from the rest of Canada by some two thousand miles of wild and uninhabited void, was already tiring of being governed from remote Ottawa, and had even let it be known it was considering an alliance with the United States. A Canadian railroad would quiet the discouraged province. Then, the Red River Rebellion of 1869–70 had made distressingly clear how difficult it was to govern a region much nearer home than British Columbia. Troops had been moved to Fort Garry overland from Toronto and other Ontario points through the dreadful country around Lake Superior only with heroic efforts on the part of Colonel Garnet Wolseley and his soldiers. It was a truly remarkable feat, carried out under the worst possible conditions, and it required ninety-six days. It was obvious that this was no manner in which to run an empire.

So, in 1872 two concerns were chartered to build the Canadian Pacific Railway. Scandals reminiscent of the Union Pacific's Crédit Mobilier marked the first years, and brought John A. Macdonald's Conservative government to grief. The government itself was starting construction and carrying on surveys.

Then, in 1878, the Conservatives were returned to power, and in their long administration the transcontinental was completed.

This is getting a little ahead of the story, but not much, for the rise of James J. Hill as a railroad prince is coincident with, and closely allied to, the building of the Canadian Pacific. There can be few examples of Canadian-American "co-operation," to use a vague term, so purposeful as that of Hill, the naturalized American, and the two Canadians, Donald Smith, whom we have met, and George Stephen. Many writers of the period liked to say that these three men were drawn together by the innate clannishness of the Scots, though one feels fairly certain that individual ability had more to do with it than a romantic Caledonianism.

The alliance of the trio had its base in Hill's idea of getting hold of the St. Paul & Pacific. He discussed it first with Norman Kittson, who thought the idea a wild aberration. But Hill was a man who "bored away," and at last convinced him to take the plunge. Even then, as he admitted later, Kittson relied on the man rather than the idea. The idea was to buy up the bonds of the Dutch, complete laying the road in time to benefit by the land grant, and let the next move be conditioned by what then seemed best.

Getting the St. Paul & Pacific, even at a bankrupt sale, would require far more money than Hill and

Kittson could raise between them. But there was Donald A. Smith, resident governor of the Hudson's Bay Company. Smith now made his home at Selkirk in Manitoba, and was beginning to take more than a little interest in the Canadian scheme for a transcontinental railway. On one of his trips to Montreal, Smith stopped over in St. Paul. Hill went to work on him. Smith had plenty of imagination, but it was perfectly under control, and Hill's bold plan first struck him as illusory. Hill, who knew more about the St. Paul & Pacific than anybody else, presently convinced Smith that the railroad was worth at least $15 million, that it could be bought for less than half that sum, *and* that its land grant, if validated by some fast laying of track, could be sold for far more than the entire property would cost.

Once he was won over, Smith approached his good friend and cousin George Stephen, just become head of the Bank of Montreal. Stephen, born in 1829 at Dufftown, Banff, Scotland, had been a herd boy before coming to Canada as a youth. Here he entered the employ of the Bank of Montreal. By 1871 he was a director; in 1876 he was elected president. The president of the Bank of Montreal was unquestionably the most powerful man of money in the Dominion.

Smith took Hill to meet Stephen in Montreal. The banker displayed uncommon interest and told Hill that he and the bank's manager, another Scot named R. B. Angus, would like to go to St. Paul to inspect the St. Paul & Pacific. Hill was ready for them. He had already been one of a party to take poor Mr. Carp, a representative of the Dutch bondholders, over the line, and he may have well stressed the worst features of what at best was less a railroad than a collection of rusty tracks that did not get anywhere and of rolling stock perfectly in keeping with roadbed and rails.

But when "Mr. Stephen was initiated into the values of the enterprise on his tour of personal inspection," Hill managed to make him see what a genuine bargain it was. There were other discussions in regard to extending the St. Paul & Pacific to the Canadian boundary, where, if things worked out, a railroad from Winnipeg would meet it; and considerable talk about attracting settlers into western Canada. The outcome of this and other negotiations was that Stephen supplied the major portion of the capital that went to buy the Dutch bonds.

To buy the bonds cheaply, Hill first made an offer that he knew would not be accepted. This offer was "to humor Mr. Carp," to "prevent him from becoming hostile," and "to prepare the way for future negotiations on a different basis." Mr. Carp responded with a plan of his own. Hill made another offer, and still another. The dickering went on for

more than a year, but in March 1878 the deal went
through—substantially on the terms Hill had first
mentioned to Stephen.

Just where Stephen got the money is still something of a mystery. It was even charged that he "bor-
rowed" it from the Bank of Montreal, but this was
never proved, and it is well to say only that he produced the major portion of the purchase price, the
sale was made, and the properties and land-grant
agreement of the St. Paul & Pacific Railroad were
presently taken over by the newly incorporated St.
Paul, Minneapolis & Manitoba Railroad Company.
The incorporators were George Stephen, Donald A.
Smith, Norman W. Kittson, James J. Hill, and
John S. Barnes, the last representing the New York
firm of J. S. Kennedy & Company, which represented,
after a fashion, the Dutch bondholders. Hill was to
manage the railroad.

Meanwhile, matters had been going forward in
Manitoba. Donald A. Smith, the Hudson's Bay Company man, had been to London to assure an adequate
share, for himself and the other Canadian partners of
the company, of the three hundred thousand pounds
that had been paid to the company for relinquishing
its rights of governing Rupert's Land, now Manitoba.
He was successful, and his superiors in London made
him chief commissioner for the company in Canada,
a position that gave him power to act in most if not

all matters without the approval of the distant Board of Governors in London. Smith was a man with the times. He had long since realized that his company's vast land holdings would soon become less valuable as a wilderness for trappers than as real estate to sell to settlers. With this in mind, the Hudson's Bay Company started a new policy of encouraging immigration.

In keeping with this policy, and with the Dominion's wish for a transcontinental railroad, Smith applied for a charter to build a line from Winnipeg to Pembina on the American border. This was the spot Hill had in mind for the northern terminus of the reconverted and rejuvenated St. Paul & Pacific. It is interesting that one of Smith's associates in his Winnipeg-Pembina road was George Stephen, who was also a large stockholder in the Canada Engine Company, Kingston, Ontario, recently organized to build locomotives.

Smith and Stephen worked fast, and in 1874 they contracted with the Dominion government to build 83 miles of road between Selkirk, Smith's home near Winnipeg, and the international border. This line would become the first branch of the Canadian Pacific. While he was at it, Smith also got a contract to build a government telegraph line from Winnipeg to Selkirk.

Now, in the fall of 1877, even while Hill and

associates were still horse-trading with the Dutch, Hill and Kittson's Red River Transportation Company was happy to load a big-stacked locomotive on a barge at Breckenridge, Minnesota, and lash it fast to their *Selkirk*. The barge and the boat were then decorated with flags and a big banner with the letters "C.P.R.," and started downstream, passing Fort Pembina to a salute of American artillery. It was greeted at Winnipeg with whistles, bells, banners, and bunting, plus a special edition of the *Manitoba Free Press*, which had announced this "Grand Rally of Citizens."

It is worth knowing that this first locomotive in Manitoba came from the Baldwin works in Philadelphia, and was christened *Countess of Dufferin*, in honor of the wife of Canada's governor-general.[1] Meanwhile, the Countess herself drove the first spike, and in little more than a year this branch of the Canadian Pacific reached the border, where Mary Sullivan, described as the big, strong, buxom daughter of the boss section man, drove "the last spike home with one mighty blow amidst the loud cheers of the multitude."

That the St. Paul & Pacific tracks were there to

[1] This same *Countess of Dufferin* stands today (1955) where it did in 1912, when the author as a cub on the *Winnipeg Telegram* often stopped to admire it on his rounds. It is a showpiece of the Canadian Pacific Railway and is to be seen in front of the CPR's Winnipeg depot and Royal Alexandra Hotel.

meet the Canadian Pacific, even though the former company was still the property of the Dutch and was being operated by a receiver, was owing almost wholly to something like legerdemain performed by Jim Hill during less than a year—which he later referred to in a magnificent understatement as a "period of trials."

V

SIGNING the agreement between the bondholders and Hill and his three associates did not mean that the property had actually been transferred. The transfer awaited court action. But large portions of the land grant, which incidentally Hill had figured would eventually pay for the bonds and much more, would not wait for court action or anything else. Dates on the calendar of 1878 governed expiration of the grants.

The stipulations provided that the rails of the St. Paul & Pacific must be laid from Sauk Rapids to Melrose, or 35 miles, on or before August 1, and must connect Melrose with Alexandria, another 33 miles, on or before December 1. A hostile legislature was ready to pounce if "suitable roadbed and rails" were not ready as prescribed.

The long haul of 160 miles from Glyndon to St. Vincent (Pembina) did not, under the contract, have to be completed during this year, a fact that was, however, of no comfort. Getting the St. Paul & Pacific to St. Vincent on the international border, to connect with the Canadian Pacific building south from Winnipeg, was of the utmost importance. Hill knew that the Northern Pacific had the same thing in mind, and though that road too was having difficulties, it might well be able to reach the border before Hill and thus be in a position to get the Canadian business. Until the Canadian Pacific had an east-west line, all traffic into and out of Manitoba and the Northwest territories would have to go through Minnesota.

Hill and his associates realized that the demoralized and bankrupt St. Paul & Pacific could not obtain credit to complete the sizable portions of track needed to win the land grant. It could scarcely keep tracks already laid in condition to operate trains. (It was a witticism of the time to remark that the steamcars of the St. P. & P. often found the prairie sod smoother and more reliable than the rails, and took off on occasion to follow buffalo tracks.)

The people of Minnesota generally were weary of the Hollanders. What they wanted was railroads, on any terms whatever, and never mind grasping Dutchmen who had expected to make fortunes from their investment. The legislature was completely in tune with Minnesota citizens, ready to vote for any threat or act that would take away the privileges or even rights of the foreigners who still owned the bonds. They hated the bankrupt railroad. It owed bills for ties, for timber, for hay, for farm produce. The ownership of a huge amount of track iron and other material was in dispute between the railroad and a contractor.

There were other complications, too, and Hill, though pressed almost beyond measure by a multitude

of harassments, kept his one good and burning eye
on the main goal: to hold the land grant. Without it,
the railroad was nothing. Whether or not Hill had a
hand in having Jesse Farley appointed receiver for
the line, it is patent that Farley was quite pliable in
Hill's hands.

Receiver Farley was running the property under
direction of the court. He was theoretically responsible
for anything done—for instance, new construction.
New construction by the railroad itself was out of
the question. Hill had a plan. He and his associates
would make a contract with the receiver to build the
portions necessary to win the land grant. Farley was
willing, but the court had to be convinced. The credit
of Hill and associates was already pledged to the limit
for the bond purchase and to carry the property. Hill
suggested that receiver's certificates against the property were the only recourse. So Mr. Farley applied
to the court for permission to complete the road and
to issue debentures for that purpose.

Two court hearings resulted only in the appointment of two commissioners "to inquire into and report
on the matters specifically submitted to them which
would determine the propriety of issuing the order requested." April was nearly done, and not a new rail
had been laid. May came on. Hill went to Davenport,
Iowa, where the report of the commissioners was to
be made. They advised that Receiver Farley be au-

thorized to contract "with any responsible party for building the line at the lowest figure he could get." The work could be financed by the debentures suggested by Hill, the payments to be made on completion of each ten-mile section.

Now, however, Judge Dillon demurred. He said that he had faith in Hill, but not in his railroad scheme. He did not decline to issue the desired order; but said that, to prevent a repetition of former troubles, he would not allow the issuance of debentures "until the road had been built." This amounted to total refusal.

Hill was discouraged, but did not give up. Instead, he went in person to see the judge and presented him "with the facts and urgent needs of the situation." The judge issued the desired order. What eloquence Hill used to win may be guessed in a remark of the judge after he had signed the permission to issue the debentures. "If Mr. Hill and his associates fail to carry it out," said he, "then they will be destroyed and I will be ruined."

It was late May 1878. Hill probably never looked at the calendar. He knew that one section of the line must be completed by August, another by December, and he meant also that the road should touch the Canadian border before the end of the year.

Hill moved swiftly enough. Before the end of May he was in New York to appear before the directors of the Northern Pacific. Hill knew that these men

expected to receive concessions if they would call off
their project to build to a Canadian connection. Instead, Hill told them bluntly what *he* was going to do.
First, he would terminate the existing agreement that
permitted Northern Pacific trains to run from Sauk
Rapids to St. Paul over the St. Paul & Pacific's tracks
at a nominal charge. Henceforth higher charges were
to be made. Yes, and possibly another charge for use
of the St. Paul's terminals.

The profoundly shocked Northern Pacific directors
retorted with a specific threat to build through the
Red River Valley, and an even more disagreeable
proposition to build their own line north from Minneapolis along the west shore of the Mississippi, thus
paralleling the St. Paul & Pacific's line on the east
bank.

Hill was neither shocked by the retort nor quite
through speaking himself. Now he outlined to the
Northern Pacific directorate a plan he had in mind.
He and his associates, he said, would at once survey
a line from Grand Forks to Fort Buford at the mouth
of the Yellowstone River. This, he pointed out, was
"a good easy line all the way, through a country as
good for agriculture as the very best portions of the
Northern Pacific"; what was more, said Hill, he was
of a mind to ask Congress for half of the land grant
promised to the Northern Pacific as far as the Rocky
Mountains. He felt sure that this request would find

considerable favor in Congress, where there were "strong interests opposed to the Northern Pacific and who would be only too glad to help us."

Letting that sink in a moment, Hill closed his remarks by saying that the interests of himself and his associates lay in developing Manitoba, but that he would not sit quietly while the Northern Pacific built lines that he believed unnecessary and useful only to hurt the St. Paul & Pacific.

At least some of the directors of the Northern Pacific were astute men. Doubtless they considered that much of Hill's talk was bluff. Yet they must have sensed the strength and determination of the forty-year-old man with the massive, shaggy head, for—to be done with this part of the story—later that year President Frederick Billings went to St. Paul to confer with Hill and to say that the Northern Pacific agreed not to build any opposing or competing line, and would no longer oppose the efforts of Hill and his associates to take over the St. Paul & Pacific.

Hill was now in more genial mood. He gracefully offered "facilities for NP traffic in St. Paul, some land there useful for a terminal, and tracking privileges on the new lines to be built by the St. Paul & Pacific on the west side of Red River." A treaty with these provisions was forthwith drawn up and signed by both parties.

Meanwhile, and though carrying the load of the

legal and business matters, Hill was also demonstrating his methods of getting a lot of railroad built quickly. With a little cash and not much more credit, he somehow managed to lay hands on rails, rolling stock, a few locomotives, and hundreds of laborers. Directing the job in person, much of the time at the railhead or in advance of it, he drove his construction crews at a furious rate, laying a mile of track a day, sometimes more. When a crew revolted and quit, Hill wired his man-catchers in Minneapolis, St. Paul, and Chicago to ship him more men, fares prepaid, with a huge thug at each car door to prevent skipping before reaching the job at the end of steel.

In clouds of June mosquitoes that set oxen to bellowing in pain and horses to leaping from their harnesses, the ties were put down and the iron laid. Under the blistering prairie sun of August, when tough men fell from prostration, the work went on with one mile a day the minimum goal—and it was reached or Hill got a new slave boss. Rattlesnakes bit a man here and there. Water with green scum and worse brought dysentery. The crews worked on. There was nowhere to go if you quit. The nights began to turn chilly; there was white on the dirty rag tents in the morning, and soon snow and sleet and hail and wind came down from the North. On went the rails in a world as white as it was bitter, and the cottonwoods along the creeks snapped and exploded like rifle fire. Come night, the stiffs were glad to huddle around the stoves in the boxcars while the Northern Lights blazed with color and crackled like fire. One mile of ties a day. One mile of iron a day.

Jim Hill was there much of the time. He'd walk the grade and watch men and material. He'd even hail a stiff whose nose was beginning to turn white, show him how to rub the frostbitten parts with snow, then lead him to thaw out slowly in a mildly warm car.

When snow drifted and slowed the pace, Hill could not always contain himself. Lee Howard, an old man living in Oregon in 1954, was in one of those gangs in '78 and recalls seeing Jim Hill get down out of his private and comfortable, if not elegant, car to snatch a shovel and start tossing snow. He spelled off one stiff after another, sending each inside to drink a dipper of hot coffee in Hill's own car which was parked on a siding.

Men *worked* for the likes of Jim Hill. Hill called them by their first names, and they stayed and worked and suffered the alternating hot and cold hells while making a railroad along the Red River Valley of the North.

Now appeared legal agents of two other railroads that had ambitions to get an early foothold in the booming Northwest. First came a man from the Chicago & Northwestern, to say that his line would like to take over the St. Paul & Pacific. Then another legal light appeared to declare that the Chicago, Milwaukee & St. Paul road, now managed by an aggressive young man named Van Horne, wanted to tap the business due from Manitoba. Just how Hill handled these men is not clear, but his general policy was to play the Northwestern and the Milwaukee "judiciously against each other," to promise first one then the other of these lines that "the other should have no part in opening up the new territory."

In October of this year on which so much depended in the career of Jim Hill, the Mackenzie government of Canada fell. All construction work on the Canadian Pacific Railway ceased, for it was not known what would be the attitude of John A. Macdonald's administration. Work ceased on the line from Winnipeg to Pembina. Its contractors went unpaid; and they moved to take over portions of the uncompleted tracks themselves. They also threatened to finish the missing links, to complete the whole line, connect it with the St. Paul & Pacific, and then operate the line themselves.

The original plan of Smith and Stephen, and of course of Hill and Kittson, was that the Winnipeg-Pembina line should be leased to the St. Paul & Pacific as soon as it was finished, for a period of ten years—or rather leased to a new company that Hill and associates were ready to organize to take over the old St. Paul & Pacific. But this new crisis of the contractors in Manitoba posed a worse threat than the combined menaces of the Northern Pacific, the Northwestern, and the Milwaukee roads. The threat was overcome by means far from clear three quarters of a century afterward.

All that is clear is that Hill, with his back to the wall in Minnesota, somehow managed to supply rails and other material to certain of the Canadian contractors, and that they finished the job.

In any case, magic had been performed, and in December the Canadian branch line reached the border. That Hill's own road was there to meet it was owing in large part to his heroic labors. Those missing links in the St. Paul & Pacific had been filled, and on January 9, 1879, the Governor of Minnesota issued a certificate that the line had been constructed according to the requirements of the acts of Congress and of the State Legislature. This was the last legal step. The land grant was certified as legally earned. Hill's credit rating immediately went soaring. We shall come presently to the grant.

Before the end of January 1879, the Pembina-Winnipeg road was leased to the St. Paul & Pacific for ten years, and Hill's trains started the unbroken run from St. Paul to Winnipeg. In May a new corporation, the St. Paul, Minneapolis & Manitoba, was organized to take over the St. Paul & Pacific properties at a foreclosure sale. The system's total mileage was 565 miles of completed road, with another 102 miles under construction. Capital stock was limited by charter to $20 million. Common stock was fixed at $15 million. Mortgage bonds for construction and improvement were authorized in the amount of $8 millions, at 7 per cent. Stock in the new concern was given in exchange for that of the Red River Transportation Company.

The incorporators were George Stephen, Donald A. Smith, Norman W. Kittson, John S. Barnes, representing the New York banking firm of J. S. Kennedy, and James J. Hill. Stephen was made president, Hill general manager. An executive committee of three members, of whom Hill was one, was appointed.

What the properties of the old St. Paul & Pacific actually cost the new concern is something that no expert in finance has cared to state without innumerable qualifications. After a great deal of digging in the records, Gustavus Meyers estimated the cost to have been $6,780,000, but even he started immediately to hedge, remarking that "the Hill coterie were not called upon to pay this sum in money. They were allowed to turn in receiver's debentures and bonds as payment for the purchase price."

The Dutch bondholders received, according to the class of bonds held, from 13¼ to 75 per cent of their par value; and one may hope that they were completely cured of a wish to finance railroads in the wilds of a wild country. But if these Hollanders continued to hold even an academic interest in American railroad affairs, they must in the next few years have come to believe they had been unmercifully hornswoggled in their dealing with Hill and his associates. For one thing, the new St. Paul, Minneapolis & Manitoba promptly disposed of a large portion, though not all, of its 2,586,606 acres of granted land, for $13,068,887. The trouble with those Dutchmen was that they lacked faith. As Hill's court biographer so aptly remarked: "Mr. Hill believed steadfastly in the American Northwest and its development."

The Dutch had been paid off, but what about Jesse P. Farley, he who had been the last receiver for the St. Paul & Pacific? Farley let it be known that *he* had not been paid off, and now in both state and federal courts, he came forward to demand that he be recompensed for his efforts. The several cases wound through the courts, term upon term, year upon year, and before Farley arrived at the end of his legal rope, the contest had spanned almost thirteen years. In the end, Farley was unable to collect so much as one dollar.

Ex-receiver Farley charged that Hill and Kittson had conspired with him to betray the courts and betray the Dutch bondholders. He was to so mismanage the affairs of the bankrupt road that the price of the

bonds would be reduced. He swore that he agreed
to keep Hill and Kittson informed of every move he
made. At the right time Hill, Kittson, and their back-
ers were to get control. As for the pay-off, said Farley,
he and Hill and Kittson were each to have a one-fifth
share in the new railroad that was to be organized
around the wreck of the old. But when the deal went
through, Farley was ignored.

It was rather audacious ground upon which to base
a suit. In dismissing it, a United States circuit court
remarked, in 1882: "Courts will not and ought not
to be made the agencies whereby frauds are in any
respect recognized or aided. They will not unravel a
tangled web of fraud for the benefit of anyone en-
meshed therein through whose agency the web was
woven." One after the other, the several courts refused to consider a secret agreement to commit fraud
(Farley had no written agreement with Hill), and
in 1893 the Supreme Court of the United States up-
held the lower courts. Hill's biographer gloried in the
contest, not only because Farley was defeated in regard to the one-fifth interest, but because Farley, who
claimed to have originated the idea of buying the St.
Paul & Pacific and connecting it with Winnipeg, was
"rejected as the author of this plan." Hence, the role of
master planner was "necessarily assigned to Mr. Hill."

While Farley was starting his court action, Hill
was already planning great things for the new railroad,

which, for sake of brevity, will henceforth be referred
to here as the Manitoba. What he wanted was to get
such complete control of the Red River Valley that
no change of heart by the Northern Pacific or any
other road would have any effect. In 1879, right on
the heels of the Manitoba's organization, he went to
see the legislature of Dakota Territory about getting
a charter for a railroad on the west bank of the Red
River. (The Manitoba ran on the east side.) But it
was not in the power of the Territory to grant a charter. Hill set his legal lights and lobbyists to work on a
general railroad law for Dakota, and by 1882 he had
his law and his charter. Only a little later he had his
tracks laid on the Red River's west side from Fargo
to the border.

With the Manitoba railroad in running order, Hill
and his associates were happy to welcome a bumper
crop of wheat, which was hauled to the already sizable milling industry located around the Falls of St.
Anthony at Minneapolis. On one day alone in October
the Manitoba moved 130 carloads. During the Manitoba's first year, the company placed orders for 12,000
tons of steel, not iron, rail. In the previous eighteen
months it had laid 26,000 tons. Hill himself also
let contracts for 225 miles of new road, about half of
which was to be laid in the Red River Valley.

It is obvious that though Hill's immediate object

was to tap the Red River Valley and Manitoba in general, his eye was already on the western United States. How far his eye roamed at this period is not known, for neither then nor later was Hill given to unnecessary discussion of his ambitions or plans. He was ready at almost any time to tell an interviewer that there was no substitute for hard work; and that honesty was, indeed, the best policy; but when it came to a specific fact, he was uncommonly chary of speech. One can believe without difficulty, however, that his threat to the Northern Pacific directors—namely that he had a mind to lay his tracks to the Rockies so fast as to pass the other's and to demand of the government one half of the NP's land grant—was much more than bluff. His subsequent career is indication that his mind, at least as early as 1878, was turned toward the immense expanse of nothing that ran from the Red River to the Cascade Range, beyond which were growing settlements and civilization. Indeed, as soon as Hill considered the Manitoba to be properly installed in Minnesota and Canada, his first steps were to take Dakota into his orbit.

At this same period, a portion of Hill's enormous energy was devoted to the affairs of the Canadian Pacific transcontinental, and this is the proper place to indicate his part in choosing a right of way, building its lines, and even supplying it with Van Horne and other talented men.

VI

THE EARLY efforts to build a railroad across Canada have been mentioned briefly. They bogged down in charges of private graft and political corruption, and the whole affair was labeled "The Pacific Railway Scandal," which carried a taint not unlike that of Union Pacific's Crédit Mobilier. With his return to power, John A. Macdonald, that magnificent politician, clubbed his Conservative party into passing a new act that provided that the railroad should be built by a private company aided by government land grants, cash subsidies, and loans.

Late in 1880 this concern was chartered as the Canadian Pacific Railway Company. Its officers included George Stephen, president, and on its executive committee were James J. Hill and R. B. Angus, general manager of the Bank of Montreal, of which Stephen was the head. Angus was also a vice-president of Hill's Manitoba railroad. Donald A. Smith appeared only as one of the stockholders. Winnipeg was the original center of operations.

The record of the division of labor of this talented crew is fairly clear. Stephen and Smith were responsible for the financing and also the political good health of the undertaking. Hill was the over-all chief of routes and construction. Angus, a native Scot, performed many quiet and useful duties, among which was to act as liaison between Hill and the Canadian associates.

Government surveys made before the company was organized indicated the best route through the Rockies was by way of Yellowhead Pass. Hill did not favor this route, and to find a new and better one he engaged a resolute character, Major A. B. Rogers, probably the first Yale graduate in Canadian Pacific employ. Hill had been attracted by Rogers's "ingenuity in discovering economical locations" for railroad lines, and Rogers was the first of the several brilliant men Hill put to work for the Canadian transcontinental.

Major Rogers became a legend in Canadian Pacific history, and deserves the mountain pass that bears his name. Fifty-two years of age when he headed into the Rockies for Hill, he had already been around, as the phrase has it. A veteran of the Indian Wars of 1862, he had served ably at the defense of St. Peter, Minnesota, having by then already shipped before the mast, studied at Brown, and been graduated from Yale in engineering. His railroad location work had been done largely on the prairies, and it had been done so well that Hill, against the custom of the time, which favored mountain-trained men for mountain work, sent him on the toughest assignment the Canadian Pacific could offer.

One of the railroad's young men of the time described Rogers as a rough and ready engineer, a true pathfinder, a short, sharp, snappy man with long, wild-flying Dundreary whiskers. He was a master of profanity. His scientific equipment consisted of a compass and an aneroid slung around his neck. His idea of a day's substantial provisions for an engineer was a plug of chewing tobacco in one pocket and a couple of slabs of hardtack in the other.

Taking a tip from Walter Moberly, British Columbia's outstanding surveyor, Rogers made his terrible way through the Rockies at Kicking Horse Creek, then over the barrier of the Selkirk range by way of Beaver Creek and the Illecillewaet River. This was the way the Canadian Pacific was to go, and the pass through the Selkirks was given Rogers's name.

It is indicative of Major Rogers's Spartan methods that the ten Indian guides he engaged for his first locating trip were hired by contract from the Oblate Mission at Kamloops, and the contract stipulated that if any came back without a letter of good report, "his wages were to go to the church, and his chief was to give him a hundred lashes on his bare back."

It is probable that by this time Hill's long-range plan was to extend his own railroad through Dakota, and so on west. But for the present, traffic income could best be increased by populating the province of Manitoba. To this end, Hill staged so successful a campaign to attract immigrants that twenty thousand settlers arrived the first season, and the Canadian Pacific pushed its rails west to Brandon. There was as yet no rail connection between Winnipeg and eastern Canada. The route was by way of Toronto to Chicago and St. Paul, then over the Manitoba to the rising Red River metropolis.

Hill now removed A. B. Stickney, his own construction boss on the Manitoba, and sent him to Winnipeg as general superintendent of the Western Division of the Canadian Pacific; and for the post of auditor of the new railroad he recommended I. G. Ogden, snatched from the Chicago Great Western. Ogden later became vice-president in charge of finance. Then, perhaps Hill's most brilliant move of all, so far as the Canadian line was concerned, he persuaded W. C. Van Horne, the young general manager of the Chicago, Milwaukee & St. Paul Railroad, to take charge of everything connected with the Canadian Pacific west of Winnipeg.

Van Horne had never worked for Jim Hill, but Hill had been impressed by the young man's ability as general manager of the Milwaukee Railroad when that line had threatened to invade Hill's territory in 1880. When Hill sent him to Winnipeg late in 1881, Van Horne was only thirty-eight years of age. Yet he had bossed the Milwaukee, and before that had managed the Chicago & Alton. He was tall, of massive build, and bearded. As a youth in Illinois, where he was born, he had wanted to be an artist, but because of family poverty and the death of his father he had gone to railroading.

At fourteen Van Horne was a fully qualified telegraph-operator for the Illinois Central. At twenty-one he was a train-dispatcher for the Alton. At thirty-one he was managing the Southern Minnesota, which he brought out of receivership. Seven years later, when Hill got him for the Canadian Pacific, he was running the Milwaukee with a sure touch and no little aggressiveness.

Van Horne took charge at Winnipeg on the last day of 1881. One of his engineers, J. H. E. Secretan, recalled that in his first interview with Van Horne, whom he called the Czar of the CPR, he was told "in a most autocratic manner" that what Van Horne wanted was the shortest commercial line between Winnipeg and Vancouver. He stated also that he intended to build 500 miles of grade that summer and to lay rails and have trains running. When Secretan expressed doubt that 500 miles of road could be built in a short summer, the Czar scowled and remarked that nothing was impossible, telling the engineer that "if I could show him the route, it was all he wanted, and if I couldn't, then he would have my scalp."

It seems agreed that Van Horne was dynamic and

ruthless. He was his own chief engineer, and made clear to his staff that he did not care *where* the lines went so long as they got there the quickest way. Speed was the first consideration. Van Horne's superior, Stephen, had told him that for financial as well as political reasons the Canadian Pacific must connect Winnipeg with both Vancouver and Montreal as quickly as possible. That was all Van Horne needed to know.

Six thousand men, and a third as many teams, drove across the prairies with all but incredible speed. The construction camps, said an observer familiar with American railroad camps, were by comparison almost military in appearance and discipline. Everything ran by command. The haste was such that the locating engineers were only a few weeks ahead of the graders. Although Van Horne did not get quite his 500 miles, the track laid that first season ran well over 400.

Meanwhile, Van Horne had induced Thomas G. Shaughnessy to leave the Milwaukee's employ and join him as general factotum, a job that this American son of an Irish immigrant filled to the complete satis-faction of the imperial Van Horne. He went on to become in good time Van Horne's successor, and Sir Thomas to boot.

While his gangs were racing across the prairies, Van Horne was obliged to divert some of his attention to the troubles of CPR construction on the line north of Lake Superior. Hill had already urged Van Horne to vote against building this line. Hill naturally wanted his Manitoba road to have the traffic incident to building some 2,500 miles of CPR west of Winnipeg; but if connection was made by an all-Canada route to Montreal, the Manitoba would suffer.

But when Van Horne went to Montreal to confer with Stephen and Donald A. Smith, he was made to realize that the CPR was not meant to be a mere feeder to an American railroad, but a Canadian transcontinental. He was also told that to maintain the backing of Premier Macdonald, this troublesome link of the CPR must be built, and the sooner the better. Van Horne went to look over the ground. It was chiefly rock and muskeg, and he remarked of this section that it was "two hundred miles of engineering impossibility." Yet the railroad must be laid, and Van Horne went to work.

Ten thousand men were soon blasting ahead in the rocks and trying to locate bottom in the muskegs. To supply them, Van Horne contracted to have materials brought by steamboats on Lake Superior. One hardy mile "cost above $750,000." In another spot, hidden lakes swallowed the track half a dozen times, along with three locomotives. In still another place, a lake had to be lowered ten feet. It was impossible either to bridge or to drain some of the coves; around Jackfish Bay, the road had to span three miles to reach a point less than half a mile distant in a direct line. Whisky-peddlers were more difficult to combat here in the wilderness than on the open prairie, and at Michipicoten a gang of them threatened Station Agent Alex Macdonald with death if he attempted to interfere with them, and staged a riot on payday.

Jim Hill did not like the look of the railroad approaching Winnipeg from the east. He was also "chagrined," said a CPR historian, when Van Horne ordered three fine Clyde-built steamers for service on the Great Lakes. Hill himself was planning something similar. The drop in the Manitoba's traffic income, caused by the fact that the CPR was now able to move its construction crews and supplies on its own ships and trains, was a sore blow to the prosperity of Hill's road, which had been getting the business when the only construction was in or west of Manitoba. The wild real-estate and business boom at Winnipeg had largely collapsed. Even worse, Hill had come to the realization that his allies, Stephen and Smith, who were still directors and heavy stockholders in his Manitoba road, were determined to finish that construction link north of Lake Superior and thus keep all traffic within Canada.

On May 3, 1883 Hill resigned from the board of the Canadian Pacific. Two months later Stephen, Smith, and Angus resigned as directors of the Manitoba, though they retained their stock. All four men remained on friendly terms, then and apparently to the end of their lives. This was not true of Hill and Van Horne. Hill doubtless believed that his protégé had done him wrong, though actually Van Horne was doing what he had been engaged for—to complete a transcontinental line, no matter who got hurt. In a later chapter we shall see how, after he resigned from the CPR board, Hill harassed Van Horne and the Canadian Pacific.

If Hill's leaving the CPR had any effect on his former protégé, it was to drive him harder than ever. Up through the dreadful canyon of the Fraser River into the Rockies went the rails from the west, while other rails were approaching from the east by way of Kicking Horse and Rogers passes. And tracks were laid only to sink again and again along the north shore of Lake Superior. By train, boat, wagon, and horseback Van Horne covered the width of the Dominion, firing, hiring, commanding—but never pleading.

His superiors were also having their troubles; cash was not coming from the government subsidy as expected, and late in 1884 it began to look as if the whole project was doomed. The crews went months with no paycar on the siding. Construction bosses were hard put to explain matters, so they lied and bluffed and threatened. It was clear, at least to Smith and Stephen, that they would certainly fail unless another government loan could be obtained. Both

Smith and Stephen had had to draw on their own
resources, pledging their own fortunes to keep things
moving. Even then work came to a halt in British
Columbia. There in the mountains the working stiffs
could wait no longer. At Beavermouth three hundred
of them, many armed with revolvers, went on a strike
and rampage. Trainloads of track-layers were intimidated and driven back to the camp. The strikers
moved to capture a bridge across the Columbia. Eight
of Superintendent Steele's Royal Northwest Mounted
Police took hold of the situation. They held off the
strikers, read the Riot Act, and by bold, cool action
got control of the camp.

Just then, which was early in 1885, rebellion
broke out in the Saskatchewan Country. Louis Riel,
he of the Red River uprising, had returned from the
United States to lead it. Collecting disaffected Metis,
who objected to the method of government surveys
on the prairies and now hated the Canadian Pacific
Railway instead of the Hudson's Bay Company, Riel
planned that *this* rebellion should be war, and not a
rather gentle rebellion like that he had staged around
Fort Garry.

Riel and his men began by raiding a store for
weapons, then attacked a post of Mounted Police,
killing and wounding several men. The Canadian
minister of defense sent wires to militia commanders

throughout the Dominion. Winnipeg's Ninetieth Battalion entrained for Fort Qu'Appelle.

Van Horne happened to be in Ottawa on CPR business when news of the uprising came. He told government men that he could get troops over the gaps in the unfinished railroad and move them into the Northwest Territories in eleven days if given a free hand. The government agreed. What followed is one of the most stirring episodes in Canada's military history.

Taking command like any field marshal, Van Horne moved five thousand troops, most of them 1,800 miles, and some 2,500 miles, into Saskatchewan. One contingent required nine days, but others made it in four. To span the gaps in construction along Lake Superior, Van Horne laid rails on ice and snow. He ran trains across frozen rivers. To speed work, he imported gangs of Chinese coolies from the United States; and turned work trains into troop trains. The weather was bitter. The mercury fell once to fifty degrees below zero, which was good for the sections where the rails rested on ice, but tough on the soldiers who had to ride on open and uncovered flatcars. Now and again the troops had to walk or ride on sleds. The artillery took seventeen hours to cross one thirty-mile gap.

Van Horne doubled the cookhouse crews in the

CPR construction camps, and they worked around the clock, brewing coffee, baking bread, and making mulligan, which were served the troops in unlimited quantities. Morale remained high despite the fact that it is possible that no troops anywhere, save perhaps in Siberia, have undergone an ordeal worse than the Canadian volunteers of the Northwest Rebellion. The Rebellion was crushed by sheer weight rather than brilliant command of the militia; and Louis Riel was hanged at Regina.

Van Horne's superb work in moving the troops had enormous effect on public opinion in establishing the military value of the Canadian Pacific. Only fifteen years previously, getting troops to Fort Garry to suppress the Red River uprising had taken more than three months. This time, and over a still uncompleted railroad, they had covered a like distance in four days. The CPR was dramatically vindicated.

Just in time. George Stephen and Donald Smith had sold or pledged everything they owned to help pay the railroad's most urgent creditors. Van Horne used to say, in later years, that the finest speech he ever heard was made in the CPR board room at this time. Ruin seemed to be just ahead. Stephen turned to Smith: "Donald," he said, "when they come they must not find a dollar." He meant that, he and Smith having spent or mortgaged all they owned, creditors of the railroad attempting to collect by suing either

Smith or himself would discover that neither man possessed one dollar of his own.

But the part played by the railroad in quelling the Rebellion had changed everything. The government now dared to lend it money. On the last day of April, while troops were still in the field, the CPR loan went through. Crews were paid across the Dominion. On November 7, 1885 the official Last Spike was driven at Craigellachie, high in the mountains of British Columbia. It was typical of Van Horne that he refused a silver spike tendered by the Marquis of Lansdowne, Canada's governor-general, and instead ordered that a plain iron spike be used. That wasn't all. Van Horne declared that anyone who came to the last-spike ceremony must be connected with the railroad or pay his fare. James J. Hill was not among the dignitaries present.

Van Horne went on to become and serve for eleven years as president of the railroad. By then he was Sir William, by reason of appointment as an Honorary Knight Commander of the Order of St. Michael and St. George. Stephen and Smith went into the peerage as Lord Mount Stephen and Lord Strathcona. Premier Macdonald became Sir John. More than any other railroad anywhere, the Canadian Pacific came to be identified with the country of its birth. Sir William Cornelius Van Horne's part in making it such was so great that it seems odd, or possibly churlish, that there is no mention even of his name in the 957 big pages of the authorized *Life* of James J. Hill.

This omission is of interest in any consideration of Hill. We may dismiss Hill's sole instruction to his biographer, Mr. Pyle, as so much wind. "Make it plain and simple and true," he had said. The biography is neither plain nor simple. Possibly it is as true as it is slavish, but it leaves all sorts of natural questions unanswered. One has to look elsewhere for clues to the character of Hill, who at any rate was not the pompous, mealy-mouthed, righteous, and almost sanctified dummy of the *Life*.

Clues about the rift between Hill and Van Horne are to be found in any serious writing about the building of the Canadian Pacific Railway. That the rift was so marked as to be dangerous to the policy of the two railroads most concerned is obvious in John Murray Gibbon's study of the Canadian line. "In 1894," he remarks, "Lord Mount Stephen paid a farewell visit to Canada and the United States, partly in the endeavour to create more amicable relations between Hill and Van Horne. This was as easy as mixing vinegar and oil."

We have seen that Hill vainly tried to have Van Horne use his influence to prevent building CPR track east of Winnipeg. Hill then thought of the line as a feeder for his Manitoba. Several years later, says Murray, Van Horne wrote Mount Stephen to say he had lost all faith in Hill. He charged that Hill's "apparently friendly disposition towards the CPR" comes from "his need of assistance of yourself and Sir Donald [Smith] in carrying out his Montana and Pacific coast plans and from nothing else." He speaks of "the hollowness" of Hill's offers to help with CPR's Soo Line problems, is convinced that Hill's influence in Washington has been "dead set against the CPR," and says he will henceforth shape his plans "on the assumption that Hill is the most dangerous enemy of the Canadian Pacific." As a clincher, Van Horne remarks that Hill "conceals his poison in friendly words."

In his work on the Canadian Pacific, Murray states that Hill, "full of brotherly love, would send Van Horne a picture for his gallery, and then issue instructions that no through tickets were to be sold to Great Northern passengers for CPR steamers to the Orient." Murray also states without qualification that the "valuable iron territory which Van Horne had virtually acquired for the Soo Line, was taken from him by the Great Northern." Well, why not? Hill was running the Great Northern, not the Soo Line. "The value of a railway," said Hill, "is in its capacity to make money."

Regardless of these sluggings and gougings, which after all were only the natural history of empire builders, the two men held certain attitudes that were incompatible. In his latter years, at least, Hill was

gregarious; Van Horne was not. Hill thoroughly enjoyed sycophants; Van Horne did not. Hill liked
nothing better than to act as judge of a cattle show;
he prided himself on having the best bulls, the best
rams, the best boars in all Minnesota. Van Horne
liked to paint landscapes, which he did very well.

One cannot quite picture Jim Hill testing his ac-
quaintances for sincerity by the methods Van Horne
delighted to use. One was his cigar test. A widely
advertised five-cent cigar in Canada was named for
Van Horne. He would send out for a hundred of
these dreadful things, have his butler remove the
bands, then put the cigars in an expensive humidor.
After dinner this was wheeled around to the guests.
This or that toady would take a deep puff. "Ah, Sir
William, what an aroma!" Another would exclaim on
the host's wonderful taste in the field of pure Havana.
Then, there was his art test. Van Horne signed one
or more of his own paintings "Théo. Rousseau," one
of the French masters of the 1860's, and took sardonic
delight in hearing the flattery of pretentious guests
who praised his taste. Hill would have considered such
capers worthy only of juveniles or, worse, dilettantes.

VII

A BUMPER wheat crop, along with continued heavy immigration into western Canada, permitted Hill's railroad to get off to a flying start. And the sale of more than thirteen million dollars' worth of St. Paul, Minneapolis & Manitoba grant lands during a short period provided the capital Hill would need to improve the line and defend his territory against the wolves of "foreign" lines, such as the Northern Pacific, the Milwaukee, and lesser roads, several of which were no more than nuisance or blackmail affairs being built, after a fashion, or merely "projected" for sale to the highest bidder.

These "foreign" lines were becoming a sort of local menace, and Hill certainly did nothing to lessen the fear in which they were held. In deploring the outside ownership of Minnesota's railroads, the report of the railroad commissioners of that state remarked: "The Manitoba is the only remaining system distinctly our own." This may have startled Donald Smith and George Stephen, respectively of the Hudson's Bay Company and the Bank of Montreal, but they were Scots, and therefore content to keep their own counsel where delicate matters of finance were concerned.

If the Minnesota railroad commissioners were a little wide of the mark in considering the Manitoba to be distinctly a home-grown affair, they were even further afield in regard to Jim Hill. In the same report, the commissioners observed glumly: "Directly Mr. Hill will be tired of overwork, and his line will pass into the jaws of the anaconda which is swallowing the smaller lines as fast as it can digest and assimilate them." When that wild statement was made, Hill was forty-three years old. Though he may even then have looked sixty, he still had thirty-five years to go, and of those thirty-five years all save the last ten days were to find him expending a remarkable amount of either physical or mental energy, or both. Jim Hill tired at forty-three! The Minnesota commissioners, to quote an apt sentence of Hill's biographer, "had no conception of the real situation at all."

As the head of the Manitoba railroad surveyed the field in 1881, he could feel that the north did not call for his attention except for his purposeful contributions to the Canadian Pacific. On his south and west was the Northern Pacific, which would have to be watched closely. Then, there were those other "foreign" lines seeking to share in the fertile lands of the Dakotas. These could be dealt with by negotiation and traffic agreements.

On the east, however, Hill must make some connection for an outlet. The Northern Pacific had started life with an outlet, Duluth, from which its road had been built westward. Touching Duluth, too,

was the former Lake Superior & Mississippi, now reorganized as the St. Paul & Duluth. Chicago-based
railroads were deeply interested in this line because
during the months of open water it could offer low
lake and rail rates to St. Paul; and by the time Hill
was able to consider it, the St. Paul & Duluth had been
quietly acquired by the Chicago roads.

Hill's road, it will be recalled, had begun life with
a sumptuous land grant, and now, in 1881, the Manitoba had money. Hill went to see the owners of the
St. Paul & Duluth, conducting the negotiations with
such dispatch that in less than a month the Manitoba
was admitted to the pool. Although Hill was never a
man who really enjoyed joint control of anything, use
of the St. Paul & Duluth would do for the present.

Still thinking of wheat, Hill observed that the
shortest available route from the Red River fields
served by the Manitoba to the head of the lakes would
have to leave the main line of his road at a point well
north of St. Paul. With little noise he picked up, for
$30,000, the charter of a strictly paper railroad, the
Minneapolis & St. Cloud, which called for a grant of
ten sections of swamplands per mile between the town
of St. Cloud and the line of the St. Paul & Duluth, a
distance of sixty miles; and four sections per mile
from there to the north shore of Lake Superior.

Hill put a construction crew to work immediately,
and the sixty-mile cutoff was built and in operation

late in 1882. It met the St. Paul & Duluth line at tragic Hinckley, which, a bit later, was the scene of one of the worst forest fires in history, when 413 lives were lost. The St. Cloud cutoff brought Duluth more than one hundred miles nearer the Red River wheat fields than it had been.

While Hill had been patching a line across Minnesota, the Northern Pacific had emerged from receivership and, under the often inspired direction of Henry Villard, was building across the northern United States, starting from both ends, the one in Dakota, the other on the Pacific coast. Villard was as different from Hill as could be imagined. Born Ferdinand Heinrich Gustav Hilgard in Rhenish Bavaria, he was three years older than Hill, and came from an important family. He was being educated at the University of Munich when a disagreement with his father caused him to emigrate to the United States in 1853. Mastering the English language with remarkable speed, he was presently ranging the western states and territories and writing articles for St. Louis, Cincinnati, and New York papers. During the Civil War he was correspondent for New York and Chicago newspapers. In 1871, while on a trip to Europe to restore his failing health, he made the acquaintance of a protective committee of German bondholders who, even as the Hollanders, had invested heavily in what up to then had been just another American mirage.

The bonds of the Germans had been issued in support of a seeming illusion incorporated as the Oregon & California Railroad Company. They had been unable to learn much of anything as to what the road had done with their money. Villard agreed to return to the United States to find out. In 1874 he arrived at Portland to investigate. He quickly perfected a working agreement among the Oregon & California, the Oregon Central, and the Oregon Steamship Company by which passengers and freight were to be exchanged as best suited to routes. Meanwhile he also joined a group of bondholders of the Kansas Pacific Railroad, and when that went into bankruptcy, Villard was made receiver. Here he had to match wits in the fast company of Jay Gould of the Union Pacific and did rather well, achieving a personal financial success.

Returning to Oregon, Villard purchased the Oregon Steam Navigation Company, reorganized it, and started to build a railroad eastward from Portland. He soon clashed with the Northern Pacific's western division, which also was building a railroad. Villard, says one of his biographers, "resolved to prevent completion of the rival road." He began by buying Northern Pacific stock to the limit of his own resources, then appealed to his friends for help. He accomplished what in railroad history is still considered one of the most notable achievements in the annals, and is remembered as the Villard Blind Pool; he asked fifty friends to subscribe toward a fund of $8 million, the exact purpose of which was not then revealed. He got the money, plus another $12 million, and bought control of the Northern Pacific, of which he was elected president in 1881.

With as much energy as Van Horne was displaying north of the border, and with infinitely more graciousness, Villard pushed construction to the utmost. The Northern Pacific, from Duluth to Tacoma, was completed in 1883. It was the second so-called transcontinental in the United States. Its land grant was something to conjure with.

When the last spike of the Northern Pacific was driven, Hill's road was creeping into and across Dakota. He had long since told his associates that he meant to lay a road to Puget Sound. If Hill meant to drive through to the West Coast, he seemed in no great haste. He told a few intimates that the Northern Pacific line was far from the best possible route. To begin with, it had cost too much per mile to build. It contained too many curves, too many heavy grades. In many places it had ignored fine advantages of terrain. Worst of all, to Hill's mind, the Northern Pacific's builders had been in too great a hurry to lay rails and had given no thought to their rear. As for Hill, he would pick a route in person. He planned to build along his route for a few miles, then, like any good military man, protect his rear.

Look at a map of the Great Northern Railroad to-day, seventy years later. Note those short branches, one after the other, taking off from the main line, heading north to touch the Canadian border. These were built as the protectors of Jim Hill's rear. From Brockston to Crookston in Minnesota; to Grand Forks, Larimore, Lakota, Devils Lake, York, Rugby, Towner, and still others in Dakota; to Bainville, Saco, Shelby, and others in Montana; to Bonners Ferry in Idaho, then to Spokane. From these the feeders went out—feeders to bring grain and cattle and lumber and ore to keep Jim Hill's traffic in good volume. They may be of less value to the road today than they were when built, but they were the means by which a railroad could pay as it went through a largely uninhabited region. It was the ideal of living off the country, the idea that was prompting inventors to devise a straw-burning traction engine that could travel from farm to farm on woodless prairies to do the threshing.

West of the Minnesota border, Hill had no land grant to sell in order to raise money. His was the first transcontinental to head for the Pacific coast without such grants in all the states traversed. But government homesteads were to be had for the settling all the way to Puget Sound. Hill would populate those homesteads as his tracks moved west. Europe was crowded with peasants who could survive this bitter climate and tame this land. There were some even nearer than Europe, a colony of Icelanders who had founded Gimli on Lake Winnipeg.

Illness, poverty, and lack of tools and equipment had brought discouragement to the people of Gimli, and when the Reverend Paul Thorlaksson went to comfort them, he was appalled. He had seen the Red River Valley in the golden harvest time. He had traveled on a fine steamboat of Hill and Kittson's Red River line, and doubtless had been exposed to the enthusiasms already being printed and distributed by Hill's agents. In any case, the good shepherd of the despairing people at Gimli bade such as would to follow him to Eden, and in 1878 they did, nearly two hundred of them, settling anew in the Red River Valley near Pembina, within sound of the whistles of Jim Hill's new Manitoba railroad, ready to take their wheat to market.

The publicity arranged by Hill through agents and newspapers was believed to have brought some twenty thousand settlers to the province of Manitoba in 1881, and almost as many to the American portion of the Red River Valley. There was to be no let-down in the colonization efforts of the Hill railroad. As his track moved westward and the stub lines went out from the main line, his well-paid agents grew in number and eloquence as they related in half a dozen lan-

guages the joys and profits of homesteading along the
St. Paul, Minneapolis & Manitoba Railroad.

Affairs of the Manitoba were going famously. In
1882 the capital stock was increased from $15 mil-
lion to $20 million, the limit permitted by the charter.
In the same year, too, the company also guaranteed a
$3 million bond issue of the Minneapolis Union Rail-
way Company. Some of this was used to supply new
connections in that city, and more went into a structure that Hill always referred to in capital letters as
the Stone Arch Bridge. There was nothing else like it
in the United States of 1882, and perhaps there is
nothing quite like it today, seventy-odd years later.

If anything were needed to indicate that Jim Hill
warranted the old cliché that he built for the future,
then the Stone Arch Bridge would do. It was laid, at
a cost that seemed reckless at the time, at an angle
across the Mississippi River just above St. Anthony
Falls in the heart of Minneapolis. It is 2,100 feet
long, 28 feet wide, 82 feet high, and built for the centuries out of St. Cloud granite. Three of its arches are
of 40-foot span, sixteen of 80 foot, and four of 100
foot. Of this neolithic monster, naturally called Hill's
Folly by lesser men than its builder, Hill himself said
it was "the hardest thing I ever had to do in my life,
the hardest undertaking I ever had to face."

In 1954 Ralph Budd, one of the great railroad figures in the United States, recalled that Hill took great

pride in the Stone Arch Bridge and liked often to talk about it. "When it came to railroad structures," said Mr. Budd, "Mr. Hill was an advocate of functional design. He had no time for frills of any kind and appreciated good lines which resulted from sound functional planning.

"The Stone Arch Bridge is now [1954] one of the oldest bridges across the Mississippi and one of the few bridges in the United States that was built in the early Eighties which, without reinforcement, still carries the heaviest modern trains and locomotives. It is a strong, graceful structure, a large part of it carrying the tracks on a curve. Mr. Hill told me that he and his chief engineer, Colonel C. C. Smith, gave a great deal of attention to the foundations, and that one of them in particular, near the west shore of the river, was very difficult. When the bridge was completed, the two men decided to make some test runs over it and for the purpose got together several locomotives of the heaviest type then in use and ran them at as high speed as was practical.

"Meanwhile, Hill and Smith stood alongside the pier and pressed their bodies against it with out-stretched arms so they could detect any tremor there might be. To their delight there was no vibration. Mr. Hill explained to me in considerable detail how they built the structure on curved alinement by tapering the piers, making them wider at one end than at the other. He also told me that this bridge is the only structure on the Great Northern Railway that bears his name and that he did not authorize placing it there. On one occasion he took me and showed me the so-called corner stone, which is a large sandstone block set in the upstream end of one of the piers. Hill's name and that of Colonel Smith are cut in large letters along with the name of the contractor responsible for placing the stone there." [1]

Surely the Stone Arch Bridge is evidence that Hill was thinking of something other than the small, if growing, Manitoba railroad, which, when the bridge was finished in 1883, had reached only to Devils Lake, less than halfway across Dakota. But the rails were still headed west, though Hill thought it well to pause briefly and build a track north from Grafton on the west side of the Red River to touch the border at Gretna, Manitoba. It was one of his first feeder lines. It also gave him a second track to Winnipeg. Best of all, it precluded interference there from the Northern Pacific. Hill heartily disliked interference.

He must have spent much time during this period going over the line. His letters to his office and his diaries show that his eye saw a great deal that needed attention. A note says that some odd lengths of rail that cannot be matched should be gathered up and sold for junk; another reports that a "platform east end

[1] In a letter to the author from Mr. Budd.

of depot wants one eighteen-foot plank for repairs";
he regrets to discover that some locomotive engineer
has "dumped his fire on the ties and burned them out
in two or three places." He finds that "flatcar No.
1269 has two broken truss rods and should be re-
paired." Here and there in his papers are rough
sketches for station buildings and roundhouses, and lay-
outs for yards, tracks, switches. He reports that a certain engineer has been kept on his locomotive too
long without sleep, which "ought not to happen." He
puts the finger on "One car repairer here, this man
smells of whiskey."

From such minor if important things, Hill goes on
to report the condition of the Manitoba railroad to
his board of directors. He tells them that though the
enormous gain in business during the first three
months of 1882 was caused in large part by freight for
building the Canadian Pacific, this fell to almost nothing later in the year because the new Thunder Bay
Branch of the Canadian road has taken away the
business "which has hitherto gone via Duluth and our
lines." It will be recalled that Hill had advised his
protégé, Van Horne, against completing this projected CPR branch on Thunder Bay. Hill was
patently disappointed.

Although Hill's railroad was now well financed
and his locating engineers were pushing on into Mon-

tana Territory, he showed no disposition to hurry matters. The stub lines must go out to tap the region between his main line west and the Canadian border. Between Grand Forks and Williston, both now in North Dakota, they were already being built, or at least had been located, and there were ten of them. Another item in Jim Hill's rear was sufficient grain elevators to handle the crops for loading. Either the Manitoba built them or Jim Hill offered inducements to have them built by others. The same was true of trackside stockyards. This country, he thought, was the place to raise either cattle or wheat. Somehow or other he found time to learn more about wheat than most farmers knew. As for cattle, he had already established his own stock farm on Crystal Bay at Lake Minnetonka, where he began to experiment with different breeds. The hardy Scotch varieties took his fancy, especially the Polled Angus. In 1883 he paid $5,000 for a single Angus bull and wrote to a farmer in Dakota that "our farmers depend too much on the cultivation of grain, which in a short time must impoverish the land. . . . What we need is a stock of cattle good for both dairy and beef."

The rails went ahead slowly. Through purchase of a short line here and there, or by actual construction, the Manitoba's mileage increased by 224 miles in 1882; by 277 miles in 1883; and by another 175 miles in 1884. These were modest enough advances, surely, but they added up. By the end of 1884 the tracks covered 1,307 miles in Minnesota and Dakota Territory, an increase of 971 miles since Hill and his associates had taken over the limping and bankrupt St. Paul & Pacific.

Jim Hill must have found 1884 a most satisfactory year on all accounts. Not only was the Manitoba doing well, but Henry Villard was virtually forced to resign the presidency of the Northern Pacific because of a combination of circumstances including "faulty estimates of construction costs which confronted the company with a huge deficit." Villard's leaving did not mean that the Manitoba's chief competitor was ready to quit the field. Not yet. But it did give weight to a letter Hill wrote a year before Villard's resignation. In it he observed that the time was at hand when any railway property would be tested to its capacity to pay net earnings, and prophesied that "we have some neighbors who will have difficulty in making both ends meet." He added that when such a time came, "we shall want to have our house in order." Jim Hill had found that he could not influence Van Horne to do anything with the Canadian Pacific except to build, not an immense feeder for Hill's line, but a railroad for Canada and the Canadians. But the continuous troubles of the Northern Pacific appeared, by 1884, to present a field for happy speculation.

VIII

SCOUTING well ahead of his Manitoba as the tracks progressed leisurely across Dakota, Hill saw that considerable extra effort, as well as subtle talents, would be needed once his road had passed Minot. Beyond that settlement, and extending almost to the summit of the Rockies, were Indian reservations. Federal law decreed that no railroad might cross or even enter lands set aside for Indians except by express permission of Congress.

This bothersome act was well meant, of course, and stemmed from the consciousness of guilt that had been accumulating over the years as the poor aborigines were driven from their home lands, one tribe after another, and herded into corrals, to be fed on government rations. The Reservation Act was not, however, quite sacred; and with or without sanction railroads had managed to lay their tracks across Indian lands.

Although Hill already had had sufficient dealings with lawmakers to make him cynical, he began his preparations to get across Montana by adopting the conventional method; he had a bill introduced in Congress to waive the Indian Reservation restrictions and thus permit the Manitoba railroad to go its way. But because, as one of his friends delicately put it, the act's terms "and the necessities of the situation were not clearly understood," it did not pass.

Hill suggested to his lobbyists that a little more heat be applied to the Congress. He himself also took direct action. Having been informed that defeat of the desired law had been inspired by Jay Gould, who just then had ironclad control of the Union Pacific and did not want Hill's or any other new line in the Northwest, Jim Hill went to New York City and to Gould's offices.

Jay Gould had long since been one of the most difficult moneyed men to see. Experience had made him that way. When one has been obliged to flee in a hack pursued by stockholders bent on murder, and to live in New Jersey for weeks guarded by an army of thugs; when one has been attacked and beaten up on a New York street—one begins to be diffident about meeting people. So, when Jim Hill came looking for Jay Gould, office clerks told him that the great man was busy in conference, or unavailable, or something or other.

Jim Hill, being a man who always took his bearings and knew where he was, surveyed the Gould offices for an instant, and then with true direction barged inside the protective railing and burst forthwith through the door of Gould's private room. R. F. Dibble, in *Strenuous Americans*, wrote that Gould looked up to see "a veritable gorilla of a man, with an abnormally

long torso and abnormally short legs, with a prodi-
giously heavy chest and neck, with thick, sinewy arms,
and limbs like granite columns. The great, dome-like
head shook so vigorously that the long, tangled iron-
gray hair and the bristling iron-gray beard tossed violently about; and the one good eye blazed like a living
coal, until it seemed to bore and burn its way straight
to the center of Gould's weazened soul. . . . Then
the beard burst asunder, the thick lips snarled back,
and from between the huge teeth there came a succes-
sion of hoarse, growling barks."

Then Jay Gould heard what Jim Hill had to say in
regard to laying tracks across Indian reservations in the
territory of Montana. "You've played the —— hog
in this matter just as long as you're going to be permitted," said the man from St. Paul. "Unless you call
off your —— Washington bushwhackers at once, I'll
tear down the whole —— business about your
ears. . . . I'll go to Washington and I'll camp there
until I nail every one of your crooks to the doors of
the Capitol by their —— ears. . . ."

This was clear enough. Hill went on to Washington, and a little later another bill, incorporating the
same provisions as the earlier bill, was passed with
little or no opposition, and approved by President
Grover Cleveland. Mr. Hill's biographer explained
piously that the bill went through because of "the
pressure of public opinion and interest." It sounded

better that way. In any case, the path through Montana, including the crossing of reservation lands, was now cleared of the chance of "harassment by the government."

Yet, there were other dangers; and during the months of waiting while the reservation-and-railroad bill was getting through Congress, Hill was not merely waiting. He must have an agency, ready to act when the time came, which could lay hands on the best available route, or at least the route selected by Jim Hill, which was the same thing. Although Hill did not appear publicly in connection with it, this agency was organized early in 1886 as the Montana Central Railroad Company. The incorporators were "a small number of Hill's personal friends." It was ostensibly organized to connect the new town of Great Falls with Helena, the territorial capital, and by virtue of its charter it could also "build to such other points in the Territory as it might elect."

Although a paper railroad to hold the Montana field until the Manitoba was ready to enter it probably occurred to Hill, the stated intent of the Montana Central was unquestionably the work of Paris Gibson, the promoter of Great Falls. Hill had known Gibson for thirty years. A State-of-Mainer who had been graduated from Bowdoin College, class of 1851, Gibson had gone west to build the first flouring mill in Minneapolis and to found the North Star Woolen Mills. In the panic of '73 he lost everything. Six years later he was raising sheep around Fort Benton, Montana Territory, and planned to build a city at the Great Falls of the Missouri.

Hill and Gibson had continued their early friendship over the years. As early as 1880 Hill was writing Gibson asking for a description of "the country lying at the foot of the mountains between the Missouri river and Latitude 49." Hill also wanted to know the number of cattle then in the Sun River, the Marais River and the Teton valleys. Gibson could, and did, supply the information. A bit later he wrote Hill of his plans for an industrial town at Great Falls. Hill went out to see for himself. Gibson convinced him. Gibson also took steps for getting title to the power sites at the falls, and also purchased near-by coal deposits. The Montana Central was organized.

Whether or not it was the plan to have the Montana Central actually build a piece of railroad is not quite clear. In any case, the urgency of the time was such, what with Jay Gould and others eying the situation, that the Central issued stock and bonds, began a survey between Great Falls and Helena, and started to make grade and lay track. At almost the same time, stockholders of the Manitoba passed a resolution fairly bubbling over with coy humor to the effect that the Manitoba's board of directors should "ascertain the volume and probable value of the business liable to originate on the Montana Central Railway" and, if it seemed expedient, to "secure a connection with that road." At a subsequent meeting of the board, who were still enjoying their coy humor, it was declared that "the Montana Central as a whole appears to us the only available route between Helena and the navigable waters of the Missouri river." The board forthwith recommended "in the strongest terms" that the Manitoba make connection with the Central and also purchase the road "if it can be brought about." The whimsy no doubt pleased both stockholders and directors, and the Manitoba proceeded to buy the Montana Central.

When the whimsy railroad started building the hundred miles from Great Falls to Helena, the Manitoba was preparing for its big drive into Montana. The Manitoba's western end in 1886 was at Minot, Dakota. Hill wanted to grade 550 miles during the next season in order to reach Great Falls. His plan was to haul material ahead of the track with an army of teams and to build bridges so that there would be no delay when the track-layers came.

To take charge of the work, Hill engaged several of the contractors he had sent north with Van Horne to lay the Canadian Pacific. They had made fine records there, and now they were to repeat in Montana.

During March 1887 the Manitoba worked day and night moving men and materials to the end of track at Minot, where a vast camp sprang up. The grading crews alone used 8,000 men and 3,300 teams. Laying track and building bridges called for another 225 teams and 650 men.

The chief contractor was D. C. Shepard. The record he kept indicates that now that there was real need for it, Hill wanted all the speed possible. Hill knew exactly what a crew of men could do; and Shepard knew that Hill would "exact it mercilessly." In summing up that summer's work, Shepard said it was "very doubtful whether 643 continuous miles of track will ever be laid again in seven and one-half months at the average of 3¼ miles per day for each working day and by one gang."

The job began April 1. A month later 35.1 miles of track had been laid down. Succeeding months saw the advance of steel as follows: May, 111.1; June, 191.7; July, 292.3; August, 407.5; and by October 1, 509.3 miles. In another fifteen days the track totaled 550 miles. Shepard recalled with obvious pride "that gigantic record of August 11, when 42,400 feet were laid between daybreak and dark." Even Hill seemed to think the over-all record pretty fair. "A long and hard summer's work," he called it, adding: "A great many people called it my folly." He said later that it was not until five years after completion that "the line to Helena earned a dollar toward paying returns on the capital invested," and recalled an "unfriendly critic writing for a magazine in the east who said the only thing the country produced was buffalo bones." The critic obviously had not heard of Butte.

Jim Hill knew about Butte. So did the Union Pacific, whose subsidiary, the Utah & Northern, was already operating between Ogden and Butte. It was common talk that the UP paid the Northern Pacific "$500,000 annually to keep out of Butte." Butte, which began as a gold camp and petered out, was astonishing the world of metals by its copper deposits. One of the copper kings of Montana was Marcus Daly, and Hill was glad to give him some good news. "When our lines are continued through to your place," he wrote to Daly, "we hope to be able to furnish you all the transportation you want, both through and local, at such rates as will enable you to largely increase your business. What we want over our low grades is heavy tonnage: and the heavier it is, the lower we can make the rates." By 1888 the Manitoba tracks had reached Butte's mile-high mountain of copper and the wildest mining town in all the West. Before the year was out, Hill had arranged with the Union Pacific for direct connection, both freight and passenger, with its lines by way of Ogden to San Francisco and by way of Pocatello and the Oregon Short Line to points in Oregon.

Hill was particularly proud of his line from Minot west to Great Falls, and he liked to call attention to what he called "the exceptional character" of its grades and curvature: "With the exception of 18 miles of temporary line, the maximum [grade] is 31.7 feet to the mile, and on about 400 miles the maximum is only 21 feet to the mile." The Northern Pacific could boast of no such evenness.

Before pushing on again for the West Coast, it was best to protect the rear, so a branch went out to Sand Coulee, where Paris Gibson's extensive coal fields were waiting. A year later this coal was finding a market in Dakota and Minnesota, adding needed traffic to the wheat and cattle before some of Butte's copper had started to move by way of the Manitoba. There were also other matters, in the extreme rear, to be attended to. At West Superior, Wisconsin, near Duluth, Hill let contracts for building a big dock and a grain elevator of 1,800,000 bushels capacity. He had great plans for the Great Lakes. But he was far from content with his joint control with other railroads of the St. Paul & Duluth, which operated between those cities. In 1887 he organized the Eastern Minnesota railway to link his St. Cloud cutoff's terminal at Hinckley with Duluth-Superior. The Manitoba now had its own direct connection from the chief cities of Minnesota and from its entire western territory with the head of navigation on the Great Lakes.

While the Eastern Minnesota was laying its 69 miles of track, Hill organized the Northern Steamship Company, which put six steamers on the Great Lakes. They were each 310 feet long and 40 feet of beam, and before the end of their first season they had moved nearly one million bushels of wheat down the lakes from Duluth-Superior.

It was becoming evident that the Northwest was, after all, something other than a void, a source of wheat, buffalo robes, and buffalo bones. By the mid-1880's most of the Chicago-based trunk lines were eager to tap this growing region. Boston and New York capital had, in spite of the expensive example of the Northern Pacific, come to see the possibilities in wheat and lumber and ore. Of the several Chicago roads building to the Northwest's gateway of St. Paul, Jim Hill selected one for his quiet yet powerful encouragement. This was the Chicago, Burlington & Northern, a brand new subsidiary of the Chicago, Burlington & Quincy, one of the oldest and strongest systems in the Middle West.

The Burlington's outstanding man was John Murray Forbes of Boston, doubtless the only railroad man whom Ralph Waldo Emerson could and did characterize as a man of remarkable force, modesty, and all-around goodness. Forbes and Hill had become friends. With Hill's blessing, the new subsidiary of the Burlington began building a line from Oregon, Illinois, to Savanna on the Mississippi, thence up the east bank of the river to St. Paul. It was finished late in 1886, when a party of newspapermen rode over the new line from St. Paul to Chicago in eleven hours and ten minutes. The Manitoba was pleased to grant the new line use of its tracks to Minneapolis, and of its railroad yards as well. The two roads presently made an official agreement to exchange freight and passengers. (Never again would Hill lack a rail entry into Chicago. Fifteen years later, as if to make certain, Hill purchased the entire Burlington system.)

If when Hill built the Stone Arch Bridge he was looking far ahead to the days of much heavier locomotives, he was also giving thought to future congestion of freight at the Twin Cities. He rightly called St. Paul-Minneapolis the Gateway to the Northwest, and he may well have foreseen the time when nine railway systems would need to break up and reassemble freight trains there. As early as 1883 he promoted and organized Minnesota Transfer, a clearinghouse for the exchange of freight cars, to be built midway between the two cities.

The citizens of both St. Paul and Minneapolis made protest, saying that Hill was trying to establish something outside the two towns. And in spite of his circumspection, real-estate men jumped in to option lands and run the price up to $700, even $800, an acre. Hill went ahead to buy the property needed, then laid out the yards on what he said, rightly enough, was "the only level place where more than a couple of lines could carry on switching." During the next several years the other roads were glad enough to buy into Minnesota Transfer, until it became a co-operative enterprise of all the lines having business in the Twin Cities.

It seems certain that by the time Hill drove the Manitoba so rapidly across Montana to Helena he had made up his mind to push through to the Northwest coast. In 1888 we see his western terminus at Helena, with Montana coal already being shipped eastward. His steamers were plying the Great Lakes. His docks and grain elevator were established at Duluth-Superior. His new branches and cutoffs in Minnesota had greatly improved the Manitoba's condition. His agreement with the Burlington augured well in regard to through traffic. He had the political situation well under control in Minnesota and in the Dakota and Montana territories.

Jim Hill was fifty years old in 1888. He had often told his associates that he would retire at fifty if by then he had accumulated his desired fortune, which he declared to be $100,000. Well, he had his fortune, and more. One of his bankers and oldest friends, John S. Kennedy, had even told Hill that he thought he was right to retire at fifty.

It is obvious now, in the light of subsequent events, that Hill's very nature would not permit him to retire, at fifty, sixty, or even seventy. There was nothing heroic or Spartan involved. It was compulsion. He knew well enough that if he decided to build his railroad through to the Pacific, he would have to build it without a land grant or government subsidy of any kind. He had been told times without number that no railroad could build across this still sparsely settled region without such subsidy.

Hill knew all these things, and had considered many other difficulties he would face if he decided to go on. But compulsion was pressing him. On September 16, 1889 he organized the Great Northern Railway Company around the charter of his subsidiary Minneapolis & St. Cloud Company. The Great Northern promptly leased the property of the Manitoba for 999 years. At midnight, January 31, 1890 the Great Northern officially took over 2,770 miles of road, together with all properties incidental to operation, of the St. Paul, Minneapolis & Manitoba Railroad. At its next board meeting the Great Northern's directors requested the management to "extend its lines westwardly from some suitable point in Montana to Puget Sound."

Even here, as was usual with any official action taken by a concern run by Jim Hill, he himself had already taken steps in the direction "requested" by his directors. He merely enjoyed humoring them. Just before the Great Northern came into existence, Hill had engaged John F. Stevens to find the so-called Lost Marias Pass through the Rockies.

IX

THE HISTORY of the American West is fairly studded with "lost" trails and passes. There are "lost" lakes, creeks, even rivers, and "lost" prairies and valleys. The number of "lost" lodes and mines is of course beyond calculation, as immense as the supposed wealth of any one of them.

Something lost presupposes a previous condition of having been found, and this was unquestionably the case with the lost Marias Pass through the Rocky Mountains, which in 1889 John F. Stevens set out to find for James J. Hill and the Great Northern Railway Company.

The Blackfoot and Flathead Indians knew of the pass, and in remote times had used it. It is more than probable that Canadian and American trappers had crossed the Continental Divide that way. In a map prepared for Congress in 1840 by Robert Greenhow appears a trail marked "Route across the Mts," and though unnamed, it follows the Marias River, a noble stream, Bernard De Voto remarks, that was named by Meriwether Lewis "to commemorate one of his many romantic attachments." Lewis had trouble with Indians on the Marias, and did not cross the Rockies by this gateway, but by the more difficult Cadotte's Pass to the south.

But the route of the Marias persisted, at least in legend, and, as related, appeared in 1840 on Green-how's map. Fourteen years later it was actually seen, though not used, by James Doty, an engineer with the Pacific Railroad Survey headed by Isaac I. Stevens, also governor of Washington Territory. Another engineer with the same party, A. W. Tinkham, believed that he had crossed the Rockies by the elusive pass, but found it so steep and rocky and narrow that he considered it out of the question for railroad tracks. Tinkham had really crossed the mountains by Cut Bank Pass, whose summit was 7,600 feet above sea level, more than 2,400 feet higher than the Marias Pass turned out to be. But Tinkham was the first white man to make a recorded journey through what is now Glacier National Park: that is glory enough for him.

When Doty and Tinkham failed to cross the Divide by Marias Pass, it was lost again for thirty-five years, or until John F. Stevens arrived. He was only thirty-six, but already had the reputation of an extremely able engineer in mountain country. He was born in West Gardiner, Maine, in 1853. His earliest work was as axman and rodman in surveying parties, and by the time he came to Jim Hill, Stevens was a location engineer of standing. He had helped to lay routes for the Milwaukee, the Duluth, South Shore & Atlantic, and the Denver & Rio Grande. He had also been in the party of Canadian Pacific engineers who found a suitable pass through the Selkirks. It is the opinion of many engineers that the Selkirk Range must have presented a proper test for the best men of their profession.

In the early spring of '89 Stevens set up his reconnaissance headquarters at Fort Assiniboine, seven miles from the Great Northern town of Havre, Montana. At Havre the railroad turned southwest to touch the Missouri at Great Falls, going on to Helena, and so to the railhead at Butte. What Jim Hill wanted was a route directly west from Havre which would cross the Rockies as far north as possible and be "the shortest and lowest passage of the Divide." Possibly the lost Marias Pass.

Stevens, with saddle horse, a wagon and mule, and one man whom he had brought from St. Paul, set out to look over the various approaches to the Rockies. They ranged north to the Canadian border and back and across the foothills. They followed canyons. The man he had brought from St. Paul turned out to need considerable fortifying against blizzards that he had encountered in the past, and drank so consistently that Stevens sent him home. At the Blackfoot Agency, Stevens tried to hire a Blackfoot guide, but nothing could induce members of this tribe to go to the headwaters of the Marias River. Stevens was glad to take a Flathead. They returned to the hills.

Winter came on. Stevens abandoned his outfit. He and his guide resumed their search on snowshoes they themselves made. Notable storms came on. Between spells of intense cold, blizzards swept the peaks and filled the canyons deep with snow. When they reached what is known as False Summit, a spot several miles east of the true pass, the Flathead guide announced that he had had enough of it. Stevens went on alone, leaving his companion to camp where he was.

In later years Stevens laid it to mere chance that he walked right into Marias Pass before he realized where he was, and continued far enough west to make certain he had really crossed the Divide. Then he turned back. At the summit he made camp—or tried to. The snow was too deep to permit a fire. He dared not lie down because of the cold, so he did what he and other men had done on occasion; tramping a solid pathway, he walked back and forth until daybreak, then started out to locate the Flathead guide, whom he found nearly dead from cold. He revived the man, and together they returned to the Agency.

Engineer Stevens proceeded to lead the Great Northern graders and track-layers through Marias Pass, and its gradient proved how thorough had been his examination; it was indeed the lowest gate through the mountains. In speaking of this feat, Ralph Budd, when president of the Great Northern, told what it meant: "The actual location of it was at an altitude of five thousand two hundred feet on a 1 per cent grade Westbound and 1.8 per cent Eastbound, and without a summit tunnel. It fully confirmed Stevens' report. At one stroke the discovery of Marias Pass shortened the proposed line to the Coast by over one hundred miles, afforded better alignment, much easier grades, and much less rise and fall." [1]

Coming down the west side of the Rockies, the Great Northern met and followed the water-grade of the Flathead River's Middle Fork, crossed the Whitefish Range to Columbia Falls, then turned north to follow the Kootenai into Idaho, and so to Spokane, "Capital of the Inland Empire," already growing from lumber and wheat and also as the center of the booming silver and lead country of the near-by Coeur d'Alene.

Hill himself was, as usual, moving ahead of his tracks, and now he visited Spokane to tell its citizens of the difficulties of building a railroad. He knew very well the local feeling about the Northern Pacific. The feeling was bitter, having turned that way during the nine years the railroad had dominated the city. The

[1] In grateful recognition of this service, the Great Northern Railway placed, in 1925, a heroic bronze statue of John F. Stevens, the work of Sculptor Cecere, near the tracks at Summit, Montana, on the very spot where he "spent that memorable night in December, 1889," on the backbone of the Rockies.

feeling was in part engendered by a device known as terminal rates, well understood by railroadmen and by no other people on earth. By this arrangement the Northern Pacific granted lower rates on freight from the East to its terminals on Puget Sound and in Portland than it did to Spokane. The rates to Spokane equaled the charge to tidewater at Tacoma or Portland plus the charges of hauling the freight back to Spokane.

But now, in 1892, here was James J. Hill coming to town to talk about railroad matters. It was reported in advance by the local press that Hill was a radical low-freight-rate man, that he would have nothing to do with the un-Christian idea of the same charge for the short as for the long haul. His arrival was the signal for great rejoicing.

In his first interview in Spokane, Hill seemed to say that the terminal rates used by the Northern Pacific were not only un-Christian, but illegal. He told Spokane people that they had made a grave mistake in taking their protest to the Interstate Commerce Commission. "You should have made a test case of it," he said. "I don't think that a jury of twelve men could have been found to decide that such a charge was legal. You could have settled it in short order."

Spokane shippers and merchants were delirious with joy, and now that Hill's own railroad had crossed the mountains and was heading west, why, it would be but a short time until Spokane had a civilized second road to carry its freight. It was taken for granted that the Great Northern would lay its tracks through Spokane on the way to the Pacific. Any railroad moving east or west *must* touch Spokane.

Not necessarily so, Hill told the shocked reporter of the *Spokane Review*, who then heard the Great Northern boss say: "You have no idea how hard your city is to get into and out of" and speak of a grade of "one-quarter of a per cent higher than we want to go." Sensing correctly that this might mean little or nothing to the public, Hill, who could be graphic enough when need be, explained the matter in relation to a train of thirty loaded cars, or a total weight of one thousand tons. "The extra quarter of one per cent," he said, fixing the *Review* man with that terrible eye, "is equivalent to having to lift one thousand tons thirteen feet in the air for each mile of road traversed."

Letting that sink in, Hill went on to show that if his line was to come to Spokane, "instead of sliding off down the inviting easy valley of the Little Spokane River," he would be obliged to cut through a summit two miles long and averaging forty feet in depth. Nor was getting out of Spokane any child's play, either, and Hill went into that difficulty in some detail. All in all, the Great Northern would be better off to pass on through Washington by the "inviting easy route" north of the Capital of the Inland Empire.

Spokane's most resolute boosters blanched when they read Hill's blunt remarks on the unfortunate geographical features around their city. They hastened to his hotel, and there protested, pleaded, and urged, until he agreed to discuss the matter before a mass meeting of citizens when they, the people of Spokane, could let *him* know exactly how much they wanted to welcome the Great Northern Railway. The meeting drew a packed hall, and Hill took the floor to rousing cheers.

Jim Hill was no Webster. He lacked the grace of classical allusion. He disdained the poetic utterance with which a Villard could captivate an audience. But he was armed as few other speakers were armed with an incredible knowledge of facts pertaining to finance, railroads, agriculture, industry, and geography. He made his points with a clarity that was blunt if need be, but clear always. He told his hearers that the Great Northern had already proved to be a road capable of doing more business than any other transcontinental that "has been built or will be built hereafter." It was better, he said, that the Great Northern keep away than to put a weak link in its chain. And was Spokane such a link?

Hill outlined the dreadful expense of laying track into and out of this city. Just to get through the town would cost one million dollars. That was twice as much as he had thought it would cost until he actually figured it. But if—if it happened that he could see a way clear to waive the easy inviting valley to the north and build to Spokane, then it would be only in case the city would do its share. Thereupon he explained what he meant by "share."

"Now, what we ask of Spokane," he cried, "is that from the time we come to the city limits you will give us the right of way, so that the building of the road will not cost anything." From the east to the west limits, he said, was five miles, and he did not think such a free right of way was an improper condition to bring the railroad hither. He closed his talk with a warming reference, saying that every man, woman, and child in the community depended on railroads and "we want as many people to depend on *our* road as possible"; and "we want to arrange our affairs so that your community and our business will be as partners, equally interested in the growth of this country." (Tremendous applause.)

It is obvious that Hill's force and magnetism, along with his common touch, completely captivated Spokane. No sooner had he left for Seattle than a Soliciting Committee got busy. When he returned one week later, Spokane was ready to present the Great Northern with the right of way. Hill accepted it graciously and responded with what must have been one of the best speeches he ever made, marked in every paragraph as reported in the press with notations of "Applause" or "Laughter" or "Cheers."

Whether or not the citizens of Spokane had heard about Fort Benton, Montana, is not on record. When that ungrateful town refused to grant Hill a right of way through its miserable collection of huts, the Great Northern tracks made a sudden loop that left the settlement a good mile from the railroad. There was no animosity in the incident. It was merely the way you built a railroad unless it was a stockjobbing affair.

While the Great Northern tracks were building to and through Spokane, John F. Stevens located the route across the prairies and rolling hills of central Washington, where the new town of Wenatchee was pleased to move from its original site to the banks of the Columbia River and the Great Northern tracks. Stevens took the line up the Wenatchee River, turned west into the foothills of the Cascade Range, then through the range by way of a low pass that bears his name. For the moment, Stevens chose to reach the summit by way of a switchback, but he also made the preliminary surveys for a tunnel, and this was later bored at the order of Jim Hill himself, a man who meant to have the lowest grades possible. From the summit, Stevens took the route west down the Skycomish River to reach Puget Sound at Everett.

Hill, of course, had been working well ahead of

Stevens, looking over the several port cities to select his terminus. He dismissed Tacoma; it was already western headquarters of the Northern Pacific. Bellingham was too far north. Seattle attracted Hill, not only because it had a good harbor, but also because its citizens were aggressive, especially toward the Northern Pacific, which had left their town on a stub line.

The difficulty about Seattle was that any waterfront entry to it seemed to be tied up by the franchise of a local railroad. One of Hill's good friends in Seattle was Judge Thomas Walsh, pioneer settler and lawyer. He and Hill got together, and Burke promptly organized the Seattle & Montana Railroad and petitioned the city council to lay out a new street, Railroad Avenue, then under water on the tideflats, and to build it on an earth fill. The Northern Pacific objected, and a bitter controversy raged for months. Burke won his point, the Seattle & Montana laid tracks along the new fill and on to Everett to meet the Great Northern. This road also continued on to the Canadian border to connect there with the New Westminster Southern, to give Hill's line a connection with the Canadian Pacific.

The last rail of the Great Northern's 834-mile stretch from Havre, Montana, to Everett on Puget Sound was laid on January 5, 1893. Train service between St. Paul and Seattle was established in July.

Seattle had planned to commemorate the event with a truly gigantic celebration. This was canceled, however, because, to quote a local commentator, of "the unsettled financial conditions at the present time." But St. Paul managed to stage festivities in honor of its new transcontinental, and in the parade was a monster log of Dougles fir, cut near Seattle and hauled by twenty horses, a sample of the major source of freight that was to keep Great Northern wheels turning until settlers should populate its main line and branches in the sparsely populated West.

The Great Northern's main line when finished covered 1,816 miles between Seattle and St. Paul, 115 miles shorter than the Northern Pacific. Its overall gradient was infinitely better; and its heavy grades were so concentrated that the use of extra engines could be economically confined to short stretches. Hill was a mortal enemy of double-headers.

Before the end of the year those "unsettled financial conditions" which had prevented Seattle's Great Northern celebration had much worsened. They had culminated in a panic that was described as a currency famine. Major industries shut down. Stores laid off help. Stocks fell. Breadlines grew. The outlook was so grave that President Cleveland felt need to call a special session of Congress. Hill was not greatly worried. In a letter to his good friend Charles E. Perkins of the Burlington, he remarked: "The general condition of the country, and particularly our part of it out here, seems to be fully as good as usual. . . ."

Surely Jim Hill had reason to feel pretty good. Of all the transcontinental railroads that had reached the West Coast, only his Great Northern could withstand the ill winds of 1893. It was a tough year for Pacific railroads. The Santa Fe went into the hands of a receiver. So did the Union Pacific. And the Northern Pacific, without astonishing Hill, failed again. Hill had predicted as much, but did not claim the role of prophet. It was clear, to his mind, that any railroad that did not pay strict attention to grade and curvature, and did not properly protect its rear, was headed for bankruptcy.

X

WHEN the Northern Pacific officially announced its bankrupt condition in August 1893, Jim Hill was ready to be helpful—in his own way. At least four months before it fell, he had been writing about it to his old friend and associate, by then Lord Mount Stephen, an international financier of imposing reputation, telling his lordship that the Northern Pacific had run its course. It was a mere matter of time before it must be wholly reorganized to "wipe out all present [common] and preferred shares." Hill intimated that a very strong financial concern, by which he meant J. Pierpont Morgan, was interested, "provided we name half the new board and find men to manage the property."

The "we" could mean only Hill, the man who had built a railroad to the West Coast without a land grant or other government subsidy. Morgan and Hill were already personal friends. One can believe that they admired each other. Surely Morgan respected a railroad-builder who told his chief engineer that "we don't care enough about Rocky Mountain scenery to spend a large sum of money in developing it," and who bade the men find the best possible route with the shortest distance, lowest grades, and least curvature. Poetry was proper in the parlor.

Hill knew what to expect, once the Northern Pacific was actually in receivership, in the way of competition with his own road. It came quickly. The rates of the bankrupt line were slashed. The Great Northern not only met the new rates, but at points where shipments originated and could be made by either road, made even lower rates. It was costly, though Hill remained cheerful, and after more than a year of it he wrote Morgan: "They [the Northern Pacific] have nothing but expenses to pay and would destroy our business. . . . Still we hold our own."

While Hill was holding his own against the Northern Pacific, Eugene Victor Debs had been organizing railroad workers in a new kind of industrial group called the American Railway Union. The ARU struck the Great Northern, along with several other lines. Higher wages was the demand. At first Hill was inclined to ignore the strikers, to send out his trains with armed guards and strikebreakers, and to open the line by force. Then, as he admitted privately later, he thought of all those "costly bridges" between St. Paul and Seattle. They could be damaged and even destroyed with a few charges of dynamite. Hill offered to arbitrate. The union refused, and Hill gave orders to open his main line by force. The strikers then agreed, the arbitration was made, and after only eighteen days off the job the crews returned. Hill's comment displayed the craft he could muster when he favored it above his natural weapon, which was force. "The newspaper reports," he said, "have indicated that the men won a great victory, and this we have been careful not to contradict."

Through rate wars and strikes, negotiations to get control of the Northern Pacific went ahead. In the spring of 1895, at J. P. Morgan's London house, Hill, Lord Mount Stephen, and Edward Tuck, a noted banker of the day, drew up a tentative offer whereby the Great Northern guaranteed payment of the $100 million of Northern Pacific bonds, plus interest not to exceed $6,200,000 a year. It was to receive in return half the common stock of the railroad, plus a majority of one on the board of directors of nine. The offer was accepted by Edward D. Adams, Northern Pacific receiver, and two men representing the Deutsche Bank of Berlin, the holder of far too many of the railroad's bonds.

The deal was scarcely agreed upon, and news of it published, when a wave of public excitement swept the Northwest. Here was a combination to dominate transportation from Duluth to the Pacific Coast. Standard Oil had pointed the way to monopoly, and now Hill and Morgan and their cohorts meant to fasten their grip on a mighty traffic monopoly. So went the comment. Thomas W. Pearson, a stockholder in the Great Northern, decided to test the validity of the agreement. Citing a Minnesota law that prohibited unification of parallel and competing railroads, he brought suit in federal court to prevent the carrying out of the merger, alleging that it would depreciate the value of his holding by making the Great Northern "the guarantor of a financially unstable system." An injunction was obtained, and the agreement halted. Months later the United States Supreme Court sustained the law.

Hill may have been disappointed, though not too much, for it was immediately apparent he had taken into consideration the possibility of an adverse judgment. He came forward with still another plan, which he had discussed at some length with Lord Mount Stephen and Morgan. It was simplicity itself. If the Great Northern as a corporation could not purchase the Northern Pacific, there was no law to prevent Hill and his friends from buying into the other road as individuals. Little time was lost, and in 1896 the Northern Pacific was completely overhauled and a new company organized in which, as a commentator discreetly observed, "Mr. Hill and his associates of the Great Northern have a large interest and the usual stockholders' voice." In reality, of course, the Northern Pacific was henceforth and for all practical purposes a second track for the Great Northern. Nobody could doubt who was to manage the Northern Pacific. That road and the Great Northern together were presently to be known simply as the Hill Lines.

The Hill Lines were due to expand, but before getting to that it might be well to consider Jim Hill briefly. He was fifty-eight years old when he took command of the two Hill Lines. Forty years had passed since his arrival on the St. Paul waterfront. For forty years he had been driving himself in a manner to wreck an ordinary constitution. The last two decades alone, or since he laid hands on the old St. Paul & Pacific, were enough to have killed many men. Yet there was no sign of physical impairment, and surely no sign of a slower pace. Hill could rest on occasion, though not for long, and when he was not resting he was something of a demon for action.

Mentally he was probably at about the height of his powers, a condition that was to continue at least another dozen years while his interests expanded to include other things than railroads. In him still, at fifty-eight, were power and ability sufficient to battle able and much younger men to a standstill.

But if his great labors and the passage of years had failed to dent his constitution, they had marked his appearance and personality. His neolithic figure stood as before, like some crag. His thinning hair was now white, his beard gray. The one good eye blazed and smoldered in turn. One day in his office in St. Paul it blazed as he yanked an offending telephone from the wall, splintered the two boxes into matchwood, then threw the whole damnable contraption out the window to the cobblestones of Fourth Street. It blazed again when a clerk in the Great Northern office did something that aroused his anger. "What is your name?" demanded Hill. "My name is Charles Swinburne Spittles," replied the clerk. It *was* Spittles, too, and Hill fired him on the spot, shouting: "I don't like your name and I don't like your face."

Occasionally, as time passed, Hill's irritability even had an effect on the Hill Lines in the field. There was the affair at unfortunate Wayzata, a Great Northern station on the shore of celebrated Lake Minnetonka. Ever since post-Civil War days, Minnetonka had been a summer resort, and over the years several large wooden hotels sprang up. Two of these, the Gleason House and the Minnetonka House, were in the village of Wayzata, and almost, but not quite, at the water's edge. Between them and the beach ran the Great Northern tracks.

It seemed to be a habit of railroad train crews to do their switching at Wayzata during the night, thus keeping the hotel guests awake. Another irritation was the way the crews left freight cars on the side track. For weeks at a time, it was alleged, no hotel guest could get so much as a view of pretty Minnetonka from the verandas. Then, there were the Great Northern depot's toilet arrangements. These appeared as twin privies placed where no one could miss seeing them. Although in that day Wayzata had no health officer, good Dr. Tibbets, the village's one physician, was either urged, or felt the need, to protest. The privies, he declared, were a menace to health. The matter was taken to court, Wayzata won, and the offending houses were moved out of range of the hotel verandas. The village was jubilant. Flushed with success, it went on to bring suit against the Great Northern to have the tracks removed from the lake front and relaid north of town. That did it. Hill exploded, then swore that ungrateful Wayzata should walk. And walk it did, for Hill had the depot moved nearly two miles east, set up again, and forthwith named Holdridge. For the next fifteen years, all freight and passengers for and from Wayzata went by way of Holdridge.

That was Jim Hill at his worst. Just as typical was another incident. It concerned Tom Wise, an old crony of Hill's, who made a living by renting boats at Wayzata. After the depot was moved, Hill happened to be passing through the village and called to see his old friend. "Jim," protested Wise, "you have ruined me by taking away the station. How in damnation can I rent boats to people who can't get off the train?" Almost immediately a crew of carpenters appeared at Holdridge. They erected a fine pavilion on the lake there, filled the building half full of glass cases, filled the cases with a full line of fishing tackle, and moored twenty-four brand-new rowboats at the floating wharf. Hill gave it to Tom Wise. "It's yours, Tom, as long as you live," said Hill.

There was the less well-known incident of Johnny Grant, a famous Montana pioneer who sold his property for $20,000 and retired to a farm near Winnipeg. He didn't need all that money around the homestead, and gave it to young Jim Hill, just then getting under way with his Red River Transportation Company. Hill invested it so well in his own business that in later years when Johnny came to need it, Hill handed him some $60,000.

For all his good deeds, one may doubt that the years brought much genuine mellowness to Hill. He just wasn't that sort of man. His temper, which in his younger years had been rather even, became wholly unpredictable; but his enormous physical strength was retained into his sixties. He was past threescore when he gave the last remembered demonstration of it. One night when Hill and his secretary, Will Stephens, were working late in the Great Northern offices at St. Paul, fire broke out in the building. Hill paid no attention to the alarm until a puff of smoke blew into his office. While Stephens hurriedly picked up papers to take them to the vault, Hill slammed shut the rolltop of his big desk, picked it bodily from the floor, and pushed it through a wide window. The desk weighed around three hundred pounds, and it crashed to the same cobblestones that had shattered the telephone boxes. The firemen would not believe Stephens when he told them how it happened.

Nearing sixty, Hill was prepared to engage in a railroad war that was to call for every bit of his strength and ability and was to last for ten years. His opponent was Edward Henry Harriman, perhaps the only railroad figure of the time fit to challenge James Jerome Hill. The Hill-Harriman battles were considered a scandal or a disgrace by many of the more sobersided financiers and railroadmen of the period. They could remember the bold buccaneers, named Vanderbilt, Drew, Fisk, and Gould, who fought over the Erie with arsenals of guns and brass knuckles, armies of thugs, and a secret printing-press that could print more counterfeit shares and bonds than Midas could have bought.

The Hill-Harriman war started on a higher plane, though before the armistice was signed it had developed a savagery reminiscent of the cave men who fought to control the old Erie in the days when the only rule was that he who won was the winner.

In appearance Harriman was the antithesis of Hill. He looked, as someone said, like a bookkeeper. Ten years Hill's junior, he was a rather frail man who wore thick glasses, had a soft voice, and was as shy as he was grave and silent. He had not, as Hill had, walked halfway across the United States and Canada to locate a route. He had never worked on the waterfront, or helped shovel trains out of snowdrifts. He wasn't that kind. Harriman got into railroads by way of Wall Street, where he had been one of the most precocious operators since Jay Gould was a lad. At twenty he owned a seat on the Stock Exchange.

After unloading a nuisance railroad on the Pennsylvania, Harriman bought into the Illinois Central, was quickly made an officer, and displayed remarkable ability in running that line. When the Morgan-Vanderbilt crowd attempted to enter IC's territory, Harriman fought them to a standstill. Next he joined a syndicate to take over the foundering Union Pacific, personally inspected every mile of the big road, then asked his directors for authority to purchase rails, rolling stock, and other items to the value of twenty-five million dollars. He got it. He went on to gain control of Oregon lines that gave the UP a Pacific port at Portland; and near the turn of the century he bought heavily into the Central Pacific and Southern Pacific railroads. He authorized building of the Lucin cutoff across the Great Salt Lake, a bold project that most engineers believed impossible.

Harriman, then, was a brilliant operator. His frail body and myopic sight were in contrast to the Horatius-like Hill of the Cyclops eye. But it is futile to try to compare the two men in ability. Hill looked like power and had it. Harriman did not look like power, but had it. Both were ruthless enough. And both meant to dominate the northwestern United States from the Great Lakes to the Pacific.

XI

AS ONE of the two Hill Lines, the Northern Pacific immediately started to show improvement. Its cost of operation fell. Business increased. Nor did the Great Northern seem to suffer. As Morgan liked to say, of this and other mergers in which he had a hand, the recognition of "a community of interest" permitted both roads to make money.

Hill knew that for some time to come his eastbound traffic would be mostly lumber, or nothing. Lumber was the chief product the far Northwest had to offer. Hill knew that the treeless prairies of the Midwest were potentially the greatest lumber market in the country. He meant to supply this market from the virgin forests that began in western Montana and continued unbroken to tidewater in Oregon and Washington. To do so, he must deliver the lumber so cheaply that even the nearer-at-hand Southern-pine people could not compete with the Northwest product in the Midwest market.

If lumber was to be his eastbound freight, that was well enough; but it would not do to haul empty GN and NP cars back to the Northwest. In Hill's eye the sight most hideous to contemplate was one of his own cars empty.

The Orient had long appealed to him, and now he sent agents there to investigate trade opportunities. They supplied Hill with a manifest of every ship that touched and cleared a Japanese or a Chinese port. He saw where the imports came from, what they were; and where exports went to. He sent agents into New England, into the Atlantic states, into the South, telling them to find out what could be made or grown in those parts that would be welcome to the Orient.

These surveys had been going on for many months before Hill, with Morgan as his ally, set out to get the railroad he wanted to complete the system already called the Hill Lines. This was the Chicago, Burlington & Quincy, with which he had been on the best of terms since the time he had helped a Burlington subsidiary to enter St. Paul and Minneapolis.

The Burlington operated from Chicago to the Rocky Mountains. It covered Hill's potential market for Northwest lumber as no other road did. It would give Hill contact with the cotton-hauling lines entering St. Louis and Kansas City; with the smelters of Colorado and the Black Hills of South Dakota. It would bring the big packing houses of Omaha into his orbit.

E. H. Harriman also wanted the Burlington. His Union Pacific ran no farther east than Omaha; the Burlington had access to Chicago. This alone would have been reason enough. But there were other reasons, too, among which was the danger that Hill might feel need to have the Burlington.

Preliminary skirmishing for what many a financial writer was soon calling "A Battle of Giants" took place during 1899 in correspondence between Hill and Harriman concerning joint operation of the Oregon Railway & Navigation Company's lines by the Union Pacific and Northern Pacific. Hill declared that such operation left the Great Northern "in a position of too great uncertainty to be allowed to continue." Harriman was not inclined to agree. The letters continued and increased in asperity, while the Hill-Morgan forces were quietly buying into the Burlington. Harriman began buying, too. But he was outbid and out-generaled by the Hill-Morgan crowd, who early in 1901 managed to get majority control of the big road. The Burlington became the third unit of the Hill Lines.

Harriman was not done. With the backing of Kuhn, Loeb & Company, New York bankers, and with Jacob Henry Schiff of that firm as his close ally, he started secretly to buy into the Northern Pacific. If he couldn't get the Burlington by direct action, then he meant to get control of Hill's second road and be in a position to dictate to Hill himself.

The Harriman-Schiff men began their campaign so astutely that neither Hill nor the great J. P. Morgan had any idea of what was going forward. All looked so serene that in April 1901 Morgan sailed for Europe, where he planned to take the waters at Aix-les-Bains, while Mr. Hill rolled across his own empire to see how his affairs were prospering on Puget Sound. He was still there in late April when he was perturbed to note a sudden, sharp rise in the price of Northern Pacific shares. This troubled him because the Hill-Morgan group owned less than half of the NP stock, and though in most cases a strong minority interest was sufficient to hold control of any railroad, Hill was no man to ignore signs and portents.

Believing that this new activity in Northern Pacific shares was something more than mere trading, Hill acted promptly. In Seattle he had his special car hitched to a locomotive, ordered the tracks cleared of everything as far as Chicago, and set off for New York City. In New York he took a cab direct to the office of Kuhn, Loeb & Company, where he demanded of Jacob Schiff to know if his suspicions were correct: was Schiff buying Northern Pacific shares for E. H. Harriman? Yes, said Schiff, he was. What was more, he already had control. (In this Schiff was either mistaken or bragging.) If the Hill-Morgan crowd would not let him have the Burlington, then Harriman was going to take the Northern Pacific.

Hill tore over to the House of Morgan to tell them they had been caught napping in the old man's absence. He reported what Schiff had said. The stunned

Morgan partners had seldom if ever been charged with dereliction. They sent a cable to Morgan in the French Alps asking permission to buy 150,000 shares of Northern Pacific common. This was on a Friday. On Saturday, while the Morgan men awaited a cable-gram, Harriman thought it would be good to own an-other 40,000 shares of NP common, just to be safe. He called Schiff's office and gave the order. Schiff was at the synagogue. The order was not carried out.

Monday was too late for Schiff and Harriman. The Stock Exchange had barely opened its doors when the House of Morgan poured buying orders into the market. On that day Morgan brokers bought 127,500 shares of NP common. The price climbed. The buy-ing continued. By Thursday, though the Morgan forces had quit buying, the price rose to 1,000. Panic hit the Exchange. Many stocks went tumbling. The panic was brief, for on that day when NP common stock hit 1,000, the Hill and Harriman forces got together and made an agreement by which the short-sellers—those brokers who had "sold" NP shares that they did not have and which could not be bought—were saved from destruction. A bit later the Hill and Harriman camps also reached an understanding: Har-riman was to have representation on the NP board, but control of that railroad, together with control of the Great Northern and the Burlington, was to remain with the Hill-Morgan crowd.

What went into stock-market history as the Northern Pacific Panic made no friends for Harriman, Hill, and Morgan. It had sent United States Steel down from 46 to 24, and the so-called "values" of many lesser shares were wholly washed out. Brokers, speculators, and mere investors took a terrible beating. "It does not seem right," wrote an observer, "that the clashing interests of three multi-millionaires should cause a tempest that has utterly obliterated the scant savings of a mass of people." When Morgan, best known of the trio, was asked by a reporter if he did not think some statement was due the public, he replied: "I owe the public nothing."

The terms of the armistice granted seats on the Northern Pacific board to Harriman and his ally William Rockefeller, but control remained with the Hill-Morgan crowd. It was at best only a sort of temporary and strictly regional peace. The Hill Lines and the Harriman System were still facing each other throughout the West. Neither Hill's advancing years nor Harriman's occasional illness could prevent a resumption of hostility.

For the present, however, Hill had a suggestion that he said would protect the Northern Pacific from raids similar to that Harriman had made. This idea presently took form as the Northern Securities Corporation, a "holding company" that would control both the Great Northern and the Northern Pacific.

Those two roads would, in turn, control the Burlington. It was capitalized at $400 million. Morgan favored it because it would put the "Northwestern lines in a company with a capital large enough so that nobody could ever buy it." Harriman at first protested, though not very hard, then voted for it. As for Hill, he thought Northern Securities would be a "strong fortress where in peace or war those who had seen the work of their hands grow great might establish it against all assaults for all time to come."

The owners of Great Northern and Northern Pacific stocks exchanged their shares for those of Northern Securities. Hill was elected chairman of the new holding company, and the Hill-Morgan directors numbered ten of fifteen members of the board. These men were to direct the affairs of the Burlington.

It is possible that the Northern Securities Corporation might have enjoyed a long and serene life had it not been for the assassination of President William McKinley in September 1901, and the consequent elevation of Vice-President Theodore Roosevelt to the presidency. Roosevelt had already, as a municipal reformer, clashed with Railroadman Jay Gould. Roosevelt had been appalled at the Northern Pacific Panic. He seems to have considered Harriman another Jay Gould whose aim in life was to wreck railroads, and to have blamed him for the Northern Pacific fracas. The forming of the Northern Securities holding company looked to Roosevelt like a new trust. Trusts were becoming a popular menace.

Early in 1902 Roosevelt ordered his Attorney General to prosecute Northern Securities on grounds that it violated the Sherman Anti-Trust Law. Morgan brought his heaviest guns into action, and litigation wound its way through the courts for the next two years. In 1904 the United States Supreme Court ordered Northern Securities dissolved. This was done. It is of interest to note that in the liquidation, the Harriman forces received a paper profit of some $58 million.

As for control of the Burlington, it remained in the hands of Hill and Morgan. Hill was philosophical about the whole affair. "Two certificates of stock are now issued instead of one," he remarked. "They are printed in different colors. That is the main difference." He complained mildly of "keeping track of two different sets of securities."

Although Hill's fawning biographer wrote: "The dissolution of the Northern Securities marked one of Mr. Hill's few great disappointments," Hill's affairs in other departments had been going very well. There was, for example, the matter of the Red River lands in Dakota. Back in 1857 Minnesota had chartered a railroad and made it a land grant. Dakota was then a part of Minnesota. Expanding his Manitoba railroad, Hill had bought the charter of this Dakota road, which had never got beyond the paper stage. Meanwhile, the General Land Office made a grievous error. Taking it for granted that these 65,000 acres in the Red River Valley did not belong to any railroad and were in the public domain, the land office gave clear titles to farmers who had settled upon it.

Now years later came Hill to ask for the land that he said belonged legally to the Great Northern Railway Company, successor to the Manitoba. In 1891 the United States Supreme Court declared that Hill was right—the grant was indeed valid. The Great Northern thereupon issued an order compelling farmers to vacate all lands in the odd-numbered sections within the twenty-mile limits of the grant. Many of these farmers had been living on the lands in question for a decade; several had been there for twenty years.

The order did not, as some writers have it, come like a thunderclap out of a clear sky. But it was shocking enough as it was—one of those things that "couldn't happen." Now it had happened, and the Great Northern quickly showed that it meant business. Actual evictions were begun.

The settlers appealed to Congress, which passed an act permitting the railroad company to select an equal area of federal lands in lieu of those in the Red River Valley. Hill already knew what lands to select. He had seen them himself. The Great Northern was happy to settle for some of the finest timber on the face of the earth, situated in Montana, Idaho, and Washington. Thus the story of the Red River grant had a happy ending after all. The farmers retained their lands in Dakota. The railroad received lands of far greater value to it than even the rich acres of the Red River Valley. Hill prevailed upon his friend and neighbor Frederic Weyerhaeuser, already the most potent figure in the lumber industry of the Lakes states, to accompany him on a tour of the Western forests, where he bought vast stands of fir and pine.

Another matter that turned out rather well was Hill's personal if reluctant purchase of the Wright & Davis lumber property in Minnesota. This included a large area of cutover land and a logging railroad that meandered through the stumps and brush. Because it was in the general area of the Mesabi Range, which just then was beginning to produce iron ore in large volume, Hill was persuaded by his sons Louis W. and James N. Hill to buy it on speculation. It turned out that underneath the stumps this property was rich in ore. Very rich. Hill leased it to the United States Steel Corporation. The corporation did the mining. The Great Northern carried the ore.

Jim Hill had made it a company rule that nobody connected with the Great Northern could "have any business that called for the transaction of business with the Company in anything along the railway where the company was interested in the carriage." When it became apparent that the cutover lands he had bought personally as a speculation were going to pay the Great Northern millions of dollars in freight charges from ore, he organized the Lake Superior Company, Limited, and "At the close of business December 6, 1906" presented Great Northern stockholders, "as an outright gift," all the shares of the Lake Superior Company. It was, as Hill's biographer remarked, "a royal gift." During the period of lease to United States Steel, the ore properties paid $45,174,225 to the fortunate holders of Great Northern stock. Meanwhile, United States Steel had paid the Great Northern freight charges for hauling almost twenty-six million tons of ore.

"The time was near," wrote Hill's biographer of this period, "to which Mr. Hill had looked forward with anticipations of mingled pleasure and regret." He was ready to "relax the bonds of duty and labor." This it was now practicable to do because he could "turn over the headship of this vast product of his brain and hands to the son whom he had trained for fourteen years to take his place." This was Louis W. Hill, about whom more in its place.

So in June 1907 James J. Hill actually resigned the office of president of the Great Northern. Son Louis was elected. Hill Senior became chairman of the board. One is not to think for a moment that Jim Hill had retired. A project he had started in 1905 still remained unfinished, and, anyway, Hill's nature would not permit retirement until nature struck him down.

In 1905 the city of Portland, Oregon, which, incidentally, was then more than 200 miles from the nearest Great Northern track, felt the need to hold an exposition like those recently staged at Buffalo and St. Louis. A hundred years had elapsed since Meriwether Lewis and William Clark had passed that way, and the Oregon affair was fittingly called the Lewis & Clark Centennial. James J. Hill was among the officially invited guests. He attended, and while in Portland was pleased to make a little speech in which he took occasion to announce, ever so casually, that he intended to "help in the development of this great state."

Now, when Jim Hill planned to help with development anywhere, it was well for other developers to watch out. One who knew as much was Edward H. Harriman. In view of his control of the Union Pacific and Southern Pacific, one of which threaded Oregon from east to west, the other from north to south, Harriman may be forgiven if he considered Oregon his own private preserve. In any case, he was alert to the threat implied in Hill's booster-like speech at Portland, and both ready and willing to take on his old opponent.

XII

IT WOULD appear that in the resumption of hostilities Hill was the aggressor. He wanted a direct line to Portland and on to the mouth of the Columbia River. Harriman's Southern Pacific reached Portland from the south through the lush valley of the Willamette River. His Union Pacific reached Portland from the east by a fine water-level grade down the Columbia, on the south bank of the great river. There was no railroad on the north bank.

Many months before Hill spoke of his intention to aid in the "development" of Oregon, his engineers had been quietly locating a route along the Columbia's north bank between Pasco and Vancouver, Washington. (Portland is across the river from the latter city.) By the time the news was out, Hill's grading and construction crews were actually at work. It happened, too, at this period that Harriman was in a hospital recovering from an operation. As soon as he was able to sit upright in bed, he called Hill by long-distance telephone to say that he, E. H. Harriman, was gaining strength daily and would soon be at the front.

With almost incredible speed Harriman started obstructionist tactics. Organizing a couple of paper concerns, which he called the Columbia Valley Railroad Company and the Cascade Railroad Company, he sent his engineers to survey a line to conflict with the Hill locations. Wherever a Harriman survey crossed a Hill survey, he applied to the United States land office, under the right of eminent domain, for certificates to build. Some of these applications were granted. They were potent stuff for Harriman's legal batteries. Even if he had no intention to build, the certificates were sufficient to slow Hill's progress down the river. He had to go into court to fight every certificate granted to his antagonist.

When the opposing forces approached the towering rock promontory called Cape Horn, Harriman pretended to begin work on a tunnel with a total crew of six men complete with picks and a wheelbarrow. On the other side of Cape Horn, Hill could display more than one hundred men and at least $30,000 worth of equipment. He took the matter into court and won.

While the Hill crews were boring through Cape Horn, Harriman withdrew his front a few miles to occupy a new position. This was an old, short narrow-gauge that had once been used as a portage around the Cascade Rapids, and was then in use for transporting salmon to a cannery. Hill outwitted the move by running his own line underground for some four miles, then getting through the narrow gorge of the Columbia on a 27-foot right of way purchased from private owners.

While the various court battles were in progress, Hill and Harriman crews staged several small, yet violent, engagements with fists, pickhandles, and rocks. Dynamite was used at least twice in attempts to destroy Hill equipment. The last court suit was tried in 1906 and resulted in a Hill victory. The last spike on Hill's road, named the Spokane, Portland & Seattle, was driven in March 1908. Trains were soon entering Portland. The line was operated jointly by the Northern Pacific and Great Northern, just as it is today.

When the first train of the Spokane, Portland & Seattle line arrived in Portland, Jim Hill was more than one year in "retirement," yet most of his time was spent out on the lines, and he had still one more fine idea for developing Oregon. The preliminary plans for carrying it out were as devious as could be imagined, and were kept so secret that nothing was suspected until it was too late. Or, rather, almost too late.

One day there appeared in the desert of central Oregon a jolly sportsman who said his name was John F. Sampson. He was on holiday and having a fine time fishing. No better stream-fishing could be found than in the swift Deschutes and its tributaries, which tumbled down the east slope of the Cascade

Range, then flowed north into the Columbia. Sampson, who carried an unusual amount of tackle and equipment, was enthralled with everything. He would arrive at this or that isolated sheep or cattle ranch, stop for dinner, and tell his delighted hosts that this was indeed God's country. What was more, he proposed to buy for himself a piece of this sportsman's paradise.

Mr. Sampson appeared to be a wealthy man. During a period of several months, during which he was constantly moving around, he took an option on a ranch here, a proved-up homestead there, paying in personal checks that turned out to be as good as gold. Nobody got around to figuring out how much of central Oregon this genial sportsman took under option, but it was generally believed that it amounted to quite a considerable lot of land. That much of the land was sagebrush, rimrock, boulders, and lava seemed to make no difference to him. Then, without saying good-by to anybody, Mr. Sampson went away.

Almost simultaneously, Mr. Sampson turned up in Portland, where lived one William Nelson, who owned the only tangible property of the Oregon Trunk Railroad. This was an elegantly printed charter, a souvenir of one of Oregon's hectic periods of paper railroads. Mr. Nelson was bemused when approached by the somewhat mysterious Mr. Sampson. He was astonished, a few days later, when the stranger asked him to come to a secluded place in one of Port-land's many parks. There, to his stunned amazement, Mr. Sampson pressed upon him $150,000 in ex-change for his stock and charter described as the Ore-gon Trunk Railroad.

Mr. Sampson thereupon dropped his disguise, and became John F. Stevens, Jim Hill's chief engineer in Marias Pass days, who more recently had finished a stint as chief of engineers on the Panama Canal proj-ect. He had come to Oregon at Hill's request to ar-range for a railroad south from Hill's Spokane, Port-land & Seattle on the north bank of the Columbia. Just where this new Oregon Trunk was heading for was not clear, though Engineer Stevens himself an-nounced that it would terminate at a tiny settlement on the Deschutes named Farewell Bend.

Stevens's announcement electrified central Oregon, where smoke of the steamcars had never been seen, nor the sound of a locomotive whistle heard. It also electrified Edward H. Harriman. He knew well enough, if central Oregon ranchers did not, that the hamlet of Bend was not the terminus Hill had in mind. Harriman guessed correctly that Hill planned to build to Bend and right on through in a direct line to San Francisco. This would not do. San Francisco and California belonged by right of possession to Harriman's Southern Pacific Railroad Company.

Harriman moved with characteristic speed. Chartering a new line described simply as the Deschutes
Railroad, he brought the able George W. Boschke,
who had just completed building the celebrated sea
wall at Galveston, Texas, to Oregon to take charge of
matters. Boschke quickly moved a gigantic crew into
the region, sent locating engineers ahead, and proceeded to make grade. It was immediately apparent
that the Harriman line was to parallel Hill's from
the Columbia to Bend or, for that matter—said
Boschke—anywhere else that Mr. Hill might have
in mind. Hill had the east bank of the Deschutes
River. Harriman's men took the west bank.

Public excitement grew. One should remember
that this was still the great era of railroad-building. The
Ford car in mass was yet to appear. For more than
sixty years railroads had dominated transportation;
they also dominated the American imagination. The
Brave Locomotive Engineer was a heroic figure. His
engine was the vehicle of romance. The train of cars
rolling across the great plains and climbing the mountains was American destiny on wheels.

Editors were quick to sense that here in the lonely
open spaces of central Oregon, a region larger than
most states, was brewing a war of a size worthy of the
opposing forces, which represented the two greatest
railroad figures of the time. They sent their reporters
to cover it, never thinking for a moment that it was

to be the very last of the wars of rails to be fought, not in the stock market, but out on the rights of way.

Old settlers in central Oregon still cherish memories of the Deschutes railroad war, the most exciting event since the cattlemen-sheepmen wars of earlier in the century. All supplies, including hay for the horses and food for the huge crews, had to be toted overland at least one hundred miles, often farther. Bootleggers heard the call and went in to set up crude establishments hidden by boulders. Paydays became hideous with noise that frightened the coyotes, magpies, and buzzards.

Immense gangs of men faced each other from opposite sides of a narrow, tortuous river. When they came to the Deschutes Canyon, a mere cleft in high bluffs of rock, the going was murderous. Although sharp-eyed men with rifles lay prone on rimrock to watch the enemy, the gangs down below paid them little heed, but carried on a running battle, exploding substantial charges of dynamite timed to have the most telling effect on the opposition. Men were killed or maimed. Now and then a great boulder, solidly in place for centuries, suddenly started to roll. At least one such boulder rolled into and over a work train, crushing one of the cars to splinters. There were numerous hand-to-hand battles with axes, shovels, and picks. A few shots were fired.

At Mile 75, just when things were at their

bloodiest, Chief Engineer Boschke of the Harriman forces received an urgent telegram, purportedly from Galveston, where, as related, he had recently built the sea wall. Said the alleged wire: SEA WALL HAS BROKEN COME AT ONCE. Boschke ignored it for the fake it was.

A mix-up of titles, surveys, and court orders and other legalities came to a head at the ranch of a man named Smith. Harriman's agents had managed to get option on a right of way from Smith. A court held that Smith had proved his right to the land. As there was no other route from this point toward Bend, Hill was forced to halt his gangs and to arbitrate. He had met his match in Harriman. A truce was made by which Hill agreed to build no farther than Bend and to permit Harriman to use the line from Metolius to Bend.

When the Great Northern tracks were completed into Bend, Jim Hill himself was on hand to drive the last spike. It was the first day of October 1911. Seven thousand people cheered when Hill, the ceremony over, stood up to pass what he said were a few re-marks. He observed that Oregon had grown to a point where it was necessary for the Great Northern "to extend a helping hand to the Southern Pacific . . . in opening up the country," and rubbed it in a little bit by adding "if they are not ready to go ahead, we will try to take the load ourselves." At seventy-three, he was still a warrior, perhaps the very last of the old-school warriors.

When the railroad reached Bend, the town's population was 536. Ten years later it was 5,415, and local boosters took the trouble to figure out that the increase was 910 per cent, claiming it "a record in the United States for the decade." Bend's sudden flowering was caused in large part by efforts of Louis W. Hill, who persuaded his lumbermen friends of the Twin Cities, the Shevlins and Hixons, the Brookses and Scanlons, to inspect the immense ponderosa pine forests adjacent to Bend. The Minnesota lumbermen found the prospect good. They came to Bend and there erected two of the largest pine lumber manufacturing plants in the world, tapping the timber with their own railroads and shipping their lumber over the Great Northern. Forty years later Bend is still one of the great lumber centers.

The Hill-Harriman truce, of course, applied only to central Oregon, and even there it was temporary. The war continued in western Oregon, where the Harriman Southern Pacific had enjoyed a virtual monopoly for many years. Hill proceeded to buy and build a number of electric lines to compete with the older road. He had already purchased the so-called Hammond road from Portland to Astoria and made it a part of his Spokane, Portland & Seattle. The Hammond line had been built, ironically enough, with the financial aid of Collis P. Huntington of the South-ern Pacific. Now it belonged to Hill. To compete with the Southern Pacific's all-rail route from the Co-lumbia River to San Francisco, Hill bought two steamers, built an ocean terminal near Astoria at the mouth of the Columbia, then put a fast boat-train on his Portland-Astoria railroad from the Oregon metrop-olis to the dock. His railroad-and-ship route made good enough time to cut into the Southern Pacific's all-rail business.

For his part, Harriman was not idle. He built extensions to Tillamook and Coos Bay and started work on a new Southern Pacific main line from Weed, California, to Portland by way of Klamath Falls. This was not completed until after Harriman's death in 1909.

To finish with the last of the Hill-Harriman wars, Jim Hill died in 1916, too soon to see the Great Northern's extension south from Bend connect with the Western Pacific in California, over which GN trains could at last reach San Francisco. Only then could the Hill-Harriman struggle be considered ended.

It is significant that at the very time when Jim Hill's Great Northern was building the last link of its connection with San Francisco, elsewhere the Great Northern, and almost every other railroad in the United States, had started to pull up the tracks of many of their branch lines, to board up uncounted depots on their main lines. Many of them were even getting into the business of moving passengers by bus over the new highways. Both Hill and Harriman died not a moment too soon.

XIII

WHETHER fighting an open war with Harriman or an undercover action against the Canadian Pacific, Hill ever kept two objects in mind: immigrants to settle along or near his railroads, and freight to haul in his thousands of boxcars, flatcars, and gondolas.

He held a number of ideas about civilization which were similar to and antedated those posed so eloquently by Frederick Jackson Turner, author of the influential *The Frontier in American History*. Hill himself often stated an abstract proposition with clarity and pungent brevity. "Population without the prairie," he said, "is a mob, and the prairie without population is a desert." No one could know this better than Jim Hill, whose empire contained a great deal of desert.

In relation to freight, it seems to have been Hill's fairly consistent policy to keep rates as low as possible and still pay dividends. His early correspondence with such of his partners as Donald Smith and George Stephen is filled with warnings that the way to make a successful railroad is to give low rates and do all possible to develop the country and increase traffic. This was long before the Interstate Commerce Commission had any authority or even influence in the

matter of freight or passenger rates. In order to intro-
duce Douglas fir and Western pine lumber to the
great Midwest market, and thus compete with Southern lumber, Hill cut the freight rate from 90 cents per
hundred pounds to 40 cents. He was ready to haul a
healthy peasant from Europe halfway across the
United States for $10 if he would agree to settle along
Hill lines; or, if it was an entire family, complete
with household effects and even a few animals, he'd
rent them a freight car for a little more.

Mention has been made of the agents Hill had
sent to investigate potential markets in the Orient.
When he had digested their reports, Hill was virtually
an encyclopedia of facts regarding the needs of China,
Japan, and India. "If the people of a single province
of China should consume an ounce a day of our flour,"
he liked to say, "they would need 50,000,000
bushels of wheat per annum, or twice the Western
surplus." He realized that these people were very
poor, he said, but if only a small fraction of them
would substitute wheat flour for rice, it would mean
the creation of a great new market.

Hill believed that United States shipping in the
Pacific suffered from high rates. In 1900 he formed
the Great Northern Steamship Company, capitalized
at $6 million, and let contracts for two huge ships, the
Minnesota and the *Dakota*, which were built and went
into service between Seattle and Yokohama and Hong

Kong. He prevailed on a group of Japanese industrialists to meet him in Seattle, where he convinced them that they should try a shipment of American cotton to mix with the short-staple article they commonly got from India. Hill told them that he would deliver the American cotton to Japan free of carrying charges—and even pay for the cotton if they did not like it. They did like it, and from that point on a steadily increasing amount of Southern cotton was carried over the Burlington and the Great Northern rails to Puget Sound. In a little while it proved really big business. So did the American export of New England cotton goods to China. Minnesota flour went across the Pacific. So did metals from Colorado.

When Japan went into a railroad-building boom and planned to order rails from England and Belgium, Hill did some quick figuring, using the cables to Middlesborough and Antwerp and the telegraph to Chicago for prices on American rails. The outcome was that Chicago agreed to sell rails for $19.50, Hill set a forty-cents-a-hundred carrying charge between Chicago and Yokohama, and the total cost to the Japanese was $1.50 a ton lower than the English and Belgian quotations. The Japanese placed an initial order for 15,000 tons of the American product.

That the efforts of Hill were really effective in creating new markets could be seen in reports of the United States Customs District of Puget Sound. In the ten years after 1893, when the Great Northern reached Seattle, exports there increased 540 per cent. Hill got great satisfaction from these figures, yet he was not wholly sanguine about the future, remarking in an interview that "this business remains to some extent a matter of conjecture." Perhaps he had come to suspect that the free-wheeling days of empire-building were passing. In any case, he did not, as originally planned, add any ships to his Great Northern line of Pacific carriers. The restraining hand of government was to be felt in many ways. The "legislative enactments and official interferences by the political authority of the government," which he feared, were increasing. The Interstate Commerce Commission was, in short, beginning to feel its oats. Neither Hill nor any other railroad mogul could any longer set such rates as he saw fit. In good time, the Great Northern ships were sold; and not long before Hill's death in 1916, the old man indicated what was the matter.

"Trade is strictly competitive," he said, "and cannot be persuaded or cajoled. At present, therefore, the laws of this country offer an effectual barrier to any activity of importance or value on the part of railroads to build up American foreign trade." New times, new ideas—bad, foolish new times and ideas. Railroads had made the United States a great nation. Now they were to be harassed, even controlled "by onerous regulations." James J. Hill could no longer prevent such strictures, but he could damn them roundly, and this he did.

Among the things that infuriated Hill were the Minnesota Rate Cases, which were to occupy the attention of the courts for nearly seven years. Hill's home state had fixed new and lower rates on several classes of freight. Hill refused to abide by the rates. He refused to pay the fines levied as penalties. He fought the many individual cases through the Minnesota courts, lost, appealed to the United States Supreme Court, and lost again.

Because these cases were instituted in his home state and prosecuted there "with virulence," Hill came to be "partially alienated in sympathy from the community where he had lived so long and served so well." In 1906 he bought a typical brownstone residence at 8 East 65th Street in New York City, and for a time thought of settling there permanently. But old ties and old ways prevented him from joining his peers in the metropolis. Even in silk hat and frock coat, Jim Hill was not to be mistaken for a conventional capitalist. Almost anyone could see through the flimsy disguise and recognize the man within as an authentic character of the frontier. It was not that Hill was markedly crude or rough. His company manners were civil enough. It was rather a deep feeling of belonging to the frontier, a milder case of Kit Carson, who preferred a buffalo robe on a plank floor to mattress and springs.

The Hills' stays in New York grew shorter. After all, they had met and married in St. Paul, and their immense home on Summit Avenue was good enough. He had filled it with paintings by his favorites, Corot and Millet and lesser men of the Barbizon School. St. Paul was good enough, too. There was the nerve center of all the Hill Lines; and at the far western terminus of the Hill Lines, in Seattle, already stood a rugged bronze bust of Jim Hill, erected by citizens as a "permanent memorial of the great man of their affection and honor."

One of Jim Hill's dreams had been to populate those great and so-called waste lands between the Great Lakes and Puget Sound. The Northern Pacific had done an immense amount of colonization work from the first. The Burlington had been even more successful in attracting settlers. When these roads became a part of the Hill Lines, their agricultural and industrial departments were continued as before, and expanded.

In the days of his Manitoba, Hill had been effective in attracting and carrying thousands of settlers to western Canada, and almost simultaneously in doing a great deal to populate western Minnesota and the Dakota country. Hill himself had much more than a financial interest in agriculture. In view of the record, one can readily believe that he was genuinely devoted to what he often called by its old name of husbandry. Even before his little Manitoba railroad had got beyond Minnesota, he was urging and supporting and attending in person several conventions of farmers to discuss drainage and irrigation. From then until the last year of his life he was ready to speak before any group that wanted to hear his ideas about farming in the Northwestern states.

In a part of Hill's remarkable mind there was room to retain a monstrous volume of world statistics about agricultural production. From this encyclopedia he could draw at will, and did so, often to the marvel of his audiences and the confusion of critics. He was no dilettante farmer, either. On his own farms, and the farms of hundreds more, he had watched plowing, harrowing, and harvesting. He asked questions. He badgered the new agricultural departments of colleges for answers. In a thirty-page pamphlet, *The Nation's Future*, written by no ghost, but by Hill himself, he condensed his ideas on the theories of Malthus and then went on to show how the gloomy implications therein could be obviated by increased agricultural production.

In the actual business of farming, Hill never failed to stress what he called the necessity for deep plowing, repeated cultivation, the rotation of crops, fertilization, and the raising of livestock. Most but not all of these practices were sound if measured by the experience of later years.

It has already been mentioned that Hill had a large farm just outside St. Paul. There he experimented with wheat and other crops, and with cattle-breeding. He laid out another farm at Crystal Bay on Lake Minnetonka, where he kept prize cattle. He sent Professor Thomas Shaw, an expert in animal husbandry to England on several trips. Among other purchases, Shaw bought fifty Shorthorn bulls, all registered, which Hill distributed free of charge to farmers along the Great Northern. To these he added fifteen Shorthorn cows purchased at an average price of $500 each, which also went free to favored farmers, and of these animals Professor Shaw remarked: "It is safe to say that fifteen cows better individually were not left in England." After another trip, Shaw returned with a herd of the first South Devons ever brought to America.

Good hogs were important to Hill, but they were most susceptible to disease. Hill badgered the Rockefeller Institute to investigate hog cholera until Rockefeller himself recommended establishment of a Division of Animal Pathology in connection with the Institute. It was set up at Princeton, New Jersey. In 1906, at Hill's order, the Great Northern prepared and sent out a train equipped with lecturers to instruct farmers, who gathered at each station, in plant and animal culture, on the prevention of disease, and on the newest methods.

The Great Northern experimental train created so much interest that it prompted Hill to greater things. In 1912 the Great Northern formed a department "for agronomic inquiry." Under the direction of F. L. Crane, late of the University of Illinois, a tract of five acres was selected on each of one hundred and fifty-two farms in Minnesota and Dakota. The owner agreed to plow, plant, and cultivate the tract exactly as directed. Selected seed was furnished to him. The produce of the five acres was his own. He was also paid for his labor. The results were enlightening. The average wheat yield for Minnesota as a whole was 15.8 bushels; for Dakota, 18 bushels. The respective yields on the Great Northern tracts were 29.86 bushels and 31.47 bushels. The comparative yields in barley and oats also went to show graphically the possibilities in the careful selection of seed.

Hill was jubilant. He demanded that the work be enlarged to include analysis of soils; and because there were no facilities equal to the scientific analysis of soils from hundreds of farms, Hill ordered the huge greenhouses attached to his St. Paul home cleared of their flora and turned over to the soil experts. Five years later Director Crane could report that his men had operated with several thousand farmers in Minnesota and the two Dakotas. Three boxcar loads of "pure seed grains" had been distributed each year free of charge. Some five hundred tons of special plant foods had been made up and distributed. The result, he summed up, was that the improved methods revealed an increase of yields ranging from 25 to 33 per cent.

Tourists and other passengers moving west over Great Northern rails never failed to be struck, during the period extending roughly from 1907 to World War I, by the display cases at scores of depots big and small. These appeared on the open platforms or inside the stations. Wheat to bug an Easterner's eye, barley and oats to marvel at, on stalks as high as a man, in handsome, fancy jars filled with golden kernels. Panoramic photographs showing monster steam traction engines at work—hauling plows, harrows, reapers, and headers; or belted to threshing machines that were beating out the gold to be found in lands along the Great Northern or, for that matter, anywhere within twenty-five miles of its tracks.

Handy to the exhibits one found a pile of booklets that told of cash prizes and fancy medals given by Jim Hill's railroad for the best samples of grains grown on dry, as opposed to irrigated, farms. Other pamphlets told of homestead lands still open to entry: "Farms Free for the Asking," said the title, and the text announced that the Great Northern was ready to show you where to locate and how to file. See Your Nearest GN Agent. . . .

To Europe went Hill's agents armed with photographic slides depicting the northwestern United States as an Eden built to heroic size. These colored pictures were thrown on screens in Scotland, Ireland, Wales, and England; and with proper captions were thrown on screens in Denmark, Norway, Sweden, Finland, Germany, Poland, and Russia.

That the pictures were basically true to conditions can hardly be doubted. It is just as certain that the conditions shown were those which prevailed on the best farms, and none other. The effect of the pictures, combined with letters home from emigrants who had long since taken farms in the northwestern United States, was immediate and profound.

At the time when the Great Northern had spanned the northern tier of states from the Great Lakes to Puget Sound and Portland, Oregon, the least-settled region was Montana. The same was true fifteen years later, when Hill started in earnest to fill the vacant homestead lands waiting for settlers. By then, too, Hill and his agronomic advisers and experimenters had left all doubt behind in regard to Montana and agriculture: those arid and desolate reaches along the Hill Lines were the finest dry-farming land in the whole country. Deep plowing one season, followed by summer fallow the next—that was the secret of success discovered by Farmer Hill's experts.

On came the settlers. They came not only from the British Isles and northern European countries, but from the eastern and southern United States. Old-time Montanans called them all honyockers, a term of contempt that probably stemmed from the "hunyak" that had been applied earlier to Slav immigrants in Dakota, Minnesota, and Manitoba. Honyocker expanded the original term to cover all "foreigners" or outlanders.

On they came, the honyockers in the immigrant trains. Some rented a Great Northern freight car. In it a homesteader was permitted to place "all second hand articles such as household goods, machinery, agricultural implements, vehicles, wagons, tools, etc.," plus the following: "Fifty bushels of grain, sufficient feed for animals in transit, 2,500 feet of lumber, 500 fence posts, a small portable house, trees and shrubbery, small stock including hogs and sheep not to exceed 20 head, or horses, mules and cattle not to exceed ten head."

However they came, they arrived in numbers. In 1909 alone homesteaders took up more than one million acres in Montana. In 1910 still more homesteaders filed on 4,750,000 Montana acres. Between 1910 and 1922, 42 per cent of the entire state was settled by homesteaders, a majority of them induced to come by the enthusiasm and perseverance of Jim Hill (who died in 1916) and his inspired agents.

The tragedy of this wave of settlement and agriculture, according to surveys made after the disaster became apparent, was that at least 80 per cent of the area settled so rapidly was unfit for crop agriculture at all, even though wheat acreage increased from 258,000 acres in 1909 to 3,417,000 acres a decade later. This was mere groundwork for the debacle.

Hill's plan for dry-farming comprised four practices: deep plowing, repeated cultivation, rotation of crops, and the raising of livestock. It was the first two that brought disaster. Although they were intended to conserve the meager moisture of the high plateau, they could not conserve the moisture very long when it did rain or do any good at all in dry years. They could and did enormously speed soil erosion through blowing.

The wind, which on the high ground of Montana seldom stops blowing, blew the soil out of—and disaster into—the region. Thousands of small personal tragedies followed. A few brief lines of statistics largely explain the tragedies: from 1900 to 1916 the grasslands of Montana yielded an annual average of more than 25 bushels of wheat to the plowed acre. In 1919 the yield was 2.4 bushels per plowed acre. The honyockers gave up and moved away.

It was one portion of Jim Hill's magnificent dream of empire-building that did not pan out as he planned it, even though he fortunately died before it was seen to have been an illusion. Had he lived, say, another twenty years, or even ten years, the sight of those abandoned shack-houses and barns along Great Northern tracks—and along Northern Pacific tracks, too— might well have killed him.

Even Hill's severest critics, such as the late Joseph K. Howard of Great Falls, Montana, grant Hill's honesty in the affair, and have expressed sympathy with his motives. Hill was deeply distressed by the nation's continuous waste of natural resources. He was in some part responsible for President Theodore Roosevelt's calling the first Conservation Congress. He believed devoutly that Eastern and Midwestern farms were on the way to exhaustion. He believed just as devoutly that such so-called waste lands as those in Montana were capable of being made into farms as productive as any on earth. Why, these farms alone could produce enough bread and beef to feed the entire population of the United States!

Decades after Jim Hill's death, one may still look out a Great Northern window and see the homesteads of his dream which have become nightmares. The high, dry climate is a preservative shroud for dreams. The unpainted house leans sway-backed and mute, the barn stands naked to its ribs. The wheat field is a desert inside the remains of a barbed-wire fence, which catches and holds roll upon roll of nervous tumble-weed. It all looks pretty hopeless to anyone who has not seen the transformation that has taken place in another portion of the Jim Hill country.

In central and eastern Washington are regions that until comparatively recently were as desolate as any-thing in Montana. Today they are green with grass, or fruits, or vegetables, and yellow with waving wheat. Irrigation made this desert bloom. Hill was right when he said that waste land was merely land that needed attention. All he needed, but did not have, was a little more time.

XIV

MR. HILL'S JUDGMENT, so wrote Frank H. Spearman in his study of *The Strategy of Great Railroads*, "has never been seriously at fault in any of his undertakings." Although the observation is a bit too optimistic, it has stood up remarkably well since it was made more than half a century ago.

The failure of Hill's dream of a Montana checkered with quarter-sections of wheat does not mean it will never become a reality. There were, and still are deserts elsewhere on the Hill Lines which are as forbidding as anything in Montana. Irrigation on a gigantic scale has been making many of them bloom, and the areas of flowering have expanded so much and so rapidly as to make many a native doubt his eyes. Item: after passing through mile upon mile of the grimmest sort of waste land in central Washington, you come without warning to Trinidad, which just happens to be a Great Northern town, and you are immediately in the middle of 120,000 acres of lush wheat fields, fields of sugar beets, and of vegetables and fruits. It is startling. Water from Grand Coulee Dam brought it about. It is only one of many such sections in this area which irrigation has transformed. The water has come from the co-operative efforts of early settlers, from private concerns, and from state and federal governments.

The city of Wenatchee, which came into being just as soon as the Great Northern tracks got there, likes to think of itself as the Apple Capital of the West, possibly of the world. Jim Hill was responsible for neither apples nor irrigation in Washington. The venerable Hudson's Bay Company planted the first apple tree there and dug the first irrigation ditch. Settlers followed the practice. Hill merely encouraged a good thing.

The Great Northern's 137-mile branch from Wenatchee to Oroville, Washington, was built in large part to encourage apple-growers and to carry their products to market. Along this branch, among scores of fruit ranches large and small, are the enormous Beebe Orchards, which ship 450 carloads of apples in an average season. It is one of the largest operations anywhere. It was established by a good friend of Jim Hill's, Junius Beebe of Boston and Wakefield, Massachusetts.

"It was Hill's pitch that influenced my father and his brother, Marcus, to go into such an extensive business in the Northwest," says Lucius Beebe, publisher of the *Territorial Enterprise* of Virginia City, Nevada. "Hill often figured in my father's conversations and anecdotes. That he had travelled with Hill in his business car was a monstrous event in our juvenile minds suggestive of Babylonish luxury and in no way connected with making money.

"Boston's interest in the West was intense and my father and his brothers were the archetypes of Boston's post-bellum capitalists. At one time or another the family had silver mines and a railroad in Old Mexico, pecan groves which seemed to be under water at high tide in Florida, a goat ranch in Arkansas, wheat fields in Manitoba, a Canadian chrome mine, water-power rights in Eastern Canada and in Central Washington. Their range of interest was catholic, and nearer home they had a factory on Martha's Vineyard for turning dead fish into something useful, vast acres of potatoes at Mineola, Long Island, tanneries and banks all over New England, and a fifty per cent interest in Vici Kid, which was a patented method for making a kind of leather popular for many years.

"Most of all my father liked to grow things—trees, corn, vegetables, every sort of flora. Combine this hobby, or failing, with the wide venture-interests of the family, and it is obvious that Jim Hill did not have to extend himself unduly to transfer some of his enthusiasm for growing apples to my father and uncle, and to convince them that the Columbia River basin, or at least that portion of it served by Great Northern rails, was the finest apple land on earth." [1]

[1] Lucius Beebe, in a letter to the author, here quoted by permission.

So the Beebes purchased land along the east side of the Columbia near where the Chelan River empties into the larger stream. The first trees planted were watered from tank wagons, then by a primitive system by which water was pumped from the Columbia with water wheels, and later by a new style of pumps with motors. This in turn gave way to pipes from the penstock of the Chelan Electric Company, a fine arrangement brought about because the Beebes had purchased all land and water rights in the townsite of Chelan Landing from three Indians. (It is recalled that the Indians involved demanded a cash sum that could evenly be distributed three ways. They were made happy with $9,000.) The trees flourished. Meanwhile, the Great Northern built the Oroville branch that serves not only the Beebe Orchards, which require cars equal to four mile-long trains annually, but also fruit-growers for much of the 137 miles along the line.

Most, but not quite all, of the big orchards on the Oroville branch were highly successful. The notoriously celebrated exception was at Bridgeport Bar, a singularly inept attempt to get rich quick, or fairly quick, by the honorable method of fruit-husbandry. Although Jim Hill seems to have had no personal hand in it, he unquestionably inspired the project, if not the exact form it took, and at least two Great Northern men went heavily into the venture.

It was one of those absentee-ownership affairs, or largely so, which have such powerful appeal to many aspiring capitalists, not unlike the incorporated silver-fox farms that came into being at about the same time in the maritime provinces of Canada. This Columbia Basin affair took form as the Bridgetport Land Company and a subsidiary, the Hudson Water Company. Land and water. That was the combination to make apples.

All you had to do was to put your cash into these two concerns. Somebody then planted the trees, irrigated and cared for them, picked the apples, sold them at a huge profit, and then, one golden day in autumn, sent you a great big check as luscious as the bountiful Winesaps that you, as a non-sweating, even non-participating, husbandman had bestowed on a grateful public. You couldn't lose. It was that simple.

The dynamo of the Bridgeport project was a man of vision and enthusiasm, Charles N. Crewdson of the Outcault Advertising Company; and his more or less devoted associates included a number of well-known people. There were J. F. Pershing, a brother of the future general; H. P. Kinsley of the Associated Press; a Mr. Morris of the System Company of Philadelphia; W. C. Watrous, an official of the Great Northern Railway Company; M. R. Brown, James J. Hill's private secretary; L. M. Herman of the Kuppenheimer clothes people; the eminent Frederick

Starr, noted anthropologist of the University of Chicago, author of *The Truth about the Congo* and other works; Mr. Dunn and Mr. Hardenbrook of Mandel Brothers, Chicago merchants; Mr. Morgan of the Morgan Envelope Company; and Richard F. Outcault, the creator of Buster Brown. In 1909, when he joined the Bridgeport Land Company associates, Outcault had made a fortune from his funny-page characters (they were not then comic strips) and from licensing the Buster Brown name to manufacturers of novelties, clothes, shoes, even bread. The genius who managed these lucrative sidelines for Outcault was none other than Promoter Crewdson.

The project at remote Bridgeport Bar went ahead full speed. The company started to plant 1,600 acres of apple trees. A pumping plant was built to raise water from the Columbia River. Irrigation ditches were dug. Reports of progress went periodically to the absentee orchardists. Few of the investors, it appears, took the trouble to look at their orchards until three or four years had passed. What they saw then caused several to abandon their interests at once.

To begin with, the trees had been planted in great blocks, with no consideration for necessary pollenization. The irrigation ditches had not been lined. They lost much of the water pumped by the somewhat erratic works of the subsidiary Hudson Water Company before it could be of much encouragement to the growth of the trees.

In 1917 the pumping plant was enlarged, and electric power installed. The increased flow was still inadequate. The plant soon ceased to function at all. Spring frosts came to plague the growers. The lack of proper pollenization resulted in chronically low yields. The color of the Bridgeport Bar apples was consistently pallid; they were hard to sell. In good time the curse of the coddling moth arrived. Heavy lead sprays were applied. At harvest time the spray residue could not be removed with local equipment. The fruit had to be shipped across the river to Brewster, a Great Northern town, where the poison could be removed.

To make short work of it, the Bridgeport Bar orchardists simply went away. Or, rather they stayed away and ceased to support the resident manager with funds. The trees decayed. Presently they were felled like so much timber and cut into fuel, possibly the most expensive fuel ever burned in the state. By 1935 much of the original project had been reclaimed by the desert. In 1953 the original 1,600 acres had been reduced to less than one hundred.

It is worth bearing in mind that the ill-fated orchards of Bridgeport Bar are less than twenty miles, as the crow flies, from the heavy-bearing trees of the Beebe ranch; and no more than thirty miles distant as a salmon would travel by the river. Management had much to do with the contrasting history of the two tracts.

Yet, just as is the case with Montana's deserted homesteads, there is still hope for Bridgeport Bar. The construction, as this is written, of Chief Joseph Dam, a few miles upriver, has brought hope to the few surviving individual orchardists in the belief that the new federal project will soon supply water to the incredibly thirsty soil.

Granted that Hill's consistent encouragement of agriculture and cattle-raising had a measure of self-interest in it, one can hardly help thinking, from the record, that he believed devoutly that tilling the soil was the basis of every human achievement. As the years came on, he devoted more and more time to state and county fairs and to all kinds of farmers' meetings. He liked to point out that he had first become convinced of the feasibility of a railroad through the Northwest when he had noted the rich black soil that showed in the ruts of the old Red River carts, back in the fifties. The many little branch lines he set to fanning out from the Great Northern were proof enough that he thought his railroad must depend on farmers.

He never let down his insistence that wheat farmers should also raise dairy or beef stock on their ranches. And when he spoke of beef or dairy herds, as he did with no little enthusiasm, he meant only the best strains. By 1913 he could say, with considerable pride, that he had distributed free to farmers no less than 7,000 head of the best cattle he could buy, including 800 thoroughbred bulls; and more than 6,000 hogs of prize stock. "I was trying," he said, "to put the people of Minnesota twenty or twenty-five years ahead of their neighbors in Iowa." Whether or not he accomplished his goal, it cannot be doubted that Hill gave an enormous impetus to interesting farmers, both immigrant and native, in better stock. And better seed, too. He urged them to experiment for themselves.

"One time when wheat was selling at 55 cents a bushel in Minneapolis," he recalled in a county-fair talk, "I thought I would try what wheat would do to feed steers. I fed a lot of steers that winter and found I had got 82 cents a bushel for the wheat I fed them. That was a lot better than selling it for 55 cents."

Occasionally, as age advanced, Hill took what he called a vacation, fishing for salmon in Labrador. But he was seldom out of touch with St. Paul. His daily intake of nicotine increased somewhat with the years, and he had always been a steady smoker; but with alcohol he was described by friends as abstemious. One finds nothing in print or the memories of those who knew him as to his likes or dislikes in the matter of food.

It is obvious he could write clear, grammatical prose. If he had a ghost writer, which is extremely doubtful, the matter was conducted with the greatest circumspection. The prose of his book *Highways of Progress* leaves one believing that Hill himself wrote every word. It is not graceful prose, but it is as clear as one could wish. He never, said an associate, used a word of Latin origin if a Saxon word would do. And he held Bunyan to be the great stylist.

Despite his biographer who works hard and none too convincingly to make Hill of genial temper, it is probable that his disposition did not improve with age. His courtier Pyle says that he had on him "the imprint of the open heart, understanding and sympathy"; nevertheless, "his glance could smite without a word" and "there were few who dared to face it then." After all, he was an emperor and he "had tasks that would brook no trifling." Because "passion goes with power," men "ran for cover when Mr. Hill's anger broke restraint."

Other than from his railroads and his work in agricultural improvement, the aging Hill probably got his greatest satisfaction from his collection of paintings. He himself thought enough of it to cite it in his sketch in *Who's Who in America*, where it is described as "one of the finest collections of paintings of the modern French school in the world." This sounds excessive. The collection was fine enough, anyway. He had started it with a Corot or two, and a good Millet; and added examples of Daubigny, Dupré, Descamps, Théodore Rousseau, and one of Delacroix's better pictures. All these artists were much admired in America. Yet, as early as the eighties, Hill purchased paintings of the younger men, including works by Monet and Renoir. This was unusual in an American collector of the time. One is inclined to the belief that Hill "never bought a picture because a dealer recommended it." Was there any reason why a man who understood the complexities of building and running a railroad and making it pay should not know exactly what he wanted in a picture?

Honors came as the years passed. Yet the years passed fearfully swift. Birthdays came closer together than when the world was young. In 1905 Sir Thomas Shaughnessy of the Canadian Pacific Railway was pleased to speak well of Hill on the occasion of his birthday. "James J. Hill," said Sir Thomas, "is the genius of the Northwest country, and I am confident that one hundred years from now his work will be much better understood in its far-reaching results than it is at present." But there was no accolade from Sir William Cornelius Van Horne, though a little later the Canadian Club of Winnipeg entertained Hill and his old friend and business partner Lord Strathcona.

In 1910 Yale awarded Hill an honorary degree of Doctor of Law and hailed him at the ceremonies as

"the last of the generations of wilderness conquerers."
They were the men who had "blazed all the great
trails which determined the nation's future." Yale did
the business with considerable grace, and properly so.
Two of Hill's sons had gone to Yale. Three of his
daughters married Yale men.

Of Hill's seven daughters, one died in infancy. The
others survived him. Mary married Samuel Hill, of
St. Paul; Ruth married Anson McCook Beard,
of New York City; Charlotte became the wife of
George T. Slade, a vice-president of the Northern
Pacific; Gertrude became Mrs. Michael Gavin II, of
New York; Clara was not married; and Rachel be-
came the wife of Dr. Egil Boeckmann, of St. Paul.

The youngest son, Walter, "engaged in farming
on a large scale in the Red River Valley." The other
two, James N. and Louis W., had since schooling
been working for the railroad. In 1907 Louis was
elected president of the Great Northern. In 1912 he
became chairman of the board of directors.

For many years it was generally understood in railroad circles that Jim Hill was grooming Louis to take
over the top job in the Great Northern; and when
Louis was made president it was assumed that the old
man's mantle had been placed on the son's shoulders.
Nobody knew better than Louis that Jim Hill's mantle
could fit no other man. Not because he thought the

elder Hill was the greatest man living—that wasn't it. It was rather that the old man occupied a place in the Hill Lines and in the Hill country that could not be filled by another. He had long since become a legendary figure, the source of anecdotes, drummers' stories, and limericks and doggerel. Editors and orators praised him as the Empire Builder or cursed him as a major scourge. Farmers and ranchers swore by or at Jim Hill. The more profane of them, given to complicated impieties, liked to start a stem-winding oath: "By Jesus H. Kee-ryst and Jim Jam Hill . . ."

Lutheran ministers and Catholic priests—and even archbishops—spoke highly of Hill's contributions to the Lord. Scandinavian comedians rocked the opera houses of Bemidji, Thief River Falls, and Yankton with song about "The Swede at the Big State Fair" who related how "Aye yoomp on Yim Hill's little red vagon . . ."

This was the same James J. Hill in whose honor Harvard University named a chair in railroad economics, the same who was a welcome and honored guest at the homes of J. Pierpont Morgan the Elder in New York and London, a man whose gregariousness was under Spartan control.

Louis Hill knew all these things about his father. As he was also a highly intelligent man, it is most improbable that the son ever thought for a moment, when he was Great Northern president, that he was in any manner filling the place of his father. The old man had nine years left of life, and before his death the actual operation of the railroad was in the hands of the young and competent executive vice-president, Ralph Budd.

XV

NEITHER as president of the Great Northern nor as chairman of its board did Louis Warren Hill seem to feel that he had actually taken the place of his father. He wore a thick black beard, looked not unlike the elder Hill, was easily irritated, had keen intelligence and considerable ability. He may well have inherited other characteristics from his father; if so, they were not clearly marked. But one can believe that he was resigned to the fact that he must live and work in the shadow of the great Empire Builder.

The sons of eminent, or even wealthy, men, no matter their abilities, are born to be watched and compared to their fathers. John Quincy Adams overcame the handicap and rose to as high a station as did his parent. William H. Vanderbilt died worth more than twice as much as the old Commodore. Yet none of Theodore Roosevelt's sons reached eminence, though some of them tried to; and no Astor in four generations did more than carefully husband the immense fortune of John Jacob Astor I. Many another huge fortune went directly to pot once the man who made it left it to his children.

Jim Hill's son Louis did more for the Great Northern Railway than is generally known outside railroad circles. It was Louis who was chiefly responsible for putting the railroad into the iron-ore business, an extremely profitable sideline mentioned in a previous chapter. Fresh from Yale, Louis went to work for the Minnesota Eastern, a subsidiary of the Great Northern, which took him into the Duluth area. The great ore deposits of the Mesabi Range were then in the process of pioneer development. Young Hill did some prospecting in person, and became convinced that the cutover timber lands of Wright & Davis, the big logging outfit, were of much greater value below the stumps than they had been above ground when the area grew thick and tall with white and Norway pine.

So, when Jim Hill himself came to buy the Duluth & Winnipeg Railroad—which had never got anywhere near the latter city—and to extend it to make an air-line route to the Red River wheat fields, Louis urged his father to buy also the abandoned logging tracks of Wright & Davis and the several thousand acres of stumps and brush which went with them. The old man could not, however, be persuaded to buy this desolation until Louis prompted D. N. Philbin, superintendent of the Duluth & Winnipeg, to urge it too. Philbin turned the trick; the logging road and stump land were bought, and under the stumps were what in time became the Great Northern Iron Ore Properties. The millions of dollars of dividends paid Great Northern stockholders over the years are thus owing in large part to the perspicacity of young Louis Hill.

In the newer field of public relations, the younger Hill, when chairman of the Great Northern board, contributed something to the railroad and to the United States. It was he, according to Freeman H. Hubbard, an authoritative voice, who coined the Great Northern slogan, "See America First," which has since become public property.

Mr. Hubbard, editor of *Railroad Magazine* and author of *Railroad Avenue*, went to some trouble to run down the origin of the slogan and the Great Northern symbol with which "See America First" was first used. This is the famous Rocky Mountain goat one sees on Great Northern rolling stock, timetables, advertising brochures, and other literature. Hubbard says that Louis Hill thought up the slogan and hitched it to the goat to make the Great Northern trademark; and that it was William P. Kenney, then vice-president in charge of traffic, who suggested the goat.

Kenney was reared in an Irish section of the Twin Cities. He sold papers, and because even then he had a sense of the value of good publicity, he hitched a pet goat to a little wagon and paraded the streets with his stacks of *Journals* and *Tribunes* and *Pioneer-Presses*. His business flourished. Later he went to railroading, and by 1912 was boss traffic man of the Great Northern. At about this period the railroad was beginning to exploit Glacier National Park in Montana, and Louis Hill thought up the inspired "See America First." Wanting a trademark for the railroad, he was over-joyed when Kenney, musing on the mascot of his paper-peddling days, suggested not just a goat, but a Rocky Mountain goat, like those to be seen in num-ber in Glacier Park, a scenic wonderland served only by the Great Northern. "Few symbols in America," Mr. Hubbard observed, "are better known than the Great Northern goat. It is generally regarded as a million-dollar idea."

It will be recalled that when Jim Hill and E. H. Harriman fought to a stalemate in the central Oregon war and Hill completed the road to Bend, the Great Northern soon prevailed on the Brooks-Scanlon lum-ber interests of Minnesota to erect a big sawmill in the Oregon town. That a fine tract of ponderosa pine was readily available through the Great Northern was ow-ing to a rather remarkable flyer Louis Hill had pre-viously taken on his own account.

Like his father before him, the younger Hill got around a good deal, saw more than most people did, and was usually fairly quick to recognize a business opportunity. In Oregon, where his father was en-gaged in what he liked to call "opening up the coun-try," Hill thought he saw a chance.

A rather sizable piece of this country was owned by the international banking firm of Lazard Frères, a little less than one million acres. Part of it was virgin timber. More could be described as range land, which meant in this case a mixture of grass here, lava there, and here and there rocks, boulders, juniper, sage-brush, and tumbleweed. How the French bankers came by it is far too complicated to go into here, and so is the long and troubled history of the tract. Briefly, it was originally a land grant to the Willamette Valley & Cascade Mountains Wagon Road Company of pioneer days, to encourage "an improved road" from the west slope of the Cascade Range eastward to the Idaho line, an over-all distance of more than four hundred miles.

Subsequently, the federal government brought suit to have the grant declared forfeit, alleging that the terms of the contract had never been fulfilled. Into court went the local attorney for Lazard Frères, Charles Erskine Scott Wood, a brilliant and erratic character who had been graduated from West Point, fought Indians, married, then settled down in Port-land to practice law. Colonel Wood, as he was known, heading a galaxy of legal talent, proved to the satis-faction of the court, if not to a vast majority of Oregon citizens, that the land grant to the ancient wagon-road company was still good and that Lazard Frères did indeed own the alternate sections along its surveyed route.

Colonel Wood meanwhile informed W. P. Da-

vidson, a capitalist of St. Paul, Minnesota, that Lazard Frères was eager to get out of the business of
speculating in Oregon lands. They were ready to sell
this huge tract at a bargain. Mr. Davidson, too,
thought it a bargain. He needed help to swing the deal,
and interested Louis W. Hill. Hill displayed immediate interest. Using his own, and not Great Northern,
resources, Hill, in the form and style of the Oregon &
Western Colonization Company, bought the land
grant that the legal magic of Colonel Wood had
validated as the genuine article.

It was some of the timber on Hill's new property
which, as related, attracted the Brooks-Scanlon interests to Bend, where they have been making lumber ever since. The lease and sale of Louis Hill's
private empire made him a wealthy man without reference to his interests in the Great Northern Railway
and its iron-ore properties. Colonel Wood seems also
to have done very well, which was no more than
proper when his great labors in behalf of Lazard
Frères are considered.

Meanwhile, and no matter who was president of
the Great Northern, the road was being ably directed
by young Ralph Budd, already mentioned. A native
of Iowa, Budd began railroading at the turn of the
century in the engineering department of the Chicago
Great Western and, after serving as chief engineer for
the Panama Railroad, entered Jim Hill's employ in

1909. Four years later he was chief engineer, assistant to the president, and executive vice-president of the Great Northern. He was running the road in 1916, when death removed the aging Empire Builder.

One of the last photographs of James J. Hill was taken in October 1915. The scene was the Ottertail County Fair at Fergus Falls, Minnesota. The picture appeared in the Sunday section of the *New York Times* on the same page with one of J. Pierpont Morgan the Younger (the old man was dead), who had undergone an operation for appendicitis. On the same page are shown two other famous Americans: Samuel W. Gompers "breaking ground for an office building for the American Federation of Labor in Washington to cost $200,000," and Ethel Barrymore, in *Our Mrs. McChesney* at the Lyceum Theater, New York.

The scene at the Ottertail County Fair is characteristic of most of Jim Hill's latter years. The old man, seventy-seven, stands on an open-air platform surrounded by Minnesota farmers, their wives, their daughters and sons. It is chilly weather. The trees in the background are bare. The audience is mostly in overcoats. Jim Hill, his hair and beard now snow white, and both longer than common, is hatless, in contrast to the square derbies, the Stetsons, the round black hats favored at the time by many Scandinavian farmers, and the pseudo-aigrets, feathers, and whole birds of the women. Hill stands there solidly on the platform. He looks intense, as though he were driving home some cherished theory of husbandry. And except for a few of the ladies, who obviously are looking at the hats of some of their sisters, the audience appears rapt by whatever the old man is saying. Even the youngsters are giving Hill their attention. If they were of too tender an age to grasp his message, they could at least look upon the greatest living legend of their time in the Northwest. There he was in the flesh, his huge hands resting on the platform rail, his huge shoulders hunched above his neck, his weatherbeaten face surrounded by snowy whiskers and hair. *He* could tell them how it had been before the pioneers came. Hill had been here at the falls of the Otter Tail River before there was so much as a shanty to mark the village named for his friend James Fergus.

That was the thing about Jim Hill. Here in his own country, or so it must have seemed, he had been almost everywhere before other white men came; and when he addressed the farmers of Otter Tail County, and the farmers or industrialists of other towns and cities along the Great Northern, Hill could speak with the incomparable authority of historical background. Whether or not he knew it, Hill was already a part of history.

While he still lived as a historical character, Hill also went into legend. Penalties went with the legend.

Long before his death, little children who never saw
Jim Hill came to think of him as they did about such
other legendary heroes and villains as Custer, Wild
Bill Hickok, and Jesse James. In Montana there was
only one man named Hill. He did not need a first or
second name, and the kids sang about him:

Twixt Hill and Hell, there's just
                                    one letter;
Were Hill in Hell, we'd feel
                                    much better.

The ditty is one of the penalties, and compliments,
of being a Great Man. It is significant that there seems
to be no similar doggerel about the men who promoted and built the Union Pacific, the Northern Pacific, or the Milwaukee. Hill stands alone. He was
the Empire Builder, praised and cursed for his building.

Before he died, Hill had somehow become a figure
of the Currier & Ives prints in connection with Litho-
graph No. 187, published in 1871 as one of their
American Railroad Scenes series. It is entitled *Snowbound*. It shows a big-stacked locomotive and its train
of passenger cars stopped by a drift deep over the
tracks. It is night. The headlamp stabs through the
gloom, revealing that the halt has occurred in a forest
of conifers. In the foreground twelve men are shovel-
ing snow, and one man is leaning on a shovel. In the

background are four men, one in stovepipe hat. Another, in blue coat and with a lantern, is probably the conductor. In at least one catalog of prints, No. 187 is described as a "small folio whose popularity has sent its value up to $250, many times that of other good prints of similar size." And the cataloger adds: "The man leaning on his shovel is assumed to be J. J. Hill."

In this old print we can see the marvelous workings of legendry. When it was issued, in 1871, Jim Hill was not a national figure. He could scarcely have been known outside Minnesota. He was not yet a railroad-man. The print was made at least seven years, and possibly more, before Hill is known to have spelled off one of his gangs in a snowstorm and sent the men into his car to have coffee. This incident, while incredibly out of character in a Vanderbilt, Gould, or Harriman, was wholly in keeping with Jim Hill. Hence, in good time, after Hill had become widely known, somebody with imagination, who might well have been a dealer in prints, heard of Hill's stint with the shovel and promptly "assumed the man leaning on the shovel to be J. J. Hill." If so, he libeled Hill. Hill might use a shovel. One cannot picture him leaning on one.[1]

There was no doubt as to how Hill stood as a man of Minnesota. When the management of the Panama-

---

[1] One of the best collections of Currier & Ives prints in private hands is that of Samuel Hopkins Adams, who told the author that in *Snowbound* "either the man in the silk hat or the party leaning on the shovel is supposed to be Jim Hill."

Pacific World's Fair at San Francisco asked each of the states to name its greatest living citizen for a Hall of Fame, the committee of five appointed by the governor of Minnesota unanimously selected Jim Hill. He had already given some thought to posterity, and had engaged an ex-newspaperman, Joseph G. Pyle, to write his authorized *Life*. Pyle also became the first librarian of the James Jerome Hill Reference Library, opened in 1917, for which Hill had set aside nearly one million dollars before the end.

Death came to him on the morning of May 29, 1916, following an "indisposition" that lasted only nine days. Ten days before, he had done a good day's work at his office.

"Greatness became him," said the *New York Times*, "and was a condition of his errand here. Whatever he had done, it had been greatly done." Many other obituary editorialists pointed out what they considered Hill's greatest achievement, that he had built a railroad from the Lakes states to the West Coast without land grant or government subsidy.

Legend-makers were busy. An editorial writer in the *Independent* recalled of Hill's youth in Ontario that "a traveller stopping at the Hill homestead tossed the young man as he left an American newspaper, and called out 'Go there, young man. That country needs youngsters of your spirit.'" The very next morning, according to this account, young Hill "chopped the last tree on the old place, then set out for the land of opportunity across the border." Not content to leave a good anecdote still credible, the editoralist went on to say of this last tree that "the stump still bears the rudely cut legend: 'The Last Tree Chopped by James J. Hill.'" Such a durable stump carrying such a hand-chopped legend belongs not in the Ontario bush of sixty-two years afterward, but in either the British Museum or the Smithsonian Institution.

Of real significance, however, is the fact that just before he died Hill had read with the greatest satisfaction a book by William Brown Meloney entitled *The Heritage of Tyre* (Macmillan, 1916). The satisfaction was that Author Meloney, even as Jim Hill, deplored the current low place of the United States in matters of world shipping. Both men believed that "with free ships and freedom from onerous regulation," Americans might "once again rule the seas commercially." When Hill had organized the Great Northern Steamship Company and put the fine new *Minnesota* and *Dakota* on the Orient run, he had dreamed that he might restore the United States "to the high position of those glorious days when our clipper ships rode proudly in all the harbors of the world." The dream had faded in the fog of "onerous regulations" on the part of his own government.

Louis W. Hill died when nearing his seventy-sixth birthday in 1948. He had lived to see the Great Northern under Ralph Budd put its (second) remarkable bore straight through the Cascade Range, and also to witness the Great Northern's entrance to San Francisco over the rails of the Western Pacific. Of Louis, the last of Jim Hill's railroading sons, the *Oregonian* of Portland said: "He was impulsive in his personal contacts, but if irritated he soon mellowed." It then went on to speak of Louis Hill not as a railroadman, but "as a painter of some ability." There was not room in one family for more than one Empire Builder.

The memory of Jim Hill should persist as long as the lounge car of each Great Northern passenger train displays a fine copy in color of the authorized portrait of the old man; and as long as the number-one train is the Empire Builder. Let the Great Northern serve as Hill's monument. He needs no other.

BIBLIOGRAPHY AND
ACKNOWLEDGMENTS

THE SOLE biography of James J. Hill is the authorized *Life* by Joseph Gilpin Pyle, in two volumes, published in 1916–17. It is more than commonly slavish. The subject is run through the courtier's gilding machine, to emerge shining like a true Christian knight battling for Truth and Right against dark and evil—or merely stupid—forces, here represented variously as government, politicians, oral and editorial critics, and any and all opponents to Hill's acts, opinions, methods, and general philosophy. The two big volumes are consistent in eulogy. They also obscure any clues to the subject's character and personality, save where the biographer's special pleading overshoots and inadvertently reveals what he is seeking to hide.

At the other extreme are the chapters dealing with Hill in Gustavus Myers's *History of the Great American Fortunes.* Although Myers is only moderately savage, compared with his strictures on, say, John Jacob Astor and Russell Sage, he still cannot concede that Hill was other than a notorious public enemy.

In his *Montana—High, Wide and Handsome*, Joseph K. Howard considers Hill to have been something of a curse on that state, yet concedes his honesty in the business of settling homesteaders there, no matter how mistaken the attempt. In *They Built the West*, by Glenn C. Quiett, Hill appears as a shrewd opportunist. Much earlier, Frank H. Spearman, writing of *The Strategy of Great Railroads*, found Hill to be nigh perfect in every department, a man whose "judgment has never been seriously at fault in any of his undertakings."

The legendry of Jim Hill throughout the Northwest, where I have lived and traveled much for more than thirty years, is without end. Some of it is important because it indicates what associates and contemporaries thought of Hill, but I have not disguised opinions or legends as documented facts.

Research for this book was done over the years in the New York Public Library; the James J. Hill Reference Library, St. Paul; the Minnesota, Oregon, and Washington Historical Societies; and the Public Library of Portland, Oregon, in all of which I was accorded the generous help of competent and courteous people. Miss Esther L. Watson prepared the manuscript.

Among the people I must especially thank for advice in bibliographical matters, and otherwise, are: Charles Beebe, Lucius Beebe, Ralph Budd, Henry W. Corbett, C. A. Gerken, Harley Hallgren, Wallace Hughes, Elizabeth Johnson, Thelma Jones, Anne Jubitz, Marion Lawrence, David Mason, Louise Prichard, Frank Branch Riley, Robert W. Sawyer, and Erskine Wood. Below are listed the works which were of much, or at least a little, help.

Bryan, Enoch A.: *Orient Meets Occident*; 1936.

Cushing, George H.: "Hill Against Harriman," *American Magazine*, September 1909.

Dibble, R. F.: *Strenuous Americans*; 1923.

Flandrau, Grace: *The Story of Marias Pass*; 1925.

Gibbon, J. M.: *Steel of Empire*; 1935.

Holbrook, Stewart H.: *The Story of American Railroads*; 1947.

——: *Far Corner*; 1952.

Howard, Joseph Kinsey: *Montana—High, Wide and Handsome*; 1943.

——: *Strange Empire*; 1952.

"James J. Hill," an obituary, the *Independent*, June 26, 1916.

Josephson, Matthew: *The Robber Barons*; 1934.

Kelsey, Vera: *Red River Runs North*; 1951.

Kennan, George E.: *E. H. Harriman*, 2 vols.; 1922.

Laut, Agnes: *The Blazed Trail of the Old Frontier*; 1926.

Lewis, John J.: "Consolidation of Railroads and the Proposed Great Northern-Northern Pacific Unification," *Harvard Business Review*, July 1928.

Linn County, Oregon, History of; n.d.

Myers, Gustavus: *History of the Great American Fortunes*; 1936.

Newson, T. N.: *Pen Pictures of St. Paul, Minnesota, and Biographical Sketches of Old Settlers*; 1886.

Pyle, Joseph Gilpin: *The Life of James J. Hill*, 2 vols.; 1916–17.

Quiett, Glenn C.: *They Built the West*; 1934.

Spearman, Frank H.: *The Strategy of Great Railroads*; 1904.

Vaughan, Walter: *The Life and Work of Sir William Van Horne*; 1920.

Wheeler, A. O.: *The Selkirk Range*, 2 vols.; 1905.

Willamette Valley & Cascade Mountains Wagon Road Company, 1864–1911, Abstract of, in Oregon Historical Society, archives.

Files of newspapers: the *Oregonian*, *St. Paul Pioneer Press*, *Seattle Post-Intelligencer*, *Spokane Review*, *Minneapolis Journal*.

INDEX

Alger, Horatio, 18
American Federation of Labor, 195
American Railway Union, 127
Atchison, Topeka & Santa Fe Railway, 125

Bank of Montreal, 48, 50, 69, 85
Barnes, John S., 50, 64
Beebe, Lucius, 177–8
Boschke, George, 154, 156
Bridgeport Bar orchard project, 178–81
Budd, Ralph, 93–4, 116, 188, 194, 201
Burlington Route, *see* Chicago, Burlington & Quincy
Burns, Robert, 8
Byron, Lord, 9

Canadian Pacific Railway: formation and construction, 45–53, 69–77; Hill resigns, 76; Hill's further relations with, 86, 96, 98
Carnegie, Andrew, 11
Carson, Kit, 164
Chicago & Alton Railroad, 72–3

Chicago & Northwestern Railway, 61
Chicago, Burlington & Quincy Railroad, 108, 138–9, 143–4, 165
Chicago Great Western Railway, 72
Chicago, Milwaukee & St. Paul Railroad, 20, 72, 85; *see also* Van Horne
Cleveland, Grover, 101
Cooke, Jay, 40–1
Countess of Dufferin (locomotive), 52
Crédit Mobilier, 46, 69
Currier & Ives, 197, 198 *n*

Daly, Marcus, 106
Debs, Eugene, 127
Dubuque & St. Paul Packet Company, 15
Duluth & Winnipeg Railroad, 190

Farley, Jesse, 43–4, 56–7, 65–6
Fenians, 29–30, 34–6
First Division Company, 40, 43
Forbes, John Murray, 108
Frontier in American History, The (Turner), 160

"Gateway to the North-west" (slogan), 109

Gibson, Paris, 102–3, 107

Gompers, Samuel, 195

Gould, Jay, 89, 100–1, 143

Grand Coulee Dam, 175

Great Northern Iron Ore Properties, 190

Great Northern Railway: *Empire Builder*, 5, 200; *Western Star*, 5; territory covered by, 6; competition with Soo Line, 83; formation and construction, 86 *et seq.*; traffic structure, 90–1; in Spokane, 117–22; reaches Seattle, 123; Harriman a director, 141; control of Burlington, 142; land-grant recovery, 144–6; Mesabi iron, 146; extension into Oregon, 148–57; encouragement of agriculture, 167–73; character of its territory today, 175–6; directorate after Hill, 186; origin of advertising themes, 191–2; *see also* St. Paul, Minneapolis & Manitoba; Montana Central; St. Paul & Pacific; Spokane, Portland & Seattle

Great Northern Steamship Company, 161–2, 200

Griggs, Chauncey W., 15, 20

Hamm, Theodore, 15

Hammond Road, 157

Harriman, Edward: comparison with Hill, 134–6; battles with Hill, 138–42, 148–58

Hatch, Edwin A. C., 11

Heritage of Tyre (Meloney), 200

Hill, Anne, 7

Hill, James, Sr., 9

Hill, James Jerome: character, 3, 130–4; encouragement of settlers, 3–4, 91–3, 160–1, 171–2; comparison with Vanderbilt, 4; death, 4, 199; appearance, 6; boyhood and education, 7–10; early travels, 10–15; life and business in St. Paul, 15–19; courtship and marriage, 20; monopolizes region's coal business, 21; relations with church, 22–3; influence of Kittson, 24–9; in Red River shipping, 29–36; rate wars with Hudson's Bay Company, 33–6; quoted on Fenian war, 34–6; forms Red River Transportation Company,

Hill, James Jerome (*continued*)

39; acquisition of St. Paul & Pacific, 42, 45–53; rehabilitation of St. Paul & Pacific, 55 *et seq.*; director of the Manitoba, 64–5; sued by Farley, 66; development of the Manitoba, 66–8; building Canadian Pacific, 69–77; resigns from CPR, 76; comparison with Van Horne, 82–4; success with Manitoba, 85–6; formation and construction of Great Northern, 86 *et seq.*; builds Stone Arch Bridge, 93–5; fights Reservation Act, 99–102; purchase of Burlington, 109; search for pass through Continental Divide, 112–17; addresses Spokane, 117–21; Seattle reached, 123; union settlement, 127–8; holdings in Northern Pacific, 126–30; comparison with Harriman, 134–5; battle with Harriman for Northern Pacific, 138–42; partnership with Morgan, 142–4; prosecution under Anti-Trust Laws, 144; resigns from Great Northern, 147; battle with Harriman for Oregon, 148–58; interest in Orient, 161–2; views on competition, 163; Minnesota Rate Cases, 164; residence in New York, 164; collector of paintings, 165, 184–5; interest in agriculture and conservation, 165–83; writer, 166, 181–2; Yale degree, 185–6; children's histories, 186; local reputation, 196–7; Currier & Ives print, 197; legends, 197–201

Hill, James N., 146, 186

Hill, Louis: influences father, 146; as president of Great Northern, 147, 186–92; develops lumber traffic, 157; death, 200–1

Hill, Mary Mehegan, 22

Howard, Joseph Kinsey, quoted, 36–7

Hubbard, Freeman, 191

Hudson's Bay Company: history, 25–8; Hill's competition with, 30–3, 37; local attitudes toward, 78; in Washington State agriculture, 176

Huntington, Collis P., 158

Illinois Central Railroad, 20, 73, 135

Interstate Commerce Commision, 118, 160–1, 163

Ireland, Archbishop, 18

Kansas Pacific Railroad, 89

Kennedy & Company, J. S., 50, 64

Kenney, William, 191–2

Kittson, Norman: early life, influence on Hill, 24–9; competition with Hill, 33; buys Hill out, 39; alliance with Hill, 45, 47, 64–6

Kuhn, Loeb & Company, 139

Lake Superior Company, 147

Land grants, railroad, 40, 68, 85, 87, 90, 144–6

Lazard Frères, 192–3

Life of James J. Hill, The (Pyle), quoted, 16, 18, 65, 66, 82, 86, 101, 144, 147, 184, 199

Macdonald, John, 46, 62, 69, 75, 81

Manitoba Free Press, 52

Manitoba Railroad, *see* St. Paul, Minneapolis and Manitoba

Marias Pass, 112–16

McKenzie, George, 15

McKinley, William, 143

Mehegan, Timothy, 20

Mesabi iron range, 146, 190

Minneapolis & St. Cloud Railroad, 87

Minneapolis Union Railway, 93

Minnesota & Northwestern Railroad, *see* St. Paul & Pacific Railroad

Minnesota Rate Cases, 164

Minnesota Transfer, 109–10

Moberly, Walter, 71

Montana Central Railroad, 101–4; *see also* Great Northern

Moore, Thomas, 9

Morgan, J. Pierpont: interest in Hill, 126; alliance with Hill, 137–8, 142–4, 187

Mount Stephen, Lord, *see* George Stephen

Napoleon, 9

New York Times, 195, 199

Newson, T. M., quoted, 14

Northern Pacific Railway: at Butte, 5, 106; formation and construction, 40–1; concessions to Hill, 57–9, 67–8; local attitudes toward, 85–6, 117–18; Hill buys into, 89–90, 98; engineering comparison to

Northern Pacific Railway (*continued*)
Great Northern, 107; battle with Hill for Seattle, 123; bankruptcy, 125–8; under Hill's control, 137; Harriman buys into, 139–42; colonization of Northwest, 165

Northern Securities Corporation, 142–4

Northwestern Packet Company, 20

Oregon and California Railroad, 89

Oregon Central Railroad, 89

Oregon Steam Navigation Company, 89

Oregon Steamship Company, 89

Oregon Trunk Railroad, 153–4

"Pacific Railway Scandal," 69

Panics: of 1857, 11; of 1873, 40–1; of 1893, 124–5; of 1901, 141

Pilgrim's Progress, The (Bunyan), 8

Plutarch, 9

Quakers, 8–9

Railroad Avenue (Hubbard), 191

Railroad Magazine, 191

Red River Rebellion, 29–30

Red River Transportation Company, 39, 52

Reservation Act, 99

Riel, Louis, 29–30, 34, 36, 78–80

Rockefeller, John D., 11

Rockefeller, William, 142

Rockefeller Institute, 167

Rockwood Academy, 8–9

Roman Catholic Church, 22–3, 187

Roosevelt, Theodore, 143–4, 173, 189

Rousseau, Théodore, 84

Sage, Russell, 42–3

St. Paul & Duluth Railroad, 87

St. Paul & Pacific Railroad: Hill's early affiliations with, 20, 28, 31; bankruptcy, 39–41; previous history, 42–5; adjunct to Canadian Pacific, 47–53; rehabilitation under Hill, 55; competition with Northern Pacific, 55 *et seq.*; acquired by St. Paul, Minneapolis & Manitoba, 63, 65–6; *see also* St. Paul, Minneapolis & Manitoba; Great Northern

St. Paul Daily Free Press, 14

St. Paul Democrat, 14

St. Paul, Minneapolis & Manitoba Railroad: acquires St. Paul & Pacific, 63; Farley suit, 66–8; local attitudes toward, 85–7; financial success, 93–6; *see also* Great Northern

St. Paul Pioneer, 14, 191

St. Paul Times, 14

Sampson, John F., *see* John Stevens

Schiff, Jacob, 139–41

Scott, Thomas, 30

"See America First" (slogan), 191

Selkirk, S.S., 32, 52

Shakspere, William, 8

Shaw, Thomas, 167

Smith, Donald: commissioner of Northwest Territories, 30; competition with Hill, 32–3; first alliance with Hill, 39; financing Canadian Pacific, 48–53, 69, 75, 77, 80–1; financing St. Paul, Minneapolis & Manitoba, 64; early correspondence with Hill, 160

Soo Line, 83

Southern Minnesota Railroad, 73

Southern Pacific Railroad, 148–9, 153, 156–7

Spokane, Portland & Seattle Railroad, 151, 157; *see also* Great Northern Railway

Spokane Review, 119

Stephen, George: finances Canadian Pacific, 47–51, 62, 64, 69, 74–5, 77–8, 80–1, 85; resigns from Manitoba Railroad, 76; attempts Hill-Van Horne reconciliation, 82–3; finances Northern Pacific, 126, 128–9; early correspondence with Hill, 160

Stevens, John, 112–16, 117 *n*, 122, 151–3

Stone Arch Bridge, 93, 109

Strategy of Great Railroads, The (Spearman), 175

Strathcona, Lord, *see* Donald Smith

Union Pacific Railroad, 40, 46, 89, 106, 125, 135, 148, 149, 197

United States Steel Corporation, 146

Van Horne, William: manager of Chicago, Milwaukee & St. Paul, 62; in construction of Canadian

Van Horne, William (*continued*)
Pacific, 68, 72–84, 96, 98; his contractors work for Hill, 104; later relations with Hill, 185

Villard, Ferdinand Heinrich G. H., 88–90, 98, 120
Villard Blind Pool, 90

Wetherald, William, 8–9
Weyerhauser, Frederic, 146

This book was set on the Linotype in a face called *El-dorado*, so named by its designer, WILLIAM ADDISON DWIGGINS, as an echo of Spanish adventures in the Western World. The series of experiments that culminated in this type-face began in 1942; the designer was trying a page more "brunette" than the usual book type. "One wanted a face that should be sturdy, and yet not too mechanical. . . . Another desideratum was that the face should be narrowish, compact, and close fitted, for reasons of economy of materials." The specimen that started Dwiggins on his way was a type design used by the Spanish printer A. de Sancha at Madrid about 1774. Eldorado, however, is in no direct way a copy of that letter, though it does reflect the Madrid specimen in the anatomy of its arches, curves, and junctions. Of special interest in the lower-case letters are the stresses of color in the blunt, sturdy serifs, subtly counterbalanced by the emphatic weight of some of the terminal curves and finials. The roman capitals are relatively open, and winged with liberal serifs and an occasional festive touch.

This book was composed, printed, and bound by The Plimpton Press, Norwood, Massachusetts. Paper manufactured by S. D. Warren Company, Boston. The typography and binding were designed by the creator of its type-face—W. A. Dwiggins.

D1236438

BURNING THE SKY

BURNING THE SKY

Operation Argus and the Untold Story of the Cold War Nuclear Tests in Outer Space

MARK WOLVERTON

The Overlook Press
New York, NY

This edition first published in hardcover in the United States in 2018 by
The Overlook Press, an imprint of ABRAMS
195 Broadway, 9th floor
New York, NY 10007
www.overlookpress.com

Abrams books are available at special discounts when purchased in
quantity for premiums and promotions as well as fundraising or educational use.
Special editions can also be created to specification. For details, contact
specialsales@abramsbooks.com or the address above.

Cataloging-in-Publication Data is available from the Library of Congress
A catalog record for this book is available from the British Library

Book design and typeformatting by Bernard Schleifer
Manufactured in the United States of America
FIRST EDITION
1 3 5 7 9 10 8 6 4 2
ISBN 978-1-4683-1417-5

The national security complex became, in the Eisenhower years, a fast-growing apparatus to allow us to do in secret what we could not do in the open.

—DAVID HALBERSTAM, The Fifties

There is the sky, which is all men's together.

—EURIPIDES

Earth changed in the black sky.

It caught fire.

Part of it seemed to come apart in a million pieces, as if a gigantic jigsaw had exploded. It burned with an unholy dripping glare for a minute, three times normal size, then dwindled.

"What was that?" Sam looked at the green fire in the sky.

"Earth," said Elma, holding her hands together.

"That can't be Earth, that's not Earth! No, that ain't Earth! It can't be."

"You mean it couldn't be Earth," said Elma, looking at him. "That just isn't Earth. No, that's not Earth; is that what you mean?"

"Not Earth—oh no, It couldn't be," he wailed.

He stood there, his hands at his sides, his mouth open, his eyes wide and dull, not moving.

—RAY BRADBURY, The Martian Chronicles

Contents

INTRODUCTION: The Middle of Nowhere   *9*

1: The Panic of 1958   *11*

2: The Elevator Repairman   *25*

3: Lines of Force   *39*

4: A Sense of Urgency   *49*

5: The Task Force   *61*

6: The Farthest Place on Earth   *73*

7: Earth in a Shroud   *85*

8: The Big Finish   *95*

9: The Veil of Secrecy   *107*

10: The Cold Glare of Day   *121*

11: The Light of Science   *133*

12: The Sky is Falling   *147*

13: A Pause to Consider   *157*

14: Bigger Bangs   *169*

15: The Sun at Night   *181*

16: The Haunted Island   *193*

17: The Fire of Damocles   *205*

18: Threats and Legacies   *215*

POSTSCRIPT: A Persistent Afterglow   *225*

MAPS   *229*

NOTES   *235*

SELECTED BIBIOGRAPHY   *251*

ABBREVIATIONS AND ACRONYMS   *254*

TIMELINE OF OUTER SPACE/HIGH ALTITUDE NUCLEAR TESTS   *255*

AUTHOR'S NOTE AND ACKNOWLEDGMENTS   *257*

INDEX   *261*

Introduction:
The Middle of Nowhere

ASIDE FROM THE TRISTAN DA CUNHA ARCHIPELAGO, CONSISTING OF THE MAIN island of Tristan da Cunha, the Nightingale islands, Gough Island, and Inaccessible Island, most of the various other tiny chunks of rock in the South Atlantic Ocean are so small and insignificant that no one has ever bothered to grace them with proper names. Only about three hundred people have ever resided permanently on Tristan da Cunha at any given time, and most of the other islands are either wholly uninhabited by humans or populated only intermittently by small scientific or meteorological crews. The islands have been a territory of the United Kingdom since the early nineteenth century, and over the years have sheltered visiting fishermen, whalers, naturalists, fugitives, and even an occasional prince or other royalty.

On the morning of September 9, 1958, some of Tristan's inhabitants were out on the slopes of the island's long-dead volcano, tending their potato patches. One of them was G. Francis Harris, who also happened to be the official administrator of the island, officially appointed by the Foreign Office back in London. Suddenly, Harris and his fellow islanders glanced up from their planting, distracted by an unusual phenomenon in those parts: the sound of airplane engines.

Two planes with US Navy markings swept overhead, low enough that the pilots could be seen peering curiously below. The friendly islanders tried waving to them, but the planes responded by abruptly turning back out to sea. "This was thought odd and most unfriendly," Harris later recounted, particularly since "the islanders had not seen an aeroplane for 15 years, apart from a helicopter, and so they were most surprised."

Harris instructed the island's radio operator to try to pick up any unusual signals that might help to figure out what was going on. He found the airwaves alive with enigmatic coded transmissions, but attempts to contact the senders were ignored. "All was in code, but we were able to advise the Royal Navy in South Africa about unusual activity, and quote to them the call signs of three or four American destroyers," Harris said. From his account, the islanders were rather put out by the experience. It caused "a good deal of consternation," he noted. "We were never told why they should have been in our area without telling us, or why they appeared so unfriendly, or why they did not pay us a social call!" he complained.[1]

Not until almost two years later, in July 1960, would Harris and the other residents of Tristan da Cunha find out the answers, when *New York Times* science reporter Walter Sullivan thought to contact them to ask if they'd happened to notice anything odd going on back in summer 1958. Barely two weeks before the decidedly antisocial US Navy airplanes buzzed the ancient volcanic island, in the depths of a cold and stormy South Atlantic midnight at the end of August 1958, an atomic bomb had been detonated about sixty miles south and three hundred miles above Tristan. Over the ensuing fortnight, two more burst in the night sky, the last only two days before Tristan da Cunha's aerial flyby.

The islanders had enjoyed front row seats for what was then the most secret Cold War operation in the world, a massive undertaking that would later be revealed to the public as "the greatest scientific experiment of all time."

And they had slept through the whole thing.

CHAPTER 1
The Panic of 1958

O<small>N</small> O<small>CTOBER</small> 4, 1957, <small>THE</small> 187-<small>POUND BEACH BALL–SIZED GADGET NAMED</small> Sputnik was launched from the steppes of Kazakhstan in the Soviet Union, announcing its presence to the world with a steady radio beeping as it circled the planet every ninety minutes. Everyone who heard it—or learned about it from the torrent of hysterical news reports—knew immediately that nothing would ever be the same.

It wasn't that the *idea* of an Earth-orbiting satellite was such a big deal. Scientists had been talking about it for years, and, in fact, both the United States and the Soviet Union had announced plans to do just such a thing as part of the newly begun International Geophysical Year (IGY), a coordinated eighteen-month program of research and exploration by more than sixty nations, dedicated to achieving a greater understanding of planet Earth. America had two separate but equally driven teams working on its satellite program: one called Vanguard, operated by the Naval Research Laboratory and strictly devoted to the civilian science ideals of the IGY, and another under the decidedly more martial auspices of the Army Ballistic Missile Agency (ABMA), led by Major General John Medaris and expatriate former-Nazi rocketeer Wernher von Braun.

Both groups had been engaging in a spirited competition to earn the official nod from the White House to launch what was then expected to be humanity's first satellite. But interservice rivalry, political maneuvering, and Cold War concerns had hampered progress. The Army—which had been steadily working on developing missiles since its postwar experiments with von Braun's captured V-2 rockets—had a definite technical lead, but the Vanguard group had a stronger civilian pedigree, which better meshed with President Eisenhower's desire to keep America's IGY and space research efforts free of any militaristic bent. For that reason, Vanguard was to be the first to make the attempt.

Everyone liked to believe that the Soviet Union was far behind the United States in science and technology. Yes, they also had atomic and hydrogen bombs, but it had taken them years to catch up, and besides, they had cheated, relying on espionage to steal American secrets. The Soviets boasted about their prowess and might, but it was all bluster. There was simply no way that such a backwards society could best the United States in the accomplishment of a technological feat that no one had ever done before.

Except now they had done it. If anyone doubted the official announcement on Moscow Radio that was being repeated and spread across the planet, they had only to tune a shortwave radio to 20 MHz. *Beep beep beep.* It was there, it was real, it was passing over the United States, and there was absolutely nothing that anyone could do about it.

Including, it seemed, ignore it. Immediate reactions ranged from fear and anger, to excitement and scientific curiosity, to outright indifference and incomprehension.

For General Medaris, at the time hosting a reception for Washington dignitaries at ABMA headquarters in Huntsville, Alabama, there was only one natural response when his public affairs officer interrupted the party to announce the news. "Those damn bastards!" Medaris snarled. The way he said it, no one knew whether he was talking about the Russians, his Vanguard rivals, or the administration officials who had refused to give him free rein. His team could have launched a satellite at least a year earlier if they'd only been allowed, or so he told his guest, newly-designated-but-not-yet-confirmed Secretary of Defense Neil McElroy. A frustrated von Braun picked up on the theme, promising McElroy that his people already had the "hardware on the shelf" to put up an American satellite in sixty days or less, if Ike would just give them the green light.

Thousands of miles away from Alabama, physicist James Van Allen took the news with a far greater degree of scientific equanimity. One of America's leading geophysicists and a driving force behind the IGY, he was aboard the USS *Glacier*, a research ship several hundred miles off the Galapagos Islands in the Pacific Ocean and en route to Antarctica when Sputnik launched. Van Allen was on the journey to launch "rockoons"— rockets lofted to high altitudes by balloons—to study cosmic ray patterns as part of the IGY. Earlier that day, he had sent off his first rockoon of the voyage.

He was busily writing up a brief summary of the day's launch when an assistant interrupted with word of Sputnik. Immediately Van Allen headed for the *Glacier*'s radio shack to confirm the news and attempt to hear the sound of Sputnik for himself. It was there, loud and clear. But a mere radio signal didn't necessarily confirm a satellite in orbit.

Ever the scientist, Van Allen proceeded to find out everything he could. He jury-rigged a paper tape recorder to chart Sputnik's signals for analysis and to measure the Doppler shifts in the signal, which would confirm that the signal was coming from a moving radio source in orbit. Everything checked out: the *beep-beep-beep* was definitely from an orbiting satellite at precisely the altitude the Soviets had announced.

After gathering as much data as possible with the equipment on hand, Van Allen sat down to write a detailed seventeen-page report, including calculations of Sputnik's probable orbit and other particulars. "Brilliant achievement!" he wrote. He added some personal observations, noting how politically-motivated delays in the US program had allowed the Soviets to trump the free world and wondering how the Russian achievement would affect the American effort. He praised the Russians' "astute" choice of 20 MHz for Sputnik's heralding frequency, observing that unlike the 108 MHz chosen for Vanguard, Sputnik's voice was readily audible not only to amateur radio operators but anyone else with a receiver that could operate at that frequency.

"Where do we stand now on Vanguard?" he scribbled in his notes, adding, "Russians have a very great scientific lead on us."[1]

IN HISTORICAL RETROSPECT, IT'S NOW CLEAR THAT FAR FROM BEING AN EVENT THAT immediately awed and terrified the world, the initial waves of Sputnik shock and hysteria didn't rack the general public so much as they did the military and political powers that be. As science historian Sharon Weinberger notes, "there was no collective panic in the first few days following the launch. It was not immediately clear—except to a small group of scientists and policy makers—why the satellite was so important . . . for most Americans, the beeping beach ball initially produced a collective shrug."[2]

Barely a month after the launch, the political posturing, bureaucratic finger-pointing, and editorial second-guessing had mostly settled down to a level only a few decibels above the usual omnipresent murmur of Cold War paranoia and apocalyptic anxiety. It helped that by October 26, the ceaseless beeping of the Soviet satellite had finally faded and passed into blessed silence. The damned thing was still up there, of course, and could still be seen passing regularly through the skies of the US on every dark, clear evening, but at least it wasn't mocking us with its radio signal anymore.

There was no denying the fact that the Soviets had beaten us fair and square, but now they'd had their fun, and it was America's turn. Soon now, Vanguard would be launched, and it would do more than just beep at the inhabitants of the planet below. It would carry actual scientific instruments that would conduct valuable research. Let the Soviets boast about Sputnik and their rockets all they liked—in the end, all they had done was pull off an impressive but ultimately pointless stunt. The United States, on the other hand, would begin the true exploration of space with Vanguard, paving the way for human beings to follow in the very near future.

But the Soviets were not about to wait. On November 3, 1957, they launched Sputnik 2. And this was not merely a carbon copy of its predecessor. It was almost a thousand pounds heavier, and also carried a living creature: a specially trained mixed-breed female dog named Laika.

Now, not only to many within the government and the military but to the American public, it was more than clear: the first Sputnik had not been a fluke, a lucky shot, a gimmick. The USSR had a real and substantial head start, and they were not going to be shy about flaunting it. Never mind the fact that they had now put a living thing in space, with all that portended for Russian intentions and capabilities for eventually sending human beings up there. With the first satellite, one could console oneself with the fact that, impressive and ominous as it was, the thing was still less than two hundred pounds—far lighter and smaller than any practical nuclear warhead the Soviets might decide to lob at us. But Laika's vehicle was far larger, an indication that they were getting into the realm of serious "throw-weight," as missile designers referred to ICBM payload capacity. By contrast, the Vanguard satellite, in the midst of frantic launch preparations, weighed barely over three pounds, and was small enough to be held in one hand.

As capitalist animal lovers around the world bemoaned the fate of Laika and pestered the Soviet Union with accusations of animal cruelty when it became clear that she wouldn't be coming home alive, others worried about the survival of the free world. Once more, questions abounded as to how Soviet Russia, a society in which washing machines and refrigerators were unheard-of luxuries, could have bested the most advanced country on Earth.

Obviously, many thought, it had to be due to more than the reasons offered by television commentators and newspaper editorialists. Even if it were true that Americans had allowed themselves to grow lazy and complacent, giddy with fancy tail-finned cars, silly TV shows, and rock-and-roll music, that couldn't explain everything. Had Communist spies stolen American secrets again, just as they had with the atomic bomb?

The only problem with that premise, aside from the lack of any actual evidence of foreign espionage in the missile program, was that if Soviet spies had stolen American technological know-how to build the Sputniks, then why hadn't America already launched their own satellites? After all, even though it was established fact that Russian spies such as the Rosenbergs had contributed to the USSR's atomic program, they had been relaying progress America had already made. As John Campbell, Jr., editor of *Astounding Science Fiction* magazine, observed: "Those Russian spies must be really good. They stole a secret we didn't even have yet."[3]

If not espionage, then, what was the explanation for Russian superiority? Why were we struggling to put an aluminum grapefruit into orbit while our mortal enemies were flying car-sized spacecraft over our country? Maybe it was simply because they knew something we didn't, some mysterious secret, a formula, a gadget that for whatever reasons of fate and chance, the United States did not have.

Physicist Herbert F. York, who had already been working for several years on nuclear weapons research and was about to become swept up in the official furor over Sputnik, wrote in his memoirs: "Many people, including some scientists and engineers who should have known better, came to believe that the Soviets knew some 'secret' about rocket propulsion that still eluded us, and even that Russian science in general was about to surpass American science."[4] Although that was decidedly paranoid, what was true, York and others came to realize after the initial Sputnik shock had faded and a more rational, if not always calmer, perspective began to take hold, was that the American missile and space program simply needed more time. The Russians had succeeded first not only because they'd been working longer and harder but also because their highly centralized, dictatorial system wasn't plagued with all the interservice rivalry, competition, duplication of effort, and plain old inefficiency of good old American democracy.

Things really weren't half as bleak as they seemed. Our civilian space program and our various classified defense efforts were proceeding apace, and all would work out in due course. Yes, we had to redouble our efforts and our determination, but there was no need to panic.

The problem was that such confidence arose from a privileged awareness based on classified data unknown to the public and the press. President Eisenhower realized that something had to be done to address

American fears and to reassure people that however dire the situation seemed, the end was not near. On November 7, four days after Laika went into space, Ike went on national television to address his agitated constituents and to defuse criticisms that he wasn't doing enough to deal with this whole Sputnik situation. He announced the appointment of MIT president James Killian as the first White House science advisor, described a slew of new American weapons systems able to bring "near annihilation to . . . any country," and showed off the nose cone of a Jupiter C missile that had just been flown into space—on a suborbital flight—a few days before. "With two Sputniks in orbit, this display of a suborbital souvenir at the president's feet in the Oval Office was hardly reassuring," Paul Dickson wrote.[5]

Eisenhower's speech, and several similar ones that followed, did little to quell public anxiety. Polls showed that many Americans were convinced that the Soviets now had the ability to rain atomic warheads down upon our cities on a whim. But at least Ike was doing something. Perhaps most importantly, the day after his speech, he gave von Braun and Medaris official permission to launch their Explorer 1 satellite on the Army's Jupiter C missile as soon as possible.

First, however, would come Vanguard. On December 6, 1957, after two days of delays, America's first prospective spacecraft barely lifted off the pad at Cape Canaveral before falling back, the booster rocket exploding in a huge fireball. Unlike the previous Soviet efforts, which weren't made public until already successful, this humiliation took place in full view of the world on live television.

Even before the debris had been cleared and the Vanguard satellite was recovered from the tall Florida grass into which it had rolled after falling from the top of its rocket, the hand-wringing, finger-pointing, and pronouncements of impending doom began anew. Senator Lyndon B. Johnson presided over congressional hearings in search of an official scapegoat, while in the next couple of weeks, just in case anyone had missed the point that America was in grave danger, a top-secret White House report was leaked to the press that spelled out that message in dire detail.

Informally, it was called the Gaither Report, although its official title was suitably ominous: *Deterrence and Survival in the Nuclear Age.* The fruit of a months-long study commissioned by the National Security Council to examine defense preparedness against the Soviet threat and propose solutions, it was never supposed to be seen by the public. The commission was chaired by the head of the Ford Foundation, Rowan Gaither, and composed of various eminent citizens and defense experts, including members of the RAND Corporation, a think tank created to advise the Air Force.

The Commission's report minced no words. America was not only in danger, she was facing the greatest threat in her history. Not only had we no defense against Soviet ICBMs, our own efforts in that department were woefully inadequate. The USSR was building far more missiles and bombers than the US, leading to an inevitable and dangerous "gap" in the coming years, and while they had shelters to protect their people from bombs and fallout, the US had practically none. The solution was obvious: immediately increase the defense budget by $44 billion over the next five years to start building more and better bombs, ICBMs, aircraft, and fallout shelters.

This was hardly the sort of thing that the ever-frugal Eisenhower wanted to hear, nor did he, as ex–Supreme Commander of all Allied military forces in Europe, think it necessary or advisable. But he faced a dilemma. Even as bits and pieces of the Gaither Report leaked to an eager press corps, Ike had hard evidence that matters were not nearly as dire as the Commission, LBJ, or the more alarmist members of the military establishment (particularly Strategic Air Command leader General Curtis LeMay) were declaring. The top-secret U-2 spy plane, which had been conducting aerial reconnaissance over the Soviet Union since 1956, had produced photos that proved conclusively that the Russians were not in fact turning out atomic missiles or bombers like sausages, as some, including Soviet leader Nikita Khrushchev himself, had claimed. In fact, it was quite the opposite. The Russians' missiles might be making more impressive headlines than the Americans', but we definitely had more of them, not to mention bomber aircraft and nuclear weapons of all kinds.

But Eisenhower knew that revealing those facts also meant revealing how they were acquired. And that meant giving up an enormous and very real strategic and psychological advantage. The Soviets certainly knew about the U-2—they routinely tracked its intrusions into their airspace—but, so far at least, they had been unable to do anything about it, which made them just as keen on keeping its existence from the public as the Americans. It amounted to a sort of Cold War "gentlemen's agreement" to keep the secret for mutual benefit. Public disclosure of the U-2 would force public protest by the Soviets and inescapable demands to stop the over-flights, thus eliminating the US's most valuable source of intelligence.

Eisenhower was forced to endure withering contempt and criticism from all sides: the press, the public, the Democrats—even many from his own party and administration described him as a wishy-washy, spineless president who cared more about his golf game than protecting the United States from a grave threat. Despite enormous pressures, he resisted the calls to officially declassify the Gaither report, knowing it would only make the entire situation worse and do no conceivable good.

The president bided his time, secure in the privileged knowledge that the U-2 had given him, confident that the United States was not in any imminent danger but was instead about to regain its bearings. He took comfort from the poet Robert Frost, who gave the president a book of his poems, inscribed with a personal note: "The strong say nothing until they see."[6]

BARRING AN ACTUAL ATTACK BY THE APPARENTLY MIGHTY SOVIET UNION UPON the humbled United States, it was hard to see how 1958 could possibly be any worse than the last few months of 1957. A deep gloom hung over the country regarding America's place in the world. There was a generous helping of pessimism about the possibility of redemption, along with good old-fashioned fear and paranoia.

Toward the end of January, that almost palpable yearning for good news, for something to celebrate, focused on the Jupiter C missile and the payload it would carry into space: the Explorer 1 satellite. Still licking their wounds from their explosive December fiasco, the Vanguard team had made several more attempts to launch, all of which had failed. So the weight of all America's hopes now fell squarely upon the shoulders of the unlikely odd couple of General Medaris and Wernher von Braun.

After two agonizing delays due to weather conditions at Cape Canaveral, Explorer 1 finally made it into space on the night of January 31, 1958. A little less than two hours later, after prodigious amounts of coffee and many cigarettes smoked by anxious technicians, scientists, and generals, it was confirmed: Explorer 1 was in orbit around the Earth. The United States finally had its satellite.

In the relief and jubilation that followed, no one paid too much attention to the fact that Explorer was really a rather puny thing, just over six feet long and weighing barely thirty pounds, small enough for three men to hoist over their heads, as Wernher von Braun, James Van Allen, and Jet Propulsion Laboratory director William Pickering did with a model at a February 1 press conference in Washington. The significant part wasn't the weight or size, emphasized the scientists—it was the instrument package. Designed and built by Van Allen, Explorer's instruments included cosmic ray and micrometeorite detectors and sensors to record temperature variations in the space environment. America's first satellite was far more than just a grandiose stunt, more than just a radio beacon or a dog carrier, like the Sputniks. It was instead a real scientific achievement.

However, the true extent of that achievement wouldn't become clear until several months later, long after the initial euphoria had faded. The more Van Allen, his graduate students, and their scientific colleagues pored over the results returned by Explorer 1, the more head-scratching ensued. At first, the cosmic ray detector seemed to confirm the data that Van Allen had collected in his many rocket and balloon tests over the previous years. Yet other data seemed to indicate no cosmic rays or other radiation count at all, which couldn't be the case. Was there some kind of malfunction in Explorer 1's radiation detectors? It seemed unlikely, not only because Van Allen's team was perhaps the most experienced in the world at designing such instruments, but also because they had purposely built the package to very conservative limits to allow for the unknown rigors of the orbital environment and stresses of space travel.

The next mission, Explorer 2, failed to go into space, but Explorer 3, which achieved orbit on March 26, cleared up the mystery. Van Allen and his team spent weeks analyzing the findings from both satellite packages, and on May 1 finally announced their conclusions to the world at a joint meeting of the National Academy of Sciences and the American Physical Society in Washington, DC. The Explorer satellites had discovered bands of radiation surrounding the Earth, trapped by the planet's natural magnetic fields. Not long after, the term "Van Allen radiation belts" caught on, and Van Allen found himself immortalized as a scientific pioneer. It was humanity's first scientific discovery of the new space age.

James Van Allen didn't find out about it until he was in the midst of analyzing Explorer 3 data, but someone else had already been speculating about the possibility of radiation belts surrounding the Earth.

At the University of California's Livermore Radiation Laboratory, a Greek-American physicist named Nicholas Christofilos had reacted quite differently to Sputnik on that fateful Friday evening the previous October. Christofilos wasn't worried about any scientific advantage the USSR might have over the United States, or about losing prestige in the IGY program. His concerns were far more direct and elemental.

It wasn't the satellite that mattered, he realized, nor the presence of the first artificial body in orbit, not even the incessant *beep-beep-beep* it emitted—even if those beeps contained some hidden nefarious messages, as some paranoid types were claiming. Apparently the satellite didn't even have scientific instrumentation, so any data it could provide would be minimal.

Before the Gaither report sounded the alarm about American vulnerability to the public, before Senator Johnson began his hearings, Christofilos had already recognized the most important fact about Sputnik: the R-7 rocket that had hurled it into space. It proved that the Soviets now had missiles powerful enough to loft objects at least hundreds of pounds in weight to vast heights and distances—and that those missiles worked.

On a peaceful October evening, a Soviet rocket had carried a harmless metal sphere bearing a couple of radio transmitters into space. On another evening in the near future, Christofilos knew, that same type of rocket—or more powerful ones the Soviets were no doubt developing or already possessed—could hurl a hydrogen warhead over the North Pole and down onto the United States. And, just as there was nothing that could be done about Sputnik except to tune in to its beeps, there would be no way to ward off Soviet warheads from devastating American cities. It was impossible to shoot down or otherwise intercept missiles traveling at thousands of miles an hour.

But, he mused, perhaps there was another solution.

Christofilos's main project, not to mention personal obsession, at Livermore was his concept for a nuclear fusion reactor called Astron. It was wildly original, revolutionary, and extremely difficult to realize on any practical level, just the sort of idea for which he had become notorious among his colleagues. Astron was strictly a civilian project—Christofilos wasn't directly involved with defense work or building weapons. But now that Sputnik had convinced him that the Soviets might be about to overwhelm us with their strength and apparently superior rocket technology, he extended his Astron ideas into a possible means to defend the United States.

In the midst of the post-Sputnik upheavals in late 1957, Christofilos went to his supervisor at Livermore, Herbert York, and laid out his idea. The thermonuclear reactions at the heart of Astron involved confining superheated plasma in a magnetic field generated by circulating electrons. He proposed to simply expand and extrapolate that idea from the small to the large, involving the entire Earth. What if a vast number of high-energy electrons could be generated above the Earth's atmosphere?

He theorized that the planet's magnetic fields would shape and focus them into an intense field or shell of radiation strong enough to disrupt and perhaps even destroy missiles and atomic warheads passing through it. The electrons, Christofilos explained, would be generated by detonating nuclear weapons in space. He had a name for the plan: Argus.

Not incidentally, there was a potential side bonus for Christofilos. The Astron machine did not yet exist; the Earth did. If Argus was successful and proved his theory, it could also help to vindicate Astron.

"His purpose was of epic proportions," York later recalled. "He intended nothing less than to place an impenetrable shield of high-energy electrons over our heads, a shield that would destroy any nuclear warhead that might be sent against us . . . Nick was completely confident that he had found the answer to the new Soviet threat, and he was eager to work it out before it was too late."[7]

York was intrigued but dubious. Not only was Argus an idea on a "grand scale," but realizing it even on an experimental level would involve satellites—something that, at least so far, the US didn't have. And even if it could be organized, it was beyond the purview of Livermore or any other existing government agency. "There was simply no place to take an invention like Nick's," said York.

But that was not going to stop Christofilos. He set out campaigning for Argus over the following months, first at the lower levels of officialdom in government and the military, and then moving steadily up the ladder. His urgent advocacy and untiring persuasiveness soon won him a growing legion of converts among Sputnik-spooked bureaucrats and military men, up to and including members of the brand-new President's Science Advisory Committee. When Secretary of Defense Neil McElroy established the Advanced Research Projects Agency (ARPA) of the Department of Defense in early 1958 as an official response to Sputnik, Christofilos finally had a place to take Argus—a place that would soon be equipped with a convenient ally when York was named the chief scientist of ARPA.

On January 10, 1958, Christofilos spelled out his proposal in detail in the highly classified paper "On the Possibility of Establishing a Plasma Shield of Relativistic Electrons in the Exosphere of the Earth as a Defense against Ballistic Missiles," a title that made his ambitions abundantly clear even to those who didn't bother to read the technical details.[8] The paper was widely circulated amongst the upper echelons of secret military and governmental circles, piquing intense interest and much discussion.

Christofilos didn't know it yet, but some people were already taking him very, very seriously. Just over a month before, on the second and third of December, Pentagon scientist Frank Shelton had briefed CIA officials on "the Christofilos concept," warning them specifically "to watch for similar Argus developments in Russia."[9] If we could think of it, so could they, was the implication. As bad as Sputnik might have been, that would be even worse.

Classified discussions continued and intensified, as anything and everything Argus-related was placed under the deepest secrecy. ARPA and the Armed Forces Special Weapons Project (AFSWP)—the Pentagon agency in charge of nuclear weapons for all the military services—set out to make preparations and plans for what Christofilos, with his characteristic self-confidence, called "the most fantastic experiment ever conducted by man."

CHAPTER 2
The Elevator Repairman

BY THE LATE 1950S, WITH CONCEPTS SUCH AS ATOM BOMBS AND RADAR AND outer space now familiar touchstones in newspapers, magazines, radio, and the new medium of television, the image of The Atomic Scientist was firmly embedded in American culture. To a great extent, that image was based on the most famous scientist of them all, Albert Einstein, who had only recently died in April 1955.

Before World War II, the Victor Frankenstein/"mad scientist" stereotype tended to prevail in films, pulp magazines, and radio shows—figures sporting vague foreign accents, wild hair, and lab coats (or, if they were truly evil, elaborately designed leather costumes). But after the war, as the atomic bomb brought renewed prominence to Einstein and introduced new science stars such as J. Robert Oppenheimer, a gentler, more benign model took firm hold. One of its earliest manifestations in Cold War popular culture was Sam Jaffe's portrayal of Dr. Jacob Barnhardt in the classic 1951 science fiction film *The Day the Earth Stood Still*. Quite consciously patterned after Einstein, Barnhardt is the film's voice of scientific restraint and reason, the rational yin to Helen Benson's (Patricia O'Neal) more emotional and empathetic yang of humanity, who together help alien visitor Klaatu navigate the paranoiac chaos of Earth society. Now that science had become so intertwined with government and the military, the few mad scientists who continued to lurk through 1950s pop culture were less Colin Clive's Henry Frankenstein than Einstein—soft-spoken otherworldliness and all.

Nicholas Constantine Christofilos didn't fit any of the popular scientist stereotypes. He tended more toward saggy blue serge suits, bright ties, and scuffed-up black shoes than the tattered sweaters of Einstein. Nor was he thin and ascetic; he was sturdy, and had an avid appetite for fine food and wine. Whereas Einstein was a famous pipe smoker, Christofilos preferred a steady stream of cigarettes. The accent was definitely there—a thick Greek variety that at times could be so heavy that some of his interlocutors wished he came accompanied by an interpreter. Calm and reserved he definitely was not. A colleague once remarked that Christofilos could easily play both roles in an argument between a pair of cab drivers.

But far more than appearance and temperament set Christofilos apart from his colleagues. His background was hardly that of the traditional academic.

He was born in Boston on December 16, 1916, the birthday of Ludwig van Beethoven, who would later become one of Christofilos's favorite composers. His parents were first-generation Greek immigrants who ran a popular coffeehouse called the Wellington Cafe, but eventually grew restless for the old country, and in 1923 moved back to Athens with their only child, seven-year-old Nicholas, in tow. While his father reestablished himself in the coffee shop business, a gadget-fascinated Nicholas began tinkering, taking apart radios and eventually learning how to build them himself, an interest partly inspired by his discovery of the novels of Jules Verne. He also displayed a passion for music, studying piano at the Athens Conservatory with the famed Greek concert pianist Gina Bachauer.

Yet it was science that truly pulled him in. By age twelve he had already proclaimed his intention to become an electrical engineer. He became a ham radio operator until forced to abandon the hobby when the Greek government banned amateur radio in 1936. But his engineering ambitions were realized with a degree in electrical and mechanical engineering from the National Technical University of Athens in 1938.

Christofilos was already thinking big. He planned to get an engineering job for a while, build up some experience, then return to the United States—and the city of his birth, Boston— to continue his education at the famous Massachusetts Institute of Technology. The job was no problem: he found a position at Wisk, Inc., a company specializing in installing and maintaining elevators. It was a good spot for someone with both mechanical and electrical talents, and there were certainly plenty of apartment and office buildings in Athens to keep Wisk in brisk business. Christofilos worked and planned for his return to America, spending his spare time reading textbooks in physics and the nascent field of nuclear science. Most of those books were in German, of course, since that was where most of the important work in those fields was being conducted by people such as Werner Heisenberg and Otto Frisch.

Unfortunately, Benito Mussolini, Adolf Hitler, and fate had other plans. In October 1940, Mussolini, drunk with hubris and a desire to grab some glory from his senior dictatorial rival in Germany, invaded Greece. The Greek army proceeded to repel the Italian forces and push them back into Albania, forcing Hitler to come to the rescue of his hapless ally six months later. The Nazis quickly occupied Greece, and Christofilos found himself under the heel of a new government.

It was definitely a blow to Christofilos's post-graduate ambitions, but an uninvited boost to his career in mechanical engineering. The puppet government installed by the Nazis nationalized Wisk, Inc., converting its function from fixing and installing elevators to repairing military vehicles. The twenty-four-year-old Christofilos was given the choice of promotion to a supervisory position or imprisonment as a potential saboteur—or a death sentence, if his intentions were deemed suspect. Christofilos took the promotion.

Despite the harsh realities of life under German occupation, Christofilos's new position was undemanding, and left him with a lot of free time, which he devoted to an even more dedicated program of self-education. If the Germans brought with them to Greece oppression, hatred, and senseless cruelty, they also brought along more of their hard-to-get scientific books, papers, and journals for an eager Christofilos to devour.

So for the remainder of the war, Christofilos led a rather mundane existence, or at least as mundane as possible under the circumstances. He spent his days at the shop, fixing Nazi trucks and riding herd on his mechanics, and his nights at home or in the library, poring over advanced texts in physics and mathematics, including some of the latest works out of Berlin: *An Introduction to Nuclear Physics* by Siegfried Fluegge, for example, published in 1942, or *Nuclear Physics Tables* by Joseph Mattauch. Christofilos was working on his own without the guidance of mentors or teachers to keep him on a more conventional and traditional pedagogical path, with nothing to keep him going save his own passionate enthusiasm for his subject and his natural predilection to follow odd ideas and invent his own ways to solve problems. Long before night school was even a thing, he was a self-styled night school student immersed in some of the most advanced, cutting-edge science of his age.

Particularly in light of later wartime developments, some of the titles of his reading material might give the impression that Christofilos was already thinking about atomic bombs. But he was not ruminating on uncontrolled, destructive nuclear power, but rather on tightly controlled energies in the service of scientific research. Back in the United States, physicist and Nobel Laureate Ernest Lawrence at the University of California at Berkeley had been building and using highly sophisticated particle accelerators since the previous decade, giant "atom smashers" that were probing the innermost secrets of the structure of matter. Christofilos was fascinated by such concepts, and was beginning to think of ways to improve upon and expand the capabilities of particle accelerators and cyclotrons—and eventually, design them himself.

By the time the occupation and finally the war ended, Christofilos was beginning to do just that, although still in his spare time. No longer a truck repairman, he returned to the elevator business, opening and operating his own company. Meanwhile, he was able to expand ever more widely the range of his scientific reading, now supplemented by visits to the United States Information Service in Athens, which provided access to important American journals such as *Physical Review*, which had been unavailable to him during the war.

His thoughts were still pointed squarely across the Atlantic to America. Before the war, the intellectual nexus of scientific research had been in Europe, but now America was on top of the world, not just politically, militarily, and economically, but scientifically as well. Most of the world's top scientists lived there, from Einstein on down, and the United States also had both the most advanced research facilities on Earth and the money to operate them and build new ones. Christofilos's restless mind was not going to be content with cornering the Athens elevator market by day while reading obscure physics books in the dead of night.

The problem was that because his circumstances and temperament had forced him to eschew the typical, accepted pathways to establishing himself in academic and scientific circles, he didn't know anyone, and nobody knew him. He had no old friends from grad school with whom to discuss his ideas, no former teachers or mentors to call on for advice and counsel or job leads. If he was going to get back to the United States as a scientist, he would have to do it the hard way, making his own path as best he could. He might not be able to dazzle the scientific establishment with fancy degrees or powerful and influential friends, so he would do it through audacious inventiveness. Already deeply versed in the theory, if not the practice, of particle accelerators and their design and operation, he began to come up with ideas.

In 1946, Christofilos had already attempted to secure a patent for a new type of particle accelerator, but further reading and research in the scientific literature now available to him soon demonstrated that he'd missed that particular elevator: someone else had already invented the thing. The machine, known as a synchrotron, had been conceived separately by Russian scientist Vladimir Veksler and Edwin McMillan at Berkeley, who built the first working example in 1945. But as usual, Christofilos was not dissuaded, and set about devising ways to improve upon their designs.

Whatever the name of a particle accelerator, whether cyclotron, Betatron, or synchrotron, such machines all perform the same basic function: generating, focusing, and controlling beams of charged particles such as electrons or protons, which can then be made to collide with each other in ways that reveal their inner structure and generate new particles from the debris. To control and direct the nuclear particles, the machines use intense electromagnetic fields that not only require enormous amounts of electrical power to generate but also huge, unwieldy, and exceedingly expensive magnets, which is why such facilities tend to be industrial-scale in physical size and electrical power requirements.

Christofilos wanted to find some way of changing all that. In 1948, he began to send letters off to the premier particle accelerator facility in the world, Ernest Lawrence's Radiation Laboratory at the University of California at Berkeley. Surely, he reasoned, once the people at Berkeley had the chance to hear and consider his ideas, they would recognize their validity, not to mention the talents of the man proposing them.

The folks at the Lawrence lab already had some passing acquaintance with Christofilos, as he'd sent them a copy of his previous patent application, which he'd filed simultaneously in Greece and the United States. No one had been very impressed then, since he had been essentially reinventing the wheel. In the new postwar age of scientific discovery and public prominence, institutions and agencies such as Lawrence Laboratory, Los Alamos, the Air Force, the Atomic Energy Commission, various universities, and most other centers of learning and innovation, along with famous scientists such as Albert Einstein or J. Robert Oppenheimer, were routinely inundated by mail from people claiming to have made The Next Great Scientific Discovery That Will Change Everything. Dutiful secretaries filed such material away in "crackpot files" and moved on to more important matters.

Still, Christofilos's first letter managed to stand out from the rest, perhaps partly because, despite the odd mathematical approaches on display, it was clear that he seemed to have some degree of expertise. The Berkeley scientists passed it around to one another, more out of bemusement than serious interest, but no one was quite able to pin down just what Christofilos was talking about.

Finally, whether out of sympathy, a sense of politesse, or simple boredom, somebody decided to sit down and write out a response, setting out in detail the reasons why Christofilos's ideas, while certainly intriguing, were wrong. His design improvements wouldn't work, and this was why. But we greatly appreciate your interest and enthusiasm, and best of luck to you, and thanks for writing, etc.

Most people would be discouraged with such a response, but Nicholas Christofilos was not most people. He plunged even deeper into reading, calculating, and thinking, refining and perfecting his ideas. He was certain he was right, somehow, even if he didn't quite understand why yet. Armed only with his own abstruse mathematics and boundless enthusiasm for his subject, he devised an approach he dubbed the "strong focusing principle," a means of manipulating alternating magnetic fields inside a cyclotron to precisely control particle beams.

He was trying to solve a problem that had been plaguing the designers of particle accelerators from the beginning. Such machines basically come in two configurations: linear and ring-shaped (disregarding the type that uses static electric fields to shove particles around, such as Van de Graaff generators). Since particles (and anything else in motion, as Isaac Newton described) tend to travel in a straight line unless acted upon by an outside force, linear accelerators seem straightforward enough, being long and straight. But what about when the charged particle reaches the end of the line? It's not a problem if your intention is to make the particles hit some kind of target—the inside of a phosphorescent screen to make it glow, perhaps, or a cancerous tumor to destroy it.

On the other hand, if you want to keep your particles moving and accelerating to ever higher energies, then sending them endlessly turning around in a circle is the clear solution, as Ernest Lawrence realized when he created the first cyclotron in 1929. But there's the problem of Newtonian physics. Since speeding protons or electrons or atomic fragments naturally travel fast and straight, a means of getting them to stay in a circular path is needed. Cyclotrons use powerful magnets for that purpose, which work well but are also big, heavy, and expensive.

And there's another problem. It turns out that while controlling a beam of charged particles in one plane—horizontally, for example—is fairly straightforward, doing so in added dimensions at the same time— say, vertically—is far more complicated. In practical terms, you can control your beam in the x-axis or the y-axis, but not both at the same time, at least not at the extreme speeds and energies required to do valuable scientific work. Try to force a beam of charged particles too strongly in one direction off the straight and narrow, and it will keep attempting to veer off in the opposite direction, trying to satisfy Newton's first law. The only solution seemed to be ever bigger, more powerful magnets to make the particles behave as desired.

Over the next couple of years following his polite Berkeley brush-off, Christofilos sought to overcome this dilemma with a new approach. "Christofilos proved mathematically that the obvious ideal, simultaneously focusing the beam in both the x and y directions, is physically impossible," wrote Elisheva R. Coleman, Samuel A. Cohen, and Michael S. Mahoney in a 2011 history.[1] But, reasoned Christofilos, doing both alternately and very quickly would create a net effect that would achieve essentially the same result. And since such an approach, which boiled down to finessing the beam path instead of wrestling it into line with brute force, wouldn't require such powerful magnets, it had the practical benefit of reducing both the construction costs and the operating costs of a cyclotron. Christofilos called it strong focusing.

The normal course for the typical academic-type research scientist would have been to write it up into a detailed scientific paper, ideally after some practical experiments as proof-of-concept, and submit it to one of the leading journals in the field, such as *Physical Review*. But that was not the sort of option open to Christofilos, who lacked any notable academic credentials or a position at an established research university or scientific institution. Again, Christofilos instead took the more direct approach of applying for a patent, titling his March 10, 1950 application "Focussing System for Ions and Electrons." Perhaps out of optimism, perhaps out of spite, perhaps out of a combination of the two, he again sent copies of the application to Berkeley.

This time, the Radiation Laboratory was not as polite. Christofilos's missive was summarily dismissed and shunted away into "file and forget" oblivion, merely another dispatch from "that crazy Greek."[2] This correspondence seems to be the origin of this particular sobriquet, which would subsequently come to be inextricably linked with Christofilos, at first only in private and professional circles and then finally by the public and press at large. There is no record that Christofilos ever seemed to mind. As Edward Teller, another scientist famous for wild ideas, but one who enjoyed a considerably more exalted professional cachet, recalled later, "Because the mathematical method was different from practices of American physicists, the Californians did not examine the proposed focusing system in full detail."[3]

By this time, even Nicholas Christofilos was beginning to have second thoughts about his career choices. But back in the United States, other events were percolating that would soon intersect with and ultimately change Christofilos's life.

On the other side of the continent from Berkeley and Ernest Lawrence's Radiation Laboratory was Brookhaven National Laboratory in Long Island, New York, established in 1947 by the Atomic Energy Commission as a place to investigate and develop peaceful uses for atomic energy. Brookhaven quickly became the East Coast hub for advanced research in particle physics, its scientists and machines the chief rival to Berkeley. The Brookhaven team of Ernest D. Courant, M. Stanley Livingston, and Hartland S. Snyder had been working with a powerful synchrotron with the science-fictional name of "The Cosmotron." Quite independently and completely unaware of the work of the "crazy Greek" who had been plaguing their colleagues on the West Coast, they developed a concept for a new accelerator design using a technique called the alternating field gradient focusing principle—or in other words, strong focusing.

Following the well-defined procedure of fully-recognized academic/professional scientists, Courant, Livingston, and Snyder published their research in the *Physical Review* on December 1, 1952, under the title of "The Strong Focusing Synchroton - A New High Energy Accelerator."[4] It was, as far as anyone knew, the first time such an idea had been put forward in the scientific world, certainly in the standard literature. Nicholas Christofilos's patent application was still making its laborious way through the innards of the US Patent Office, while his previous letters detailing his ideas, complete with his wonky mathematics, remained buried and forgotten somewhere in the correspondence files of the Berkeley Radiation Lab.

And Christofilos himself—still in Athens and well out of the loop of the scientific establishment—remained blissfully unaware that anyone else, let alone a trio of American researchers in Long Island, New York, had just gotten the credit for the thoughts that he had painstakingly worked out through countless hours after long days installing elevators in office buildings and apartment complexes, all on his own and without the use of great multimillion-dollar research instruments staffed by technicians and graduate students.

But, even though he certainly didn't get the latest issues hot off the press from the US Information Service, he dutifully kept up with his reading. Which made it inevitable that sooner or later he would discover that he had been scientifically scooped.

Sometime in late 1952, Christofilos learned of the Brookhaven research, though accounts differ on whether it was from gathering hints and rumors from pre-publication sources and gossip or from the actual *Physical Review* publication of the Courant, et al., paper. Whatever the case, he wasted no time in taking action. The concepts in the Brookhaven paper were essentially the same as those he'd earlier proposed to Berkeley in his follow-up missives after his initial letter had been gently rejected and corrected. He knew that different scientists working independently often came up with the same basic ideas; that was how science and invention had always worked. After all, other people had thought of the electric light, the telephone, the airplane, evolution by natural selection, and various other ideas long before Edison, Bell, the Wright Brothers, or Charles Darwin came along. But the names history remembered were the people who had stayed with their ideas, developed them, fought for their acceptance. And in his own way, Christofilos had been doing likewise. Maybe he hadn't published in a major (or even a minor) scientific journal, but he had a patent pending on strong focusing.

He engaged a big Greek law firm with connections and offices in Washington, and with some advance money from them, set out to return to America to investigate and stake his proper claim. In January 1953, he arrived in New York, went to the New York Public Library to read further on the Brookhaven paper and related work, then headed out on Long

Island to confront his as-yet-unknowing rivals. He told them of his work in detail, explaining how the *Physical Review* paper had essentially laid out what he'd already presented to the Berkeley Radiation Lab, and how those good folks had summarily dismissed him. He wasn't necessarily accusing anyone of stealing his ideas—he knew all about coincidence and simultaneous discoveries—but given his primacy of interest, shouldn't he at least get some substantial acknowledgment?

This was not the way that scientists generally received recognition for their work.

The Brookhaven people were suitably chagrined and not a little surprised. Normally, this argumentative Greek might have been dismissed as just another crackpot, but if there was a legitimate patent application involved, they couldn't afford to ignore the situation. They promptly got in touch with their Berkeley colleagues to check into Christofilos's tales of woe and scientific one-upmanship.

"Retrieving his manuscript from the file, red-faced Berkeley scientists saw that while the details of his scheme differed from those of the Brookhaven scientists, the principle was the same," wrote historian Robert P. Crease.[5] They, as well as the Brookhaven group, gracefully acknowledged that Christofilos deserved the primary credit for coming up with the strong focusing idea. After consultations with Christofilos's lawyers and the Patent Office, the Atomic Energy Commission agreed. Finally, Nicholas Christofilos had been recognized as a serious, authentic, and creative scientist, and all without a fancy Ph.D. His conception of strong focusing was officially acknowledged in a letter published later that year in *Physical Review*.

Not that everyone was really happy about it. Crease quotes a peeved Brookhaven accelerator scientist, Kenneth Green, who later wrote to a colleague: "When it turned up that [Christofilos] had independently conceived the strong-focusing idea, we were intrigued and impressed. However, his mathematical work . . . was less advanced, and his calculations were scarcely suitable for the design of an operating machine . . . The time had become ripe for the invention of strong-focusing and it was inevitable that someone would happen upon it. To be historically correct, the principle was really laid down in a paper by Thomas in 1938."[6] It is unknown whether the paper of which Green speaks was a part of Christofilos's voluminous self-education in the years before, but whatever the case, in this particular instance his diligence, imagination, unconventional approach, and most of all his foresight to file for a patent had paid off handsomely.

And not just in prestige, but financially. Following negotiations among Christofilos's lawyers, the AEC, and the Brookhaven Laboratory, Christofilos was granted a $10,000 licensing fee to allow Brookhaven the right to use strong focusing techniques in their new accelerator. The prestige factor turned out to be even more valuable than the money, however. It was now undeniably clear that here was a brilliant and inventive scientist who was far too valuable to be allowed to languish in Athens fixing elevators.

As usual, he was bursting with ideas, most of them now dealing with harnessing the power of nuclear fusion for peaceful purposes after the first hydrogen bomb had been detonated by the United States less than a year earlier. The United States was already putting together a fusion reactor program dubbed Project Sherwood, and Christofilos presented his own concepts at an early meeting of project personnel in April. "He made his presentation with the unbridled energy that would always characterize him—voice raised, arms flailing with the force of his gestures, wild scribbling engulfing the blackboard," described Coleman.[7] The assembled physicists were suitably enthralled by the performance—and the ideas. Christofilos's Astron proposals "seemed to combine the best features of the rival existing approaches to fusion . . . and therefore was something they wanted to pursue."

There was, however, a problem. Research in fusion reactors, even if it had little to do with fusion weapons, was still highly classified, and Christofilos had no security clearance. Even during his Astron presentation to the Project Sherwood crew, this issue had caused some consternation when, running out of blackboard space to scribble his equations, Christofilos had moved the board aside to find another board underneath covered in classified data which he wasn't supposed to see.

To some people, this eccentric figure was already suspicious. Herbert York recalled, "The security people had their doubts. They found it hard to believe that 'an elevator mechanic' had accomplished all that Nick [Christofilos] claimed. He must be, they thought, some kind of mole that the Russians, who also knew about accelerator technology, had pumped full of ideas not his own."[8]

Whatever the case, it was obvious that Christofilos was somebody that should be working on the fusion project, but getting him security clearance would take a while. What to do with him in the meantime? Fortunately, Brookhaven had already gotten over its feelings of chagrin at being upstaged, and offered Christofilos a staff position to work on their new accelerator. Meanwhile, he could continue to develop his Astron theories and calculations, then pick up with serious fusion work back in California after his security clearance came through. He enthusiastically accepted, beginning work at Brookhaven in June 1953.

It seemed like an excellent plan. Christofilos would delve into fascinating, practical work at Brookhaven on accelerators and particle physics, the sort of stuff he'd been doing only in theory back in Greece, while still continuing to work on Astron and any other ideas that arose from the depths of his imagination. Then he would move into the secret, classified world, working not on weapons but on a source of energy that could transform the planet. He would never again install another elevator.

And he was back in the United States at last, but this time to stay. He loved Greece, the home of his parents and ancestors and the place where he had spent most of his life up until now, but ultimately he considered himself an American. He had never stopped being an American citizen and to him, the United States, not Greece, was truly his country. Now he would be able to use his gifts to serve that country and her people.

As he settled into Brookhaven, Christofilos also settled into a new life. In spring 1954, his Greek girlfriend, Elly, arrived in the US, and they married on April 27. Although Christofilos was in his element, finally working at the forefront of his chosen field, Elly did not take well to life in America, a problem to which her husband seemed to pay little attention. It was an oversight he would eventually live to regret.

But for the time being, all was well, and Christofilos would become a vital member of the Brookhaven team for the next three years. In 1956, his security clearance finally came through, and Nicholas Christofilos was deemed loyal enough by his native country to be entrusted with its vital secrets.

Now he could truly get down to business. America's fusion energy research was centered in California at the Lawrence Radiation Laboratory, which had spun off from the Berkeley Radiation Lab, mostly for the purpose of developing nuclear weapons in competition with the Los Alamos Laboratory, which had created the world's first atomic bombs. In December 1956, Christofilos, Elly, and their baby son, Nicholas Jr., left New York for California. For Elly, it was another disrupting, upsetting change of environment and lifestyle. For Nicholas Christofilos, it was an entry into a heady realm of secret science, political intrigue, and the chance to determine the future of not only his country but the entire planet.

CHAPTER 3
Lines of Force

BY THE TIME AN AGITATED NICHOLAS CHRISTOFILOS FIRST BURST INTO HERBERT York's office with the idea for Argus, America had been in the atomic testing business for quite a while. Ever since the first atomic explosion on July 16, 1945, the United States had detonated close to a hundred nuclear devices. Many of them had been in the continental United States, first in New Mexico, then at the Atomic Energy Commission's Nevada Test Site beginning on January 27, 1951. Many other more powerful weapons, including a number of hydrogen bombs, had been tested at the Pacific Proving Grounds, where the US made use of islands captured from the Japanese in World War II. And two had exploded over Japan in August 1945, killing and maiming hundreds of thousands of human beings.

In 1957 alone, before Sputnik unleashed a different kind of explosion within the scientific community, the United States had tested twenty-nine atomic bombs, all in Nevada. Plans were underway to test more hydrogen weapons in the coming year in the Pacific, even as concerns about atomic fallout and worldwide protests were forcing reluctant national leaders to contemplate a testing moratorium.

The tests conducted by the AEC were of a dizzying variety. To most average folk, a Bomb was a Bomb, but the weaponeers of Los Alamos and

Livermore, not to mention the Pentagon strategists who devised the ways and means to use them, knew better. Nukes came in all physical sizes and levels of explosive power, from small weapons that could fit in the back of a truck, shells that could be fired by artillery pieces, and huge, monstrous devices that weighed tons and could be carried only by airplanes or ships. Atomic weapons could wipe out soldiers on the battlefield, a flotilla of ships or submarines, an air or naval base, or an entire metropolitan area, including the suburbs. Explosive yields ranged from a mere few hundred tons of TNT to multimillions.

But wherever the weapons were tested, whatever their design, all the tests had been conducted with one of three main objectives: trying out a new weapons design; studying the immediate effects of the nuclear explosion on buildings, bridges, animals, materials, or people (psychologically if not physically); or devising military tactics for their use in warfare. The test series and individual "shots" (atomic detonations) were given odd, nonsensical code names such as GREENHOUSE or TUMBLER-SNAPPER or UPSHOT-KNOTHOLE[1], and were complex logistical undertakings that took a year, usually more, to organize, and involved thousands of people, from scientists, military brass, and governmental administrators at the top all the way down to construction workers, technicians, and enlisted draftee soldiers at the bottom.

Testing Christofilos's ideas would be quite a different proposition. It would literally be a scientific experiment on a global scale, using the entire planet as both laboratory and test subject. It wouldn't require any special new weapons design—an off-the-shelf nuke would do fine, as long as it was detonated high enough in the atmosphere. The extreme altitude would ensure that any direct effects on people or things on the ground would be minimal if not nonexistent. As to the military utility of the entire enterprise—finding that out was essentially the whole point.

Though Christofilos wasn't aware of it at the time, military planners had already been thinking about high-altitude nuclear explosions. According to the official history of the Defense Nuclear Agency, Pentagon strategists worried about what might happen with nukes in outer space. "Christofilos' study was an extension of the DoD's [Department of Defense] interest in the effects of nuclear explosions in the outer atmosphere. In the early years of the missile age, military planners feared that electrons emitted by such large-altitude nuclear blasts could become trapped in the Earth's atmosphere and might possibly block the operation of ballistic missiles and defensive radar systems." A 1955 test series in Nevada, TEAPOT, had raised concerns about an electromagnetic pulse (EMP) generated by atomic weapons, and "there were numerous questions about the effects of missile-launched weapons and detonations in space, especially the effects of EMP on radio communications and equipment."[2] Now that the Soviet Union had made the missile age a dangerous reality, leaving America struggling to catch up, such questions were more urgent than ever.

The next big nuclear test series, dubbed HARDTACK and set for the Pacific in the new year, included some high-altitude shots, but none high enough to test Christofilos's theories. And there was another wrinkle that Christofilos himself introduced soon after approaching York. "A week or so after Nick first opened the floodgates on this stream of new ideas, he came in with an addendum. He had made a new calculation that showed there is already a 'background' of electrons of natural origin trapped in the Earth's magnetosphere, and he said we had to measure it before we did any experiments with a bomb."[3] Otherwise, how could scientists possibly tell the artificially generated radiation apart from the natural background? It made sense to York, and fortunately James Van Allen and his colleagues at the State University of Iowa had already designed instruments capable of detecting electrons in space.

Unfortunately, of course, such instruments would have to actually be placed in orbit, something that the US had yet to accomplish. "Such devices were coming along, but we had not yet flown any," York noted. For the time being, at least, Christofilos would have to do something which went against the grain of his usual predilections: he would have to wait. Or so York counseled him.

He was not about to do that. Neither were other people, especially after Sputnik. Herbert Scoville, for one. As the Deputy Director for Science and Technology at the CIA, Scoville had read Christofilos's classified paper on Argus and was also aware of the concerns about high-altitude nuclear explosions. Thinking ahead to the near future when America would finally get its own satellites aloft, Scoville "worried that the Soviets might be thinking along the lines of Christofilos' paper and use a nuclear weapon to form a long-lasting trapped radiation belt and interfere with US satellites."[4] It might not be as apocalyptic a scenario as Christofilos's fears of incoming Soviet nuclear missiles, but it was far more likely, and something that the US would be helpless to counter.

The flipside of the coin, of course, would be that if the United States did it first, it could be a powerful weapon against the Soviets. Or perhaps a quasi-weapon, since it wouldn't involve any sort of direct military attack—which only made the whole idea more intriguing.

Anxious to get moving, and persistently prodded by Christofilos, York decided to go to the President's Science Advisory Committee, otherwise known as PSAC. Chaired by James R. Killian, PSAC authorized further study of Argus and its military potential. In early 1958, Christofilos got the chance to strut his stuff in a presentation of his Argus paper before the entire PSAC in Washington. "Christofilos presented, in his brilliant and vigorous way, his theories about the 'Christofilos effect,'" Killian recalled. "By temperament effervescent, intense, and highly emotional, Nick could make any meeting explosive in discussion. [He] was in good form that day."[5]

PSAC was duly impressed, both by Christofilos's arguments and the other considerations that had already been circulating among Pentagon officials for months. They knew of the upcoming high-altitude HARD-TACK shots, and that, while they might provide some interesting data, they wouldn't conclusively settle the question of the widespread effects of such detonations. Argus promised to do so.

PSAC recommended that Christofilos's theory be tested "as soon as possible." The wheels were turning now. On March 6, Killian and Herbert York, now ARPA chief scientist at the Pentagon, briefed President Eisenhower, who approved undertaking further study in preparation for testing the Argus concept. He also approved the idea of launching a satellite to monitor the Argus effects.

An alphabet soup of governmental agencies were now involved. Aside from ARPA, Eisenhower instructed that efforts be coordinated among the Atomic Energy Commission (AEC); the Armed Forces Special Weapons Project (AFSWP), which was in charge of atomic weapons development across all the military branches; the Department of Defense (DOD); and of course the place where it had all started, Lawrence Livermore National Laboratory (LLNL), the defense-oriented offshoot of Ernest Lawrence's University of California Radiation Laboratory (UCRL). Conferences, consultations, and secret meetings ensued in Washington, California, and elsewhere.

In the meantime, the United States had finally begun successfully launching satellites. At least, it had managed to put two of them into space, Explorers 1 and 2. Both of the satellites, and the upcoming Explorer 4, carried scientific instruments designed and built by James Van Allen, who, along with rocketeer Wernher von Braun, was suddenly a scientific superstar in the public eye.

Nicholas Christofilos's own superstar charisma may have been hidden in the classified shadows, but it was of little concern to him. As long as he could focus on proving his theory and, in doing so, protect the United States, Christofilos was perfectly content to work away in the dark. If he had any frustrations about anonymity, he took them out on his piano at night, playing Beethoven and Bach, mostly all *fortissimo*, to the consternation of the neighbors. Meanwhile, he continued work on the Astron project.

On April 21, 1958, Killian and the White House received the official approval for the Argus operation from both the Secretary of Defense and the Atomic Energy Commission. Now it was solely up to one man to give the final go-ahead: the president. Killian promptly scheduled a meeting with Eisenhower on Thursday, May 1.

THAT SAME DAY, JAMES VAN ALLEN WAS IN WASHINGTON AT THE GREAT HALL of the National Academy of Sciences (NAS) for one of the biggest moments of his life. This one promised to surpass that crazy night only a few months past, when Explorer 1 became America's first satellite in orbit. That had really been more von Braun's and William Pickering's triumph, since they'd been the men who put Explorer into space, while Van Allen's instruments had just been along for the ride. (Von Braun would later make light of his celebrity status, telling Van Allen and his colleagues, "You're the important ones. I'm just the trucker.")[6]

But today, it was all about science and discovery in their purest forms. Van Allen and his team at the State University of Iowa (SUI) had spent the months since that January night collecting and analyzing the data from their instruments on Explorer 1, as well as its follow-up satellite Explorer 3. As required under the rules of the International Geophysical Year, under whose aegis the Explorers had been launched, Van Allen had reported his discoveries to IGY officials in April. Now the time had come to tell the rest of the world.

The session began promptly at 9:45 AM at a joint scientific conference of the NAS and the American Physical Society, with Van Allen reporting his findings to an amazed audience of colleagues, followed by a press conference at which Van Allen explained things in less esoteric terms for the benefit of reporters. One reporter asked for clarification, asking the scientist if the radiation he'd detected could be described as a "belt" encircling the Earth, and Van Allen agreed. The term "radiation belt" was born, to be further codified: "At a scientific conference in Europe soon after, NRL [Naval Research Laboratory] physicist Robert Jastrow used the term Van Allen radiation belt for the first time and the name quickly defined a permanent new landmark in the heavens," wrote historian Abigail Foerstner in her biography of Van Allen.[7]

While Van Allen was enjoying his moment in the scientific spotlight, a few blocks away at the White House, James Killian was laying out for President Eisenhower all the plans and preparations for the Argus experiment that had been worked out over the previous months. The president listened, considered, and gave his approval for the nuclear tests and the rest of the operation. It became official with the issuance of ARPA Order #4: Argus was a go.

Before the day was over, Herbert York informed Van Allen that Argus was going ahead, and that he and his team at the State University of Iowa would be participating. Van Allen was pleased: it was another chance to go into space and do more science.

It did not come as a complete surprise, however. He had already known the broad outlines of Argus for a few weeks, and the probability that satellites would be tasked to detect the Christofilos effect. This practically guaranteed that Van Allen would be asked to participate, since he and his crack team of graduate students had more experience in building space-based radiation detectors than anyone else on the planet at the time.

A couple of months earlier in March, a meeting had been called at the Jet Propulsion Laboratory (JPL), ostensibly to discuss the preliminary results from Explorer 1. Aside from people already quite familiar to Van Allen from Explorer, such as JPL director William Pickering and Army general John Medaris, the meeting was also attended by scientist Wolfgang Panofsky, who had been working discreetly with Christofilos on Argus ideas.

It seemed a bit odd at the time, since Explorer 1 had been in orbit just over a month, and it was early to be talking about any definitive "results" from anything. In effect, however, it was Van Allen's audition for the Argus project.

Van Allen's graduate student George Ludwig recalled in his memoirs: "Although the meeting was openly billed as a gathering to discuss Explorer 1 results, those results were still so tentative that, in retrospect, a meeting of such senior personnel for that purpose was certainly premature. No one in our small Iowa team had made any outside hint of our growing suspicion that the Earth might be surrounded by a previously unknown region of high-intensity trapped radiation. The stated meeting objective was certainly a cover for its true purpose—an early examination of the possibility of orbiting a satellite suitable for detecting and quantifying the Argus Effect."[8]

Van Allen was far from naive. "There were vague allusions at this meeting to the possibility of radiation experiments at high altitudes by the AEC," he remembered.[9] After the JPL meeting, Van Allen kept in touch with Panofsky with phone calls about Explorer 1 results, picking up further hints here and there. As Ludwig noted, "Although none of us at Iowa knew of

Argus planning by then, we subsequently became aware of it by degrees."[10]

The following month, when Van Allen informed the officials of the space program and IGY of his Explorer 1 and 3 findings in April, he was formally read into the Argus planning. "At that time, I was introduced to the secret plans for the conduct of the high-altitude bomb tests, later called Argus," he recalled.[11] He found out that it had been his friend William Pickering at JPL who had suggested Van Allen and his Iowa stalwarts for the job.

There was another disturbing revelation. "I also learned that, despite the absence of definitive information, some officials of the Atomic Energy Commission believed that the Soviet Union might have already conducted such tests."[12] If that were true, it was suggested, then it was possible that the radiation belts Van Allen had detected weren't a natural phenomenon—an alarming proposition not only from a military standpoint, but also from the viewpoint of a scientist who had just claimed to make a major discovery.

So Van Allen agreed to come on board, for a variety of reasons. "I was eager to participate in the Argus tests because of their apparent national importance and more particularly because of the possibility of distinguishing between a natural and an artificial population of geomagnetically trapped particles,"[13] he wrote. He, like Christofilos, was sure that what he'd found was not the result of Soviet nuclear meddling. But learning how to distinguish between natural radiation and that caused by nefarious high-altitude atomic activity was obviously a high priority.

Van Allen brought George Ludwig and fellow graduate student Carl McIlwain into the secret. After the formal approval of Argus by the president, matters began to move very quickly. Less than two weeks later, another meeting was held at JPL, and there it was made official: Iowa would build the scientific payload for the upcoming Explorer 4, which would monitor Argus in space. Plans were coordinated between JPL and the Army Ballistic Missile Agency that would launch the satellite, track the craft and collect data. But time was crucial in order to make the launch window for Explorer 4. "The meeting assigned Iowa an unbelievably tight schedule of deadlines," Foerstner noted. Van Allen's team had a mere seventy-seven days to get it all done.

For a research scientist like Van Allen, it all might have been something of a conflict. In a very real sense, he was in fact co-opting his scientific work to the military, an arrangement that many scientists would consider a deal with the devil. But Van Allen had already been working under the auspices of the military for most of his career. In World War II, he had worked on proximity fuses and, as a naval officer, helped test them in combat. His postwar sounding rocket and balloon research had been conducted hand-in-hand with the military, using their rockets, ships, and aircraft to carry his instruments to the upper atmosphere and into space. For him, this was a logical extension of all his previous work. Until the establishment of the civilian space agency—NASA—that would come later in 1958, the military controlled access to space.

"While he had fought against military control of scientific space research, [Van Allen] had no qualms about partnering with the military for a defense mission," wrote Abigail Foerstner.[14] They were the ones with the rockets, after all. And it was certainly not the same as building weapons, as many of Van Allen's colleagues were doing. True, his findings might have defense applications, but they were also important science.

But secrecy had its own complications. "Explorer 4 was announced as part of a peaceful IGY satellite program, but the design and construction of the instrument package was top secret, and it was used for military purposes," observed historian James Rodger Fleming. Scientific laboratories and workshops were traditionally bastions of openness and free access for everyone, at least for everyone who was a student or professor or otherwise part of the institution, but Van Allen and his team couldn't work that way anymore. As they began a frantic quest to build the Explorer 4 instruments in less than three months—"breakneck speed" as Ludwig put it—somebody put up a sign in the lab: "This job is so secret, even I don't know what I'm doing."[15]

CHAPTER 4
A Sense of Urgency

As Argus planning accelerated, secrecy spawned further complications. That was nothing new in the world of atomic weapons and the military, but Argus took matters to an entirely new level. Not only did the purpose and concepts of Argus need to remain classified, so did the very existence of the entire enterprise. The reasons were not just military, but also political, diplomatic, and even scientific.

If Christofilos was right and Argus worked—if electrons and charged particles generated by a high-altitude nuclear detonation could be trapped in the Earth's magnetosphere to create an artificial radiation belt—the effect, by definition, would probably be global. The Christofilos theory predicted that particles would spiral around the magnetic lines of force, beginning at the point of generation, whizzing north or southward toward one of the Earth's magnetic poles, then heading back in the other direction toward the opposite pole along the next magnetic force line, jumping from one to the next in an east-west direction. If intense enough, the net effect would be that the field of charged particles would spread longitudinally to eventually circumnavigate the globe and form a "belt."

Obviously, such a phenomenon would not be a localized event like a thunderstorm or even a hurricane. As an official history later explained:

"If an ARGUS detonation performed as predicted, it would produce world-wide disturbances in the upper atmosphere that could be monitored by any nation with properly emplaced instrumentation."[1]

No one could do anything about the Soviet Union or anyone else getting lucky and detecting Argus all on their own, of course. That was a risk that had to be taken. But permitting the public or other governments to know about the tests in advance would make it much easier for the Soviets to eavesdrop. Both the US and the USSR routinely monitored each other's nuclear tests and most other military maneuvers from a respectful distance, using aircraft, submarines, ships, and fishing trawlers (spy satellites, though in the works, were still a few years away). That was just an accepted part of doing business in the Cold War, and to be expected when atomic tests were announced in advance. But there was no point in making it easier for the Soviets, especially with something as potentially important as Argus.

Officials became even more troubled when the Soviets launched their third Sputnik on May 15. Unlike its two predecessors, Sputnik 3 featured a suite of scientific instruments to support its IGY mission. That was fine for science, but potentially threatening for Argus. "Since the satellite contained instrumentation for measuring atmospheric radiation, it might be able to detect Argus, if the Soviets knew when and where to look for it," wrote Lisa Mundey. "American officials worried that the Soviets, should they be given advance warning, might send up specialized satellites to measure the American experiment."[2] Soviet space activity was yet another reason to keep a tight lid on the project.

Not everyone agreed. At the May 1 meeting at which Eisenhower gave Argus his final stamp of approval, the issue of secrecy versus a public announcement was discussed, briefly but heatedly. "While the DOD [Department of Defense] opposed an announcement," noted Mundey, John Foster Dulles, then Ike's secretary of state, "insisted on one."[3] AEC head Lewis Strauss, though no fan of governmental openness himself, also pointed out that because he would have to inform Congress of the test, as was the case with all nuclear tests, leaks would be inevitable.

Everyone at the meeting was quite aware that this was a wholly unprecedented case. The United States had only ever tested one atomic weapon in total secrecy, and that had been the very first one on July 16, 1945, in the midst of a world war. But now the world was at peace, and attempting to detonate atomic bombs in secret came with the possibility of various unpleasant international repercussions.

There was also the question of the ongoing International Geophysical Year, the IGY, led by the United States and USSR and meant to be a completely open, nonmilitary, purely scientific endeavor, with all data shared freely among nations. That didn't matter when discussing a non-IGY activity such as setting off nuclear weapons, but launching satellites that were ostensibly scientific, such as Explorer 4, was another matter. How was Explorer 4's true mission going to be kept secret if the US was obliged to openly publish its scientific data?

It was clear that Argus was simply going to be too big, too wide-ranging, too ambitious an effort to conceal completely. At the State University of Iowa, Van Allen and his graduate students could simply keep their mouths shut and put up a couple of funny signs around the lab, but that wasn't going to work outside of Iowa City. Cover stories were going to have to be invented for practically everything. To make matters even more confusing, a new secret code word, FLORAL, was officially assigned to the Argus project in order to avoid the nuclear test connotations that the original "Hardtack Argus" designation had acquired. "These plans were to conceal the true intentions of all phases of the ARGUS operation, not only from other nations but also from the majority of DOD personnel participating in the tests themselves."[4]

Which meant that at that moment, thousands of men serving in the US Navy, US Air Force, and US Army were now destined to participate in one of the most secretive operations of the twentieth century, completely without their knowledge. Aside from the problem of explaining the movement of men, ships, planes, and other military equipment to unknown and unspecified destinations, there would be the problem of organizing, supplying, and carrying it all out.

And where would they all go? Where was Argus to be conducted, particularly given the need and desire to keep its purposes obscured, if not completely secret? Obviously the usual test sites in Nevada and the Pacific were out. It would not be possible to detonate one or more atomic weapons several hundred miles above Las Vegas without the entire US west coast knowing about it. As for the Pacific, it might be easier to keep away curious eyes, but there were other considerations.

On March 1, 1954, the US had exploded a hydrogen bomb dubbed Castle Bravo at Bikini Atoll. It was a test of a new H-bomb configuration, and it exceeded everyone's expectations, including its own designers. Expected to produce a yield of about five megatons, it was a monster, generating three times that yield. Because of the unexpectedly high yield and tricky winds that shifted the predicted fallout patterns, Castle Bravo ended up dousing a lot of people with radiation, including the civilian crew of the *Lucky Dragon*, a Japanese fishing boat. All of them were affected with radiation sickness; one later died. It was a massive public relations disaster for the US and the AEC worldwide, and became a major impetus for protests that would ultimately lead to the cessation of atmospheric nuclear testing.

Though the radioactive fallout of Castle Bravo had long since faded over the Pacific, the political fallout still persisted for AEC chairman Lewis Strauss. Though he had previously demonstrated little to no concern for the fate of Marshall Islanders or errant Japanese fishermen, he didn't want to risk any further public or press outcry over the testing program. Better, thought Strauss and most others in the AEC and DOD, to find another place to give Christofilos his trial run.

It was bad enough to attempt something as huge as Argus under a shroud of secrecy and deception. But there was also a clock ticking, and it was one that could not be ignored.

Even though President Eisenhower had purposely centered much of his national security policy around nuclear weapons, a concept he called the "New Look," he had been thinking about stopping the testing of atomic weapons for some time, at least since before the 1956 presidential election. From the time he took office in 1953, he had been dedicated to the notion of the "peaceful" atom, the use of nuclear energy for peaceful civilian purposes such as electrical power, scientific research, and medicine, and in general converting atomic swords into civilian plowshares. As a career soldier, he was intimately aware of the military's endless thirst for more weapons and more resources, and the Strategic Air Command, AEC laboratories, and the rest of the nuclear establishment in particular were endlessly rapacious. The Pentagon fought him at every turn, whether by directly opposing his efforts or issuing dire warnings about the mortal danger facing America.

"Eisenhower . . . had long been concerned about the nuclear arms race and where it was leading us," Herbert York recalled. "Ever since the 'Bravo' nuclear fallout accident in the Pacific in 1954 had raised world consciousness about nuclear tests, [Eisenhower] had mulled over the possibility of a nuclear test ban both as a solution to the fallout problem and as a means for slowing down the arms race."[5] Ike had been forced to back off the issue for political reasons when Adlai Stevenson adopted it as a major part of his platform in his 1956 presidential campaign against Eisenhower. But Ike had been re-elected, and the time was ripe to take action.

Earlier in the spring, Ike directed PSAC to examine the issues concerning a possible nuclear test ban or moratorium. Some scientists in the nuclear arms establishment, such as Edward Teller, were strongly opposed to such a move, arguing that it would gravely imperil America's strategic position. Others, including the members of PSAC, thought otherwise, noting that the US had a firm technological lead in nuclear weapons technology and that the fallout problem needed to be addressed directly.

Eisenhower approached Nikita Khrushchev on April 20 to formally propose an international meeting of experts to talk over a moratorium, and Khrushchev agreed. Soon, serious negotiations were underway for a test moratorium to go into effect before the end of 1958.

That didn't leave much time for an operation on the scale of Argus. The US already had the HARDTACK atomic test series in the works for 1958, divided into two parts: HARDTACK I in the Pacific and HARDTACK II later in the year in Nevada. Given the mind-boggling complexity of organizing and conducting HARDTACK, completing an entirely separate test series from scratch was going to require a herculean effort.

And while HARDTACK was scheduled to include some high-altitude detonations, they would be nothing like Argus: far lower in the atmosphere, far from outer space. That gave added urgency to the necessity of Argus. Another test-ban technical report, this one from a panel of both scientists and military men, observed: "If the high altitude shots at HARDTACK are successful, the U.S will possess weapons effects information important to AICBM [anti-ICBM] and other military developments that will not be available to the same extent to the USSR until a similar test is conducted. But much more effects information will be needed than HARDTACK is likely to provide because the instrumentation for the HARDTACK tests is incomplete, and there are likely to be further important effects that will not have been tested (e.g. ARGUS)."[6]

So Argus was carrying the weight of a great many hopes and expectations. And everything had to be completed before the year was out. The spring of 1958 had been one of secret meetings and conferences, but now that Eisenhower had given the green light, the time for talking was over and the time for action beginning. The first, most basic task was to decide a location for Argus, if not the Pacific or Nevada. Fortunately, Herbert York at ARPA had some good ideas. "I vividly recall poring over maps (something I've always enjoyed) looking for an appropriate site, discovering that Gough Island was in the right place, and then and there personally deciding on that location," he wrote.[7]

Gough Island is a lonely place in the South Atlantic Ocean not far from an even lonelier place, Tristan da Cunha, and an extinct volcano called Inaccessible Island. They form an archipelago far from shipping lanes, tourist havens, and civilization in general, inhabited by exotic wildlife and a tiny population of several hundred people. From the point of view of Argus planners, the area also had the distinct advantage of being far distant from the Soviet Union or any of its various worldwide interests or allies. In other words, it was perhaps the unlikeliest place on Earth for any stray Russian trawlers, submarines, or aircraft to happen by.

Aside from its geographical obscurity, the area enjoyed another feature that especially recommended it for the Argus experiment. It lay east of a dip in the Earth's magnetic field called the Brazilian or South Atlantic Anomaly, where the magnetosphere was closer to the surface and thus encountered more air molecules. If Argus electrons hit the Brazilian Anomaly, they would be absorbed by air molecules, interfering with and possibly derailing the expected Argus effect. Detonating the atomic devices just east of the Anomaly, however, would give the Argus radiation belt—if it formed—time to expand, grow, and spread eastward around most of the planet before dissipating, allowing ample opportunity to detect and measure it.

Also, it was imperative to observe the "magnetic conjugate point"—the area where the Argus effects were expected to be mirrored along the north-south direction in the magnetosphere. A detonation point in the South Atlantic near Tristan da Cunha and Gough Island placed the Argus conjugate point near the Azores in the North Atlantic, where naval ships could easily assemble and monitor the tests remotely—and without arousing any undue suspicions.

But such a remote operational area as the South Atlantic also posed some serious problems. For one thing, if all went according to plan, it would be August when Argus was conducted, which meant it would be winter in the South Atlantic, with rain, snow, and freezing temperatures—challenging conditions for naval operations under normal circumstances, much less while trying to launch a nuclear missile from the deck of a ship, something that had never been attempted before. Such weather conditions would also complicate routine matters such as the task force ships finding and rendezvousing with one another, refueling and supply, even communications. It was not going to be a pleasure cruise by any means.

An experienced sea hand and administrator would be needed to run the operation. Fortunately, one was available. Captain Lloyd M. Mustin, who was just preparing to assume command of the US Navy's Destroyer Flotilla Two and accept a concomitant promotion to Rear Admiral, was wrapping up a family vacation in San Francisco and preparing to report to his new station in Newport, Rhode Island, when he received orders on May 19 to report to the Chief of Naval Operations (CNO) in Washington instead.

The CNO informed Mustin that his new duty assignment, though not his promotion, was going to be delayed a bit. The Argus task force, which was going to include not only naval forces but Army and Air

Force as well, needed a commander, and Mustin had been chosen. A Naval Academy graduate with considerable combat experience in World War II and a Navy family pedigree that stretched back as far as his great-great-grandfather and the War of 1812, Mustin had had no direct experience with nuclear weapons in his military career, but he had a lot of experience in commanding large, diverse military forces.

Mustin was given office space within the headquarters of the Armed Forces Special Weapons Project (AFSWP) in the Pentagon and began receiving a flurry of technical briefings. The new task force would need a name as well. "We realized that we would need an operational designator of some sort, in order to get all of the communication facilities and the control and the command structure network and so on," he recalled in an oral history. "We asked for, and got, from the commander in chief, that designator, Task Force 88 [TF 88]."[8]

Meanwhile, the skipper of the USS *Norton Sound*, Captain Arthur R. Gralla, was getting some unusual orders of his own. He discovered that his vessel, which had begun her unglamorous life as a seaplane tender in World War II and later become a guided-missile ship, had been selected as the launching platform for the Argus experiments. It was a natural choice, since the *Sound* had been conducting missile tests, launching sounding rockets, and sending off weather balloons since her conversion a decade earlier.

"It was pretty sure that the *Norton Sound* would be the launch ship," Mustin recalled in a 1980 interview. "[She] had that big after-deck . . . in addition, *Norton Sound* had a lot of tracking equipment—telemetry, receiving equipment, so on . . . she was optimum."[9]

This particular job, however, was not going to be her usual routine. The ship would require further extensive modifications in order to handle the missile that had been chosen to launch the Argus warheads—the multistage Lockheed X-17a—and to increase its fuel capacity for the extended voyage. Gralla got his orders, his briefings, and returned from Washington to his ship's home port, Port Hueneme, California, to take his vessel up to the San Francisco Naval Shipyard for refitting. His crew had no idea as yet just what was going on, or where they would be sailing. But that was life for the average sailor.

Mustin put together the rest of his task force. Matters were somewhat complicated by the fact that while the *Norton Sound* was based on the West Coast as part of the Pacific Fleet, the remainder of the assigned ships were in the Atlantic Fleet, based on the East Coast. But if coordination and communications were affected by that reality, such complications also helped to enhance security and to bolster the developing cover stories as to the true purpose of Task Force 88 (TF 88): "TF 88 was identified as consisting of Atlantic Fleet units. This force ostensibly was established by CINCANTFT [Commander in Chief, Atlantic Fleet] to conduct a series of tests of new equipment being introduced into the operating forces. These tests were to be conducted over a wide range of sea and climatic conditions, necessitating a prolonged period of operations at sea."[10] As for the *Norton Sound*, she was said to be "involved in special missile operations requiring preliminary tests on the Pacific Coast Point Mugu Missile Range before conducting a series of firings in a remote area of the Pacific Ocean."[11]

For another TF 88 member, the USS *Albemarle*, the Argus assignment was going to provide a welcome break from some intense duty. The ship had been picked as the floating base of the Navy's newfangled nuclear bomber program, centered on a graceful but ultimately impractical jet aircraft called the Martin P6M SeaMaster. In the era before nuclear submarines and submarine-launched ICBMs, the Navy had been desperately casting about for some entree into the nuclear business, since that was where the lion's share of Pentagon money was to be found. Money had been pouring into the Air Force and its Strategic Air Command bombers for a decade, and the SeaMaster project was the Navy's bid for a piece of the pie. But the project had been plagued with difficulty, including test-flight crashes and fatalities, and would ultimately be cancelled.

"The *Albemarle* was a seaplane tender that . . . had been taken out of mothballs, and millions of dollars spent in converting her into a tender for that jet seaplane, the P6M, that the Navy spent so much money and time on for so long," recalled Mustin. "It was somebody's supposed secret entry into the strategic nuclear bombing realm, I often thought. But it wasn't very successful . . . the P6M program was about to be canceled, but it was delayed enough so that *Albemarle* was available."[12]

For the summer of 1958, however, the *Albemarle* would get a break from SeaMaster tests and refittings to serve as the northern monitoring station for Argus in the Azores. She would be positioned at the conjugate point in the North Atlantic, watching for artificial auroras and measuring whatever other Argus phenomena might manifest themselves.

To preserve security, she was not officially designated as part of Task Force 88, but as a vessel that, having just undergone an extensive overhaul at the Philadelphia Naval Shipyard, was in need of a routine shakedown cruise. That would be her cover for the Argus voyage. The Navy also announced that the ship would be working with the Air Force on some long-range communications tests—which was true, after a fashion.

Mustin had other concerns besides security and logistics. One of them was just how many Argus shots would actually be fired. As an experienced sailor and ship handler, he knew very well how rough the seas and the weather could be in the South Atlantic winter, and worried about the prospect of trying to launch a ballistic missile from the deck of a ship—especially one carrying a nuclear warhead. Even disregarding the possible safety issues, it was reasonable to expect that such a feat would take more than one attempt.

It was an issue that, as Mustin discovered, had apparently been given little consideration. "I think initially that's how the thoughts lay, that we would go down there and we would fire one, and that would be that."[13] When he found that several missiles would be available for Argus, he pushed for additional shots. "Somewhere along the line, it became apparent that we could get two of these X-17 rockets modified to carry the warhead. So immediately the plan was to take along two. I hadn't been thinking this thing over very long before the word came from Lockheed that there were enough components around to assemble a third. So I took steps to get that done . . . when the *Norton Sound* sailed, she was actually carrying three . . . I know that my thinking, before we ever left, was that if things permit, I would certainly expect to fire all three."[14]

The three-stage Lockheed X-17a rocket chosen for Argus was a thin needle-like research vehicle forty feet tall, developed for the Navy's Polaris missile program as a test bed for heat shields on missile cones. In that capacity, it would be launched straight up, pass through the peak of its ballistic arc, then head straight back down through the atmosphere to subject a missile nose cone to the intense friction heat that would be encountered by a re-entering ICBM warhead.

"It had been used in places like White Sands proving ground and so on, out in the desert, just from crude, simply fixed launchers that you'd aim up in the sky and light her off, and off she'd go," Mustin said. "We, on the other hand, had to launch it from the deck of a ship. It's kind of a cliché to say from the deck of a rolling ship, till you stop and figure what the forecasts are for weather in that part of the world. Almost any time of the year, you name it, that part of the world is pretty uncompromising . . . down in that part of the Atlantic, there's practically no data, because nobody goes there; the weather is so lousy. The average wind force was gale. We expected the weather would be a factor in anything we did."[15]

But the X-17a had not been designed to carry nuclear warheads. It was simply too small and not powerful enough to loft most of the weapons in the US stockpile, which tended to be large, bulky, and heavy objects.

Still, the weapons labs had been making great progress in warhead miniaturization—one of the payoffs of all the testing in the Pacific and especially in Nevada. It was an effort driven by the ever-expanding plans for more diverse and versatile nukes made not only for the confined spaces of submarines but for use in artillery shells or backpack bombs. The W-25 warheads destined for Argus would be of this generation: low-yield weapons originally intended for air-to-air missiles. They were meant not to obliterate cities, but merely to knock enemy planes and missiles out of the sky.

Which, as Mustin realized, was of little comfort when considering the prospect of such a weapon accidentally detonating in the middle of a naval task force. "This nuclear warhead had nothing but the simplest fuze," he recalled. "It was ignited by the acceleration of the rocket. It was going to run for whatever the time was—700 seconds, or thereabouts, as I recall it—at the end of which time it was going to detonate that nuclear warhead. That's all there was to it. Once it was started, there was no way of turning it off."[16]

In other words, it was not set to go off on impact, but at a fixed time after launch. If a missile were launched off the proper trajectory, or failed to reach sufficient altitude, a disaster could ensue. "The combination of fairly easily predictable malfunctions could find you coming down with a live nuclear warhead, with a fuze that had been armed and was going to go off at some unknown time. This could be anywhere within a radius of quite a few miles from you, at some launching accident or other. So the launching point we picked was more than 1300 miles from land, in all directions."[17]

Quite aside from the possibility of inadvertently nuking someone else, Mustin well knew that "the hazard of this thing coming back down right within our own force was not negligible. And, of course, in later years, to conceive of the AEC ever agreeing to any such thing as this is just so remote that I can't tell you how remote it seems to me. But I suppose the general consensus was that, 'We have no choice; we've got to do it. This is absolutely the best that can be done. An alternate solution of let's don't do it is not permissible. So the heck with it, let's get on with it.'"[18]

As spring melted into summer, that was the attitude that prevailed throughout all the various agencies, organizations, and institutions engaged in Argus. There was a deadline to meet, objectives to be achieved. It may not have been wartime, but it certainly felt like it. For those involved, nothing less than the survival of the free world seemed to be at stake.

CHAPTER 5
The Task Force

T HAT SUMMER OF 1958, NEWLY-MINTED REAR ADMIRAL MUSTIN WAS NOT THE only one with rockets on the mind. ARPA, which remained in operational charge of America's space program until the new and decidedly civilian National Aeronautics and Space Administration (NASA) took over officially in the fall, was making preparations for the Argus satellite missions, Explorers 4 and 5. Two of the Army's Jupiter C missiles, originally scheduled to launch inflatable spheres into orbit, were retasked for Argus, while James Van Allen and his team busily continued building the equipment payloads back in Iowa City.

Other rockets were also being readied. The Air Force was preparing to launch a bevy of sounding rockets from three different sites on the East Coast in conjunction with each of the Argus shots. The rockets would provide both a backup and a supplement to the data acquired by the satellites, passing through the Argus radiation shell at different altitudes and trajectories.

Although not directly part of the project, the fate of another pair of rockets would be watched closely by Argus personnel: the two Redstone missiles that would launch the high-altitude nuclear shots of HARDTACK, dubbed Teak and Orange. Everyone knew that while these tests wouldn't negate the necessity or the motivation for Argus, they still held the promise of some intriguing results that would be directly related to and perhaps even markedly enhance the impact of Argus in scientific and military circles.

Unlike the comparatively humble X-17as that would carry Argus into space, the Redstone was a serious missile, almost seventy feet long with a thrust of over 61,000 pounds. In its modified Jupiter C configuration, it had carried America's first satellite, Explorer 1, into orbit, but was capable of lofting far larger payloads, such as the hydrogen warheads of Teak and Orange, which were weapons that weighed about three tons and gave a nuclear yield of 3.8 megatons.

As with all the other Pacific nuclear tests, secrecy was not a major issue for these shots. Johnston Island, already well-established as part of the US Pacific Proving Grounds, underwent massive preparations before the shots, including the construction of a launching pad, liquid-oxygen fuel plant, concrete observation bunkers, and extensive instrumentation arrays for monitoring, photographing, and recording the proceedings. A variety of aircraft were assembled for observation, recording, and search-and-rescue operations, along with a flotilla of ships. Unlike the wilds of the South Atlantic, Johnston Island was one place where the US military and scientific establishment could set up everything precisely as they wanted it.

Originally, the Teak and Orange shots had been scheduled for launch from Bikini, but AEC Chairman Lewis Strauss, in an uncharacteristic display of concern for the native Marshall Islanders, whose entire way of life had been disrupted by the test program ever since it began in 1946, worried that the high-altitude bursts, which would be visible over a far greater range than usual, might injure or permanently blind indigenous personnel, not to mention anyone else who happened to be in the area. The memory of the Castle Bravo debacle and the resultant bad publicity was still fresh in his mind.

Upon further study, the Department of Defense and the government labs concurred. "Results of theoretical calculations on the optical thermal yield of these weapons when detonated in the upper atmosphere became available indicating that such detonations would be bright enough to cause permanent retinal injury to observers of the bursts," noted a Defense

Department history of HARDTACK. "These calculations had only recently been completed by the DOD. Because some 11,000 Micronesians would have been close enough to view the very high altitude bursts at the EPG [Eniwetok Proving Ground], thus risking retinal damage, the Secretary of Defense and the Chairman of the AEC decided on 7 April to change the location of the test to Johnston Island."[1] There were not going to be any further *Lucky Dragon*–type public-relations fiascos this time. Johnston Island was suitably remote, more than five hundred miles away from the nearest inhabited areas, even if moving the operation there entailed greater logistical difficulties.

But the shots would have other repercussions, which would not come as a surprise to Nicholas Christofilos and would also provide further impetus for Argus. Teak was launched shortly before midnight on July 31, 1958. Set to detonate over water some distance away from the island, a guidance system glitch instead caused it to explode directly over Johnston Island at the planned altitude of about fifty miles, causing something of a shock to observers on the ground. By all accounts, Teak was a spectacular sight, creating an enormous, brilliant, multicolored fireball in the sky that not only dazzled the official observers in the immediate area but was also visible as far as seven hundred miles away in Honolulu.

Hawaii got more than just a dazzling light show. The blast poured electrons into the ionosphere, blacking out radio and radar over a broad range of the Pacific as far as Australia. "The red glow remained clearly visible in the southwestern sky for half an hour," recounted a Defense Nuclear Agency history.[2] It was an apocalyptic sight: "One air force officer watching the display fantasized that this was what a nuclear war might look like," noted James Fleming.[3]

The people on the scene at Johnston Island seemed to have suddenly dropped off the face of the planet—or perhaps, had been blown off of it. "In Honolulu, military and civilian air traffic communications were interrupted for several hours. At the AFWSP's offices in the Pentagon, [AFSWP commander] Admiral Parker grew concerned for the personnel on Johnston Island as hour after hour passed with no word regarding the test. Finally, some eight hours after Teak had occurred, the word that all was well came from

[A. R] Luedecke, the commander of Joint Task Force 7 . . . The communications blackout worried others as well. Later AFSWP learned that one of the first radio messages received at Johnston Island once communications had been restored was: 'Are you still there?'"[4]

The Orange shot about two weeks later, though nearly identical in design, was something of an anticlimax, occurring at a lower altitude and proving to be considerably less picturesque. It also failed to produce the widespread electronic havoc of Teak, though some effects were still reported.[5]

The final verdict was somewhat equivocal. Though Teak and Orange, along with a low-yield balloon shot at low altitude called Yucca, weren't enough to conclusively confirm or deny Christofilos's ideas one way or another, they did demonstrate that something unusual happened up there when atomic weapons detonated in the twilight zone where the Earth's atmosphere transitioned into the void of outer space. But not everyone was satisfied. "While some valuable information had been gathered from Teak and Orange, many scientists in the nuclear weapons community considered the tests to be only partially successful," noted the DNA history. "Neither detonation had occurred where it had been planned and, due to cloud cover, detailed photographic coverage was incomplete."[6] There were some calls to repeat the Teak test, but these were dismissed in the face of the impending nuclear test moratorium.

All of which served to place further emphasis on Argus. As preparations accelerated relentlessly, anticipation grew. After all, Teak and Orange had not been specifically designed and targeted to create the Christofilos effect. What would happen with Argus, intended to do just that?

IT HAD BEEN A BUSY SUMMER FOR ALL CONCERNED, FROM THE HALLS OF THE PENTAGON and the offices of Admiral Mustin, to the basement lab of James Van Allen in Iowa; from the shipyards of San Francisco, Philadelphia, and Norfolk, to the decks and compartments of the *Norton Sound*. After completing refits in San Francisco, Captain Gralla had taken the *Sound* back into the Pacific off the southern coast of California, to the Naval Air Missile Test Center Sea Test Range. Under the tutelage of technicians from Lockheed

Missiles Systems Division, the crew practiced assembling and preparing the X-17a missiles for firing in a ten-day training course in Van Nuys, California. While the *Sound*'s crew were experienced missileers, this particular vehicle was a new animal for them, and there could be no margin for error.

Back in Iowa, the Van Allen team was laboring to prepare the Explorer 4 and 5 instrument packages for launch. Fortunately, the importance of the project helped to grease the wheels: "The Argus Project was helped immeasurably by the assignment of a very high military priority that helped to cut through the red tape and delivery delays," remembered George Ludwig.[7] That was a good thing, because apart from the technical challenges, constant coordination was necessary among all the project principals. Ludwig, Van Allen, and the rest of the team had both civilian and military aircraft readily available to fly themselves and equipment between Iowa City, Washington, and Huntsville, Alabama, where the Jupiter rocket that would loft Explorer into orbit was being put together. Tests had to be made to ensure that the instrument package would work flawlessly with spacecraft systems, communications setups, and even that it would fit inside the confines of the rocket shell. Again, there was no margin for error. The satellite data was going to be all-important, because ground observations and sounding rocket flights were not going to provide enough hard data to confirm and characterize Christofilos's predictions. That would require sustained measurements of the predicted radiation shell that could only be provided by a satellite. And with a project deadline of September 1, 1958, now firmly imposed by the powers that be, there would be no opportunities to repeat the Argus experiment. "We had to get it done by the first of September, or our name was mud," Mustin recalled.[8]

Ludwig himself took two trips to Huntsville in June, carrying first the Explorer instrument package prototypes and then the actual flight units for various tests and preparations. The classified nature of the entire business was something of a mixed bag. "Despite the secrecy, we could build all of the equipment in the open, since the satellite and its instrumentation served officially as an International Geophysical Year (IGY) program to extend our investigation of the natural radiation discovered by Explorers I and III," Ludwig wrote. "Only the second mission to study the nuclear blasts was held in strict confidence by a small group of us who were build-ing the instrument. In fact, only Van Allen and [Carl] McIlwain had access to the full range of details. My knowledge was limited to a basic under-standing of the mission and to details necessary to build the instrumented satellite, test it, and interface it with the launch vehicle."[9]

He wasn't the only one working in the dark. Out on the West Coast, the *Norton Sound* spent the month of July test-firing X-17a missiles from her fantail launching area. The test version—a configuration of the X-17a known as the Winder missile fitted with a special warhead loaded with telemetry equipment—turned out to be a tricky beast. While the first test-firing at sea went well, hurtling to an altitude of 302 miles, matters quickly became more problematic.

Navy missileman Dick Culp worked as part of the telemetry station team aboard the "Snortin' Norton." "The missile itself was originally de-signed as what was called a nail-driver," he remembered. "The first stage would take it out of the atmosphere, then it would topple and the second two stages would fire and drive it down into the atmosphere." The purpose was to test the reentry characteristics of different nose cone shapes and ma-terials. But for Argus, Culp said, "we just sent them all straight up."

As with many other rocket designs, the X-17a first stage employed a spin package—small retrorockets that would fire upon launch to send the missile spinning on its long axis, imparting greater flight stability. The spin motors would be automatically jettisoned once the missile was in flight and on course. "The idea was once it came off the launch pad, they would fire and they would get the ballistic motion going," Culp noted. "In the early years, the retros were slightly overpowered and they unscrewed the rest of the rocket and it all collapsed."

On the second test-missile firing, said Culp, "they used a captive fin configuration which worked well." But not well enough, apparently. About twenty-five seconds after launch, "it basically took itself apart," apparently because of resonant vibrations that were too much for the mis-sile's structural integrity. The third test suffered a similar fate.[10]

Something obviously had to be changed. A missile coming apart over the ocean loaded with nothing but telemetry equipment was a reasonably innocuous picture, but the same scenario involving a live nuclear warhead was not acceptable. After a tense conference, the missile team decided to dump the spin rocket package and make some adjustments to the stabilizing fins. That seemed to do the trick, and a fourth test on July 24 was successful, soaring to 362 miles.

Still, that made only a total of two successes in four attempts. A 50 percent success rate might be good enough for many endeavors, but nuclear weapons demanded a far greater batting average. Unfortunately, it would have to do, because time was rapidly running out. Only three more X-17a missiles remained available, and they would all be needed for Argus. And with a long voyage ahead of her, the *Norton Sound* needed to get underway.

The *Sound* left the Navy's Pacific missile test range and returned home to Port Hueneme to get ready. Lockheed missile technicians worked twenty-four-hour shifts to finish the assembly and preparations of the remaining missiles and to get them loaded aboard ship. Sometime in those remaining few days, technicians from Sandia National Laboratory quietly loaded three 1.7 kiloton W-25 nuclear warheads aboard the *Norton Sound*, their presence known only to Captain Gralla and a select few.

Among the discreet visitors to the *Norton Sound* before her departure was a bespectacled civilian with a taciturn, serious manner: Dr. Frank Shelton, the technical director of AFSWP. "One of the things I wanted to discuss with Captain Gralla was the role and help the Sandia Corporation people would provide on board the *Norton Sound*," he recalled. "They would take care of arming, fusing, safing and firing of the nuclear weapons. Having been employed at Sandia, I was very familiar with these people." After witnessing one of the test launches on a brief trip aboard the *Sound*, Shelton returned to the Pentagon and met with Nicholas Christofilos to discuss the Explorer 4 and 5 Argus satellite measurements. Meanwhile, the ship's company was joined by Commander Bob Wertheim, who would serve as Argus missile officer.[11]

Most of the rest of the crew had no idea of what they were about to undertake. "We knew we were going on a cruise that would be about sixty days," recalled Navy electronics technician Keith Mayfield. "No information as to where or what for."[12] Dick Culp concurred: "We knew we were going to be doing something fairly major, and nobody had any idea where it was." Everyone knew that the mission would have something to do with firing missiles—that was the ship's job, after all. And obviously, it was reasonable to assume that they would be working with the same Lockheed X-17a system they'd been training and practicing on for the last couple of months. But firing the missiles from where, and carrying what, exactly? As usual in the military, such details were only for those deemed to have a "need to know," and the crew, at least for now, didn't need to know much.

Neither did many other people. "Secrecy was the watchword," Admiral Mustin confirmed. "It was thought that if the Russians found out what we were doing, they might choose several courses of action, any one of which we wouldn't like much." For one thing, given the international feeling at the time regarding atomic testing and a possible test ban, Mustin thought that one thing the Russians could do "would be to raise a big hue and cry and appeal to the ban-the-bomb freaks and so on, and get the test called off." Or on a less political, more practical level, "if things worked out more or less as expected, they [the Russians] could put up some instrumentation, too. They could learn a lot of technical results from our test and perhaps get as much information out of it as we did."[13]

Security and secrecy involved not merely silence, but outright deception. "There was a lot of both cold weather and tropical weather gear brought aboard, so there was a lot of speculation as to where we were going," Keith Mayfield said.[14] The word went out that the Navy was going to be conducting unspecified test operations in the Arctic. Crew members were even shown films about the Arctic and cold weather operations. Such subterfuge extended all the way up the chain of command and beyond as *Norton Sound* departed Port Hueneme at 6 PM on August 1st, sailing for parts unknown to most.

"We had an elaborate cover scheme," Mustin recalled. "She sailed from Point Mugu, Port Hueneme. She sailed west, and she was bound for test operations in the Pacific, ostensibly." Unlike most vessels traveling from the Pacific to the Atlantic, the *Sound* would avoid the Panama Canal.

As AFSWP technical director Frank Shelton explained, "We did not send the ship through the Panama Canal for security reasons. The Russians noted all naval vessels transiting the Canal."[15]

Mustin continued, "All of the ship's radio traffic was broadcast on the Pacific Fleet schedule. And we had made arrangements that all this traffic was then recorded by a naval communications station somewhere, I've forgotten where, encrypted in full, including the call signs—we didn't have encrypted call signs in those days—and rebroadcast on the Atlantic schedule. So she, to anyone trying to find out anything about her by radio traffic analysis, was still in the Pacific, obviously, because traffic addressed to her was being transmitted to the Pacific. But it was reaching her completely covered."[16] Another tactic was the use of plain-language cover messages containing coded meanings.

With the ship safely underway and any contact with the outside world now strictly controlled, the crew learned a few more tantalizing details. "The crew was informed that we would be going to the South Atlantic," said missile telemetry crewman Ken McMaster.[17] Recalled Dick Culp, "It was after we left. That's when they told us we'd be going around Cape Horn and firing in the South Atlantic. That's basically all they told us."[18] Until the end of Argus—a term that even the *Sound*'s crew had not yet heard—the *Norton Sound* would be a ghost ship, alone, silent, cruising toward a mysterious rendezvous in the middle of nowhere on a most secret mission.

Which, of course, only encouraged speculation both above and below decks. "During the cruise I learned, through scuttlebutt, that we had atomic warheads aboard," Ken McMaster remembered. Were they for testing purposes, scientific research, or was the *Sound* on her way to begin World War III? No one knew for sure, but such questions made for spirited discussions around the wardroom and in the berthing spaces.

The crew of the *Sound* had other distractions, however. Captain Gralla kept the missile-handling teams busy with repeated drills and simulated launches, not just in good weather and daylight but at night in the poorest conditions they could find. They practiced wrestling the X-17a onto its portable launch trailer on the *Norton Sound*'s fantail deck, trying to de-

termine the worst conditions under which a launch might still be conducted. After much trial and error, the missileers found that launching was
possible in winds of up to forty knots and sea swells up to sixteen feet,
which were fairly alarming, if not uncommon, conditions. Finally, the crew
demonstrated that they could get a missile out of storage, rolled out on the
deck, secured in place, and erected in firing position in just about forty-
five minutes. No one realized quite yet just how valuable all this exhaustive
practice was going to prove.

In the days after *Norton Sound* set sail for the South Atlantic, the eight
other vessels of Task Force 88 left their ports on the East Coast, including
the *Albemarle*, the oiler *Neosho*, the destroyer *Warrington*, and the venerable
aircraft carrier USS *Tarawa*, which would serve as Admiral Mustin's flagship for the task force. Most of the ships sailed south, while the *Albemarle*
headed for station at the Azores. Operating under the same strict security
blackout as the *Norton Sound*, the crews aboard these vessels kept occupied
with their own drills and exercises, which included launching small
Loki/Dart antiaircraft missiles at sea to practice radar tracking and other
Argus support functions.

Far above the Atlantic and Pacific, in an orbit ranging from 164 to
1381 miles, Explorer 4 was ready. It had been launched on schedule at 10
AM on July 26 from the Cape Canaveral Air Force Missile Test Center, just
in time for the Teak test that closed out the month. The Teak and subsequent Orange shots provided a bit of a shakedown for Explorer 4, but were
still at far too low an altitude to do much more than gently tickle Van
Allen's onboard instruments. Most of the charged particles emitted by the
blasts were soaked up in the dense lower atmosphere, as expected. But the
satellite and its instrument package had proved to be healthy, functioning,
and ready for Argus.

Unfortunately, Explorer 4 would be conducting its spaceborne observations of Argus all alone. After several delays, its intended companion,
Explorer 5, launched from Cape Canaveral on the morning of August 24.
But the final stage of the Jupiter C missile failed to fire, and Explorer 5,
along with Van Allen's painstakingly designed and crafted instrument
package, fell back to sea to a final destination at the bottom of the Atlantic.

No matter. All was in motion: plans made, ships sailing, everything coming together. The first phase of Operation HARDTACK was wrapping up in the Pacific, to be followed by its Nevada phase in the fall, and then, assuming that international agreements and political goodwill prevailed, the nuclear test moratorium would take effect, for however long that goodwill persisted. Back at Lawrence Livermore Laboratory in California, Nicholas Christofilos knew that the Argus tests would be among America's last nuclear tests for quite a while—perhaps even forever, if some people got their way. If his theories were going to be proven correct, if he was going to be vindicated, this was the time, the only opportunity he might ever have.

It was now or never.

CHAPTER 6
The Farthest Place on Earth

FOR MOST PEOPLE, THE SOUTH ATLANTIC OCEAN IS LESS A DESTINATION than just a place to pass through on the way to somewhere else. Very few tourists or other casual visitors venture there, probably due to the lack of amenities and easy communications with the outside world. Admiral Mustin described it as "almost a maritime desert. It's just been a place that people stayed away from."[1] All of which made it a perfect stage for Operation Argus

Mustin, now aboard his flagship *Tarawa* and leading Task Force 88 southward, busied himself with various preparations. His meteorology officer had discovered weather maps of the South Atlantic drawn years before by South African observers, and poring over them gave Mustin a good idea of the fickle and infinitely changeable weather patterns in the area. Mustin brought together the captains of the other TF 88 vessels for highly secret briefings, ferrying them over to the *Tarawa* by helicopter. "I had told them what we were going to do, and why we were going to do it; and what the security implications were, and what the hazard implications were; and that they could tell no living soul except their exec [executive officer], and he could tell nobody," said Mustin.[2]

Launching the Loki sounding rockets from the deck of the destroyer USS *Warrington* gave the task force practice at radar tracking and detection. "This gave us a pretty good rehearsal," Mustin recalled. "It also added a lot of visible activity, of a perfectly innocent nature, for all the ships' crews and so on to see. The story was that we were doing some high-altitude experiments."[3]

The *Tarawa* and her aircrews also had the opportunity to practice what would be one of her main duties during the Argus operation: maintaining security. "We knew that we would need a considerable degree of surveillance around the area, for safety's sake and others," Mustin said. Airplanes and helicopters from the *Tarawa* would patrol a perimeter around the task force, keeping an eye out for Russian trawlers, submarines, and other suspicious observers. None were definitively sighted, but Mustin was ready for them, with plans in place to turn away from any unwanted company and if necessary even split up the task force, spread out his ships over a wide area, and rendezvous again later at some predetermined point.

An ocean away on the other side of the planet, *Norton Sound* continued ahead on her own solitary odyssey. The missile handling and launching drills were briefly interrupted by the traditional "shellback" initiation festivities for the "pollywog" crewmen who were crossing the equator for the first time. It provided a mostly welcome diversion from below-decks scuttlebutt, daily routine, and the mysterious mission on which the vessel was embarked, the details of which were still unknown to most of the crew. The official "Crossing the Line" certificates awarded to the new shellbacks had been among the various supplies loaded aboard the *Sound* and the other task force vessels before departure—in cartons all labeled Top Secret and delivered personally to ship captains in order to preserve security.[4]

Another highlight for the *Sound* crewmen came a few days later on August 17, as the ship went "round the Horn" of South America and entered the Atlantic. Becoming a shellback and going around the Horn on the same voyage granted them the exalted status of "horned shellbacks"—something of which few US sailors could boast.

It was obvious by now that whatever the *Norton Sound*'s ultimate destination, it was not going to be a tropical paradise, nor would it be the Arctic. But the transition from summer in the Northern hemisphere to winter in the Southern hemisphere was striking and obvious, marked not merely by the occasional iceberg passing by but also with the icy winds and choppy seas that lashed the ship. With a length of 540 feet and beam of almost seventy feet, the *Sound* was a fairly large vessel. The design of her hull made her stable to roll, but, as Mustin noted, "surprisingly prone to pitch." As sea and weather conditions grew steadily more challenging, the value of all the practice drills insisted upon by Captain Gralla at the onset of the cruise became clear.

After steaming south for most of her voyage thus far, the *Norton Sound* now headed north, bound for the farthest place on Earth. The first vessel to arrive on her assigned station was much farther north, the *Albemarle*, which took up her post in the Azores on August 23. Meanwhile, the rest of Task Force 88 arrived in the Argus operational area, the lee of Gough Island in the Tristan da Cunha archipelago, miles from the nearest land. "The weather was lousy," said Mustin. "Gigantic swells were rolling past." But then, they had been expecting as much.

Fortunately, they wouldn't have long to wait for the star performer of the upcoming show. Late that afternoon, lookouts on the *Norton Sound* reported to Captain Gralla that they had sighted the *Tarawa*. The *Sound*'s radioman dispatched a droll message to Task Force 88: "Doctor Livingstone, I presume?"

One of the most unusual military operations in the history of the world had officially begun. In the next several days, the men aboard this small flotilla in the middle of nowhere would attempt to do something that had never been done before.

As the military contingent of Argus continued to gear up, so did the scientific corps. Data tapes from Explorer 4 poured into the Iowa City lab bearing data from Teak and Orange, all of which needed to be reduced and analyzed before the impending Argus shots added to the already impossible workload of Ludwig, McIlwain, and the other Van Allen acolytes. The failure of the Explorer 5 launch added to the pressure, since it left Explorer 4 the sole orbital observation post for Argus.

But there would still be some backup for Explorer. While the Explorers, blessed with the official imprimatur of the International Geophysical Year, were at this point the only public operation connected with Argus (though not, of course, to the public's knowledge), other preparations were also coming together in August 1958. One was an audacious, frantically conducted effort by the Navy, originally conceived in the rush of post-Sputnik panic less than a year earlier.

Officially, the Navy already had a dog in the fight for American satellite dominance with the Vanguard program, notorious for its embarrassing launch failure on December 6, 1957. While the Army Ballistic Missile Agency (ABMA) famously saved America's pride at the end of the following month with Explorer 1, Vanguard also redeemed itself not long afterward by finally launching the second US satellite on March 17. The Vanguard project was destined to be taken over by civilian hands upon the birth of NASA on October 1, 1958.

Unofficially, however, while Vanguard and ABMA vied to even the satellite score with the Soviets as well as each other, the people at the Naval Ordnance Test Station (NOTS) in China Lake, California, where the Navy developed and tested weapons under top secrecy, had their own ideas. At first they focused on the conventional concept of launching satellites from the ground, but the ABMA had a lock on the requisite rocket technology. Then, an inspiration: what if a smaller rocket was launched from a jet fighter at high altitude to kick a satellite into space?

Much like Argus, it was another of those "so crazy it just might work" notions that flourished in the frenzied atmosphere of the Cold War, and the NOTS scientists and engineers set to work devising Project Pilot, later unofficially but universally dubbed NOTSNIK (NOTS for Naval Ordnance Test Station, with the -NIK suffix as a nod to Sputnik). The NOTS team proposed using a specially-modified Douglas Skyray F4D-1 jet to launch a small multistage rocket carrying an even smaller satellite. The reporters who had derided Vanguard's first unsuccessful satellite as an aluminum grapefruit would have been even more amused by the NOTSNIK satellite package, an eight-inch-diameter plastic donut stuffed with rudimentary electronics weighing just over two pounds.

Still, the NOTS team managed to wrangle some research money out of Navy officials in Washington, and set to work under complete secrecy, hoping to startle the world. In a canny move, they soon got more money by proposing that NOTSNIK could serve as a backup for Explorer 4's Argus observations. That hope became the driving force for the project—under, as with most everything else associated with Argus, impossible deadlines.

Unfortunately, despite its best intentions and clever conception, NOTSNIK would turn out much as Vanguard's first effort, though thankfully wholly out of the public eye. Several launch attempts in late July and in August before the Argus shots were all unsuccessful, and the Navy pulled the plug. Still, some of the NOTSNIK ground stations did manage to collect some useful Argus data from Explorer 4 to supplement other observations. (It would not be the end of the concept of aircraft-launched space vehicles. The Air Force would revisit the idea in the 1980s as a possible means not of launching satellites, but of shooting them down.)

The quiet failure of NOTSNIK didn't leave Explorer 4 entirely on its own, however, nor would the Navy get all of the Argus action. While the Navy was busy assembling task forces and attempting to launch rockets from fighter planes, the Air Force Special Weapons Center was preparing Project Jason, in which a series of high-altitude sounding rockets would be simultaneously launched from various sites along the East Coast to pierce the expected Argus radiation belt and make scientific measurements.

Though scheduled to coincide with the Argus launches, one Jason experiment was conducted early, both as a sort of dress rehearsal and also to provide a calibration measurement for the later shots. On August 15, several days after the Orange high-altitude nuclear test over Johnston Island in the Pacific, a Jason rocket was launched from Patrick Air Force

Base at Cape Canaveral. As with the Jason shots that would follow, it was a five-stage solid-fuel rocket loaded with instrumentation, including radiation sensors and telemetry equipment. The three sites set for the big show were Patrick; the National Advisory Committee for Aeronautics (NACA) station at Wallops Island, Virginia; and Ramey Air Force Base in Puerto Rico, with each station respectively dubbed Papa, Whiskey, and Romeo. Shortly after the Argus rockets left the deck of the *Norton Sound*, each site would send forth its rockets. Since they would penetrate the presumed Argus radiation shell from the ground up in a more or less perpendicular direction, and only for a brief period, the Jason sounding rockets weren't expected to provide as comprehensive a data picture as that expected from Explorer 4. Still, they would serve as an important complement to and perhaps confirmation of whatever Explorer had to report.

Argus would also be heavily monitored from below, an effort officially designated as Project Midas. This would include the observations from Task Force 88 vessels, including the *Albemarle* at the North Atlantic conjugate point, as well as ground stations and aircraft from airbases in Portugal and Spain. Further monitoring would be conducted at other locations around the globe.

Whether visual phenomena, geomagnetic disturbances, radio interference, or something else completely unexpected, the effects of Argus were not about to go unobserved. Everyone involved realized that here was a unique opportunity that might never come again.

BACK IN THE FRIGID, TURBULENT SOUTH ATLANTIC ABOARD THE *TARAWA*, Admiral Mustin was worried about the weather.

It was not looking good. His meteorologist, Commander Max C. Jack, had continued to study whatever historical data he could find about weather patterns in the area. Most of the major storms in the South Atlantic, he discovered, appeared to originate around two major points: one just off the tip of South America, and the other near Buenos Aires. After formation, a storm would usually follow a very predictable path eastward across the Atlantic. Whichever origin point, the paths happened to converge in a most unfortunate location: "the spot that was our chosen launch point," Mustin remembered.[5]

But that was only in theory. Reality was bad enough. "It snowed and all sorts of things," Mustin said. "It really was truly winter. It would be bright sun one minute, and just horizontally driving snow the next. Wind from the east, wind from the west, whoever knew what. These circular storms would go by."[6] Even routine operations, such as refueling the task force vessels from the oiler *Neosho*, became hazardous tests of endurance in the rough, cold seas.

The only up-to-date weather observations available came from low-power radio stations broadcasting from South Africa, Rio de Janeiro, Buenos Aires, or the Falkland Islands, and reception was spotty at best. Since the presence and purpose of Task Force 88 remained top secret, direct inquiries to outside civilian weather stations were out of the question. Further complicating matters was the fact that it was generally impossible to apply whatever limited data could be obtained from South American stations and those in South Africa to make any kind of coherent forecast. Mustin decided to deploy the two destroyer escorts in Task Force 88 to serve as a weather picket. "The reason was that the prevailing winds were from the west, and the storms approached from the west," he said. "These little ships were better in that kind of heavy weather than the World War II destroyers" (also serving in Task Force 88). The two destroyer escorts took turns on weather station, deploying about three hundred miles west of the main task force, which gave the main force about seven hours advance warning of bad weather.[7]

It was going to be a day-to-day, hour-to-hour situation. The value of the repeated missile drills, both those in good weather off Point Mugu on the other side of the world and those conducted in forty-knot winds and sixteen-foot swells was becoming painfully obvious. The Argus shots were not going to go off in ideal conditions.

As the man in charge of the entire ball game, Mustin had more to think about than simply launching atomic missiles off of a ship. The weather would also play a key factor in the observations that could be made and the data that would be collected. The worldwide network of other observers on sea, earth, air, and in space would be unaffected by the weather in the South Atlantic, but that was still where the action was going to happen, the ringside seat. The other ships of Task Force 88 would be conducting their own observations, as would specially instrumented aircraft from the *Tarawa*. Heavy cloud cover, much less snow and wind, would spoil the show for everyone, not to mention increasing the hazards. Mustin noted that he didn't much like the idea of his aircraft "up there in the dark, above the clouds, then coming down through a 20,000-foot cloud layer, to land in the black of night on a deck with blowing snow on it."[8]

For Argus to work, the X-17a missile had to be launched from the *Norton Sound* at a nearly vertical trajectory, which meant being able to predict and compensate for the winds as precisely as possible. The missile launcher was not designed for continuous adjustments, "like, for example, a modern naval gun that stays aimed at a fixed point in space while the ship moves around underneath it," Mustin explained.[9] Because of the great acceleration of the missile, the wind would have little if any effect after launch, but launching at a proper trajectory was critical.

One small consolation, both for Admiral Mustin and the task force crew in general, was that fallout was not going to be an issue. Almost all other atomic tests in the Pacific and in Nevada had to pay close attention to the weather not just to ensure optimal conditions at test time but also to predict and prepare for possible fallout wind patterns after the shot. With the Argus detonations occurring at an altitude of several hundred miles above the earth, there was no reasonable possibility of fallout. Whatever else happened, there would be no Castle Bravo/*Lucky Dragon* fiasco with Argus.

The issue of radiological safety had been a somewhat delicate subject for Argus planners, however. The typical procedure, as practiced for nuclear tests in the Pacific, was to issue film badges to all personnel who might conceivably be exposed to radiation. But in those cases, everyone knew going in that they were about to participate in a nuclear test.

Not so with Argus, being conducted in utmost secrecy at the bottom of the world. "The security aspects of the Argus experiments precluded the operation of the type of radiological safety program that is common to nuclear testing," said the final task force report, adding ominously, "It was therefore decided that the interests of the government should be protected against possible future lawsuits by a radiological safety program that would not reveal to personnel of the task force that nuclear testing was involved in their operations."[10]

Although as per standard practice, the Navy had obtained four thousand film badges, enough to supply every member of the task force if necessary, they were actually given only to select people, those already aware of the true nature of Argus. *Norton Sound* crewman Dick Culp wasn't one of them. After developing bladder cancer later in life, he eventually received $75,000 through a compensation program established by the Department of Justice in 1990 for veterans who contracted certain types of cancer linked to atmospheric atomic testing. "I think there were a fair number of people who actually got compensation for that," he recalled. "And even some that were not out on the high decks. In the engine room there were a couple of them that I know were compensated." But without any kind of radiological exposure records, a direct causal link is impossible to establish. "Basically, if you could prove you were on the ship and you had medical records that proved you had one of the selected cancers, you got your payment," said Culp. "I don't know that anything can be taken from [that], other than it happened."[11]

Said Mustin, "We couldn't accept issuing every man in the task force a film badge . . . because this would establish beyond a shadow of a doubt the nuclear association of what we were going to do. We simply couldn't afford to have that revealed until quite a bit after the fact."[12]

So only select personnel, including the pilots of the aircraft who would conduct airborne observations and the personnel aboard the *Norton Sound* directly involved in handling the nuclear warheads, received radiation film badges. Additional film packets were surreptitiously placed in exposed open-air locations on all the task force ships to monitor post-shot radiation, if any. Meanwhile, during the shots, the *Norton*

Sound would be buttoned up as tightly as possible under the same precautions prescribed for an atomic attack—just in case.

Such precautions, of course, did not preclude the possibility of a launch mishap bringing a 1.7-kiloton nuclear warhead down in the middle of the sea to obliterate Task Force 88.

The troublesome weather also helped to somewhat mitigate another concern, namely operational security. The *Tarawa* had already been conducting routine air patrols twice a day with her squadron of Grumman S2F Tracker fixed-wing aircraft, ensuring that no unwanted company came near the task force, whether accidentally or intentionally. While the patrols continued in the lead up to the test shots, the bad weather did help to ease fears about uninvited guests in the form of Russian submarines or fishing trawlers.

With Explorer 4 also up and humming along in orbit, yet another complication arrived for Mustin to deal with. "We were supposed to launch [the missile] so as to get the detonation at a time when the satellite was in a certain spot on its path around the earth."

It all amounted to an intricate operational dance of ships and aircraft, which also had to be coordinated with the *Albemarle* up north at the magnetic conjugate point, the Jason sounding rockets, Midas observation planes, ground observers, and all the other monitoring stations around the world.

But there was time for one more dress rehearsal. On August 25 and 26, the *Norton Sound* fired off four small Deacon sounding rockets to simulate the main event, giving everyone a chance to practice their jobs and coordinate techniques. One of the most challenging jobs fell to the Grumman S2F Tracker aircraft. "We wanted—if we could get it—to have some kind of visual observation above the clouds. So quite a while before launch time, we would launch four S2Fs to struggle up to get on top of the clouds, which really was just about at, if not slightly above, their intended operating ceiling," explained Mustin. The S2F was, after all, designed as an antisubmarine aircraft, intended to operate at relatively low altitudes above the water to search for enemy subs, not to pierce the heavens like a jet fighter. Unlike fighter aircraft, they also didn't carry oxygen for the crews to accommodate high-altitude operations. The crews had portable oxygen equipment, but that limited their range.

"We would station them such that, at a certain point in the countdown, the four planes would be at the four corners of a square, centered above the launching ship. Each one would start in the same direction around the perimeter of this square so that, hopefully, when the rocket went by, they'd be in a position . . . [to] get a pretty good look at it."[13]

Aboard the *Norton Sound*, Lockheed personnel along with select Navy missilemen and Sandia technicians prepared the first X-17a for launch. With the missiles on their portable wheeled gantry, "getting them out there [on deck] in the weather was rather interesting," missileman Dick Culp wryly recalled.[14] Again, this was where the repeated practice drills—not to mention the heavy cold-weather gear that had been loaded aboard back in Hueneme—paid off.

The September 1st deadline was rapidly approaching, the weather was closing in, and time was running out. The countdown to the first shot began.

CHAPTER 7
Earth in a Shroud

ANOTHER COLD AND ICY NIGHT IN THE TRACKLESS VOID OF THE SOUTH ATLANTIC. Somewhere in the darkness, a small group of men clad in heavy hooded parkas clustered around a missile launcher on the fantail of the USS *Norton Sound*, illuminated only by a set of makeshift floodlights mounted on poles. As they worked, a biting wind whipped around them, blowing snowflakes across the deck, whirling around the tall, thin missile resting on the launcher, and passing beyond into the inky blackness of the ocean.

Their preparations completed, they slowly, cautiously, began raising the missile to its fully upright launch position. As it rose, seeming to grow in stature against the dark skies, some of the men rested their gloved hands on guide ropes or the launcher frame, as if to urge the missile on, or perhaps, to reassure themselves. Atop the narrow structure of the missile, looking like the end of a Q-Tip, was an odd bulge: a small nuclear warhead.

Finally the men withdrew, leaving the Lockheed X-17a missile alone on the deck, standing in defiance of the choppy twenty-five-knot winds that occasionally shook it on its launch platform. Everyone knew those winds weren't nearly strong enough to tip over the forty-foot, six-ton rocket with its nuclear warhead, much less the launch gantry. Or so they hoped.

Most of the ship's crew, save for the launch technicians and a select few others, were below decks and behind closed hatches, their only connection with the event about to transpire consisting of terse announcements over the ship's public address system. In the superstructure above deck, in the command spaces and telemetry room and radio shack, officers and sailors busied themselves watching instruments, staying in contact with the other ships and aircraft of the task force, and waiting.

The final command to fire the missile and send it on its spectacular one-way journey would come not from a human being, but from a machine. When the ship's skipper, Captain Arthur Gralla, issued the order, an officer would press an "intent to launch" button that released control of the firing to an analog computer system tied into the gyroscopes deep within the *Norton Sound* that helped her navigate. Only when the constantly moving deck of the ship and the waiting missile atop it were at the properly determined angle would the Thiokol XM20 Sergeant solid-fuel first stage fire with its forty-eight thousand pounds of thrust and start the rocket on its way.

Gralla's command was accepted and executed at 0220 hours Greenwich Meridian Time on August 27, 1958. Even in the unsteady seas, everyone aboard felt the ship's stern momentarily drop with a shudder under the sudden thrust of the missile, the brilliant light of its first-stage engine revealing other vessels of the task force nearby. Then the ship steadied and the light congealed into a hurtling, glowing ball, followed by a mere point of bright light and then nothing at all, as the missile vanished into the heavy cloud layer above. In a few minutes, if all went well, the skies would be illuminated again by the detonation of the 1.7-kiloton warhead far above.

The missile technicians and the crew of the *Norton Sound* breathed a well-earned sigh of relief. Whatever else happened, the X-17a had been fired safely and successfully, and there was now one fewer atomic warhead on board. They had made some history: for the first time, an atomic ballistic missile had been fired from the deck of a ship at sea. Argus 1 was on schedule.

Unfortunately, it was not quite on target.

"There was something wrong, and we couldn't be sure just what it was," recalled Admiral Mustin. "The first thing we were sure of was that our calculations of the ballistic wind, and its effect on the weather cocking of the rocket, had been wrong. The rocket had not achieved a vertical trajectory." As the rocket climbed higher, tracking radars picked it up and calculated its course, and at least two of the S2F aircraft in the murky sky above the ocean had managed to see the rocket trail. The rocket was not about to fall back onto the task force or any other unsuspecting people on Earth, but it was quickly becoming apparent that it was not going to achieve its planned altitude.

Mustin initially suspected that the rocket's second stage had somehow failed to fire. Later analysis more or less concluded that a combination of the tricky, ever-shifting winds nudging the Argus 1 missile unpredictably, along with errors in the trajectory firing calculations, had resulted in an improper launching angle. It remained to be seen whether the final altitude of the warhead detonation would be enough to achieve the Argus effect and vindicate the predictions of the "Crazy Greek."

The W-25 warhead dutifully exploded about seven minutes after departing the deck of the *Norton Sound*, at an altitude of about 110 miles and a position of 38.5 degrees south latitude and 11.5 degrees west longitude. The pilot of one of the S2F aircraft was flying at 22,000 feet and reported "a great luminous ball" about 40 degrees above the horizon. Back on the surface of the ocean, the few men standing outside on the *Norton Sound*, as well as a somewhat larger audience topside on the other task force vessels, saw the cloud layer above them glow brightly from horizon to horizon, flickering, then dimming. There was no sound save for the cold, howling winds.[1]

Those who saw the fireworks, such as they were, of Argus were fortunate. Particularly aboard the *Norton Sound*, most of the participants saw little or nothing of the fruits of their months-long work. "We opened the hatches," recalled Quintin Owens, one of the tracking radar operators aboard the *Sound*. "The sky lit up brightly with a green tint." Dick Culp didn't even see that much, working in the telemetry station. Ken McMaster recalls watching the launch while standing in a hatch near the hangar door—"the noise and fire [were] frightening"—but he didn't see the detonation at all.

At first, Argus 1 seemed to be pretty much a dud, at least scientifically speaking. The warhead had obviously detonated, but not at an optimal altitude, probably too low for any definitive results. But the visual observers, at least those who were airborne, certainly got their money's worth. "For the next 30 minutes the aircrew observed and photographed an awesome auroral display as colors and shapes changed," noted a government report.[2] The witnesses down at sea level weren't as fortunate; the cloud cover prevented them from seeing much beyond the initial flash of the explosion.

Still, the presence of auroral phenomena was a good sign that something was going on up there. About an hour after detonation, the first of the Jason rockets was launched from Patrick Air Force Base at Cape Canaveral. In the ensuing hours, three more launch attempts were made from Patrick, Ramey, and Wallops, but only one was successful.

Martin Walt, a young physicist with Lockheed working under contract with the Air Force for the Argus project, was sitting in the telemetry center at the Cape, eyes glued to an oscilloscope, watching for signals from the radiation detectors aboard the rockets. "I watched intently during the 10-minute flights," he recalled. Every one hundred seconds, he took readings and plotted the data, looking to confirm that the rocket had passed through the Argus band of electrons. "The results were disappointing as only the normal background had registered. At that point we ceased launching and reported that no significant effects had been seen"[3] —most likely because of the errant trajectory and relatively low altitude of Argus 1.

Those farther north in the Atlantic, up near the conjugate point in the Azores where the *Albemarle* was waiting, didn't get to enjoy the show that the southern observers had witnessed. An Air Force C-97 observer plane reported an orange glow in the sky about twenty-two minutes after the detonation, and strong radar echoes were picked up by the *Albemarle* and other monitoring stations in the area, but no auroras or other visual fireworks were evident.

It took Explorer 4 to demonstrate conclusively that there was indeed an Argus effect. About three and a half hours after Argus 1, the satellite passed through the geographical region where the Argus radiation shell was expected to form. Sure enough, Van Allen's instruments immediately began registering a sharp rise in electron flux, far above the natural background that had been carefully monitored and confirmed previously by Explorer 1 and over the past several weeks by Explorer 4. "The 'Argus effect' was easily and promptly observed," Van Allen wrote later in a paper. "The great peak which was intersected at 0608 UT on August 27 had no precedent in four weeks of previous observations of the natural radiation. Moreover, it was encountered on the first observed intersection with the planned magnetic shell following the Argus I detonation."[4] Repeated passes by Explorer 4 showed an electron shell extending and spreading, following the Earth's natural magnetic field lines—just as Christofilos had predicted.

Still, it wasn't much of a payoff, considering the enormous amount of effort that had been expended thus far on the entire project. Even if the first shot had been an unqualified success, another shot, which would provide more confirming data, would have been an irresistible proposition. Since the results of this first attempt had been rather equivocal at best, and since the *Norton Sound* was already in place with two more missiles and atomic warheads at the ready, not to mention the rest of the task force, why not try again? The powers-that-be certainly agreed. "Because of the negative results from other projects . . . headquarters concluded that a second shot was required,"[5] said an official history. Mustin recalled, "We told Washington . . . we were getting ready to launch the second one."[6] In a terse cable to the Pentagon about Argus 1's faulty trajectory, he said, "Still seeking reasons."[7]

Because the *Albemarle* and other northerly-located forces hadn't seen much, the decision was made to change the launching site and thus the detonation point, which would move the all-important magnetic conjugate point farther north and hopefully closer to the Azores and the *Albemarle*. Mustin took his flotilla farther south, closer to the South Pole and into even colder, less hospitable seas. Sailors aboard the *Norton Sound* and the other vessels amused themselves by snapping pictures of passing icebergs.

Meanwhile, the Lockheed missile technicians checked and rechecked their charges. "These rockets were really just castoffs," Mustin noted. "They were the leftovers of an earlier phase of the Polaris program, modified to our purpose." That was the reason for the "a" part of their X-17a designation. "The main thing to calculate was how far off the vertical must we launch this thing so that it would fly a vertical track."[8] Nobody wanted another wonky trajectory, as with the first shot.

By the night of August 29, everyone was on station. The S2F planes were once again aloft, flying their observation box pattern. The weather was once again marginal, with winds at twenty-two knots, but everyone was used to that by now. Unfortunately, at about quarter after ten that evening, the missile beacon system began to malfunction. By the time it was fixed, it was well after midnight. Finally, at 3:10 AM, Argus 2 left the deck of the *Norton Sound*.

This time, things looked better. "We were satisfied that it had gone vertical," Mustin said. "Everybody in the planes caught it right where it ought to be, as it came up . . . and our radar plots showed it going vertical."[9]

The trajectory was good. Then a different problem: once again, the missile was not reaching proper altitude. "They saw the second stage ignite, but they didn't see the third stage," Mustin said.[10] Several minutes later, the sky again lit up from horizon to horizon as the warhead detonated. Except for the aircrews, however, the light show was more disappointing than with the first shot, not only for Mustin and his South Atlantic forces but also for the *Albemarle* up north, again thanks to heavy cloud cover. Neither the observer aircraft nor the radar stations in the North Atlantic detected much, if anything, from Argus 2. No aurora, no glow in the sky, no doubt to their considerable disappointment.

The Jason team was considerably more successful, however. This time, they managed to successfully launch ten out of twelve rockets, beginning just under half an hour after Argus 2 and continuing until about four days later. The readings from the rocket instruments provided a good picture of the Argus 2 radiation belt. "We all felt elated at that point," Walt remembered.

And Explorer 4 came through again as well, although with a bit of confusion. The initial data reports seemed to be coming from an orbital position that should have coincided with the Argus 1 shot, not the Argus 2 event. Finally the analysts realized that Explorer 4's course had shifted several minutes in latitude, throwing off the predictions. Compensating for the orbital shift solved the discrepancy; the Explorer data nicely complemented the Jason results as well. "The rocket instrumentation was more elaborate and gave the best determination of the energy spectrum of the electrons," explained Walt.[11]

"But we hadn't done what we set out to do, so we got the third rocket ready," Mustin remembered.[12] The third and final Argus shot would prove to be the most memorable of them all.

MUSTIN AND THE REST OF TASK FORCE 88, NOT TO MENTION ALL THE OFFICIALS at the Pentagon and ARPA and Lawrence Livermore Laboratory and everyone else even tangentially aware of Argus, had done everything possible to maintain the most scrupulous security from the very beginnings of the enterprise. No less a personage than President Eisenhower himself had emphasized from the start that Argus had to remain top secret for reasons both military and political. Even by the time atomic warheads began exploding in the midwinter darkness over the South Atlantic, many of the participants in Argus, from the sailors at sea to technicians at ground observation posts and labs around the world, still had only a vague notion of what was really going on.

So confidence in the clandestine nature of the proceedings remained high. Even Frank Shelton, Argus technical director, was confident that it would be possible to "indefinitely maintain that [Argus] had never occurred."[13]

Unfortunately, secrecy and security are concepts of the human mind, not the natural universe. As scientists such as Albert Einstein, J. Robert Oppenheimer, and their brethren throughout history have repeatedly warned those in power, the so-called "secrets" of nature are open to anyone and everyone who cares to discover them, whether they involve how to make a fire, carve a better arrowhead, or build an atomic bomb.

Van Allen's discovery of the natural radiation belts girdling the Earth did more than simply galvanize Nicholas Christofilos into making Argus a reality. It also inspired countless other scientists around the world and aroused their scientific curiosity and inventiveness, getting them to ask questions and propose experiments to find answers. Among them were Edward Ney and Paul Kellogg, a pair of scientists from the University of Minnesota.

"Upon hearing of the Earth's newly discovered trapped radiation in May 1958, [they] suggested that a nuclear device might be detonated some 250 miles high near the southern auroral zone to see what effect it might have on the radiation belt," George Ludwig recounted.[14] There was no frantic talk about stopping Soviet missiles or defending the US from the Red hordes, or knocking out enemy satellites that might be spying on us or preparing to drop H-bombs on America from outer space. Ney and Kellogg were simply scientists, excited about a new discovery and eager to explore its nature and implications, for no motivation or purpose other than pure intellectual curiosity. "Those discussions took place in the absence of any knowledge by Ed or Paul of the Argus Project," Ludwig emphasized.[15] Perhaps, thought Ney and Kellogg, the concept would be an interesting project for the ongoing International Geophysical Year, a way to extend Van Allen's discovery into new areas of spaceflight and experimentation.

They took their idea to friends in Washington at the Office of Naval Research, the same folks who had been launching (or trying to launch) Vanguard satellites. The response was decidedly chilly. Cease and desist, the researchers were told in no uncertain terms—though they were not told why. Undeterred, Ney and Kellogg next decided to approach Herbert York at ARPA, but were firmly dissuaded from that notion as well.

Finally, they settled on the time-honored practice of all scientists: publishing in the open scientific literature, in this case, the venerable journal *Nature*. "When the Pentagon learned of that, their consternation changed to full-blown alarm," wrote Ludwig.[16] Gently but firmly, Ney and Kellogg were persuaded to hold off on publishing their work. No, we can't explain why, but you'll find out soon enough.

However, Ney and Kellogg might have been spared some grief had anyone at the Pentagon or CIA pondered the universality of nature and the evanescence of supposed "secrets." Less than a year later, on March 8, 1959, two Russian scientists, I.S. Shklovskiy (who would later become famous for his ideas on extraterrestrial intelligence and his work with Carl Sagan) and V.I. Krasovskiy published an article in the Soviet newspaper *Izvestiya* reporting the detection of high-energy particles in the lower Van Allen belt—speculating that the phenomenon might be artificial. "It is not to be excluded that this zone has, if we may say so, an artificial origin," they wrote. "High-altitude explosions would be fully sufficient for the formation of the lower zone of fast charged particles."[17] In their article, the researchers referred to some of the recent US tests in Nevada that had been conducted from high towers or balloons.

Such musings by Soviet scientists did not, of course, mean that the USSR either knew anything about Argus or was plotting such experiments itself. But it's clear that Christofilos was hardly alone in his wild ideas of atomic bombs and radiation belts. "The idea of injecting charged particles into the Earth's magnetic field by nuclear detonations did, as it turned out, also occur independently to the Soviets," as Ludwig wrote. "It is unknown when the idea first occurred to them—it might have been either before or after they learned of our discovery of the region of high-intensity radiation."[18]

A survey of foreign scientific literature on ionospheric research conducted for the US Congress about ten years after Argus noted, "It would appear much more likely from subsequent Soviet articles, however, that not only the USSR, but other countries, had foreknowledge of the [Argus] tests and were monitoring them."[19] That was a thought that would certainly have given Admiral Mustin, Nicholas Christofilos, not to mention President Eisenhower, a severe case of insomnia. The report also noted that the worldwide monitoring efforts encouraged and supported by the IGY program would have made the conduct of secret nuclear tests such as Argus very difficult if not impossible, another thought of which the Argus people were already keenly and painfully aware.

While Admiral Mustin's patrolling S2F aircraft and destroyer screen kept away any nosy Soviet trawlers or submarines from the Argus operational area, the global nature of the Argus experiments and their effects couldn't be so easily contained. Ludwig observed that "The Soviets also had ample opportunity to see the results of the Argus tests by receiving the *Explorer IV* signals at their receiving stations. On one specific occasion, as *Explorer IV* was transiting one of the Argus-generated shells, it was easily within range of their Tashkent receiving station."[20] Even worse, it wasn't just the Russians: similar French geophysical stations also detected them.[21].

At the time, neither the Soviets nor the French quite realized yet just what their instruments had stumbled upon, nor would they know conclusively until several more months had passed. For the moment at least, only the privileged few who were privy to Argus knew precisely what was going on down in the South Atlantic.

CHAPTER 8
The Big Finish

IF ADMIRAL MUSTIN AND THE FOUR THOUSAND OFFICERS, SAILORS, TECHNICIANS, and assorted support personnel of Task Force 88 had any hopes of wrapping up their mission quickly and setting sail for home and the warmer climes of the northern hemisphere, they were soon disappointed. The grand finale of Argus—at least, the part involving rockets and atomic explosions—was going to take longer than planned, and for a reason that surprised absolutely no one: the South Atlantic weather.

The third Argus shot was set for two days after the second, on September 1st, just in time to fulfill the deadline set months before. That deadline had been mostly arbitrary, even though President Eisenhower had announced the successful conclusion of negotiations with the Soviet Union for a nuclear test moratorium just over a week earlier. Officially, however, that moratorium wouldn't go into effect until midnight on October 31st.

Technically speaking, then, the United States could go on detonating nuclear weapons until then, and in fact, the second phase of the HARDTACK test series was set to begin at the Nevada Test Site in only a couple of weeks. But even had Task Force 88 brought along enough X-17a rockets and atomic warheads to continue piercing the upper atmosphere and lighting up the sky, nobody wanted to hang around in the frigid, squally South Atlantic that long.

So everyone was quite anxious to see off *Norton Sound*'s final nuclear-tipped rocket as August ended and September began. Even the Pentagon couldn't help nudging Mustin along. "It is a real pleasure to observe how well all of you are doing a tough job," noted a cable to Mustin from AFSWP chief Admiral Parker back home in Washington. "A final good one to start September off would be wonderful."[1]

The South Atlantic had other ideas. The winds refused to let up, and launch preparations had to be scrubbed and the missile returned to the hangar. In search of better weather and also to perhaps move the magnetic conjugate point closer to the *Albemarle* up north, Mustin moved the task force farther southward, with the destroyer escort USS *Hammerberg* on weather picket duty about 250 miles west of the main force.

The Lockheed technicians again wheeled out the Argus 3 missile onto the *Norton Sound*'s fantail on September 5. The seas were rougher than ever, but still deemed within launch parameters, so the countdown proceeded. Finally, at around 10:30 that evening, Captain Gralla gave the order, the "intent to launch" button was pressed, and . . .

Nothing happened.

The Argus 3 missile sat calmly on its launcher, unmoving, unconcerned, as the South Atlantic winds blew and the *Norton Sound* pitched and rolled in the waves. By now, everyone was more or less used to the disconcerting experience of a slight delay after the launch was ordered, but this was taking too long.

"It was like 4, 5, 6 minutes gone by," Dick Culp recalled. "We were all sitting there thinking, okay, we've got a 2 kiloton nuclear warhead sitting on top of a three-stage rocket in the South Atlantic in a storm."[2] What was the best way to get the damn thing off the fantail without obliterating everyone within five miles?

Fortunately, that wasn't going to be necessary. Technicians quickly determined that the missile had simply failed to ignite—a common phenomenon in the rocket business, and something that was relatively easy to correct. The September 5 launch was officially scrubbed, the missile taken down, and corrective measures quickly applied. "One of the destroyers sent us a book of matches with a comment that maybe these would help,"

Keith Mayfield remembered. "That gave us all a good laugh."[3]

Twenty-four hours later, everyone was again in place, the sea conditions were unsurprisingly lousy, and the X-17a missile was ready. This time, no book of matches or any other extraordinary measures were required. At shortly after 10 PM, the button was pressed, the ship rolled, and the rocket launched.

Everything went precisely as planned. There were no trajectory problems, no glitches with the rocket staging, no other unforeseen difficulties. Even the skies cooperated, the cloud cover opening up in time for the *Norton Sound* and the other vessels of Task Force 88 to be rewarded with the sight of the Argus 3 warhead detonating at almost five hundred miles altitude. Following the explosion, they also watched as an artificial aurora formed, shimmering and coruscating in the night. Far to the north in the Azores, the *Albemarle* also reported seeing a brilliant auroral display, as well as detecting the predicted radio and radar effects. They had hit the magnetic conjugate point more or less dead on at last.

An observer watching from the fantail of the *Albemarle* vividly described the sight:

> The effect began as a blue-green 'spear' starting close to the horizon, climbing in back of a cloud, and reappearing above the cloud. The effect first appeared about a half a minute after detonation . . . a short time after the onset of the effect, a red crown developed at the head of the bluish spear. The red was distinct but not as bright as the green. For the next minute the red spread out while the blue-green lost intensity. The red aurora deepened in color, began to fade, and after 4 minutes was no longer visible. The blue-green spread out and became an indistinct luminous glow covering about 45 degrees of horizon up to about 30 degrees high. This glow slowly faded and was gone about 32 minutes after the aurora began. The brightest part of the initial display was extremely intense as the edges of the cloud which obscured the center of the display were outlined clearly, as if the moon were behind the cloud.[4]

The display witnessed by the Task Force 88 contingent down south was even more spectacular. The various observation aircraft reported "a bright diffused white light which lit up the sky," followed by "a long streak in the sky . . . with a fish-tail or 'X' of electric-blue . . . extending southward with a brilliant magenta," "pastel lines of blue, green, and rose," and brilliant streamers of colored light against a background of stars, followed by auroras. Though no equally picturesque eyewitness descriptions seem to have survived from the shipboard audience, the light show they witnessed was undoubtedly no less spectacular.[5]

From its orbital vantage point, Explorer 4 was also suitably dazzled by Argus 3, observing the electron shell forming and spreading around the planet. It would provide the only space-based observations this time, as the sounding rockets of Project Jason remained grounded for the Argus finale.

"This one went completely as planned, in all respects," Admiral Mustin later noted with satisfaction. "This was the beginnings of a whole new realm of nuclear effects knowledge."[6]

Not to mention vindication for a "crazy" Greek-American physicist, who had just witnessed his nutty idea evolve from scorn and ridicule to a massively ambitious operation of the US military and scientific establishment, all in less than a year.

CONSIDERING THAT HE WAS THE MAN WHO HAD STARTED IT ALL, WHOSE RATHER outlandish idea had grown in less than a year from an off-the-cuff discussion in a Livermore office between himself and his bemused supervisor into a massive, globe-girdling operation involving thousands of people working in utmost secrecy, Nicholas Christofilos is curiously absent from almost all contemporaneous accounts of the Argus tests. Aside from AFSWP scientist Frank Shelton's meeting with Christofilos at the Pentagon at the end of July 1958, Christofilos is unmentioned in the available records as a participant in any of the frantic activity that ensued over the following weeks. If he was indeed the man of the hour, the person who had posed the questions that so many people were now striving and risking their lives to answer, then just what had he been doing all this time?

Argus's extreme secrecy, combined with the highly accelerated planning, scheduling, and execution of the entire operation, were not only unique for US nuclear test series but posed a frustrating problem for historians: the project didn't generate the usual mountains of documentation typical of a huge joint governmental and military undertaking. Even the most comprehensive official history of Argus, the Defense Nuclear Agency report performed as part of the United States Atmospheric Nuclear Weapons Tests/Nuclear Test Personnel Review in 1982, noted this difficulty: ". . . a larger than normal amount of the planning and coordination was done in person, without the usual amount of formal preplanning, agenda preparation, and position papers being written."[7] As if that weren't enough, many of the records that did exist have been destroyed in routine housekeeping in subsequent years, while some, such as the small number of radiological film badges used by Task Force 88, have simply been lost. Still other records remain classified.

Which nevertheless does not preclude informed speculation on some matters, such as Nicholas Christofilos's activities during the Argus shots and their immediate aftermath. He was certainly being consulted on occasion, as in his Pentagon meeting with Shelton, but undoubtedly spent most of the rest of August and September 1958 back at Livermore, concentrating mostly on the Astron project but keeping an ear to the ground for word from the South Atlantic. When the news finally came that his theories had been confirmed and a "Christofilos effect" had indeed been observed, one imagines him nodding in satisfaction, enormously pleased with himself—and not at all surprised. He had, after all, known all along.

And then he surely went right back to work, waiting for the data from Van Allen's Explorer 4 and the various other scientific observations, his mind already churning with the possibilities of their application to Astron and ever more outlandish ideas. As always with an intellect such as Christofilos's, answering one question only led to many more.

THEIR MISSION ACCOMPLISHED, THE MEN OF TASK FORCE 88 PREPARED TO SAIL for home, hearth, and family, with the crew of the *Norton Sound* perhaps especially relieved by the fact that they were no longer carrying live nuclear warheads along as part of their cargo. Though she had followed a solitary course on her outward bound journey from Port Hueneme, the *Sound* remained with her six other task force companion vessels for now, steaming northward toward the equator and the summer. Deciding that the men under his command had earned a break, Admiral Mustin requested and was granted permission to take his ships to Rio de Janeiro, from which the civilians from Lockheed and Sandia could leave the *Norton Sound* and fly home. Meanwhile, on the way, his aircraft carrier flagship USS *Tarawa* continued routine daily flight operations.

The mission may have been over, but not the secrecy. Except for official communications back home, radio contact with the outside world was still prohibited. "There was no noticeable effect on the morale of ship's personnel," said Mayfield. "We were sailors doing our job." Still, noted *Norton Sound* petty officer Bobby Terrell, "We were told not to say anything to anybody about where we had been and what we did."[8]

Which, of course, did not preclude speculation, especially once the sailors of Task Force 88 were set forth on liberty in Rio and began mixing with the civilian population. Even if the crew kept their mouths shut, such restrictions didn't apply to non–US Navy personnel. Some of the wilder theories about the doings of the *Norton Sound* and Task Force 88 involved, predictably, the Russians. Although Sputnik 1 had long since fallen back to Earth in January, as had Sputnik 2 in April with its unfortunate canine passenger, Sputnik 3 was still beeping away happily as the Soviets' 1958 representative in Earth orbit. "Many people said that our mission was to target this satellite and shoot it down," recalled Quincy Owens. "Of course, this wasn't true." Still, not an unreasonable assumption to make concerning a guided missile ship operating in remote waters, far from established sealanes. But the only involvement of the *Norton Sound* with Sputnik 3 was an occasional sighting of the transiting satellite by ship's lookouts during those nights that were free of clouds and storm squalls.

As Dick Culp recalled, however, the *Norton Sound* did have an encounter with Sputnik 1 the previous year. "We were off of Central America, off of Panama basically, looking for some weather to test missiles in, and that was when Sputnik was launched. In the telemetry shack, we played around and we finally picked up the signal. We must have sat there for two hours, just listening to that damn thing go ping, ping, ping."[9]

Admiral Mustin took immediate steps to preserve the secrecy of Argus upon arrival of the task force in Rio on September 15. "As soon as I got in, I approached the local US security types in the embassy, who would have been CIA people, of course," he recounted. "We had in Brazil a rather numerous military mission, commanded by a rear admiral. And we had naval communications security, and so on. I told them what the problem was and alerted them. At the conclusion of our visit of about a week, more or less, there had been no talk in the bars or anywhere. Of the 4,500 men in the task force, the few who knew kept their mouths shut, and those who didn't know had been successfully diverted off to some other explanation of what was going on."[10]

Presumably, that explanation did not involve taking potshots at Sputnik 3. "We were told that it had something to do with the discovery of the Van Allen radiation belts," said Bobby Terrell.[11] (Which of course was technically true, if in an oblique manner.) As Mustin explained, "You never can get away with just telling people, 'Oh, we're doing something that's so secret we can't tell you.' That just gives rise to all kinds of speculations; you've got to give them some other explanation that's plausible." The missile firing drills and weather preoccupations of the task force suggested a reasonable cover: "some sort of high-altitude weather observations or something." It seemed to work, as Mustin recalled. "There was no leak from that task force picked up by security agents who were deliberately alerted to look for it."[12] Although, as the final official Argus report noted, "the press displayed keen interest," the official line that TF 88 had been "testing new antisubmarine-warfare and long-range communications equipment, taking upper-air soundings, and generally conducting operations normal to such a force" was readily accepted.[13] Operation Argus remained comfortably classified—for now.[14]

In any case, the sailors of Task Force 88 were far more interested in blowing off steam, meeting girls, and enjoying the back pay they had just received than in revealing secrets. They enjoyed their liberty blissfully unaware of being shadowed by security men ever vigilant for indiscretions. "Rio was a blast," said Ken McMaster. "We had lots of liberty and two months' pay in our pockets. The people were extremely friendly and helpful." Without going into detail, Bobby Terrell simply said, "I will always remember Rio."

Even Admiral Mustin called it "an absolutely delightful stay." Not only were there no security problems, there were none of the usual incidents routinely expected whenever a group of young sailors hits port after months at sea. Mustin noted, "When we left, the local provost marshal told me, 'Oh no, we didn't expect any trouble, because trouble always comes when sailors start to fight over a girl in a bar somewhere. But in Rio, there are so many more girls than there are sailors that they never have to fight over them. If there's any fighting, it's the girls fighting over the sailors.'"[15]

Finally the Rio excursion ended and the ships of Task Force 88 set sail for home. After crossing the Equator once more, the force began to break up, its individual vessels heading for their own home ports along the East Coast. The California-based *Norton Sound* was on her own again, stopping in Trinidad for a two-day visit before heading for the Panama Canal, the Pacific Ocean, and the final leg of her long trip home to Port Hueneme.

Mustin began to collect messages of congratulations from higher echelons. Chief of Naval Operations Admiral Arleigh Burke cabled,

YOUR TASK FORCE HAS ESTABLISHED AN UNQUESTIONED RIGHT TO A PROMINENT PLACE AMONG THOSE WHO HAVE DEMONSTRATED TO THE FREE WORLD THAT IT MAY BE THANKFUL FOR THE CALIBER OF OFFICERS AND ENLISTED MEN IN OUR NAVY X TO ALL HANDS IN TASK FORCE EIGHTY-EIGHT A MOST HEARTY WELL DONE.[16]

Now that the sailors, pilots, missilemen, radar operators, and all the other practical, nuts and bolts, hands-on participants of Operation Argus had essentially completed their work, the focus shifted back to the place where it had all began: the laboratories, the blackboards, and the restless minds of the scientists. There was a prodigious amount of Argus data to be reduced, examined, collated, interpreted, and analyzed. Much of it came from Explorer 4, and it went to the physics building in Iowa City, to be processed and parsed by James Van Allen and his stalwart graduate students. As expected, the satellite finally went dark in mid-September, its batteries exhausted, but it left reams of data as its legacy.

The pervasive secrecy of Argus proved inescapable. "As in the case of the earlier Explorers, paper strip-charts were produced as a first data reduction step for Explorer IV," explained George Ludwig. "But for Explorer IV, the process was a bit more complicated because of the highly classified nature of the Argus Project." Before the Argus tests, nothing was classified, but that changed quickly. "During the month following the first nuclear burst, i.e. during the times that portions of the data showed the effects of the tests, Carl McIlwain served as a data screener," Ludwig noted. "He diverted the charts containing indications of the Argus tests for special handling, where he served as the primary data reader."[17]

Those initial results were shared only with a highly select group of individuals within government and scientific circles. The intent was not merely to hide that the United States had just conducted three nuclear tests without the knowledge of the rest of the world. There was also the fact that those tests had been worldwide in their effects—and that the "Christofilos effect," now also known as the "Argus effect," had graduated from an intriguing hypothesis to scientific reality, with implications that ranged far beyond the scientific and academic into the military realm.

As Van Allen later wrote, "In each of the three cases, a well-defined . . . shell of artificially injected electrons was produced." The Argus shell initially formed at the upper atmosphere detonation point, with electrons zipping back and forth from magnetic pole to magnetic pole, then steadily progressed eastward, just as Christofilos had theorized. For those worried about Soviet skullduggery, Argus also provided some welcome reassurance: "Also, we found that the physical nature of the Argus radiation, as characterized by our four Explorer IV detectors, was quite different than that of the pre-Argus radiation, thus dispelling the suspicion that the radiation observed by Explorers I and III had originated from Soviet nuclear bomb bursts."[18]

But the good news was also tempered with some bad. Although the Christofilos effect was real, it also proved exceedingly weak. The Argus electron shells persisted no longer than a few weeks, and not very intensely at that. It seemed unlikely that Christofilos's "radiation shield" would even inconvenience incoming Soviet warheads, much less completely incapacitate them. There might be some effect on satellites that happened to pass through, but even that would be limited and slight.

Initial disappointment in some quarters, however, soon yielded to a renewed enthusiasm. Of course the Argus effects were modest, argued some. It was only a proof-of-concept thing, after all. The warheads were barely firecrackers, not even two kilotons, and aside from the third shot, they hadn't even really gone off at a properly high altitude. But what would happen if we got serious: detonating a thermonuclear weapon hundreds or even thousands of miles up, pumping megatons, not mere kilotons, into the magnetosphere? Wouldn't that give us our missile-killing radiation zone? Proponents of the notion even had a code name picked out for a repeat performance of Argus at the megaton scale: Willow-Argus.

Such ideas might have seemed attractive and even sensible to some in the Pentagon, but any serious proposals along such lines were quickly squelched. With the impending nuclear moratorium at midnight on Halloween, there would be no more plans for nuclear tests in the immediate future. The HARDTACK series was wrapping up in Nevada, but it was far too late to make any such grandiose changes in its schedule to sneak any Argus-type experiments under the wire. And megaton-range tests were out of the question anywhere except the distant Pacific test site.

As the Iowa team continued to study Explorer 4 data, the Project Jason and Midas teams performed their own analyses of the information collected from the sounding rockets, aircraft, ships, ground stations, and radar and radio observations. By the beginning of November, even as the analyses and head-scratching over Argus data continued, enough had been pieced together for presidential scientific advisor James Killian to report preliminary results of Argus to President Eisenhower in a detailed memo on November 3.

Significantly, Killian concentrated his emphasis on the military aspects of Argus, not the scientific. "This historic experiment, probably the most spectacular ever conducted, provides the first verification of the existence of several phenomena of military importance when a nuclear explosion takes place in space above the earth's atmosphere," he wrote. "The results yielded by the experiment verified and confirmed the earlier predictions. They affect the design requirements for the electronic and warhead components of intercontinental and intermediate range ballistic missiles, the design of ballistic missile and air defense radar equipment, and, especially, military short wave communications equipment."[19] Already, Killian was thinking ahead to the implications for America's ongoing ICBM programs.

Still, in keeping with his official role, Killian mentioned the scientific value of Argus, even as that was still being determined by Van Allen and the various other researchers involved. "The experiment bore out the theoretical predictions of Christofilos in a beautiful manner," Killian waxed enthusiastically, "and provided scientific information of great value about conditions surrounding the earth." Though he didn't mention it in his memo to Eisenhower, Killian was also quite aware that the new detail provided by Argus on the space environment and radiation conditions was going to be vital for the nascent manned space effort.

Killian also praised the "extraordinary accomplishment" of all involved. "Especially notable was the successful launching of a large solid-fuel rocket carrying a nuclear payload from the heaving deck of a ship in the squally South Atlantic. Scarcely less so is the fact that the whole experiment was planned and carried to a completely successful conclusion in less than five months."

On top of all that, noted Killian, "Impressive, too, is the fact that no leaks have occurred despite the large number of civilian and military personnel involved."[20]

Unfortunately, though neither Killian, Eisenhower, nor most anyone else concerned with Argus knew it at the time, the leak had already occurred, and would soon burst forth into a flood.

CHAPTER 9
The Veil of Secrecy

GIVEN HIS WARTIME NAVY SERVICE FOLLOWED BY YEARS OF SCIENTIFIC WORK using military resources, James Van Allen was no stranger to the peculiar world of official secrecy and classification. But there was always a fundamental tension there, between the requirements of secrecy and his identity as a scientist dedicated to the principles and long-standing scientific traditions of open research and freedom of knowledge. Most of the time, he had been content to walk that sometimes shifting line, reasoning that he was working with the military, not for it; under its tent, perhaps, but not under its thumb.

Now that reasoning was beginning to feel somewhat hollow, and the continued restrictions on Argus and his Explorer 4 results were beginning to chafe. He could understand perfectly why Argus had to be kept secret beforehand, and during the actual nuclear shots. But that was all over with now; mission accomplished, the job done. What possible justification, he began to ask, was there to keep everything in the dark indefinitely?

There were other considerations besides basic principles. Explorer 4 had been publicly planned, announced, and conducted as a part of the International Geophysical Year. The IGY's raison d'etre was that it was completely public and international. All data was to be gathered by the sixty-seven participating nations in a spirit of complete scientific openness and collegiality. That meant all was to be shared freely. The IGY was supposed to represent the nations of the earth coming together in peace and friendship to explore and study the planet that they all shared in kind. Including even the USSR, and of course, the United States.

So all of the data collected by Explorer 4, as an IGY project, had to be shared with the world. There had to be time allowed to collate and analyze and interpret, but eventually, the data had to be made public. It was more than just a matter of scientific principle and cooperation—the US had signed an international agreement to that effect. If they held something back, if they refused to share some of their findings, then they were not only breaking that agreement, but everyone—most particularly, the USSR—would wonder just what the hell the US was hiding, and why.

This had been a topic of some concern from the very beginnings of Argus. A few of the scientists involved, such as Herbert York at ARPA, had pointed out the IGY issue, something which became even more of a problem with the necessity of borrowing (or perhaps, commandeering) various IGY equipment and resources for Argus in order to maintain the impossibly tight project deadline. That problem directly conflicted with another: the need to keep Argus hushed up so as not to endanger the ongoing negotiations for a test ban treaty or at least the prospects for a moratorium.

At first, such concerns were briefly considered and then mostly brushed aside, under the pressures of time and planning for Argus. But now that the operation had been successfully accomplished, the missiles fired, warheads detonated, data collected, and everyone sent home (and the testing moratorium safely in place for the moment), the questions arose anew, and at a greater volume than before.

As far as the Pentagon and the military were concerned, there was nothing to talk about. They were perfectly happy to keep Argus under wraps indefinitely. "The satellite instrumentation records that disclose the Christofilos effect are classified and are not being made available to International Geophysical Year authorities," stated the Navy's final Argus report from Task Force 88, and that was that.[1]

The problem was that events were transpiring to make such a position difficult to sustain, if not ultimately impossible. Not only were pesky scientists such as Van Allen pushing for more openness, so were others in government, including members of the President's Science Advisory Committee (PSAC). As 1958 transitioned into 1959, the Argus secrecy that had been simmering along contentedly in a slow, rolling boil was threatening to boil over.

"A great debate within government developed as to what kind of public announcement should be made, if any," Killian recalled. "There was a tricky question involved related to the International Geophysical Year because some of the data-gathering facilities that were employed were IGY facilities, and there was a general IGY commitment to publish the data from work done under the program . . . while recognizing that there were important military uses for the data yielded by the experiment and that this information should be kept secret, nevertheless there were strong convictions in PSAC that the experiment should be made public and such results as could appropriately be published should be made available for the benefit of the scientific community."[2]

That community was already quite restless, both in and out of government. So were several members of the fourth estate, who, though so far unbeknownst to Killian or most anyone else in scientific or government circles, were already quite aware of the Argus saga.

Hanson Baldwin, longtime military correspondent for the *New York Times*, had found out about Argus at least several weeks before any missiles had left the deck of the *Norton Sound* in August 1958. Apparently the leak originated with someone from James Van Allen's lab back in Iowa. Possibly a graduate student, possibly a technician—the identity of Argus's own whistleblower has never been definitively ascertained, even after six decades. (Killian's successor as PSAC chairman, George Kistiakowsky, later noted in his diaries that "Roy Johnson of ARPA has investigated this leak and has definitely traced it to the No. 2 man in the Van Allen Laboratories," which would seem to indicate Carl McIlwain, though this is not confirmed.)[3]

Baldwin knew he had a big story, but as a Pulitzer Prize–winning war correspondent, graduate of Annapolis, and savvy observer of all things military, he knew the serious ramifications of revealing such a secret operation, especially before it even happened, not only for the military but for the delicate test-ban negotiations ongoing in Geneva. He decided he needed some guidance on the scientific aspects of it all, so he confided in his *Times* colleague, science reporter Walter Sullivan.

"About the end of June, 1958, [Baldwin] put his head in my office and asked if he could talk to me privately for a few minutes," Sullivan later wrote in his book-length account of the IGY, *Assault On the Unknown*. "He had learned, he said, that the United States planned to fire several atomic bombs in space."[4]

Baldwin explained his reluctance about going public too soon. In the meantime, Sullivan suggested consulting a friend of his who was "so centrally involved in the United States space program that he would be sure to know of the operation." That was Richard Porter, chairman of the IGY Panel on Rockets and Satellites. Sullivan was sure that Porter would also "give us his candid personal opinion, rather than merely an official line."[5]

Porter was "both horrified and amused" when Sullivan told him what he and Baldwin had already uncovered. "I can't tell you not to print it, but I can say this: If you do, the operation will never take place," he told the science reporter.

To emphasize the point, about an hour later Sullivan got a call from ARPA's head of security, William H. Godel, imploring him to hold the story. Sullivan assured the nervous security chief that he and Baldwin had already resolved not to publish anything before the Argus operation actually took place, which seemed to calm Godel for the moment. In exchange, they had ARPA's assurance that Argus would be officially announced and revealed to the world after it was all over, and that the *Times* would be informed in advance so they could be the first to break the story.

Realizing that they'd obviously struck a very sensitive nerve somewhere within the bowels of the Pentagon, Sullivan and Baldwin agreed to sit on the story—for the time being. Which didn't, of course, preclude further probings on their part, as they attempted to piece together their fragments of information into some sort of coherent whole.

Whatever his own misgivings about secrecy, Van Allen himself was as yet unaware of impending leaks. Aside from busily continuing to analyze the treasure trove of Explorer 4 data and preparing for new space missions, he had been busy helping to publicize the aspects of Explorer 4's accomplishments that could be publicized. In the fall of 1958, he contacted several of the companies that had provided components of Explorer's instruments, sending them photos of their contributions and granting them permission to use them in advertising materials.

"The enclosed photo shows a few of the 2N338, 2N335, and 608-C transistors and diodes employed in the Explorer IV satellite," he wrote to electronics manufacturer Texas Instruments (TI) on October 22. "You are free to use this photo for publicity purposes, advertisements, etc., provided only that the State University of Iowa is mentioned in the release . . . Explorer IV was developed on an extremely tight schedule [Van Allen couldn't reveal exactly why, of course] and we wish to express our appreciation for the cooperation received from you and your Company which enabled us to carry the project through to a successful conclusion."[6] The company wasted no time in making good use of Van Allen's offering, just a month later sending him a work-up of a full-page ad for the upcoming January issue of *Scientific American* mentioning the "added reliability and economy" of "TI transistors for Explorer IV." Noted the cover letter, "Please note that credit for the photo is being given to your fine university in the ad."[7]

Slowly but inevitably, the dark curtain of secrecy and security cloaking Argus wore thin. By the end of 1958, it had become little more than a veil, concealing details but not the general outlines of its subject. And to their increasing alarm, Baldwin and Sullivan began to feel their exclusive scoop beginning to slip away.

Much to Sullivan's chagrin, in October 1958, the man who started it all, Nick Christofilos, presented his ideas of creating an artificial radiation belt of electrons around the Earth at the Chicago meeting of the American Physical Society. "The only major point he omitted was the use of an atomic bomb to provide the electrons," Sullivan later complained.[8] Instead, Christofilos proposed the rather outlandish idea of generating the electron shield with an orbiting nuclear accelerator, something like what he'd been working on at Brookhaven and then at Livermore labs. Perhaps because he already had a well-established reputation for engagingly bizarre ideas, no one seemed to take special notice. Of course, Christofilos neglected to mention that what he was proposing in theory had already been proven in fact experimentally over the South Atlantic several months earlier.

Then came the annual meeting of the American Association for the Advancement of Science (AAAS) in Washington, D.C., just after Christmas, which Sullivan duly attended as part of his usual *Times* science beat. At the meeting came more rumblings of Argus from other quarters, including a paper presented by noted astronomer Fred Singer on "Artificial Modification of the Earth's Radiation Belt," and a press conference with Singer and James Van Allen. A *Newsweek* reporter kept asking Van Allen and Singer about any possible connections between the radiation belts and high-altitude nuclear explosions, such as the HARDTACK tests that had occurred that summer, and whether Van Allen's Explorer 4 had detected them. Sullivan realized that his *Newsweek* colleague was really asking about Argus, albeit indirectly and perhaps somewhat shooting in the dark.

Old pros that they were, Sullivan and Baldwin realized that journalistically speaking, if other reporters had caught the scent, then the game was almost up. They decided to take more decisive action in order to guarantee an exclusive for the *Times*. Sullivan wrote to Herbert York, who had just been promoted from ARPA Chief Scientist to the Director of Defense Research and Engineering at the Pentagon. Sullivan mentioned to York some, but not all, of what he knew of Argus, and requested a meeting to discuss going public, emphasizing that the *Times* didn't believe it could continue to hold the secret indefinitely. "Because IGY data was open to all, I said that we—or anyone else—could unearth the Argus effect with a certain amount of 'concentrated effort'," Sullivan recalled.[9]

That was enough to set off some alarms at the White House and Pentagon. York consulted with James Killian, noting "I know that he [Sullivan] knows considerably more than he has written." He also pointed out to Killian that while the AEC wanted to keep the secret, scientists such as Van Allen were increasingly pressing for publication of Argus scientific data, as required by IGY agreements.[10]

To help prove his point that Argus could be uncovered with a little "concentrated effort," Sullivan checked with the IGY monitoring networks and casually inquired whether there had been any indications of unusual magnetic storms around the end of August and beginning of September. He was informed that yes, there had in fact been a "rather remarkable event" around that time that couldn't be associated with any definite solar disturbance of the sort that generally created such phenomena. Sullivan also checked around with other official sources, including overseas, for reports of unusual magnetic or auroral activity around that same time period. He detailed his poking around in another letter to York.

In a meeting at the Pentagon with York and his assistant on January 14, Sullivan laid out the case for going public. "They had studied my letters and apparently had discussed them with James Killian," said Sullivan. But they thought that the evidence Sullivan and Baldwin had collected was "inconclusive." Sullivan argued that since knowledge of the radiation belts and ideas for Argus-type experiments were already quite public, any disclosure of the Argus shots wouldn't tell the Russians anything they didn't already know. York agreed in a general sense, but pointed out that information on the explosions, such as their altitude, yield, and geographic location, was indeed sensitive and had to be concealed for national security reasons, and again officially asked the *Times* to hold the story.

As York later remembered: "In the first week of January 1959, on my first or second day on the job as director of defense research and engineering, he [Sullivan] came to my office and tried to strike a bargain. We will, he said, hold the story indefinitely if you will promise to give us twenty-four-hours' notice of any release on this subject. I was totally inexperienced in such matters, so I immediately reported the whole thing to Quarles and Killian. They rejected his proposal. The White House joined the Pentagon in trying to persuade the *New York Times* to suppress the story."[11]

Sullivan was far from satisfied by the entire encounter, suspecting that the real reason the Pentagon wanted Argus kept secret was political. "I am convinced that the only reason we are being discouraged by the Pentagon . . . is to postpone the day of diplomatic reckoning," he told Baldwin.[12] Specifically, he thought that with the test-ban negotiations still ongoing in

Geneva, the last thing the government wanted was to reveal that the US had been secretly blowing up atomic bombs in space. Scientists involved with Argus had been telling Sullivan the same thing.

There was indeed a rapidly growing rift between the scientists pushing for declassification and openness on one hand, and the Pentagon striving to maintain secrecy on the other. It had been inevitable from the beginning, as soon as Argus planners hitched their star and their A-bombs to the IGY wagon in the frantic rush to save time and complete Argus as soon as possible. Reluctantly, and under the relentless prodding of journalists such as Sullivan and scientists such as Van Allen, the administration and the Pentagon were beginning to realize and accept the reality that they couldn't keep Argus secret forever. But if they couldn't, how best to limit the damage, and just how should they go about telling the world?

A memo to Killian on January 14, the same day as York's meeting with Sullivan, noted that "it is to be expected that fragmentary unauthorized releases and leaks will occur," and that "enough have already occurred to have attracted the curiosity of many scientists." Declassification "would have beneficial effects on our own scientific community since it would equip them with working knowledge and would stimulate them to develop new ideas and inventions based upon the newly demonstrated effects." In other words, it might encourage the development of new weapons or defenses based on the Argus effect, not to mention saving money by, for example, not building radio equipment susceptible to interference from Argus-type effects.[13]

Aside from coalescing around military and scientific poles, the intramural debate began to settle down into two broad options, which were set out by Presidential Special Assistant Karl G. Harr to Killian in a memo on January 20. "There appear to be two contingencies: first, the publishing of information about the shots as a result of leaks and, second, the voluntary release of information by the Government . . . If the *New York Times*, or anyone else, breaks a substantial part of the story, our alternatives appear to be: 1. Neither to confirm nor to deny such leaks; 2. To disclose all that we may safely do from a national security point of view." Harr pointed out that waiting for the story to break on its own would mean that "we would have lost control over the manner and timing of such release." He proceeded to recommend, among other things, that "appropriate scientists prepare a report" and that Congress and the appropriate foreign powers, including the Soviets, be officially informed as well. He even provided a handy set of guidelines to govern such a public release, including emphasizing that "the detonations produced no radioactive fallout"; that "there was no violation of our IGY commitments" because unclassified satellite data had been released; and that "this was not the test of a weapon in the usual sense, but a scientific experiment." The Administration and the Pentagon would find that last suggestion in particular quite handy over the coming few months.[14]

Sullivan and Baldwin as yet knew nothing of all the consternation they had caused within the hallowed halls of the White House and the Pentagon. As far as they were concerned, in the previous summer they had made a gentleman's agreement to keep the secret of Argus until it was all over and made public, and now their reasonable expectations to at last publish the story were being summarily dismissed and endlessly delayed.

Sullivan decided that the time had come for a direct approach, one closer to the top. On February 2, James Killian happened to be in New York City to make a speech. Sullivan figured that was his chance.

After Killian finished his speech, wrote Sullivan, "I appeared on a dais with a letter in hand, summing up our case for publication." He handed the sealed letter to Killian personally, making sure it wasn't going to be intercepted and round-filed by some trusty assistant running interference for his boss.

As the banquet hall emptied after the speech, Killian and Sullivan took seats. Killian opened and read the letter as Sullivan waited.[15]

The letter patiently spelled out the *Times'* position. "We were given repeated assurances that we would be given sufficient prior notice of any announcement so that we should be the first to publish it," Sullivan had written. "To avoid inadvertent disclosure, knowledge of the project has been limited, on the *Times*, to Hanson Baldwin and myself." Despite prior assurances, however, Sullivan noted that, apparently, "a policy decision was made some months ago not to make any disclosure about Argus."

But that position, Sullivan argued, was no longer sustainable. He detailed the various reports on Argus effects that had come out in the scientific literature, not to mention "questions asked by science writers at the AAAS annual meeting" that "suggest that some of them are on the track of Argus." Given all that, continued the letter, "we doubt that we can continue to withhold publication of at least a limited account of Argus." Scientists they had consulted were unanimous that revealing Argus "would not disclose anything which was not already known, from the scientific and military point of view." And Sullivan again pointed out the US obligation to publish Explorer 4's IGY data.[16]

Killian didn't argue with Sullivan's reasoning, but sidestepped it by pointing out that disclosure of Argus could derail the Geneva test-ban negotiations. "The Russians would be handed the argument that the only untrustworthy participant in the talks was the one that had sneaked off to fire atomic bombs far from its own shores," as Sullivan paraphrased him. When Killian said that he also couldn't provide any advance notice in case the government went public, Sullivan asked if at least someone could tip off the *Times* informally. "His reaction to this seemed to be assent, but we were still left in an uneasy situation."[17]

Providing still more ammunition for Sullivan's position was a short article published in a British paper, *The Observer*, a couple of weeks later. Although it didn't mention Argus specifically, and obviously the unidentified "scientific correspondent" who penned the piece had no knowledge of the project, the article, titled "Radiation Belt May Monitor A-Tests," noted that "the newly-discovered belt of intense radiation surrounding the earth . . . may provide a new method of detecting high-altitude nuclear explosions."[18] The piece cited the work of Kellogg and Ney at the University of Minnesota which had earlier caused such consternation in the US government. Finally, they had been allowed to publish in *Nature*, proposing "a scientifically controlled high-altitude nuclear explosion to test the accuracy of their assumptions." Now a foreign newspaper was onto it. Even the most obtuse governmental official had to realize that this did not bode well for the continued secrecy of Argus.

But the scientists were getting restless as well. Later in February, a highly secret ten-day scientific meeting was convened at Lawrence Livermore Laboratory to talk over Argus results in detail. Along with the planned scientific discussions, a large part of the meeting ended up dealing with the question of Argus classification. According to George Ludwig, who attended along with Van Allen, "the arguments were, at times, heated."[19]

As a later summary to York described, the debate split fairly evenly between scientific and military arguments. The memo summarized the scientists' position as "the scientific value and possible scientific prestige associated with publication of full reports on the scientific aspects of this experiment outweigh national security advantages of continued security." It was perfectly possible, argued most of the scientists, to separate out all the scientific aspects from the few military-type secrets such as the exact shot yield and firing locations.

Advocates of the "military" position, which turned out to be a decided minority, claimed that "the general national security value of the experiment outweighs the scientific and possible scientific prestige value to the country to be gained by release. Maintain necessary security. The impact on future military applications and implications may be larger than scientific or other values to be gained by open publication."

After hammering out the wording of these two propositions at great length, the group decided to vote for either "Proposition 1" (the scientific viewpoint) or "Proposition 2" (the military viewpoint). Not surprisingly, most of the scientists, including Van Allen's group, favored Proposition 1, which got seventeen votes to Proposition 2's five. Even the usually militaristic Edward Teller voted for open disclosure and Proposition 1. Only Nick Christofilos, always the gadfly, decided that he didn't quite like the wording of Proposition 1 but would vote for "a slight modification or reinterpretation" that he would write himself later.[20]

Van Allen felt strongly enough about the whole issue that, shortly after the Livermore conference, he sent an extended summary of his own views to Killian, using his unique preeminence within the scientific community to further emphasize and detail the virtues of openness. "Prompt and full public report of the tests and observations will contribute greatly

to the international prestige of the United States as a leader in the application of atomic devices to scientific purposes," he wrote.

"The possibility of conducting Argus-type experiments has been suggested publicly by a number of persons both in the United States and
abroad," Van Allen pointed out, noting that the existence and character of
the Earth's natural radiation belt were already widely known, including by
the Soviets, who were perfectly capable of carrying out similar experiments.
"It may reasonably be presumed that they are already preparing such experiments, if indeed they have not already conducted them," he said.

And because the successful Argus tests "undoubtedly constitute the
greatest geophysical experiment ever conducted by man," trumpeting that
success to the world would "contribute enormously to the international
prestige of the United States as a leader in scientific endeavor." Otherwise,
he warned, "the US will quite likely be again 'Sputniked' in the eyes of the
world by the Soviets."[21]

Now that the Argus team had come down on the side of publication,
it remained only for Killian's PSAC to make their own judgment. At their
monthly meeting on March 16, PSAC decided that "continued security
classification . . . is not of significant military advantage to the US." While
PSAC had originally recommended that Argus be classified Top Secret,
"there are no longer any scientific or technical considerations which can
justify the continued classification of the FLORAL [Argus] tests."[22] PSAC
also reiterated the argument that revealing Argus would enhance American prestige and thereby offset any political fallout that might result from
inadvertent leaks. The upcoming meeting of the National Academy of Sciences in April would be the perfect venue to tell the world about Argus,
thought PSAC.[23]

The participants in all this debate and discussion were fully aware
that the New York Times was lurking in the wings, straining at the bit to publish the whole story but patiently awaiting some stamp of official approval.
But they weren't going to wait forever, particularly when Hanson Baldwin
got wind of the rapidly building momentum within the government and
even the Pentagon to go public. After being so patient and conciliatory for
almost a year now, it seemed that Baldwin, Sullivan, and the New York Times

were about to be scooped by their own government. "We feared that, once the decision was made in Washington, the machinery might move so fast that we would be left hanging in the dust," wrote Sullivan.[24]

If that was the case, then it was pointless to sit on the story any longer. Baldwin and Sullivan went to the top: *New York Times* publisher Arthur Hays Sulzberger, president Orvil E. Dryfoos, and managing editor Turner Catledge. After hearing the case laid out for them by their long-suffering reporters, the *Times* brain trust gave the go-ahead for publication—with the proviso that Sullivan and Baldwin notify the White House first as a courtesy. If the White House protested that publication would seriously harm national security, the *Times* would continue to hold off.

Around 4 PM on March 18, Sullivan tried to call Killian, but the science advisor was out of the office. Sullivan laid out the situation for Killian's assistant, R.M. Briber. "He said that matters had proceeded too far to withhold publication of the story any longer," Briber wrote in a memo. "When I asked if this was an irrevocable decision, he said that it had certainly proceeded far enough to make such a change very difficult; that it was essentially irreversible." Sullivan promised "to keep the yield, time, place, and height of the experiment in vague terms."[25]

Baldwin called ARPA and spoke to its director, Roy Johnson, basically giving him the same pitch: the *Times* was about to publish. "After Johnson hung up with Baldwin," wrote historian Lisa Mundey, "he immediately informed Deputy Secretary [of Defense] Donald Quarles of the conversation. Soon after, phones rang across Washington, as news of the impending story spread through agency circles. Before long, nearly every top official involved in Operation Argus in the White House, DOD, and AEC knew that a very public security breach was imminent."[26] The administration began to circle the wagons, deciding who would be responsible in which agency for answering what questions, and in general deciding on the officially approved story. Everyone settled in to await the coming onslaught.

Sullivan and Baldwin spent the rest of the evening scrambling to write the main Argus story along with supplemental material, and to prepare accompanying maps, photographs, and diagrams, all while waiting for a fateful call from the White House that could yet stop everything dead.

"Hanson and I watched the clock tick away the final minutes until the great presses in the basement began to thunder. They rolled. No call ever came. And the world learned of Argus."[27]

Much to the relief of Sullivan, Baldwin, and a great many scientists including James Van Allen, the White House for whatever reasons had apparently decided to bow to the inevitability of the free press and the might of the *New York Times*. On the morning of March 19, 1959, one of the greatest secrets of the Cold War became one of its biggest stories.

CHAPTER 10
The Cold Glare of Day

PRESIDENT DWIGHT D. EISENHOWER WAS DECIDEDLY ANNOYED ON THE MORN-
ing of March 19, 1959. The Argus story was emblazoned across the front
page of the *New York Times*: "US ATOM BLASTS 300 MILES UP MAR
RADAR, SNAG MISSILE PLAN; CALLED 'GREATEST EXPERIMENT'."
Finding a top secret US military project all over the most prominent newspaper in the world was not the sort of thing a president wanted accompanying his morning coffee.

On the *Times* front page, as befitted their journalistic roles, Baldwin
covered the military/operational side of Argus while Sullivan handled the
science. Though they were working from incomplete information and were
missing some pieces of the story here and there, they still managed to get
most of the details right, and definitely succeeded in conveying both the
scale and the significance of Argus.

"In a military sense the findings have great potential significance to
the development of an anti-ballistic missile system and to the security of
the nation's early warning and global communications system," wrote Baldwin. He described the role of Explorer 4 in studying the Argus effect and
the failure of Explorer 5, noting that "partly because of the lack of adequate
instrumentation and the complex nature of the experiment there is consid-

erable controversy among scientists and military experts as to the exact interpretation of the data available. Nearly all agree, however, that the information . . . is still imprecise and that more experiments are needed."

Baldwin also discussed the military implications of high-altitude nuclear explosions interfering with radio and radar, and the original Christofilos notion that "neutrons released by an exploding nuclear warhead from an intercepting missile could cause the detonation of an incoming enemy warhead—without actual physical contact between the missiles." And he considered what Argus might mean for the ongoing test-ban negotiations: "If high-altitude tests can go undetected, as Argus did, there is apparently a substantial argument in favor of those scientists who hold that no monitoring system can possibly detect all test violations."[1]

Sullivan's story on the other side of Page 1 concentrated more on physics and the scientists involved. "It has been said that geophysics is a science 'in which the earth is the laboratory and nature conducts the experiments.' In this case the space surrounding the planet was the laboratory, but the experiment was conducted by man." He described the Argus auroras and the radiation shell resulting from the detonations, noting that "although the lifetime of the man-made shell of radiation has been kept secret, it is reported to have been limited." Sullivan also detailed how Christofilos had conceived of the Argus effect and the role of Van Allen and his Explorer 4 instruments, along with the detection of Argus phenomena reported by various IGY stations, noting that "although the results of Argus are still secret . . . they appear to have been world-wide."

Sullivan included another rather alarming idea in his story. "Some physicists would like to see a 'ladder' of nuclear explosions, climbing into space in a manner that would disclose the patterns of magnetism and other phenomena in the entire region lying within 15,000 miles of the earth," he wrote. But, he added, "In view of the present stalemate on suspension of nuclear weapons tests, further explosions in space would raise political problems."[2]

The *Times* also featured additional stories on "volatile scientist" Nicholas Christofilos, the Argus secrecy debate, and diagrams, maps, and photos of the *Norton Sound* and key personnel. It was impressively comprehensive coverage, and this was only the first day. More Argus stories would follow the next day and in the coming weeks, not only in the *Times* but in various other newspapers and magazines.

Even though the administration had known the security lid was about to be blown off, it was still something of a nightmare. Eisenhower's assistant, Brigadier General Andrew J. Goodpaster, explained to the president what had happened and the steps being taken to best control the damage. Herbert York would handle any inquiries directed to the Pentagon and "confirm that tests were held for the dual purpose of testing important scientific theories . . . and ascertaining other high altitude weapons effects of military interest," which, of course, had to remain classified. Meanwhile the AEC would confirm that three high-altitude nuclear tests had indeed been conducted in the South Atlantic, but that there had been no significant fallout. If anyone asked why they had waited so long after the tests to announce them, the answer would be that they had needed to complete data analysis and evaluate military factors before any public announcement could be made.

Eisenhower was only partially placated by the efficiency of his underlings. "The President commented with vehemence upon the action of the *New York Times* in breaking security on this matter, and upon the irresponsibility of participants in the operation who leaked the information," Goodpaster impassively noted in a memo. Later that morning, meeting again with Goodpaster and now joined by Killian, Eisenhower had calmed down, agreeing that a statement could be issued noting that "it had already been planned to hold a symposium on those scientific aspects of the project which did not have military implications." He also put Killian in charge of handling all news inquiries on the scientific aspects of Argus.[3] Killian decided what could be revealed and what couldn't, separating the Argus scientific wheat from the military chaff.

Meanwhile, it was time for the administration to face the press directly. At 11 AM at the Pentagon, Deputy Secretary of Defense Donald Quarles held a press conference, joined by York, ARPA Director Roy Johnson, and Argus scientists Frank Shelton and William Thaler. They were not facing a friendly audience.

As Sullivan later noted, for Quarles it was "probably the most discomfiting press conference of his career."[4] The Deputy Secretary had to walk a fine line between the appearance of openness and the needs of security, and he had to do it before a roomful of skeptical reporters. He stuck to what had become the official line from the DOD and White House: "Like all programs where we are probing space and science in this area, we see the potentiality of military implications; but the program, the experiments as conducted were essentially in the spirit of scientific experiments." Quarles made sure to emphasize the IGY connection and to assure all present that scientific data would be released as IGY rules required.

Predictably, the reporters were not satisfied. Quarles easily fended off questions about the yield of the Argus shots as classified, and in any case "the yields in these explosions are not part of the International Geophysical Year experimentation." That didn't stop further questions about the military side of Argus. Another reporter inquired whether Argus was "directly involved in the antimissile program."

Quarles deflected further queries about the relevance of Argus for missile defense systems then under development, sticking to the emphasis on the science angle. He announced that because the National Academy of Sciences would soon be publishing all the scientific data officially, he would have to "reserve the answers to questions of that kind for the scientific publications."

"Are we to infer from your remarks that all of this information is being withheld from the public by the National Academy of Sciences?" asked someone.

Of course not, replied Quarles. "What I said is that the National Academy of Sciences is organizing for the publication through normal scientific channels . . . I did not mean to imply that everything we know is going to be published, nor did I mean to imply that the National Academy of Sciences is holding up everything we know from publication."

That didn't sit well with the press. "Well now, Mr. Quarles, let me get this straight," challenged another reporter. "Were these experiments not financed by the American people at taxpayer expense, and if this is true do the results not belong to the American people rather than the property of the scientists?"

"The results are not the property of the scientists," Quarles retorted. "Of course the scientists publish those things which we collectively judge to be in the interest of the American people to publish. There is no inherent right of publication, and in fact, the public interest will prevail in deciding what will be published and what will not be published . . . I think it would be inappropriate for me or my associates here to attempt to even brief for you the scientific results."

The press tried a different tack: Well, in that case, how about some broad information in layman's terms? In response, Quarles let York answer some general questions about the Argus effect and its measurements through Explorer 4 and sounding rockets.

The press conference was becoming something of a Mexican stand-off by this point. Another reporter inquired that if Argus really was intended as a scientific experiment, and given the public's great interest in science, "Why can we not just have a general briefing right now explaining the general results of this? We are fairly intelligible [sic] men, Mr. Quarles, and we can convey this in turn to the American people"—most of whom, he noted, did not read relatively obscure scientific journals. ("Hear, hear!" someone added.)

Quarles continued to walk the line. "I would like to make it clear that we do not represent this to be solely a scientific experiment any more than the first reactor that went critical near Chicago was solely a scientific experiment. The scientific aspects of it were exceedingly important, but there were other aspects of it that were exceedingly important." And not open for public discussion, in other words.

"Sir, we have been here more than an hour and we still don't know what your basic purposes were in the experience," complained another journalist. "We would stay many more hours if we thought it would be useful."

As the *New York Times* noted the following day, the news conference "was characterized by heated exchanges between [Quarles] and newsmen who charged they were not getting sufficient details . . . Mr. Quarles refused to permit the officials and scientists with him to respond to questions without his specific permission in each instance."[5]

Uncomfortable and trying as it may have been for Quarles and the assembled newsmen, Quarles succeeded in holding the ground for the administration. As Lisa Mundey points out, "Quarles managed to give less information about the test at the two-hour press briefing than Sullivan and Baldwin had presented in their stories."[6] The *Los Angeles Times* complained, "His answers were so guarded that it was virtually impossible to learn specifically what had been accomplished in the tests."[7]

One thing that Quarles did reveal, whether inadvertently or on purpose, was his displeasure at the whole affair. "He announced that he was sorry that the project was no longer a secret, noted the *New York Times*.[8] Walter Sullivan observes, "What seems to have distressed him in particular was the fact that the timing of the announcement of so momentous an event was determined by a newspaper and not by the government."[9] He quoted Quarles: "It isn't playing the game with the Department of Defense just the way I would like to see it played." Still, the *Times* pointed out that "Mr. Quarles, however, would not confirm that he was, in effect, accusing the *Times* of a security breach."[10]

But whether the Pentagon, the White House, and the military liked it or not, Argus was now public knowledge, and that meant it was fair game for the press corps, as James Van Allen found out that day. He was in California on the morning of the Argus revelations, attending a symposium on "The Realities of Space Exploration" along with the Jet Propulsion Laboratory's William Pickering and several other luminaries. Though he had of course seen the morning papers and knew in advance that the story was going to break, he was perhaps unprepared to face questions on Argus just yet, and declined to comment on specifics. But a reporter from the *Los Angeles Times* hit him: "If a host of neutrons could be released at great altitude, could they split the nuclei of a missile warhead and detonate it?" Fortunately, Van Allen was used to handling impertinent questions from nosy newsmen. He answered carefully, "Yes, if there were enough of them," stressing that he was speaking purely hypothetically. That didn't stop the *Times* from headlining the article "Space Blast Can Stop Missiles, Expert Says."[11]

The next day's edition of the *New York Times* featured more coverage, focusing not only on the Quarles press conference but also implications for the test-ban negotiations and a profile of Frank Shelton, the enigmatic DOD scientist, technical director of the Armed Forces Special Weapons Project "responsible for developing military requirements for atomic weapons and for conducting atomic tests," and scientific director of Argus.

As the story rapidly spread from the *New York Times* to the wire services and various other newspapers, and news outlets strove to find different angles on the fairly limited information that had been so far released, several figures in the Argus story found themselves the objects of unaccustomed, mostly unwanted attention. For men such as Shelton or Admiral Mustin, who were most comfortable working in the shadows of official obscurity, publicity was anathema. Fortunately for them, the most colorful character of Argus—and thus the one most attractive to the press—was the man who started it all, Nicholas Christofilos.

Beginning with the *Times* initial coverage on March 19, which featured a biographical sidebar on Christofilos and a photo captioned "Can argue as well as a Paris taxi driver," the "Crazy Greek" quickly became the vaguely whimsical public face of the Argus project. His unconventional background and personality coupled with his by-his-own-bootstraps life story were just too good to ignore, and nearly every paper featured a prominent sidebar about Christofilos with their Argus coverage. Whether he wanted to be or not, the scientist had become something of a media star.

It probably mattered little to Christofilos personally. Individualist that he was, he had always been rather indifferent to what anyone else thought or had to say about him, and he had other problems. Not long after the Argus story broke, he filed for divorce from his wife Elly in Berkeley, California, citing "extreme cruelty."[12] Unfortunately, his new celebrity made such personal matters fair game for the press.

Married for about five years, they had already been separated for four months, but Elly still claimed it was a surprise. "I never expected him to do this," she told reporters, sobbing and clutching their two-and-a-half-year-old son Nicholas Jr. "I cling to the hope he may not go through with it." An article in the *Washington Post* noted, "She expressed amazement at the grounds her husband selected. It was plain that to her the words 'extreme cruelty' implied more than what they have come to mean in the United States divorce context."[13]

The Argus revelations affected another principal player in a very different way. While Walter Sullivan was delighted with the big exclusive that he and Hanson Baldwin had brought to the *Times*, noting that "particularly within the scientific community and in the press, the disclosure was welcomed," it had caused Baldwin considerable personal anguish. Baldwin's biographer Robert D. Davies noted that Baldwin "agonized" over revealing the Argus secret. His dual identity as a reporter and as a former naval officer and Annapolis graduate made either decision—to publish or to keep quiet—a betrayal of his personal principles. "His dilemma was acute," Davies wrote. It was only when he heard rumblings that the Pentagon was about to go public anyway at the upcoming NAS conference that he decided to publish.

The story made Baldwin and Sullivan heroes both at the *Times* and among their journalist colleagues. *Time* magazine, for example, praised Baldwin and Sullivan for having "played the game at its best—with initiative and responsibility."[14] But Baldwin was not consoled by such accolades. "Baldwin felt a responsibility of the Times to the public, as well as to the country and the freedom of the press," said Davies. "His military contacts thought that Baldwin, as a newspaper writer, had had no right to determine what the public should read on military-political subjects, but he would reply that that was what a free press was all about . . . the Argus Project was to Baldwin just another example of the 'developing attitude of the government that the public must know only what the government thinks it is good for it to know'"—a sentiment of which Donald Quarles would no doubt have approved.

Baldwin decided he needed to make some amends. "A week following the story's release, he felt obligated to write to his old friend and valuable news source, Admiral Arleigh A. Burke, the chief of naval operations," noted Davies. Baldwin "confessed that he had 'played the game completely and in fact bent over backwards to avoid injury to the country which all of us serve.' He was very upset that the Navy had been blamed for leaking the story . . . a lie that he wanted to set right with Admiral Burke."[15]

Because of Argus, Davies concluded, Baldwin "was forced to reassess his views on the Washington bureaucracy. The press corps and government officials no longer shared the belief that they were on the same side, as was the case during World War II . . . with considerable passion, Baldwin told Admiral Burke that the real issue in all this was neither the security of information nor the denial of data to the Soviets; instead, it was the issue of 'controlling information and . . . issuing when the government wanted to and under the terms it wished.' In his view, Washington's concern to maintain secrecy had exhibited a 'fundamental failure to understand the first principle of good public relations and of democratic government.'"[16]

A few days after Argus broke, reactions from other quarters began to appear, including from the American citizens who, as a reporter had noted at the Pentagon press conference, paid for the whole thing. Referring to reports that Soviet scientists had in fact detected the Argus explosions, a letter to the editor in the *New York Times* noted, "the Pentagon kept secret from the American people something which was known to the Russian Army. One wonders who is fighting whom and why."[17] Another reader asked, "By what right can any nation or group proceed to envelop our earth in a band of radiation, the harmful effects of which are still open to debate? . . . What will be the verdict of future generations, if any remain, on the irresponsibility of conducting nuclear tests without more concern for human welfare and moral issues?"[18]

Others weren't as troubled by such grand moral issues. An editorial in the *Washington Star* noted, "Certain data will remain classified, regardless of those who clamor about the public's right to know. Such secrecy seems reasonable and necessary. After all, given an age as dangerous as the one we live in, there is much to be said for holding one's tongue on occasion . . . why should we publicize in detail what he have learned? Why should we shout about it from the rooftops?" The *Star* went on suggest that perhaps more high-altitude tests should be conducted, both for the sake of scientific and military knowledge. "Why should man debar himself from these probings? Indeed, how can he do so without enchaining his own mind and sinning against his own questing nature?"[19]

It was not only Pentagon officials and American taxpayers who were exercised about Argus secrecy and the question of revealing it to the world. Seeing the Argus story hit the papers on March 19, Senator Clinton P. Anderson, chairman of the Joint Committee on Atomic Energy (JCAE), was quite annoyed that, as administration officials had previously agreed, the JCAE had not been informed of the release in advance. He promptly wrote to General Herbert Loper at the Pentagon, who was the official liaison to Congress on atomic matters, and demanded an explanation. Loper sent a conciliatory answer, detailing the drama that had transpired within the Pentagon before the *Times* story and accepting full responsibility for failing to notify the JCAE. He had been briefly in Walter Reed Hospital on the evening of March 18 and so had missed hearing about the *Times* informing the government it was about to go public.[20]

Anderson wasn't mollified. He had been pressuring the Pentagon and AEC for more data on fallout, in preparation for public hearings on the issue later in the year, but the administration had been stalling and dragging its heels. Anderson viewed this latest fiasco over Argus as yet another example of deliberate obstructionism. As political payback, he released to the press some of his recent correspondence with the government on the fallout issue, stating, "The process of making public the ARGUS and fallout information is an example of how difficult it is to make available to the public the information it is entitled to have."[21]

Another prominent member of the Senate, Margaret Chase Smith of Maine, worried about possible fallout from Argus. Apparently reacting to a letter from an aggrieved constituent, Smith wrote to the AEC asking for more information about Argus's safety. AEC General Manager A. R. Luedecke responded promptly, assuring the Senator that because of the small Argus yields and the great altitude of the detonations, Argus did not "in any way represent a health hazard to human beings at the altitudes of air transport or on the surface of the earth." As to the secrecy of Argus, Luedecke noted that "all nuclear test detonations by the USSR have always been conducted in secrecy. It is possible that an experiment similar to 'Argus' has been conducted by the Russians."[22] If the Russians did it, then so could we, seemed to be the implication.

Meanwhile, preparations were underway behind the scenes, as Killian's PSAC and others in government debated over how much more to reveal in an official White House release at the end of March, and at the upcoming NAS conference the following month. At long last, after playing ball with the government and military and dutifully keeping their secrets, the scientists were about to have their day in the sun.

CHAPTER 11
The Light of Science

A DRAFT SCIENTIFIC REPORT WAS SHUTTLED AROUND THE PENTAGON, WHITE House, IGY Committee, and AEC, undergoing revisions and refinements to ensure that no more secrets were revealed than was already the case. The AEC was concerned only with disclosing the yield of the Argus shots, so that material was duly removed. After some further tweaks here and there, White House Press Secretary James Hagerty released the report on March 25, with Herbert York providing the scientific perspective.

For the administration, it was an exercise dedicated to emphasizing the position that Argus had essentially been a massive IGY science experiment with perhaps some military aspects, rather than a military project that happened to involve some science that could be conveniently shielded by the IGY. A memo from Assistant Secretary of Defense Murray Snyder to General Goodpaster offered some helpful suggestions for talking points to accompany the scientific release, complete with possible questions and answers.

For one, on the issue of delaying the release of the story, the memo noted that "despite rumors to the contrary" (apparently an oblique reference to Senator Anderson), the JCAE had been fully informed of the military implications of Argus and had opposed publication for that reason just as much as the Pentagon. Snyder mentioned the *Washington Star* editorial that had gone on about the "reasonable and necessary" need for "holding one's tongue on occasion" and suggested that reading a few lines from the piece might come in handy. In response to the question "was the publication of this story a breach of security?", Snyder suggested a response of "it should be obvious that the original disclosure of the plans for the Argus project, weeks before it occurred, was a serious security violation and a reprehensible thing," adding that efforts were underway to identify the source of the original leak to Baldwin.[1]

The report released by the White House glossed over any military questions to focus solely on science, describing the theories of Christofilos, the observed Argus effects, and how the various IGY resources were used to observe and record them. "The scientific aspects of these experiments . . . are regarded by many participants as one of the major achievements of the International Geophysical Year," said the report. Still, "it was clear that the undertaking involved a mixture of scientific and military interest."[2] The *New York Times* reported that "Despite the intensity of the artificial radiation, Dr. York dismissed the possibility of creating radiation belts with atomic explosions to kill the passengers in any future space vehicles."[3]

Not everyone in the scientific community agreed with that assessment, however. Victor Weisskopf of MIT, physicist and Manhattan Project veteran, suggested at a meeting of the American Physical Society that Argus had demonstrated that the radiation environment of outer space was threatening enough that future space travelers might have to restrict themselves to the polar regions, where "escape hatches" allowed a sort of "end run" past the radiation into outer space. As reported by the *Montreal Gazette*, "The Project Argus high-altitude nuclear explosions strengthen a view that the first launching stations for spaceships probably will have to be placed in Polar regions." Also, Weisskopf "did take issue with some of the published reports about things we might be able to do as a result of the Argus test," specifically the notion that, as some sources had reported, "neutrons from nuclear bombs exploded at high altitudes could be used to 'trigger' an A-bomb warhead in an enemy missile prematurely."[4]

While some scientists questioned a number of the official and unofficial contentions swirling around the whole Argus story, others dismissed the entire enterprise as "a total failure." Joseph H. Irani, radiation laboratory director at defense contractor Aerojet General, felt so strongly about the matter that he called the *Los Angeles Times*. The paper requested that he send them a letter explaining himself, which he proceeded to do in great detail.

"Today, when the free world is faced with a ruthless enemy who has no gods nor conscience, the United States is toying hopelessly with a wasteful and trivial experiment," Irani claimed. "Such an undertaking aimed to build up our defenses against incoming missiles can result only in draining our economy, creating false confidence, increasing fallout and eventually losing both cold and hot wars. So far the results from Project Argus show nothing that we did not know before or can not prove on paper or in the laboratory." Specifically, Irani took issue with the idea that radiation from an Argus-type shield could ever be strong enough to knock out warheads, or to effectively blackout radio and radar. Despite being hailed "as tremendous by some and as spectacular by others," Irani argued that to the general non-scientific public, "it is whatever the official and scientist calls it. It may be called a success while in truth it is a failure. On the other hand, the Russians may be concentrating on more tangible and less screwball ideas than we are." Irani also raised the specter of nuclear fallout from high-altitude tests, tying in his objections to the ongoing test-ban campaign. Although he made clear that he was speaking only for himself and not for Aerojet, Irani proclaimed Argus "a desperate attempt on the part of our so-called eminent scientists to find a solution for anti-missile missiles."[5]

Some in the scientific community assailed Pentagon secrecy as the cause for overblown and misleading expectations about Argus. "It is not . . . the delay in publication of the scientific reports which most needs attention. It is instead the mistaken conclusions in news reports that a magic film of radiation may shield us from missile attack," wrote physicist William Selove, vice chairman of the Federation of American Scientists, to the *New York Times* and several other major newspapers. That assertion, said Selove, "is a delusion . . . More candor in the statements from official quarters would lead to much less self-deception by the public." And such self-deception could only lead to disaster: "Unless the people and the governments make a real effort to understand the overwhelming effects of nuclear war and the fact that a real defense against intensive intercontinental ballistic missiles H-bomb attack does not exist and quite possibly never will, we shall probably stumble into devastation."[6]

Aside from such voices of dissent, however, the White House release seemed to do its job to almost everyone's satisfaction. "According to the White House, Argus had always been considered part of the IGY, and the test had not been previously announced so that scientists could follow normal procedures and sort out the militarily relevant information from the scientific," wrote Mundey. "What had been born a military test had been rechristened an anti-militaristic civilian scientific experiment."[7]

Still, the largely successful attempt to recast Argus in the innocuous and noble light of scientific inquiry didn't explain why the Pentagon remained so exercised about its release to the public. Testifying before Congress several weeks later, Snyder was asked whether he considered the Argus story a breach of security. "In my opinion it was a breach of security to print this story unless it was declassified," he responded, explaining that once the Department of Defense had been informed that the story was about to be published by a certain newspaper, it hurriedly declassified the scientific aspects to limit the damage. "The name of the newspaper was not mentioned," the *New York Times* noted archly.[8]

President Eisenhower also commented in a statement that "we regret that unknown persons gave out information prematurely and selectively to a single newspaper about the Argus experiments. This unauthorized step removed the decision on release from the orderly processes of Government. It is clear that whoever made this information prematurely available did so without any authorization on the part of the Government. In my judgment it is not in the overall interest of the United States for individuals to decide, on their own, whether and when restricted material should be made available to the press."[9]

Another reason for the administration's reluctance to reveal the existence of Argus was the reaction of foreign governments—not merely the obvious and understandable desire to keep the Soviet Union ignorant of the entire affair, but the political difficulties of carrying out such an enterprise without the consent of—or even consultation with—allies and other affected nations. For example, Brazil, in whose general neighborhood the United States had proceeded to detonate nuclear weapons without any sort of notice. Their reaction was less than enthusiastic. The Brazilian press railed about "atomic dust poisoning men in South Brazil" and that "the radioactive cloud produced by three bombs already may be producing effects on men, animals and vegetables." Brazilian scientists warned of "birth monsters," though others reassured their citizens that no excess radioactivity had been detected.[10]

As the National Academy of Sciences Argus symposium approached at the end of April, efforts continued to figure out what else needed to declassified, both to comply with IGY agreements and to portray Argus as chiefly a scientific experiment. The Pentagon, naturally, continued to play things quite close to the vest, while the scientists, led by Van Allen, pushed for the release of more data, such as shot yields, exact times, and precise latitudes and longitudes.

In a letter to Killian shortly before the symposium, US IGY satellite committee chairman Richard Porter and IGY US executive director Hugh Odishaw set out the scientists' case. "Such data are necessary if the various papers having to do with observed effects are to be scientifically meaningful," wrote Porter and Odishaw. They pointed out that because "a competent scientist" could already figure things out fairly accurately from the already-released data, there was no useful purpose to be served by keeping it classified. And exact data would be far more valuable. "It will not suffice to permit a few US scientists to use these data and then, without disclosing their calculations, state that a particular theory has been verified or not verified." Scientists, Odishaw and Porter were saying, needed to show their work. They argued that such information could easily be disclosed while still keeping secret military details such as the types of warheads and rockets used.

Again, there was also the issue of international prestige and politics. "It is important to give the greatest possible appearance of frankness in order to offset the impression that the United States has not lived up to its responsibilities in an international program," the scientists warned. "Even though the Argus experiment, as such, was not officially a part of the IGY"—as the White House was claiming, went the implication—"their relationship appears now to be inextricable. Both the domestic and foreign press have accused the United States of cynicism in conducting a secret military experiment within the framework of the International Geophysical Year program . . . if data basic to scientific understanding are withheld, the world will question US conduct in this matter." Greater openness would also "aid in deflecting alarmist interpretations of the experiment, particularly with reference to fallout."[11] After further discussion with York, Killian recommended the release of more—but still incomplete—details.

On April 29, Christofilos, Van Allen, and the rest of the Argus scientists finally presented their (mostly) complete results to the world in a packed house in the Great Hall of the National Academy of Sciences in Washington. With the imposing (at least to the lay public) title of "Scientific Effects of Artificially Induced Radiations at High Altitudes," the NAS symposium was intended to cover the full range of Argus scientific results, with all the major players participating and presenting papers on everything from the Explorer 4 satellite observations to the Jason sounding rocket measurements and other ground observations.

In his introductory remarks, symposium chairman Richard Porter also added to the general confusion. "Despite some newspaper stories to the contrary, there was no commitment under the IGY to exchange information with other nations on the Argus experiment," he stated. "Argus was not an IGY program; it was a Department of Defense effort." But because "the Department of Defense and the Atomic Energy Commission have now released the information you are about to hear this morning so that it can be made part of the synoptic geophysical record," he proceeded to disclose reasonably approximate times and locations of the Argus shots.[12] The scientists had won this particular argument, at least to some degree.

Then the presentations began. First up was Nicholas Christofilos himself. He sketched out the background of Argus, including how he had

originally conceived of the whole idea and how it had grown out of his Astron fusion reactor research. The Astron reactor, he explained, involved the
idea of creating a cylindrical layer or "bottle" of electrons to contain a high-
temperature magnetic plasma. Because he became interested in space after
the first Sputnik was launched, "it occurred to me to extrapolate this idea
of the electron layer to global dimensions."

No doubt to the relief of both Pentagon officials and scientists in at-
tendance, Christofilos neglected to mention the possible military implications of such an idea, noting instead that "it is obvious that the scientific
aspect of such experiments is extremely important." He recounted the discussions at Livermore, his first classified paper, and the Argus proposal it
eventually inspired, confirming that it was Van Allen's discovery of the
Earth's natural radiation belt that tipped the balance and convinced everyone that Argus had to be done.

After completing a general summary of the project and the observed
scientific results, Christofilos argued that they were just beginning: "Con-
tinuation of the Argus experiments . . . may yield new information in addition to that anticipated . . . there is now available a new tool for exploring
the part of outer space encompassed by the geomagnetic field, and for clar-
ifying the phenomena of interaction of the earth's magnetic field with various charged particles of natural or artificial origin."[13]

As befitted his lone-wolf reputation, Christofilos presented his
paper solo, but the remainder of the presentations were team efforts. Next
up was Van Allen, with Carl McIlwain and George Ludwig also credited
as authors on the paper titled "Satellite Observations of Electrons Artificially Injected Into the Geomagnetic Field." Van Allen explained again
how "the discovery of the existence of the natural, trapped radiation
served as an over-all validation of the Argus proposal." He proceeded to
spell out the Explorer 4 data in great detail, with a great array of charts,
graphs, maps, and other visual aids. And he emphasized that the satellite
data proved both that the Argus effect was a reality, and that the radiation
belt he had discovered the previous year was indeed a natural phenomenon and not somehow created by secret Soviet atomic blasts. He also
noted that despite previous estimates, the Argus radiation shell had per-

sisted at least until the previous December. The Pioneer 3 space probe, launched on December 6, 1958, in an unsuccessful attempt to reach the Moon, nevertheless reached an altitude of slightly over 63,000 miles, and before falling back to Earth managed to pick up some faint vestiges of the Argus radiation shell, weak but still active even after three months. Those traces had disappeared by the time the next Pioneer was launched in early March 1959.[14]

Explorer 4 may have been the most visible part of the Argus project before the whole thing became public, but the Jason sounding rocket observations also attracted a lot of interest once they were revealed. The Air Force scientists in charge of that effort—Lew Allen, William Welch, and several other colleagues—detailed their part of the story. The data collected by the Jason rockets "agree qualitatively with those measured by the satellite Explorer IV," they reported, noting that the rockets also collected some additional information not possible with satellite observations.[15] That was followed by two other members of the Jason team, Jasper Welch and William Whitaker, who offered a heavily mathematical presentation on the theory of trapped electrons. Finally, Philip Newman of the Air Force Cambridge Research Center and Allen Peterson from Stanford gave separate presentations on the various Argus data collected from the ground, including radio, radar, and visual observations.

Over the next several days, the scientists dominated the world news. Newspapers presented their findings with elaborate diagrams and graphics. Perhaps as a bit of Cold War propaganda boasting of an American triumph, even the United States Information Agency got involved, featuring Argus on their "New Horizons in Science" English language radio program broadcast on the Voice of America on May 7. The show featured recorded excerpts from Porter and Peterson at the NAS symposium, and though it didn't do the same for Christofilos (possibly because of his heavy Greek accent), it reported his declaration that Argus provided "more accurate knowledge of the true shape of the Earth's magnetic field, knowledge that may be of practical importance in radio communications and weather predictions."[16]

Christofilos, however, did speak about Argus on a different Voice of

America program broadcast in the Greek language. His proud parents, still in Athens, listened in on one of the still-operating radios their son had built himself during his youthful electronics tinkering days.

The scientific details of Argus were fascinating enough for geophysicists and space scientists, but they also pointed to definite military and political considerations for anyone who cared to approach them from that perspective. Although it had perhaps not been the intention of Van Allen and his colleagues, the wealth of data they had now released also demonstrated quite conclusively not only the possibility of detecting high-altitude nuclear explosions, but more importantly, precisely how to do it—and the vast amounts of data that could be gleaned from such observations. Naturally, anything that American scientists could do, Soviet scientists could do as well, a fact not lost on the Pentagon and White House. These, of course, were much the same arguments that Van Allen and others had used to fight for the declassification and release of Argus data.

At the symposium, the scientists had alluded rather obliquely to such concerns, including the mention of how high-altitude nuclear detonations could interfere with radar and radio communications and Christofilos's observation that, as the internal newsletter of his employer Livermore Lab later reported, "Such experiments must be restricted to small bombs in the kiloton range, because megaton fission released in the proper location in outer space could create a radiation hazard for several days or more for outer-space travelers."[17] Some in the press seized upon this to play up the radiation shield angle. "Expert Says One Bomb Can End Satellite Life Around World," declared a *Washington Post* headline. The accompanying story opened with the alarming lines: "A 1-megaton atomic bomb exploded at the proper point in outer space can girdle the earth with a band of lethal radiation within minutes. A man on a satellite within that band would be dead in less than 3 hours."[18]

But whether such a phenomenon was ultimately a hazard or a weapon depended upon your point of view—and on the identity of the affected space travelers, spacecraft, or missiles. The Christofilos Effect (or alternatively, the Argus Effect) had been conclusively, if only weakly, demonstrated by the low-yield Argus tests. What would happen with more powerful nuclear explosions? Could the Argus Effect be used as Christofilos had originally intended, to destroy enemy missiles, and if not, to at least cripple them? And if that wasn't possible, what about using it to disrupt and knock out enemy communications and radar systems?

Such questions were on the minds of congressmen at a closed hearing before the House of Representatives Committee on Science and Astronautics a couple of weeks before the NAS symposium. York and Shelton, as the top Pentagon scientists for Argus, both testified. Committee chairman Overton Brooks and his colleagues managed to learn some intriguing things about Argus that had not been revealed in the news articles, the White House release, and the NAS symposium.

York laid out the general chronology and details, including the reasons for keeping certain information classified. Some of the confusion in the press had actually been working to the government's advantage. "The newspapers published the altitudes as 300 miles. We have simply let it stand there. All we have said is that the shot burst was well outside the earth's atmosphere. The reason for keeping this classified is that one of the ideas and—practically everything that was seen in this experiment confirms the ideas of Christofilos."[19]

As for the locations and times of Argus, "The reason for keeping the precise time secret is that when you explode a bomb anywhere around the earth, there are certain radio signals which are produced," explained York. "The observation of these radio signals are important in connection with detecting explosions." So specifying the shot times within about ten minutes before or after "is good enough to be useful in connection with the scientific applications of this data, but it is vague enough so that we think that the Russians can't work this down to the point where they know what kind of signals this produced." York also pointed out that because the Argus shots were relatively small, press reports of worldwide effects "are based on a confusion of these shots with the high-altitude shots in the Pacific which did produce large-scale disturbance"—a reference to the Teak and Orange shots that had preceded Argus in 1958.[20]

Because the hearing was conducted in secret, the questions focused more on the military ramifications of Argus than its scientific discoveries.

The congressmen seemed particularly intrigued by the effect of high-altitude nukes on communications, especially when York observed: "If instead of being small, if this bomb had been very large, then shooting it in the South Atlantic would probably have interfered with communications across the North Atlantic. So that it gives you the odd opportunity of firing a bomb in a completely remote part of the world which is under your control—or under no one's control, perhaps—and producing a communications interference at a place which is not available to you. In other words, if we fired this bomb in the Indian Ocean we could have disrupted shortwave communications in the vicinity of Moscow." Although that "would take a bomb of large yield and not this little bomb," it was "a rather interesting possible weapons effect . . . if you do it in the South Pacific, somewhere around the tip of South America, you can interfere with communications in Washington."[21]

Pennsylvania's James Fulton, after some queries on Argus science, returned to the military implications, asking York if such an effect might be used "to get through radio, radar, and other communications that Russia or any Iron Curtain country might have set up as a defense . . . to have our strategic air force pass into Russia without detection?"

"That is one of the things people had in mind here," York responded. He emphasized that there was still much that remained unknown, making it difficult to seriously discuss specific strategic or tactical military possibilities. Was there even a consensus that there was any point in striving for some kind of missile defense system? "I think there is simply a divergency of opinion here," said York. "There are people who feel it is worth continuing. There are a few who feel it is worth speeding up. There are a few who feel that there just is not anything along this line at all . . . that is why we have to keep at it all the time."

Another congressman wanted to know about fallout from these high-altitude explosions. "We are still working on that question," said York. "We do not know the answer." He noted, however, that because fallout from high-altitude explosions takes much longer to return to earth, most of it is probably decayed by the time it reaches the ground.

The politicians were highly exercised by the secrecy issue, especially how a supposedly classified project was uncovered by a newspaper. How was such a serious security breach possible? Was everything being done to locate the source? Shelton assured the Committee that it was. That didn't placate Frank Osmers of New Jersey, who worried that if the *New York Times* could find out about Argus, then "I presume the Soviet Union knows as much about it." Congressman Emilio Daddario of Connecticut, not accepting York's assertion that Hanson Baldwin and Walter Sullivan had just been supremely persistent and dedicated newsmen, even raised the specter of a possible spy ring: "Apparently there is a chain which got the plans into the hands of these people . . . and any program of whatever importance we put through from this point on, we have to assume it is not only in the hands of the newspaper but in the hands of the enemy as well. If someone has so little regard for the security of the country, then they certainly would not have any less regard for the security of giving it to the agents of a foreign country."

"In this case the Soviet Union did not seem to have it," York replied patiently. "If they had it, it would have been to their advantage to release it." As Shelton had previously testified, had the story broken publicly before the Argus operation, "we probably would not have conducted the experiment."

"We have paid for a fine piece of research for Russia to use against us," complained Leonard Wolf of Iowa, worrying about what would happen if the Russians decided to disrupt communications in Washington by detonating a bomb at Tierra del Fuego.

"If you want to interfere with communications in Washington, the best thing to do is put the bomb right here," York said dryly. He agreed that "you can do it by putting it in Tierra del Fuego," but observed that "it is of much greater concern if they put it right here, because then they can interfere with communications by killing us all."

The hearing ended on an appropriately apocalyptic note, as Utah representative David King noted that many of his constituents "seem to be very concerned about these experiments that go off in the areas that carry such lethal potentiality with regard to the human race. They seem to feel we are tampering with great forces, the implications of which we

Nicholas C. Christofilos, Greek-American physicist, photographed in 1971. (*Credit: Lawrence Livermore National Laboratory*)

Physicist James Van Allen, here pictured posing in his Iowa laboratory with one of his rockoons. (*Credit: University of Iowa Libraries*)

A full-scale model of Explorer 1, America's first satellite, held by its creators. The team was gathered at a press conference at the National Academy of Sciences in Washington, DC, in the early hours of February 1, 1958, to confirm that the satellite, which had launched a few hours before, was in orbit. *From left to right:* Jet Propulsion Laboratory director William Hayward Pickering, James Van Allen, and Wernher von Braun.

(Credit: NASA / Jet Propulsion Laboratory–Caltech)

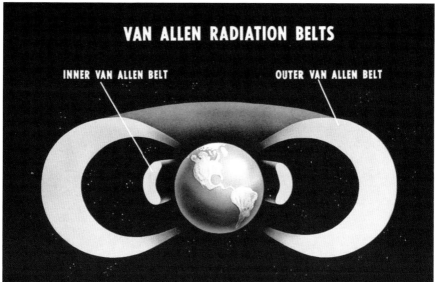

The data from Explorer 1 and Explorer 3 resulted in the discovery that the Earth was encircled with bands of radiation, trapped by the planet's natural magnetic fields; these became known as the "Van Allen radiation belts."

(Credit: NASA)

Christofilos explains his latest "crazy idea," which he coined the Argus effect.

(*Credit: Lawrence Livermore National Laboratory*)

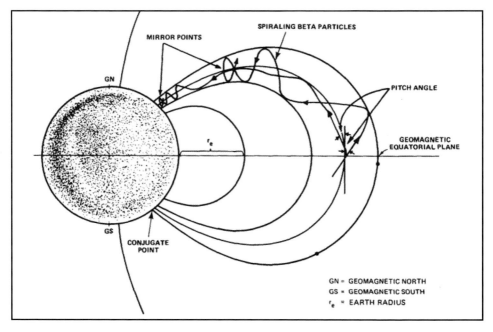

A diagram of the Argus effect.

(*Credit: Defense Nuclear Agency*)

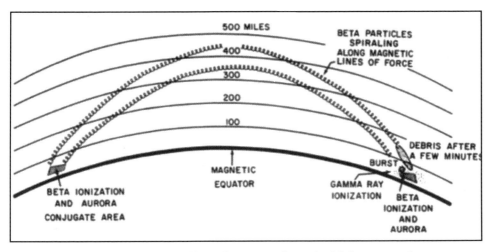

Another diagram of the Argus effect, illustrating how the high-energy electrons produced by an outer space nuclear detonation travel back and forth along the Earth's magnetic lines of force. *(Credit: United States Department of Defense)*

Christofilos explains how a magnetic field encompasses the Earth. He theorized that, if a nuclear bomb was detonated along the planet's magnetic field, some of its radiation would be trapped and would travel along lines of magnetic force to a point at the opposite end of the line (known as the magnetic conjugate area), spreading around the Earth in a thin shell of electrons. Christofilos suggested the possibility that the Argus effect could be used defensively. *(Credit:* Life Magazine, *1959, reprinted in* Annals of Iowa, *Volume 70, 4, Fall 2011)*

Rear Admiral Lloyd M. Mustin, reluctant commander of Task Force 88, which was formed by the Pentagon's Armed Forces Special Weapons Project to carry out the highly clandestine Operation Argus. (*Credit: Mike Green, NavSource Naval History*)

The USS *Tarawa*, the aircraft carrier that served as Task Force 88's command ship and Mustin's headquarters during Argus.

(*Credit: Mike Green, NavSource Naval History*)

The USS *Norton Sound* (AVM-1), the ship that would launch the first nuclear weapons into space. The *Sound* had a vast aft deck that made her a perfect missile-launching platform. *(Credit: United States Navy)*

Two of the Grumman S2F Tracker aircraft of Tarawa's VS-32 "Norsemen" squadron that patrolled the Argus operations area for unwanted intruders and also conducted observation flights during the tests. *(Credit: Allyn Howard, NavSource Naval History)*

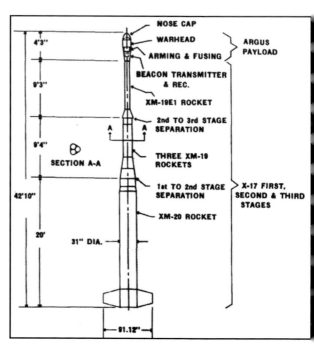

Left: A sequence of frames from an X-17a test-firing film on the *Norton Sound*. Note the spin retrorocket package falling away in the final frame.

(Credit: Department of Defense)

NOSE CAP

WARHEAD

ARMING & FUSING

ARGUS PAYLOAD

BEACON TRANSMITTER & REC.

XM-19E1 ROCKET

2nd TO 3rd STAGE SEPARATION

4'3"

9'3"

9'4"

SECTION A-A

THREE XM-19 ROCKETS

42'10"

1st TO 2nd STAGE SEPARATION

X-17 FIRST, SECOND & THIRD STAGES

20'

XM-20 ROCKET

31" DIA.

91.12"

Above: Diagram of the Lockheed X-17a rocket that would loft the Argus warheads into space from the deck of the *Norton Sound.*   (*Credit: Defense Nuclear Agency*)

Right: X-17a missile ready for test firing from the *Norton Sound.*

(Credit: United States Navy)

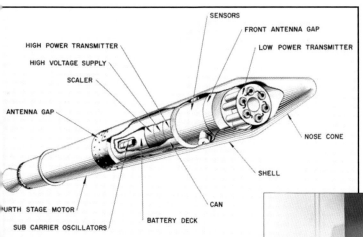

Explorer 4, Van Allen's satellite that would monitor the effects of Operation Argus in space.
(*Credit: University of Iowa Libraries*)

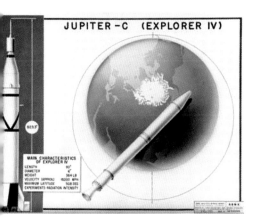

The Jupiter-C launch vehicle that would hurl Explorer 4 into orbit.
(*Credit: University of Iowa Libraries*)

Before shipping it off to Cape Canaveral, Van Allen plants a farewell kiss on the Explorer 4 instrument package as Carl McIlwain (center) and George Ludwig look on. (*Credit: University of Iowa Libraries*)

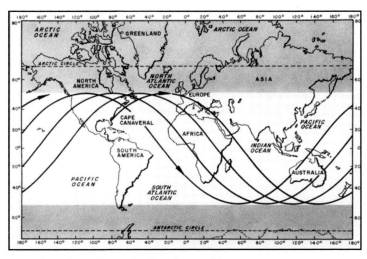

The plot of Explorer 4's first four orbits.
(*Credit: University of Iowa Libraries*)

STATE UNIVERSITY OF IOWA IOWA CITY

Department of Physics

309054

21 February 1959

R

Dr. James R. Killian
Office of the President
White House
Washington 25, D. C.

Dear Dr. Killian:

1.   I enclose for your consideration a memorandum entitled "Expression of Views on Declassification of Argus" dtd. 17 February 1959 (SECRET). This is an extended version of a similar one submitted at the Conference on Argus on 18 February 1959 in Livermore, California.

2.   As you will note, my views are: (a) that continued security classification of the Argus-Hardtack tests is of little practical avail, (b) that a prompt and full public report of the tests and observations will contribute greatly to the international prestige of the United States as a leader in the application of atomic devices to scientific purposes, and (c) that if we fail to do (b) the U.S. will quite likely be again "Sputniked" in the eyes of the world by the Soviets.

Sincerely yours,

J. A. Van Allen

A. Van Allen

Enclosures (1) "Expression of Views on Declassification of
Argus" dtd. 17 February 1959, 3 pages (SECRET).
(2) Excerpt from "The Observer", English newspaper
of Sunday, February 15, 1959 entitled "Radiation
Belt May Monitor A-Test" (UNCLASSIFIED).

After Operation Argus proved a success, the US once again decided to detonate nuclear weapons in space to test the limits of the now-confirmed Argus effect. Called Operation Fishbowl, the test series was launched from Johnston Island in the Pacific, with various shots at different altitudes and nuclear yields. An array of sounding rockets carrying instrumentation for scientific measurements undergoes liftoff preparations before the Operation Fishbowl high-altitude nuclear tests.   (*Credit: Defense Nuclear Agency*)

Operation Fishbowl's Bluegill Prime launch pad explosion would require major cleanup, including decontamination of the irradiated launch site. Workers in radiation suits inspect the remains of the Thor missile engine after Bluegill Prime.   (*Credit: Defense Nuclear Agency*)

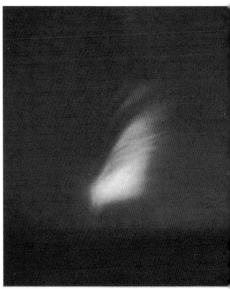

Photos of the effects of the Starfish Prime shot, which produced a light show and boreal effect in the nighttime sky. (*Credit: Defense Nuclear Agency*)

The detonation of Starfish Prime seen through a cloud layer in Honolulu.

(*Credit: Defense Nuclear Agency*)

The Starfish Prime fireball from Hawaii.
(*Credit: Defense Nuclear Agency*)

An upper atmospheric photograph of the Starfish
Prime explosion.   (*Credit: Defense Nuclear Agency*)

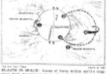

On the morning of March 19, 1959, one of the greatest secrets of the Cold War became one of its biggest stories when Walter Sullivan and Hanson Baldwin ran their story on Operation Argus in the *New York Times*.

(*Credit:* New York Times *archive*)

On October 7, 1963, President John F. Kennedy signed the Limited Test Ban Treaty, officially ending the era of nuclear testing in the atmosphere and outer space.

(*Credit: JFK Library*)

The Astron fusion experiment at Lawrence Livermore National Laboratory, the center of Nicholas Christofilos's work after Argus. The photo shows Christofilos's linear electron accelerator. (*Credit: Lawrence Livermore National Laboratory*)

Christofilos in 1968. He died in 1972, never realizing his grand dreams for Astron.

(*Credit: Lawrence Livermore National Laboratory*)

know not. We are going willy-nilly not knowing where it will take us. If we make a mistake we will sterilize half the race. They take a dim view of the whole thing."

"I know that people do," York replied. But he reassured the Committee that these high-altitude experiments "just don't do that . . . I don't know how to prove that to somebody who doesn't want to believe it." He added that "I suppose it is possible we could stumble on to something. We do consider this as carefully as we can . . . I guess anything is possible. We are as sure as we can be that it is not possible, that it isn't dangerous."[22]

However, it was becoming increasingly obvious that, spurred by the revelations of Argus, the Teak and Orange tests of the previous summer, and the rapidly growing campaign against fallout and nuclear testing that had led to the test moratorium, a great many people both in the US and around the world weren't quite so confident with official reassurances. In fact, just as others pondered the possibilities for further Argus-type experiments after the test moratorium lifted, the public was worrying more and more about what might happen if atomic and thermonuclear weapons continued to be detonated with such careless abandon all over the world—and how it could be stopped once and for all.

CHAPTER 12
The Sky is Falling

AS THE BIGGEST PUBLIC CELEBRITY OF THE ARGUS SCIENTIFIC CONTINGENT—AND undoubtedly the one most experienced in dealing with the press—James Van Allen was invited to write and speak further on Argus in the coming months. Perhaps the most exotic invitation came not from yet another American university, chamber of commerce, or Sunday newspaper supplement, but from the Soviet Union.

Now that the IGY had officially wound up all its worldwide activities and closed up shop as of December 31, 1958, the multitudes of participating scientists were deep into analyzing, interpreting, and presenting the fruits of the eighteen-month enterprise. That included the Russians, who hosted the Cosmic Ray Conference of the International Union of Pure and Applied Physics in Moscow in July, 1959. As one of the world's foremost authorities on the subject, Van Allen was invited as a matter of course, but especially to discuss his work on the Argus project. Although the NAS conference at the end of April had been completely open to the national and international public, the papers that Van Allen, Christofilos, and the rest of the scientists had presented there were still in press and had yet to appear in the official journal of the NAS, *Proceedings of the National Academy of Sciences*. Van Allen's Russian colleagues, not to mention other international researchers, were eager to hear the details of Explorer 4's probings of the Argus effect from the man himself.

The Russian scientists were sincerely concerned with the scientific aspects of it all, but with the test-ban negotiations between the US and USSR dragging on in Geneva, such information obviously also had political ramifications. Those may have been exacerbated by the June 1959 release of a joint report from the Atomic Energy Commission and the Defense Department on the effects of 1958's high-altitude Teak and Orange shots, which revealed how the tests had disrupted and partially blacked out radio and radar for thousands of miles over the Pacific, from Australia to Hawaii—and also noted how rabbits, used as test subjects, were blinded even at great distances by the intense flash of the explosions.

Coming close on the heels of the Argus revelations of secret high-altitude nuclear testing, these new reports added to the already fair amount of consternation in the press. "High A-Blasts 300 Mi. Away Damage Eyes," headlined the *Chicago Tribune*. "Radio Was Snarled By H-Bomb Blasts in '58," said the *New York Times*, also noting that by "'sheer coincidence,' according to officials, the report was released on the same day on which the nuclear powers agreed at Geneva to hold further technical discussions on the problems of detecting atomic explosions at high altitudes . . . the report also clearly indicates that hydrogen bombs exploded in the stratosphere could prove to be a valuable method for disrupting radio communications and radar warning systems in advance of an enemy missile attack or bomber raid."[1] These stories merely served to emphasize a Bureau of Standards report released about a month earlier that, as the *Washington Post* reported, "the blasts disrupted for hours radio circuits between Sydney, Australia, Wellington, New Zealand, Honolulu, Vancouver, and San Francisco. Some circuits . . . were out for days."[2] The news reports did distinguish between the Argus shots and the Pacific tests, explaining that unlike the relatively small Argus blasts, the latter tests were hydrogen bombs exploded at much lower altitudes.

As if all this wasn't alarming enough, York and Shelton's congressional testimony in April had also been released in heavily censored form. The papers jumped on York's musings that a high-altitude nuke over the

Indian Ocean could black out Moscow, or one over South America could do the same to Washington.[3] That was alarming not merely on a visceral level but on a political one. As the Federation of American Scientists noted in their newsletter, "[T]hat we have in fact been testing nuclear weapons in space makes it clear that some sort of arrangement with regard to such explosions will have to be discussed at Geneva."[4]

So as the summer of 1959 settled in over the world—along with the radioactive fallout from the extensive US and Soviet testing of the previous year—high-altitude atomic bombs were on everyone's mind. Military officials worried about the threat they posed (while also keen to exploit their strategic and tactical potential); negotiators in Geneva worried about the political complications they created for a test ban; civilian activists and the general public worried about fallout and helpless blinded rabbits; and scientists enthused over the geophysical secrets they were revealing about the outer space environment.

It was in this unsettled climate that Van Allen journeyed to Moscow in June, along with some of his American physicist colleagues, on a $1,200 travel grant from the National Science Foundation. But not before he received a visit from an enigmatic government official, who had a special favor to ask of him.

"The federal agent asked him for a 'trip report' covering questions in eleven areas of interest, including a full description of recent cosmic ray developments, names of institutions and leading scientists, leads on anyone who was secretive or evasive, and all the materials from the conference," wrote Van Allen biographer Abigail Foerstner. In short, Van Allen was asked to "evaluate the status of cosmic ray research in the Sino-Soviet bloc," and given a list of ten locations of interest he might visit.[5]

Ever dutiful, Van Allen agreed, and departed for Moscow. While in the USSR, he assumed as a matter of course that, as a prominent American and particularly one involved in research related to military issues, he was under discreet KGB observation, and his Russian counterparts had probably been given similar instructions to feel out their American colleagues for any interesting tidbits of information. But he proceeded to present his Explorer 4 observations and Argus results just as he had already done at the National Academies symposium, to the fascination of the Russian researchers. Van Allen toured Russian labs and research facilities; he met his Soviet counterpart, Sergei Vernov, who had designed the scientific instruments for Sputniks 2 and 3. As was usually the case among professional scientists, it was all friendly and collegial, even if the activities were being constantly shadowed by incognito KGB officers.

Van Allen later admitted to a twinge of concern when colleague Leonid Sedov invited him to a seminar at the USSR Academy of Sciences to talk further about Argus. It hadn't been part of the previously scheduled itinerary, and as George Ludwig noted, "Everyone was edgy during those Cold War years . . . it was not unknown in those days for visitors to the USSR to disappear."[6]

But the invitation seemed legitimate, and after all, Van Allen was there to talk science to his Russian opposite numbers. As a bit of insurance, he asked two fellow Americans and conference delegates, physicist John A. Simpson of the University of Chicago and MIT's George W. Clark, to join him at the Academy. "I figured that if all three of us disappeared, someone would certainly investigate," he explained later.[7]

His talk at the Academy turned out to be enlightening not only for the Russians but for the Americans. Van Allen learned that both nations had originally suspected that the Van Allen belts weren't a natural phenomenon but a result of secret nuclear testing by the other side. But now that particular suspicion had been defused. "They could see for themselves . . . how different the Argus belts were from the natural belts. That pretty much laid the question to rest."[8] It was a telling example of the value of international scientific cooperation and the sharing of data.

Van Allen's Russian odyssey had gone over so well, in fact, that it led to a visit in November by Soviet researchers to Van Allen's lab in Iowa. The atmosphere of tension between the two nuclear superpowers may have been continuing as steadily as ever, but scientific cosmopolitanism was at least helping to mitigate its worst aspects here and there.

Meanwhile, back in the States, the debates over government secrecy that Argus had helped fuel were raging, now dealing less with Argus than with the fallout controversy, which by this time had grown into a major worldwide political issue. Senator Clinton Anderson, in a political pique at being kept out of the loop on the Argus *New York Times* leak, had released secret correspondence between the AEC and the Joint Committee on Atomic Energy. They had brought some extremely disturbing facts to light, and Anderson wasted no time in making them the center of the JCAE fallout hearings he was then chairing.

The letters between the JCAE and several Pentagon and AEC officials, including Herbert Loper, Willard Libby, and A. R. Luedecke, confirmed that despite previous public reassurances that the dangers of fallout from atmospheric testing were minimal, high amounts of dangerous radioactive particles had been falling to earth and entering the food chain far faster and at greater intensities than formerly believed. "It looks like strontium-90 isn't staying up there as long as the AEC told us it would," Anderson observed. Even worse, "the fallout is greatest on the United States."[9] While there was no real intimation of intentional deception on the AEC's part, the correspondence made clear that there was far less confidence on the issue among the Commission's scientists than had been known to the public.

Still steaming about the Argus matter two months later, Anderson published a lengthy editorial in the *New York Times* in early May just as the hearings were about to begin, decrying the administration's fetish for secrecy and classified data in general, as well as its conduct regarding Argus and strontium-90. "Where should secrecy end and freedom of information begin?" he asked. "Does it make sense for defense information to be labeled 'top secret' and yet released in full to the newspapers? Why are questions about the nation's atomic energy programs met again and again with the reply: 'It's classified'? Is the secrecy surrounding the atom justified? Or is the secret stamp perhaps being used as a convenient shield behind which to hide information which someone somewhere happens not to like or to agree with?" Anderson made it clear that he believed that far too often the latter was the case, much to the detriment of the public good. Beyond the public's right to know, said Anderson, "suppression of information prevents discussion which might produce solutions to the problems at hand. It is impossible to say how many valuable scientific breakthroughs have perhaps been delayed—or even prevented—because scientists were not free to exchange information; how many Christofiloses have gone undiscovered because of secrecy . . . I am hopeful that our fallout hearings this week may provide some answers."[10]

The JCAE hearings did not provide any final answers to the dilemma of openness versus secrecy, or a completely satisfactory solution to the problem of radioactive fallout. But they did serve as yet another reminder to all the world's nuclear powers that fallout was an issue that could not be ignored, disregarded, or covered up. It had first come to general public awareness with the US Castle Bravo test way back in 1954, and went on to become one of the major issues of the 1956 presidential election and a political hot potato ever since.

But now, Ike didn't have to worry about politics. "Eisenhower, late in his second term, was determined to burgeon his legacy as a peacemaker," notes the Defense Nuclear Agency history. "For the President, the moratorium on nuclear testing was the harbinger of a relaxation of tensions that would hopefully lead to a nuclear test ban treaty, nuclear disarmament, and overall detente with Moscow."[11]

Such noble aspirations were all very commendable and played well with the multitudes of ordinary citizens worried about strontium-90 isotopes showing up in milk and the bones of their children, but the testing moratorium, to say nothing of the prospect of a complete or even partial end to nuclear weapons testing, had raised considerable alarm in other quarters. Not only were Pentagon planners and military brass worried about Soviet cheating and national security, but the weapons labs such as Los Alamos and Livermore and the vast infrastructure that had been constructed to conduct and maintain America's nuclear testing capabilities was now being directly endangered. Even the AEC admitted privately that public opposition had become so passionate that the US would soon be forced to give up atmospheric testing entirely.

But there were practical concerns as well, with the US testing establishment essentially in mothballs since the previous Halloween. Noted an official AEC history, "As summer 1959 dragged on with no perceptible progress in the Geneva talks, pressures began to build within the Administration for resumed testing. During the moratorium the Commission's laboratories had accumulated various requirements for tests. They also needed to develop warheads for new types of missiles, to proof-test new weapons entering the stockpile, and to gather more information on weapons effects."

It wasn't merely a case of institutional ennui. "In the meantime, both the Department of Defense and the Commission had to live with the fact that the voluntary moratorium was denying them the full potential of the nuclear stockpile. Just as worrisome to both agencies was the possibility that by the end of the year the President might once again extend the voluntary moratorium."[12] If the nuclear weapons establishment remained idle for too long, there were fears that the best scientists and technicians would be forced to leave the weapons labs and military for private industry and academia, a "brain drain" that could seriously cripple US military capabilities.

There was also the problem of getting back up and running if the moratorium did end and testing operations resumed. The military had to decide what units to keep operational and which to deactivate; what facilities at Nevada and in the Pacific to close down and which to keep open; and in general, how to maintain everything on a sort of reduced alert status without losing proficiency or allowing morale to evaporate. One major decision was the disbanding of the military's Joint Task Force Seven, the massive organization which had been conducting the Pacific test operations. Los Alamos scientist and historian William Ogle called this "possibly the most serious single move made during the moratorium toward winding down our capability to test in the atmosphere."[13]

Alternatives to atmospheric testing meant either underground—or, once again, in outer space. The latter possibility sparked renewed discussions over the more ambitious sequel to Argus, called Willow-Argus or simply Project Willow.

That idea had been briefly discussed around the time of the Argus operation but abruptly abandoned when the impending testing moratorium made it a moot point. Now seemed a good time to dust off the concept, but there were still considerable difficulties. "Even underground and high-altitude testing was not free from political complications," noted the DNA history. "The public controversy over ARGUS six months after the fact had less to do with testing *per se* than with the nuclear agencies' failure to keep Congress informed of their plans. The implication, disquieting in light of the ongoing test ban negotiations, was that tests conducted in outer space could go entirely undetected. Nevertheless, it was the fallout question that absorbed public attention immediately after the ARGUS revelations. To what extent was high-altitude testing safer than atmospheric tests? How high was high enough to prevent radioactivity from returning to earth? Congressional hearings in May of 1959 produced warnings from AEC, DASA [Defense Atomic Support Agency, formerly AFSWP], and public health experts that even a shot thirty miles up offered only a 50 percent margin of protection. However, at much higher altitudes—ARGUS had taken place approximately 300 miles above the earth—fallout dropped off automatically. For DASA planners, this turned deep space into the next frontier for nuclear testing once the moratorium was lifted."[14]

So perhaps Argus had paved the way for the eventual salvation of nuclear testing by opening the door to outer space. Whereas Argus had been an initial probing, a proof of concept for the Christofilos effect and its potential, Willow would be far more extensive, involving higher altitudes and far more powerful weapons, building upon the lessons learned and the phenomena observed during Argus and the Teak and Orange shots in the Pacific. It would include far more comprehensive tests of the effects of high-altitude nuclear explosions on radio and radar communications, and soon Pentagon planners envisioned even more: "After the spring 1959 hearings, discussions began between DASA and the AEC to expand the scope of Willow to include AEC requirements for high-altitude testing, detection, and evasion."[15] Although the Argus results had seemed to discount the possibility, Christofilos's original idea of an antimissile defense might still become a reality through Willow.

Discussions regarding Willow had been going on since at least the previous year, and estimated budgets were being prepared for it as early as January 1959, calling for $60 million for the project. That already high preliminary price tag didn't include money for the missiles and launch support facilities, which didn't bode well for the future of the entire enterprise, particularly since the 1960 AFSWP/DASA budget appropriation was only $17 million.[16]

With the moratorium in effect, DASA and the military continued to debate Willow, and somewhat quixotic efforts to keep it alive would drag on until about the end of the following year. "One could hardly make a persuasive case for a project which, if nothing changed, would never be productive," observed the DNA history.[17] Whether the test moratorium was continued for another year or ultimately led to a permanent test ban, Willow could probably never be conducted. For the time being, at least, the weaponeers would have to wait.

The scientists, however, didn't have that problem, and continued to pore over their Argus data. Later in the year, Army Signal Corps scientists announced evidence of a second Argus radiation shell in their analysis of the Explorer 4 data.[18] If the military and strategic potential of Argus had been stalled somewhat by the test moratorium and political obstacles, the scientific bounty was there to be reaped.

But the military contingent was about to get some encouraging news. On December 29, 1959, reluctantly yielding to pressure and hoping that it might kick start the Geneva test-ban talks with the USSR that had stalled over technical issues, Eisenhower announced that the US would end its "voluntary moratorium" as of December 31, though it would not resume actual testing without giving public notice in advance. The Soviets responded that they would refrain from testing as long as the US did likewise.

For the weaponeers, it wasn't yet a return to the glory days, but it gave hope that perhaps they might soon be back in the game. Another sign came less than two months later on February 13, when France tested its first atomic bomb in the Saharan desert and became the world's fourth nuclear power, following Britain's first test in 1952.

Clearly, despite the best efforts of disarmament advocates and the prevailing tides of world opinion, the era of nuclear testing was not yet past. Whether it would resume its frantic pace of the past ten years in the open air of Earth, be driven off the planet into space, or banished deep underground remained to be seen.

CHAPTER 13
A Pause to Consider

WITH THE EISENHOWER ADMINISTRATION ENTERING ITS FINAL YEAR AND A PRES-
idential election on the horizon, nuclear testing and the Cold War in general
seemed to have settled into an uneasy lull. Nikita Khrushchev's visit to the
United States in the fall of 1959 had gone well and seemed to augur an eas-
ing of tensions, but there were major issues between the US and USSR yet
to be resolved, such as the test ban treaty. The Geneva talks continued fitfully with US negotiators struggling to develop new strategies for dealing
with the Soviets, but it was becoming increasingly probable that any substantial breakthroughs would have to wait for the next administration. Still,
Eisenhower and Khrushchev were planning a summit meeting for May
1960 in Paris, and perhaps progress there would translate to other areas.

Meanwhile, the nuclear testing establishment kept itself occupied at
a greatly reduced but steady pace. Scientists at the weapons labs still had
mountains of data from all the tests of 1958 to analyze, and at the continental test site in Nevada, there were other non-weapons projects to keep
things humming along. The AEC and NASA worked on experiments for
Project Rover, with the aim of creating a nuclear-powered spacecraft, while
the Air Force busied itself with Project Pluto, a nuclear ramjet cruise mis-

sile. Such efforts involved the use of nuclear reactors and radioactive materials, but not nuclear explosions, so they were fair game whether the test moratorium was considered in force or not. Livermore continued low-level work on Plowshare, their pet project for the use of atomic explosions for civilian purposes such as digging mine shafts and creating harbors. Although the moratorium prevented full-scale experiments involving Plowshare ideas, Livermore scientists were free to test concepts with conventional high-explosive devices at the Nevada Test Site. And it was also possible to continue technical work on finding ways to detect nuclear explosions through seismic and other kinds of sensors, research that was directly relevant to the Geneva test-ban negotiations.

"Tunnels were dug. Contractors kept working. Radiation safety and weather groups remained in place. Overall, a level of readiness was maintained so that nuclear weapons testing could successfully resume when needed," noted a DOE history, also observing that "the moratorium was not entirely unwelcome in the testing community. After a record seventy-seven nuclear weapons tests in 1958, the testing system, noted one participant, 'was tired, tired, tired.'"[1]

Ever restless, Nicholas Christofilos had already moved on from Argus, continuing work at Livermore on his main passion, the Astron fusion reactor, and supervising construction of a linear accelerator to test Astron concepts. Turning away from outer space to the depths of the oceans, he had also devised a system for communication with submarines using extremely low frequency radio waves.

He was also undergoing some profound personal changes. His divorce from Elly became final in May, and at the end of June he married a coworker from Livermore, Joan Jaffrey, in Chapala, Mexico.[2] It would not prove to be a happy ending, however, as the emotional and legal fallout from the divorce would persist for some time to come.

James Van Allen was also deep into new projects and space missions, but still found himself talking and writing about Argus. Whether consciously or not, he continued to downplay the military aspects of the enterprise in favor of the scientific. Speaking at Ohio State University early in 1960, he echoed what had now become the standard Argus line,

calling it "one of the greatest experiments in pure science ever conducted." At the same time, noted Walter Sullivan, "he spoke out strongly
against its secrecy, which he termed a 'masterpiece of administrative stu-
pidity,' for when the project finally became known, it appeared to be 'a
sinister sort of military experiment,' instead of the great scientific achievement that it was."[3]

Despite such protestations, none of the direct participants in Argus
such as Van Allen, nor those who had been more indirectly involved, as
Sullivan had, harbored any illusions about the dual nature of Argus. Sullivan, still with the *New York Times,* had begun work on a book about the
International Geophysical Year, and decided to devote an entire chapter to
Argus, knowing a good story when he'd broken one. Van Allen was among
the many experts Sullivan contacted for help and to read over drafts. Sullivan would also include a detailed account of just how he and Hanson
Baldwin had broken the Argus story and the challenges of dealing with
the byzantine world of government secrecy and official classification.

Unlike his colleague Hanson Baldwin, Sullivan apparently had no
second thoughts about his role in revealing a classified story to the public.
In one of his letters to Van Allen, he commented, "Yesterday I received the
text of a talk you have recently given to some engineers in which you discussed the security aspects of Argus with forthright candor and also referred to a new, exciting—and secret—experiment to be carried out in
space. I can only say that this time there is no soul-searching going on at
the *New York Times.*"[4] The "secret experiment" Sullivan refers to is unknown, but the jaded attitudes of both men about the vagaries of government classification comes through loud and clear.

As part of his research, Sullivan also tried contacting those who may
have been the great invisible, if unwitting, audience for Argus: the inhabitants of Tristan da Cunha. In March 1960, he sent letters to both the current
British administrator, P. A. Day, and the one present during the time of the
Argus shots, G. Francis Harris, inquiring about whether they or other islanders had seen anything unusual.

The mail service to the ostensible "farthest place on Earth" was
painfully slow, so Sullivan's inquiries didn't reach the island until July—

which turned out to be the first time that anyone on Tristan da Cunha had heard anything about Argus. "When the letter reached the island . . . its 294 inhabitants learned for the first time that on Aug. 27, 1958, an atomic bomb was fired sixty miles south of their island," Sullivan later wrote in the *New York Times*.

In his response, which Sullivan didn't receive until October, Harris recounted how the islanders had indeed noticed some strange things going on during that brief but odd summer of 1958, including the occasional passing Navy aircraft and mysterious shortwave transmissions. Somewhat more ominously, current administrator Day's response to Sullivan included observations of fallout measurements on the island having increased to about three times their normal levels from late summer to October 1958. Sullivan checked with an expert at the New York AEC office, who told him that the brief rise in readings at Tristan was most likely not related directly to Argus but was simply a result of increased fallout all over the world during that period, given the high number of US and Soviet tests that had occurred that year: "October [1958] was a pretty darn meaty month all over the world," said the AEC. There may have been a slight increase in fallout at Tristan from the first Argus shot, but "probably slight compared to the general world-wide increase at that time."

It seemed hard to believe that anyone could be unaware of atomic bombs going off in their own backyard, but as Sullivan explained, "Official word of the staging of Project Argus was withheld for some time, and when the news was finally printed the location of the atom shots was not revealed. Hence the islanders and their British administrators may have heard about Project Argus without relating it to the September flight of planes over their island."[5]

WHATEVER HOPES STILL REMAINED FOR EISENHOWER TO ACHIEVE A TEST BAN treaty or a more permanent detente with the Soviets evaporated on May 1, when an American U-2 spy plane was downed over Sverdlovsk and its pilot, Francis Gary Powers, was captured alive. Khrushchev was genuinely outraged, considering the incident a betrayal of the goodwill he believed he had been building up with Eisenhower. But more than that, he also recognized a golden propaganda opportunity, which he proceeded to exploit to the fullest. The initial US denials, disproved by the capture of Powers and the U-2's reconnaissance equipment, didn't help. Eisenhower refused to accede to Khrushchev's demands for an apology, and the Paris summit rapidly collapsed in rancor and recrimination. A disappointed Eisenhower had to return home knowing that he had failed in his great dream to leave a legacy as a peacemaker.

Fortunately, the U-2 affair didn't completely destroy prospects for a test ban treaty. In the wake of the episode, both Eisenhower and Khrushchev reaffirmed their commitment to pursuing disarmament. The talks continued in Geneva, but with the atmosphere chillier than ever. The spirit of trust, or at least wary friendliness, that had been slowly blossoming between the US and USSR had vanished, and it would be left to Eisenhower's successor to pick up the pieces.

One of the many contentious issues in the Geneva talks was the problem of verification: if both sides did agree to stop testing nuclear weapons, how could they be sure the other side wouldn't cheat? In other words, was it possible to set off a nuclear explosion without anyone knowing about it? As Sullivan had discovered in his correspondence with the Tristan islanders, it was at least theoretically possible, since apparently they hadn't known about Argus until he told them about it. But if anyone on Tristan had happened to be awake in the middle of the night and looking up at the time of an Argus shot, they may have seen something.

It was clear that atmospheric tests in the open air wouldn't escape scrutiny for long. Even if they were conducted in a remote enough location, fallout debris would inevitably spread around the world for anyone to detect; indeed, that was how the US had initially learned about the very first Soviet A-bomb. And since one of the major motivations for a test ban was to stop atmospheric testing and the spread of fallout, detecting such tests wasn't really an issue. The sticking point was whether tests deep underground or at very high altitudes—in the upper atmosphere or outer space—could be effectively concealed. A joint US-Soviet conference of scientific experts in summer 1958 had concluded that methods for detection of clandestine testing were largely reliable, which helped convince both sides to undertake the temporary moratorium.

The prospect of policing a permanent test ban was still daunting. Detecting underground tests with seismometers posed the problem of distinguishing a nuclear detonation from natural earthquake activity. Detecting high-altitude tests might be possible with satellites or earth-based means, but it wasn't as straightforward as it seemed.

Some disquieting news also came out of the Soviet Union near the end of 1960, when Russian geophysicist Valeria I. Troitskaya, who had headed the Soviet IGY effort, reported that her analysis of data from various Soviet "telluric current" monitoring stations had picked up unmistakable signs not only of the Argus shots but also of the Orange high-altitude H-bomb test in the Pacific. Troitskaya's work had already demonstrated that magnetic storms caused by solar activity can "twang" the natural geomagnetic current in the Earth's crust. As her detectors demonstrated, the Argus shots and Orange had done essentially the same thing. The data pinpointed both the times and the locations of each detonation, and the publication of Troitskaya's data was in fact the first public announcement of the actual shot times. "Dr. Troitskaya pointed out . . . the official times given by the United States for the shots erred somewhat. This, according to scientists associated with the project, was so because they were required, for security reasons, to make the times approximate," reported Sullivan in the *New York Times*.[6]

Although the Soviets hadn't realized the true nature of their odd geophysical observations at the time, the reality that they had in fact detected the supposedly secret Argus shots was not comforting to Pentagon officials. But for those working and hoping for a permanent test ban, it provided further evidence that cheating would be readily uncovered. It did not help to resolve debates in Geneva over other issues, however, such as on-site inspections and yield limits for underground tests. The negotiators soldiered on, even as John F. Kennedy won the November election and Dwight D. Eisenhower prepared to leave office.

In his farewell address to the nation on January 17, 1961, Eisenhower famously warned against the excesses of the "military-industrial complex," lamenting the fact that while in the past the United States built weapons only in times of war, in the new atomic age "we have been compelled to create a permanent armaments industry of vast proportions." In an often overlooked corollary to his warnings of the "undue influence" of the military, he also spoke of "the equal and opposite danger that public policy could itself become the captive of a scientific-technological elite." Ironically, though perhaps with the best of intentions, Eisenhower himself had done much during his presidency to foster and expand both.

That irony did not escape the wise old warrior and statesman. Mentioning the imperative of disarmament, and with the failure to achieve a permanent nuclear test ban weighing on him, he said, "I confess that I lay down my official responsibilities in this field with a definite sense of disappointment. As one who has witnessed the horror and the lingering sadness of war, as one who knows that another war could utterly destroy this civilization which has been so slowly and painfully built over thousands of years, I wish I could say tonight that a lasting peace is in sight . . . so much remains to be done."

The work of achieving "a lasting peace" would now fall to John F. Kennedy. He took office as something of a contradiction, part "peacenik," part dedicated Cold Warrior. Although he had campaigned against a nonexistent "missile gap" between the US and USSR, and now promised to "oppose any foe" to "assure the survival and the success of liberty," proclaiming that "only when our arms are sufficient beyond doubt can we be certain beyond doubt that they will never be employed," he also called for "serious and precise proposals for the inspection and control of arms." During his years in the Senate, Kennedy had been a strong and outspoken supporter of a nuclear test ban, and many test-ban advocates were confident that the new president would finally achieve that goal.

The Soviets also seemed reasonably optimistic and receptive to renewed discussions. Nikita Khrushchev himself began pressing for a summit meeting with Kennedy even before the new president was inaugurated. For a brief but heady moment, the "New Frontier" seemed to be more than lofty rhetoric. And although both sides had publicly declared themselves no longer bound by the testing moratorium, they were continuing, quite voluntarily, to observe it anyway, based on a gentleman's agreement of "I won't do it unless you do it first."

Meanwhile, not everyone was happy with the new administration. The Pentagon and the AEC were growing increasingly restive, uneasy with the ongoing moratorium, fearful about falling behind the Soviets, worried about hanging on to their scientists, struggling to maintain some kind of operational readiness to resume testing while uncertain what form it might take if it did resume. Despite the relentless worldwide public opposition to atmospheric testing that had led to the moratorium in the first place, many in the testing establishment knew that there were no guarantees that the USSR would continue to play along. Perhaps for now, it suited their propaganda purposes to do so, but that could change abruptly. And who was to say that the Soviets couldn't—or wouldn't—test in secret while still professing to be observing the moratorium? And if that happened, how badly would it affect American security and the effectiveness of our own atomic stockpile?

Even assuming good faith on the part of the Soviets at present, it was still quite conceivable that for whatever reason the US could decide to resume testing on its own accord. If so, would it be underground? In space? In the atmosphere? Would it take place in Nevada or the Pacific? Both? Someplace else entirely—even back in the frigid South Atlantic? As the Kennedy Administration settled in, such questions were endlessly discussed, both in administration circles and within the halls of the Pentagon and the AEC.

Kennedy's new team of advisors and cabinet members also debated options for the next round of test-ban negotiations, which, after closing down the previous December to await the new US administration, resumed in Geneva in March 1961. It was not an auspicious start. Perhaps reenergized by the break and deciding to test the mettle of the new administration, the Soviets assumed a tough stance, rejecting American proposals on verification and inspections and offering problematic counterproposals. Any hopes for a quick and substantive breakthrough were quickly dashed.

Matters only grew worse as spring turned to summer. The abortive Bay of Pigs fiasco in April didn't help US-Soviet relations, nor did the first meeting between Kennedy and Khrushchev in June in Vienna. The young president tried to hold his own against Khrushchev, but the domineering chairman seemed to largely overwhelm him, especially as Khrushchev issued an ultimatum on the long-troublesome Berlin situation. Kennedy left Vienna feeling demoralized, while Khrushchev went home newly confident. Before the summer was over, the Berlin Wall would be raised, and two months after that, US and Russian tanks would confront each other in a brief but tense standoff at a border checkpoint between East and West Berlin.

After all the hope and optimism with which 1961 had begun, it was hardly the climate for sweeping disarmament agreements. As if to emphasize the point, the USSR finally decided to abandon the test moratorium. On August 30, they announced that they would resume testing, laying the blame squarely on the United States for its failure to accept its supposedly reasonable proposals for the test ban and disarmament. The Soviets proceeded to conduct their first nuclear test since 1958 two days later—in the open air. They followed that up with more tests, with no concerns about fallout or public reaction. (In response to accusations that they had broken the moratorium, the Soviets had a convenient loophole: they pointed out that they had only pledged not to test as long as the "Western powers" did likewise—and that "Western powers" included France, which had indeed continued to explode bombs quite independently in utter disregard of any US-USSR agreements.)

Kennedy's reaction, reported his special assistant and speechwriter Ted Sorenson, was "unprintable." He had tried to avoid it for as long as possible, but politically, practically, and militarily, he no longer had a choice. On September 5, he announced that "In view of the continued testing by the Soviet Government, I have today ordered the resumption of nuclear tests." But Kennedy still had a political card to play. The new American tests would only be conducted "in the laboratory and underground, with no fallout." The USSR might be cavalier about nuclear fallout and world opinion, but not the US. "We have taken every step that reasonable men could justify," said Kennedy. "We must now take those steps which prudent men find essential." He also noted that "our offer to make an agreement to end all fallout tests remains open until September 9."

Underground tests resumed in Nevada ten days later under the name of Operation Nougat. Compared to the renewed Soviet activity, it was a fairly modest effort, though the weapons labs and test personnel were pleased to be back in business. Unfortunately, Kennedy's promises about "no fallout" didn't quite pan out: some of the Nevada tests nevertheless ended up venting some radioactive debris from their underground tunnel shafts into the air. Still, it was minor and limited only to the immediate vicinity, unlike the product of the new multi-kiloton and megaton Soviet tests.

That disparity, however, started to grate on some within the testing community. Why should the United States continue to restrain itself while the Soviet Union had resumed open testing of all sorts of large, dirty weapons aboveground without any regard at all for the rest of the world? Aside from that nagging question, there continued to be new weapons designs and problems that could only be effectively resolved with the testing of larger devices, either aboveground or at high altitudes. Pressure began to build on the Kennedy Administration to return to a full-fledged program of atmospheric testing instead of one timidly hiding away in deep underground caves and tunnels.

All of these alarming developments had not escaped the notice of American popular culture. In the midst of international tensions, a minor yet oddly appropriate movie was released in July of 1961 called *Voyage to the Bottom of the Sea*. Directed and co-written by Irwin Allen, previously known mostly for nature documentaries and an adaptation of the Arthur Conan Doyle novel *The Lost World*, *Voyage* centered on the advanced scientific research submarine USOS *Seaview*, designed and built by genius scientist and engineer Admiral Harriman Nelson. When meteors ignite the Van Allen radiation belts, lighting a fire in the sky all over the world that begins to melt the polar ice caps and literally cook the entire world, Nelson devises a plan to use the *Seaview* to save the Earth by launching a nuclear missile to explode within the belts, extinguishing the fire and presumably wiping out the belts as well.

Although a scientifically preposterous scenario, Allen's fanciful premise is oddly reminiscent of Project Argus. Unlike Argus, Nelson's scheme is quite public and vocally opposed as too risky by many scientists and governments, forcing an obsessive Nelson to evade various obstacles before he ultimately achieves his mission and saves the planet. It's unknown whether Allen and his co-screenwriter Charles Bennett were directly inspired or influenced by Argus in conceiving the story, but it's likely that they were at least aware of the project, and attempting to tie in their film with current newsworthy events, including not only Argus but also the International Geophysical Year, nuclear testing, and especially the recent launch of the world's first nuclear submarine USS *Nautilus*, using the canny commercial instincts on which Allen built his subsequent career in film and television. (And of course, the film's themes of worldwide catastrophe, melting icecaps, and attempts to stave off worldwide climate change in the face of political denial and opposition have a sad new relevance in the twenty-first century.)

While hardly the equal either artistically or technically of other contemporary films involving themes of nuclear testing and weapons, such as 1959's highly influential *On the Beach*, *Voyage to the Bottom of the Sea* (which spawned a successful television series several years later) is an intriguing cultural artifact of a tense era, a moment in history in which imminent catastrophe seemed to hang over the entire world, not in the form of a burning sky but of nuclear Armageddon. Although neither Irwin Allen nor almost anyone else realized it at the time, his potboiler film would prove eerily prescient of the very near future, if not to such an apocalyptic degree.

The sequel to Project Argus was about to be born.

CHAPTER 14
Bigger Bangs

ON OCTOBER 30, 1961, THE LARGEST EXPLOSION EVER CREATED BY HUMANS occurred over the remote Arctic archipelago of Novaya Zemlya. It was a hydrogen weapon called the Tsar Bomba, designed, built, and tested by the Soviet Union with an announced yield of fifty megatons, but actually somewhat higher than that, with later analyses revealing a yield of fifty-seven megatons. Though the bomb had originally been designed to create a 100-megaton explosion, that was apparently too much even for the Soviets, who modified the weapon for a lower yield after realizing the amount of fallout such a weapon would create, not to mention the fact that it would certainly immolate the bomber crew dropping it and even from that desolate location possibly kill or injure a number of Soviet citizens. It was the ultimate in saber-rattling.

It did not come as a surprise. That past summer, Khrushchev had already warned that the Soviets might test a 100-megaton weapon, and earlier in October he had announced his intention to test a fifty-megaton version of that weapon. But the advance warning did little to diminish the political—and physical—impact of the test.

Even in its more modest form, the bomb's effects were felt around the world. Buildings were damaged and windows shattered hundreds of miles away, and the seismic shockwaves traveled around the world three times, echoing both the voice of doom and the defiance of the USSR.

Despite all the wrangling in Geneva about test detection and cheating and on-site inspection, this was not the sort of test that could be kept secret. Nor was that the point. Nikita Khrushchev had intended it as a demonstration of his country's strength, determination, and stubborn independence. And on a more visceral level, Tsar Bomba was simply meant to scare the world. Khrushchev wasted little time in boasting of the Soviet achievement and warning that the USSR possessed far more powerful weapons.

As might be expected, worldwide reaction outside the Communist bloc was universally negative. It wasn't only the monstrous scale of the weapon—seemingly beyond any reasonable military purpose—but the callous disregard of the fallout from such an enormous detonation, particularly since the USSR had voluntarily refrained from atmospheric testing for almost three years previously (though they had resumed almost two months before Tsar Bomba). The Vatican called the test "an insane decision, morally, politically, socially, economically, and humanely deprecable," that had shown the world "the true face of Communism . . . reflecting the tension of hatred." The Norwegian Parliament, geographically closer than most to the site of the detonation, declared that it "showed a cynicism unparalleled in history," while West Germany accused the USSR of "ruthlessly risking the health of all mankind."[1]

The US was also critical. Former presidential candidate and outspoken test-ban advocate Adlai Stevenson, now US ambassador to the United Nations, proclaimed that the Soviet Union had "started a new race for deadly weapons."[2] Also predictable was that this latest Soviet provocation increased by orders of magnitude the pressures upon Kennedy to resume testing in the atmosphere, rather than limit the US to innocuous "no fallout" underground detonations. After all, if the Soviets weren't going to restrain themselves, why should the United States?

Also, the problems that had arisen during the extended moratorium—such as maintaining test capability and resources—hadn't gone away, even with the resumption of underground testing in Nevada. And the labs continued to insist that certain categories of new weapons and their effects couldn't be effectively evaluated without full-fledged atmospheric testing. Opinion was almost unanimous that, as presidential assistant Arthur Schlesinger later wrote, "This final atrocity made it impossible to put off our own preparations for atmospheric testing any longer."[3]

Still, a reluctant Kennedy continued to resist. Although he announced shortly after the Tsar Bomba test that the US was preparing to resume atmospheric testing "in case it becomes necessary," and approved funds for such preparations, he balked at issuing final, definitive approval. Even in the face of domestic and international outrage over Soviet testing, he met opposition from certain quarters, most notably from British prime minister Harold Macmillan. That was a major difficulty, since test planners had decided that with the deteriorated resources of the US's former Pacific testing sites, new tests would require a fresh site: Christmas Island, which happened to be British territory. In a December summit meeting with Kennedy in Bermuda, Macmillan agreed to go along with the resumption of US atmospheric tests and the use of Christmas Island, as long as the US made one more sincere attempt at Geneva to achieve a test ban treaty.

That seemed to clear the path to resume, but Kennedy continued to drag his heels. His new AEC chairman Glenn Seaborg, who was, naturally, deeply involved in the discussions, wrote that "following the Bermuda summit, the decision to test in the atmosphere seemed to have been made. Yet two more months were to elapse before the decision was announced. During this period the president repeatedly sought reassurance, in meeting after meeting, that it was the right thing to do, that there was no alternative . . . what Kennedy seemed to hope for was some eleventh-hour agreement with the Russians that would make testing unnecessary."[4]

Alas, it was not to be. On March 2, 1962, Kennedy gave a lengthy address to the nation outlining the reasons for deciding to resume atmospheric testing. "It was as though he were addressing the judgment of history," Seaborg noted.[5]

Kennedy discussed the continued Soviet tests and the technical and military gains they were achieving, and explained that resuming US atmospheric tests would make the Soviets realize that the United States would no longer sit idly by and allow the USSR to catch up and surpass us—which might make them more open to further negotiations and the long-sought test ban treaty. Furthermore, he said, "If the Soviet Union should now be willing to accept such a treaty, to sign it before the latter part of April and apply it immediately—if all testing can thus actually be halted . . . there would be no need for our tests to begin."[6]

The Geneva talks resumed a couple of weeks later, but the impasse continued with the Russians over technical and verification questions. The United States moved ahead with its preparations in the Pacific, including at Christmas Island, where the UK had officially granted access more than a month earlier.

The new series, officially dubbed DOMINIC, would be an ambitious, wide-ranging operation, with thirty-six shots planned, from airdrops to weapons on barges and towers, and the first operational test of the Navy's new Polaris submarine-based missile system. As if to make up for lost time since the interminable moratorium, it would be the largest nuclear test series yet conducted by the United States. And in a major part of DOMINIC called Operation Fishbowl, the US would once again detonate nuclear weapons in outer space for the first time since Argus. But this time, the project would be conducted without the same constraints and uncertainties. The Argus/Christofilos effect was real. What could be done with it? It was time to extend the intriguing results of Argus into an entirely new level of power and technical ambition.

The Fishbowl events wouldn't be the first nuclear detonations in space since Argus, however. As part of their busy operations since abandoning the test moratorium, the Soviets had already fired several high-altitude shots, including at least one experiment in which they fired a missile through the fireball of another detonating warhead to observe and measure the effects. That was disquieting for Pentagon planners, since it indicated that the Russians were aware of the possibilities of "fratricide"—the inadvertent destruction of one warhead by another aimed at the same target—and trying to find ways to either mitigate it or use it to advantage.

"One of the grave concerns felt by the administration about the Russian tests of 1961 was that they might have made progress toward an antimissile missile," said Seaborg. "It was evident from our analyses of the tests that the Soviets had made an effort in that direction. The implications of this were frightening. If one side could prevent penetration by the other side's missiles it would have achieved an enormous and tempting advantage."[7] Further high-altitude tests by the US were needed to keep pace.

Planning for Fishbowl had been in progress for quite a while before Kennedy announced the resumption of US atmospheric tests. Anticipating that possibility not long after the Soviet fifty-plus megaton supertest, he had ordered the testing facilities to make serious preparations, including the establishment of a new joint military task force to conduct tests in the Pacific. Joint Task Force 8 (JTF-8) was formed under the command of Army Major General Alfred Starbird. To command the naval forces of JTF-8, Starbird tapped Argus veteran Rear Admiral Lloyd M. Mustin.

"There was a lot of scurrying around the Navy Department to see who would be the Navy deputy," Mustin remembered in an interview. "Well, I had never had any interest in being involved in the nuclear weapons business, in any way . . . But people began looking at me pretty closely because of that Argus business."

Mustin wasn't happy about the idea. "Nobody wanted the job," he said. But as it happened, he was the only naval officer with the necessary rank and experience. "I said, 'I'm pretty sure that I can do the job, but it's certainly not something I'm asking for.'" But "be that as it may," orders were orders, and "I found myself ordered to be the Navy deputy of Joint Task Force Eight."[8]

Mustin would not be quite as directly involved with the high-altitude Fishbowl tests as he had been with Argus, however. The shots would be launched by Thor missiles, placing them under the aegis of the Air Force part of JTF-8. A preliminary planning document was already completed in November 1961, months before Kennedy actually gave formal approval for DOMINIC and Fishbowl to proceed. Long before then, plans and proposals for additional high-altitude tests had been under discussion, stalled at first by the test moratorium and later by Kennedy's reluctance to resume testing. But now speculation and possibility had become reality.

According to the initial November 1961 plan, Fishbowl would consist of three shots: Bluegill, Starfish, and Urraca, each at different altitudes and nuclear yields, all launched by Thor boosters from Johnston Island, the same place from which Teak and Orange had been launched in 1958 and the only spot in the Pacific with the necessary launch facilities. (Conveniently, it was US sovereign territory, avoiding the need for any pesky negotiations with allies.) The objective was to further study and define the various intriguing phenomena that had been revealed by the earlier Teak, Orange, and Argus tests, and to evaluate their defensive—and offensive—military implications. The earlier tests had been interesting, but as a Pentagon official commented, "poorly instrumented and hastily executed," such that the data provided by them, including Argus, was of only limited value. But a series of dedicated high-altitude tests, carried out with all the elaborate instrumentation, measurements, and control of a laboratory experiment, would fill in all the blanks and answer all the questions remaining from 1958.

"It had begun to become desperately clear that there were, indeed, all sorts of results to be expected from detonations at altitude that we simply had to have information on," Mustin recalled. "They could be of catastrophic proportions on a national basis, if they were not adequately known, so that adequate considerations could be made for them."[9]

One of those considerations was what came to be known as EMP, or electromagnetic pulse. Although the existence of EMP as part of the phenomena accompanying a nuclear blast had been known to scientists almost from the beginning of the atomic age, it had been considered a relatively unimportant side effect compared to blast, radiation, and the other far more obvious phenomena. But the Teak event in 1958 had started to change minds, and Orange and Argus only served to convince more people that EMP was something that had to be better understood. "I had never even heard the term during [Argus], but in the interim, some pretty alarming possibilities had begun to be recognized in this country," Mustin said. Such as knocking out the entire US power grid and communications network "by one single nuclear burst above Kansas, or some such thing."[10]

Another consideration involved the possibility that the intense X-rays generated by a high-altitude or outer space nuclear burst, unimpeded by atmosphere, might cripple or destroy enemy warheads—a sort of extension of Nicholas Christofilos's original idea. If so, perhaps defensive missiles could be designed to maximize their X-ray output for better efficiency and killing power.

So there was much to learn, much to catch up on, all driven by the omnipresent Cold War fear that the Russians would learn it all first and go on to use it against us. Now armed with the president's reluctant approval and full authority, preparations moved ahead quickly, if not smoothly. Getting the vast American nuclear testing machine fully back up and running after such a long layoff, especially for such an ambitious and extensive enterprise as DOMINIC, proved to be a daunting task. Under the pressures of an impending deadline, Project Argus had managed to go from an odd idea in the mind of an eccentric scientist to a successfully completed operation in less than a year. But DOMINIC dwarfed even the massive undertaking that was Argus. And while Starbird, Mustin, and the various other planners of DOMINIC weren't facing the same deadline pressure of 1958, they did have orders to be prepared to begin testing anytime beginning in April of 1962.

There were facilities to be built, observation stations and instrumentation to be set up, equipment to be moved, and endless administrative and logistical problems to be resolved. Somehow, it all got done, and Operation DOMINIC opened on April 25, 1962, with Adobe, the first airdrop shot at Christmas Island. More tests followed in short order, including the first firing of a live nuclear-armed Polaris missile from a US Navy submarine, the *Ethan Allen*. Making a return appearance in that operation was the Argus veteran USS *Norton Sound*, now serving not as a missile platform but as Admiral Mustin's flagship for the operation. Immediately after the Polaris test, the *Norton Sound* returned home to Port Hueneme, her cameo appearance in DOMINIC completed, and with it, her career in nuclear test operations. The vessel continued to serve as a testbed for various Navy weapons systems until finally decommissioned in 1986.

Meanwhile, as preparations for the high-altitude Fishbowl tests continued over at Johnston Island, some decidedly nontechnical complications arose. One of them, which had already been somewhat taken into account in the planning of the operation, was the eyeburn problem. Detonating a nuclear weapon at high altitude meant that the intense light of the fireball would be visible over a much broader area than in a surface or tower shot, thus exposing civilians far removed from the test area, even as far as Hawaii, to the possibility of temporary or permanent eye damage if they happened to be looking in the wrong direction when a bomb went off. The problem had first been recognized back in 1958 with Teak and Orange, when some native islanders had been affected. But the Fishbowl events would occur at much higher altitudes, exposing a much wider area to danger. Aside from choosing the most remote and sparsely populated location possible for the tests and evacuating any potentially affected areas, the only solution was to make certain no one strayed into the danger area around shot time. That task would fall to the Navy's patrol planes and ships.

Another complication was more political and thus, less easily resolved. As had been the case ever since both the USSR and US resumed testing, protests had commenced worldwide. Three thousand people demonstrated in Tokyo after the first DOMINIC shot, and 350 protesters were also arrested on the other side of the world at the US embassy in London. On April 29, President Kennedy hosted a formal White House reception and dinner for forty-nine Nobel Prize laureates and other scientific luminaries, including J. Robert Oppenheimer, the former scientific leader of the Manhattan Project. But another dinner guest, Nobel laureate Linus Pauling, was outside the White House, part of a huge crowd picketing against nuclear testing. Several anti-nuclear advocates even went to more extreme lengths, sailing boats into the quarantined safety zones around the Pacific island testing sites, attracting the attention of Admiral Mustin's ever-patrolling security screen of P2V aircraft and destroyers.

For those in the atomic testing game, such annoyances had become part of doing business. But the announcement at the end of April of the impending high-altitude tests brought protests from an entirely different quarter: the international scientific community. The pioneering British radio astronomer Sir Bernard Lovell, director of Jodrell Bank Observatory, worried that the Fishbowl shots, particularly the test planned for the highest altitude, Urraca, would seriously disrupt or even destroy the Van Allen radiation belts, or at least the inner belt.

"The operators of this project should be restrained by all possible means from this presumption of moral right to interfere with the environment of the earth," Lovell declared. "A small group of military scientists, unknown and unidentified to the world at large," were doing nothing less than preparing a "sledgehammer blow at the radioactive environment of the earth."[11] The influential and persuasive Lovell managed to convince a large contingent of scientific colleagues, mostly British and European, that Fishbowl should be stopped, or at least delayed until the possible consequences could be thoroughly and properly examined.

As the more conventional atmospheric tests continued unabated in the Pacific, the Fishbowl controversy played out in the press and scientific community. It seemed to degenerate fairly quickly into an Old World/New World tiff, with the stodgy Brits and hidebound Europeans feeling put out over the Yanks insisting on some foolish childishness. Or at least it was portrayed that way, thus conveniently avoiding the real scientific questions that Lovell, astronomer Fred Hoyle, the International Astronomical Union, and others had raised.

Such an attitude wasn't even strictly limited to this side of the pond. A BBC producer, writing to James Van Allen to thank him for a television interview on the controversy, opined that "It is clear that . . . there is still a considerable residue of resentment in this country against the Americans' ability to do things which we can't afford or haven't the skill to carry out!"[12] In other words, the objections of Lovell and his colleagues supposedly weren't the result of legitimate concern, but simply professional and nationalistic jealousy.

Indeed, little of the protest seemed to come from American scientists. While British scientists such as Dr. Martin Ryle from Cambridge University feared that "the Van Allen radiation belt will be so badly bent that it may never be quite the same again in my lifetime," Americans such as former IGY scientist Richard Porter denied that the Fishbowl tests would cause any lasting damage to the Van Allen belts.

So did the man who had discovered them, James Van Allen himself. Publicly at least, he declared the new high-altitude tests "a magnificent experiment" that "can and will add greatly to the knowledge of all mankind." As to the concerns of Lovell and his other scientific colleagues abroad about the space tests, Van Allen noted that "within a few weeks I expect we would not be able to tell it had ever happened."[13] Privately, however, Van Allen was not as confident as his press statements implied. He would soon have cause to regret his sunny facade.

In the weeks leading up to the commencement of Fishbowl, the press remained ambivalent. While Walter Sullivan mused that the tests "may prove to be the greatest show in scientific history,"[14] the *Los Angeles Times* noted that "It is at least possible that an H-bomb this country plans to fire high over Johnston Island in June or July will inflict a grievous wound on the bottom side of the thick radiation zone around the earth."[15] The *Wall Street Journal* declared that "If indeed any danger is associated with this experiment, there is also danger involved in not doing all we know how to do to explore those reaches of space about which much is conjectured and little is known . . . after all, the people who believed the world was flat thought it almost sacrilege when Columbus dared to try to prove it wasn't."[16] England's left-wing *Guardian*, however, felt that "a nation has no right to interfere with the environment of the entire earth on no wider authority than its own decision . . . assurances that all will be well by American scientists, however distinguished, have a tawdry, unseemly ring . . . [B]y carrying out experiments which affect the whole environment the Americans are setting a series of precedents . . . [S]ome procedure should be worked out for deciding which global experiments are acceptable and which are not."[17]

The controversy was persistent enough that Kennedy finally decided to put together a committee to study the question, including Van Allen, Nicholas Christofilos, and other prominent scientists. Under time pressure and constrained to deliberate only on very specific questions, the committee quickly concluded that the Fishbowl tests did not pose any significant problem either to scientific research or to manned spaceflight. Van Allen would later characterize these conclusions as "tentative," but for the time being, they were good enough for the government to proceed. At a press conference on May 9, in response to a question about whether the upcoming nuclear tests would jeopardize Kennedy's stated position that the US would conduct only peaceful operations in space, Kennedy responded, "No, I don't think so. I know there's been disturbance about the Van Allen belt, but Van Allen says it's not going to affect the belt, and it's his!" The reporters laughed.[18]

In the midst of it all, the AEC found itself inundated with letters from concerned citizens, which had either been sent to the AEC directly or forwarded by other government agencies. Finally the Commission's Deputy Director of Public Information, Philippe Jacques, was forced to devise a form letter in response, addressed "To Those Who Have Inquired Regarding the Van Allen Belts." Jacques wrote reassuringly, "The reasons for our high-altitude tests over Johnston Island and their importance to our national security, together with the safety aspects of such testing, have been carefully considered at the highest levels of the Government." He went on to explain that "outstanding scientists, including Dr. James Van Allen, discoverer of the belts which bear his name," has concluded that any effects from the tests would be minor and would disappear quickly. Also, "none of the possible effects on the Van Allen belts would constitute a health hazard . . . there is no need for concern about any lasting effects on the Van Allen belts or associated phenomena." Whatever comfort Jacques had hoped to provide may have been undercut by his remark that "Because these tests are being conducted for the purpose of acquiring significant national security information, it is not possible to reveal all the data concerning the tests."[19]

A few weeks later, as June began, and Fishbowl was finally about to commence over Johnston Island, all the political, administrative, and technical obstacles seemingly vanished. But as challenging an endeavor as Argus had been, Fishbowl was about to prove even more fraught with adventure and danger.

CHAPTER 15
The Sun at Night

So FAR IN 1962, EVEN AS THE UNITED STATES CONTINUED TO RAMP UP ITS nuclear testing activities, the Soviets had been unexpectedly quiet. They had conducted an extremely low yield test at the beginning of February, but nothing since. No one expected this state of affairs to continue for very long. Obviously they were simply analyzing data from their 1961 shots and making preparations for a fresh round of shots.

Which didn't mean that the Russians were ignoring US activities. They might be unable to snoop around underground tests in Nevada, but DOMINIC in the Pacific provided a new opportunity to monitor American activity. "There was a Soviet ship, well known to us," Mustin recalled. "It wasn't a trawler; it was a big ship that cruised slowly through the Pacific . . . it was an intelligence-gathering ship with massive facilities for electronic interception and so on." The vessel had been tracked by Navy patrols at least from the vicinity of Midway Island, and Mustin's planes kept watch on her as she approached Johnston Island. The Soviet ship, however, was careful to stay outside of the restricted waters surrounding the testing sites, an easy task since the boundaries had been made public to all marine traffic as a safety measure. "They stayed out there for a while," Mustin said, "long enough to confirm, to their own satisfaction, that we were detonating devices over there. She was about 500 miles away." At least one of Mustin's P2V aircraft stayed in sight of the Russian spy ship continually, rotating with other planes based on Christmas Island.

It was a hazardous duty, stretching the P2Vs to their limits of range and endurance. One plane was almost lost at sea when it experienced an engine fire. "Those men flying those long over-water patrols were really facing a very real risk every minute they were airborne," Mustin remembered.[1]

JTF-8's scientific deputy, William Ogle, noted that while the British were permitted to make scientific measurements of the Christmas Island shots as part of the agreement for letting the United States "borrow" the island, no such arrangements existed with the Soviets. "The Russians also made measurements with no formal agreement," he wrote later. "The Task Force and the Commission discussed the subject, but there was really nothing we could do about it except watch and keep fairly close by to make sure that they did not come within the danger area." Sometimes it was difficult to be quite so tolerant. At one point during a stopover in Fiji, JTF-8 commander General Starbird was dining at a small restaurant and happened to notice the captain of the Russian ship relaxing nearby, apparently taking a break with some of his officers. "Starbird did not want to chance an international incident, and therefore, did not have a discussion with the Captain," Ogle noted.[2]

Unwanted audience or not, the Fishbowl part of DOMINIC had already begun unofficially on May 2, with the launch of an unarmed Thor missile from Johnston Island. It had essentially been a full dress rehearsal for all the various tracking, monitoring, and experimental stations on land, sea, and air. One of the primary reasons that the Thor missile had been selected, aside from its supposed reliability, was that it had the ability to carry pods which could be released from the missile at predetermined altitudes. Each Thor would carry three of the two-meter-long pods, which contained instrumentation and experimental equipment. After ejection from the booster, the pods would make soft landings by parachute in the open ocean, where they would be retrieved by Navy ships and Marine helicopters. At least, that was the plan.

The May 2 rehearsal, named Tigerfish, went reasonably well, although two of the three instrument pods encountered problems with their recovery systems and were damaged. More dry runs for the various support forces, without any missile launches, followed over the next several weeks. Finally, on June 2, the first nuclear shot, Bluegill, was ready to go.

Shortly after midnight, the Thor missile bearing the Bluegill device was launched. All was going perfectly well at first. The main radar tracking facility for the Johnston Island launches was a ship with the appropriate if not picturesque name *Range Tracker*, which was operated by the Air Force with a civilian crew as part of its Pacific Missile Range. Moored to the Johnston Island pier less than half a mile from the Thor launch pad, the *Range Tracker* had to follow the missile, which was shot into the skies nearly vertically, from almost directly beneath it. "This meant that as the missile climbed on up to hundreds of miles in the sky, with horizontal separation at the ground of a couple of thousand feet, it really required the radar to track very near the zenith, which is a tough problem for a radar," Mustin explained. Somewhere along the way, as Bluegill approached its highest altitude, the *Range Tracker* lost it.

That was a major problem. Somewhere high above the Pacific Ocean with ships and airplanes spread out in all directions, a nuclear-tipped missile was reaching the peak of its ascent as its engine burned out, preparing to plummet back to Earth under the inevitable command of gravity. Without a radar fix, there was no way to know precisely whether the missile was still following its planned trajectory, and thus no way to know where the missile—and its live nuclear warhead—was going to fall. One does not take chances with live nuclear weapons, and there was no time to consider the problem at leisure. JTF-8 commander Starbird gave the only possible order. The range safety officer pressed the destruct button, and the Thor missile exploded, taking Bluegill with it. There was no nuclear explosion, so the entire experiment was a failure. For now at least, the Bluegill shot would have to wait.

Adding to the general consternation over the loss of a valuable missile and even more valuable (but more easily replaceable) nuclear warhead—not to mention the failure to collect any of the desired data—was the discovery that Bluegill had actually been on its proper trajectory, as subsequent data analysis proved. Although there had been no way for Starbird, the range safety officer, or anyone else to know it at the time, there was no need to press the destruct button. Starbird reported as much to Washington in a terse cable two days after the incident: "Preliminary evidence available indicates that the Bluegill missile probably flew a normal trajectory and, if we could have known this, the detonation could have been made to occur in a place to give a safe firing and successful data." Although he noted that "the warhead-missile system had extensive protective systems in it to prevent any except a high-altitude [nuclear] burst," he had decided that "if I could not know from satisfactory tracking that the trajectory could not target near the ship array, I would not authorize arming of the warhead. Unfortunately, the missile tracking system lost the track before we could secure guarantee of safe trajectory. The missile was not commanded to arm therefore but was commanded to destruct." Looking on the bright side, he noted, "the fact that . . . the destruct worked in Bluegill as commanded, indicates the firing safety system is sound."[3]

It was a chastening situation for all concerned. "There was plenty of agonizing going on, including some by me after I got into the act, to try and figure out what had gone wrong and what we could do to safeguard ourselves against this," Mustin remembered. One obvious solution was to have more radar coverage. "It turned out that we had a number of resources, right there on the island, which indeed had been tracking this thing throughout its flight. If only they had been asked, they could have told us that it was exactly on course . . . but nobody had thought of that or made any arrangement of that nature."[4]

Also disappointed were the people who had gathered on the beach at Honolulu watching for Bluegill's nuclear light show. In any case, an official statement assured civilians that the mishap would not "cause hazardous levels of radioactivity in the water" or "constitute a hazard to human health." Perhaps the best epitaph on the anticlimactic debut of Fishbowl came from Ogle as Bluegill's pieces fell into the Pacific: "Best damn dry run we ever had."[5]

While the three instrument pods were recovered from the missile (two of which, it was discovered, had failed to eject properly), nothing else was retrieved. There was nothing more to do but pick up the administrative and operational pieces and continue on. The next shot would be Starfish, planned for June 19. The intervening time would be spent in further rehearsals, including better tracking procedures to prevent a repeat of the Bluegill fiasco.

On the night of June 19, another Thor sat poised on the Johnston Island launch pad, ready to boost Starfish into space. Two of the three experimental pods were replaced by dummy RVs (reentry vehicles) intended to test the effects of X-rays from a nuclear blast on warhead materials, with an eye to decreasing the vulnerability of US warheads. Everyone was optimistic that the snafus of Bluegill had all been adequately addressed.

A few minutes before midnight, Starfish was launched. It flew straight and true into the night for just under a minute, then it all went wrong. The Thor missile sputtered and flared and began going out of control. This time, it was clear that something was dreadfully amiss, and at sixty-four seconds into the flight, the range safety officer again hit the button to destroy the missile and nuclear warhead.

It had still been early in the missile's trajectory, however, and it had not yet moved very far from the vertical above Johnston Island, ending its existence at an altitude of only 30,000 to 35,000 feet. Debris from the explosion fell onto Johnston Island, causing no major damage but creating quite a mess. Parts of the missile, one of the RVs, and the remaining instrument pod were scattered over the island, and more debris fell into the lagoon and surrounding waters of Johnston Island. As the Navy recovery divers soon discovered, some of the junk was contaminated with plutonium from the Starfish warhead.

The cleanup effort consumed the next several weeks. Analysis of the debris along with other data revealed that one of the dummy re-entry vehicles had been the culprit, disrupting the missile's exhaust flow and weakening it until the Thor's engine tore loose and collapsed into the fuel tanks.

The other DOMINIC shots were proceeding apace, but Fishbowl was beginning to look decidedly jinxed. Fixing the problem that had caused the destruction of Bluegill had done nothing to save Starfish from the same fate. And only a limited supply of Thor missiles, instrument pods, and other necessary equipment was available, so continuing to lose them at this rate for no appreciable return was obviously unacceptable.

The displeasure wasn't simply felt by the test personnel, but extended all the way to the top. "These two failures presented us with the problem of what to try next at Johnston Island," AEC chairman Seaborg remembered.[6] Because Starbird had made it clear that to allow time for all the necessary preparations it wasn't possible to conduct further missile shots closer than fifteen days apart, and because Fishbowl had already been operating for more than a month with nothing to show for it, President Kennedy was beginning to ask embarrassing questions, with the implied possibility that the rest of the high-altitude program might be curtailed or even cancelled entirely.

At the end of June, Seaborg visited the Pacific test sites along with several aides and JFK's national security advisor McGeorge Bundy. They watched a shot at Christmas Island and then proceeded to Johnston Island to tour the facilities and, perhaps, to provide a little incentive and encouragement. "We saw the launching pad and the complicated diagnostic facilities operated by the Air Force and several laboratories," Seaborg wrote.[7] Upon his return to Washington, Seaborg sent a message to General Starbird, telling him not to rush the upcoming second attempt at Starfish. The luxury of failure, always a fragile thing in the best of circumstances, was gone. For the next shot, everything had to work.

As discouraging as they may have been, at least the failures thus far encountered hadn't resulted in casualties to anything other than equipment. For all aspects of Operation DOMINIC, safety had been a prime consideration from the first planning sessions, and continued to be emphasized throughout all operations. No shot, whether on or near the ground, high above, or in space, would be fired unless all weather conditions were good and the potential affected area had been swept clear of any unauthorized or unneeded personnel.

That was relatively easy for the more conventional tests; whether dropped from aircraft, carried aloft by tethered balloons, or detonated underwater, no human being was required to be nearby when the weapon burst into life. But the Fishbowl shots posed a unique problem. Someone had to be there on Johnston Island to prepare and launch the Thor missiles needed to carry the nuclear devices into space. And liquid-fueled missiles such as the Thor were infamous for blowing up when no one wanted them to. Even the crew of a B-52 bomber, sitting mere feet away from a megaton weapon cradled in their bomb bay, were safer than a crew working a half mile away from a megaton warhead sitting atop thousands of gallons of volatile, highly explosive liquid fuel. The rain of debris that had fallen all over Johnston Island from the failed Starfish test was a grim reminder of the possibilities.

There was only one option. "Our practice was to evacuate the island, the late afternoon immediately before the shot, of everyone except those absolutely required for the conduct of the test," Mustin said. "It soon turned out that the only way to do this was to evacuate them by helicopter to a ship." Because there might be as many as a thousand people on the island during test activities, that required a large ship, preferably an aircraft carrier.

Mustin first secured the *Iwo Jima*, which was later replaced by the *Princeton*, both carriers that hosted Marine helicopter squadrons to handle the evacuations. "These Marines really made a precisely organized and executed operation of evacuating 2000-2500 [sic] men off the island in a couple of hours," remembered Mustin. "Of course, it required that the people being evacuated respond precisely to organization and discipline. And this was not something they were accustomed to. They were a heterogeneous bunch of stevedores and cooks and bakers and scientists and engineers, a certain proportion of military, and so on. But the need was apparent and the mechanism was there. The Marines knew exactly how to do their part. It really went beautifully, and we never had an accident in quite a number of evacuations of the island."[8] Other documents cite the usual complement of evacuees as only around 800, but whatever the number, it was nonetheless an impressive operation.

Once an evacuation was completed, the carrier would move away from the island and out to sea, clear of the trajectories of the warhead-carrying Thor as well as the various instrumented rockets that would be fired for the test. "The main danger, we were told, would not be from the nuclear explosion, but from the barrage of instrumented Nike missiles which would be launched to take readings on the detonation," recalled one test veteran. "The impact points for these missiles were unpredictable."[9]

Aside from observing the shot, there was little to do. "Many of the people brought to the ship were relatively highly paid scientists, engineers, etc., who had nowhere to go and nowhere to spend their salaries," observed a website for Johnston Island veterans. "Rumor has it that many high stakes poker games could be found on the USS *Princeton* as these folks waited for the all clear signal to return to their work stations on the island."[10]

From its safe vantage point, the carrier became the main observation point and command post, with constant secure communications channels to Washington. Before Fishbowl finally came to an end, the wisdom of the pre-shot evacuation policy would become even more evident than after Starfish.

The second attempt at Starfish, now called Starfish Prime, was ready to go on July 4, a coincidentally appropriate date to get Fishbowl back on track with a huge fireworks display. Unfortunately for happy coincidences, the winds were too high for a safe Thor launch, and the shot was postponed. For the next few nights, the weather was too cloudy over Johnston Island and vicinity, precluding the necessary observations and measurements of the high-altitude fireball. Postponements on account of weather were par for the course in nuclear testing, but in this case, they were becoming particularly frustrating.

Finally, just after 11 PM on July 9, Starfish Prime was launched. Starbird was reportedly so nervous about the outcome that he refused to watch the closed-circuit television of the launch at his command post. But for once, he had nothing to worry about. Everything went perfectly: the launch, the Thor missile, the trajectory, the radar tracking, the launch of the experimental rockets, the positioning and operation of the observation ships and aircraft. Precisely as planned, the Thor missile reached an apogee of about seven hundred miles, then nosed over and began its ballistic trajectory back to Earth. Finally the actual detonation of the 1.4 megaton Starfish Prime device took place at an altitude of about 250 miles.

What followed was perhaps the greatest light show ever seen over the Pacific Ocean. Starfish Prime lit up the entire sky from horizon to horizon, from Hawaii all the way to New Zealand, opening with a flash of white light brighter than the sun, which gave way to intense auroras, shimmering curtains of green, yellow, and red—an awesome, primal spectacle of energy on a scale that dwarfed into insignificance all those who witnessed it.

Mustin happened to be 1200 miles away on Christmas Island during Starfish Prime, but he didn't miss a thing. "I just went out and sat on the edge of the sand dunes there and watched the sky," he recalled, as above him was "a complete unbroken sheet of yellow light."[11]

The civilian spectators back in Hawaii, who had been so disappointed when the previous shots had turned out to be duds, finally had their patience rewarded. Some had been waiting on the beaches, while others were guests of several hotels offering rooftop bomb-watching parties, just as some Las Vegas hotels had been doing for years with the Nevada shots. "Except those in a few isolated areas where rains blotted out the sight, residents on all the major islands of the state saw the explosion," reported the *New York Times*. "The most fortunate observers here were those on the heights overlooking Honolulu. They had a clear field of vision when the blast illuminated the horizon south of the city. The brilliant flash sent yellow fingers stabbing through the broken clouds. Some observers believed the color was greenish. The sky turned pink and then a tomato red. It was Hawaii's second sunset of the day and was visible for nearly seven minutes." The paper also featured before and after shots at Waikiki Beach, showing clearly how the night had temporarily become day.[12]

At Kwajalein Island, 1400 miles west of Johnston, an Air Force major reported that "a brilliant white flash burned through the clouds rapidly changing to a green ball of irradiance extending into the clear sky above the overcast. From its surface extruded great white fingers, resembling cirro-stratus clouds . . . to be replaced by spectacular concentric cirrus-like rings moving out from the blast at tremendous initial velocity, finally stopping when the outermost ring was 50 degrees overhead. They did not disappear but persisted in a state of frozen stillness. All this occurred, I would judge, within 45 seconds. As the greenish light turned to purple and began to fade at the point of burst, a bright red glow began to develop on the horizon at a direction of 50 degrees north of east and simultaneously 50 degrees south of east expanding inward and upward until the whole eastern sky was a dull burning red semicircle . . . obliterating some of the lesser stars. This condition, interspersed with tremendous white rainbows, persisted no less than seven minutes."[13] Reports from the launch site back at Johnston Island were similarly vivid, describing multicolored glows, streamers, and discs in the heavens.

Other reports came from civilian planes, such as a Canadian Pacific Airlines in flight to Sydney, Australia. Seeing the sky to the north come alive with fiery auroras, the captain turned the plane to give his passengers a better view. In New Zealand, Fiji, and all over the Pacific, observers marveled at the brilliant flash and the active colorful auroral display that followed. "An interesting side effect was that the Royal New Zealand Air Force was aided in anti-submarine maneuvers by the light from the bomb," noted a later technical report.[14]

There were also official technical observers spread across the Pacific, manning over two hundred stations in Samoa, Fiji, Okinawa, Wake Island, and other remote spots. A *New York Times* reporter was stationed with the Samoa group. "Word of the explosion was greeted jubilantly—and with a sense of relief," he reported. The hours leading up to the test were lazy and relaxed, as the men lounged about house trailers and tents with their instruments. "As the hot and humid afternoon wore on, scientists, technicians and military observers performed the few routine tasks in preparation for the big show, as they had done twice before in vain. Then most just sat and talked or read or had a beer or two as the countdown sounded over the shortwave radio."[15]

And Starfish Prime was felt and observed far beyond the Pacific. In Boulder, Colorado, needles on scientific instruments monitoring magnetic atmospheric and earth currents at the National Bureau of Standards were pegged violently when the device detonated. Similar effects occurred in other labs across the country. "Many American scientists . . . were amazed at the intensity of the long-range effects," noted Walter Sullivan.[16]

Unlike the situation during Argus, when the number of satellites circling the planet could be counted on one hand, the orbital population had increased considerably during the past four years. Among them was Ariel I, the UK's first satellite (though launched in collaboration with the US at Cape Canaveral), and Injun 1, the latest satellite from James Van Allen and his crew at the State University of Iowa. Injun 1 would follow in the footsteps of its predecessor Explorer 4 to provide data on Starfish Prime, while Ariel, as well as several other satellites, would soon suffer a less dignified fate.

Not everyone who witnessed Starfish Prime that night responded with awe and wonder. Many natives on various Pacific islands reportedly feared that the sky was literally falling on them, fleeing into churches or other refuges. "Crazy white man!" one Samoan exclaimed. Military and test personnel were supposedly obliged to reassure panicky people. Noted the *Times* reporter on Samoa, "Observers not connected with the nuclear test program felt that much of the commotion among the natives could have been avoided if the Samoans had received more advance information on the nature and purpose of the nuclear experiment."[17]

Some reactions were less primal and far more political. The American embassy in London was again besieged by demonstrators from the Campaign for Nuclear Disarmament, as it had been since the opening of DOMINIC. The President of Ghana protested to Kennedy in a formal diplomatic note: "Is there no way wherein you . . . can resolve the present cold war anarchy? Is it not real wisdom to suspend this dangerous arms race until efforts being made for peace . . . can result in a general disarmament treaty?" Moscow, predictably enough, condemned Starfish Prime as a "crime" committed by US "atom-maniacs." Proclaimed the Soviet news service TASS, "The United States exploded a nuclear device in space despite strong protests of all mankind . . . [and] confirmed yet again that it is following the course of whipping up the nuclear arms race." Meanwhile, noted the *New York Times*, "In contrast to the Johnston Island nuclear shot of 1958 [a reference to Teak], which took Hawaiians by surprise, there was little criticism today of the hydrogen bomb explosion [in Hawaii]."[18]

Regardless of whether the rest of the world was delighted by the spectacle or outraged by its political ramifications, the US test authorities, military, scientists, bomb designers, and support personnel were all enormously pleased. There had been a few minor glitches, of course; a couple of instrument rockets had failed, and one or two experiments hadn't worked here and there. But all of the major elements had gone well. The smoothness of the entire operation seemed to wipe out all the frustration and disappointment of the previous failures.

It soon became evident, however, that smooth and spectacular as it was, Starfish Prime had been something far more than just another nuclear test shot. Even as the magnificent visual displays diminished and then disappeared from the night skies, and all those involved in the operation congratulated one another and basked in success, the effects of Starfish Prime were not about to leave the stage quickly or gracefully.

Nor were the demons of Fishbowl banished for good. They were, in fact, about to become far worse.

CHAPTER 16
The Haunted Island

THE UNPRECEDENTED LIGHT SHOW OF STARFISH PRIME HAD ONLY BEEN ITS MOST immediate and obvious manifestation, perceptible to anyone under the Pacific skies on that July night. But for those who had long planned, prepared, and finally carried out the operation, it was also the least important part. The purpose of detonating a nuclear weapon high in outer space was not to create pretty fireworks, after all. It was to evaluate its military potential.

The purpose of the entire Fishbowl operation was spelled out on the first page of a preliminary planning document: "The primary objective of the overall series is to obtain data regarding the interference to radar and communication systems produced by a high altitude nuclear burst." Such data would be useful in more ways than one. Teak, Orange, and Argus had already demonstrated that "blackout has serious implications for critical defense systems such as BMEWS [Ballistic Missile Early Warning System], Nike-Zeus, ICBM penetration and many communication systems, and conversely that its employment may be an effective ICBM offensive tactic."[1] A later report described Starfish Prime's major objectives including: "1. Evaluation of missile kill mechanisms produced by a high altitude nuclear detonation; 2. Evaluation of a high altitude nuclear detonation on electromagnetic surveillance capability; 3. Evaluation of the effects of a high altitude nuclear detonation on long range communications," along with investigations of how such phenomena would affect systems that detected nuclear blasts.[2]

The ionosphere all over the Pacific had received a huge jolt, perhaps comparable only to what it would receive naturally in a major solar storm, with a massive sudden blast of electrons injected into the D layer, the radio-reflecting lowest region of the ionosphere. It was the Christofilos/Argus effect writ large—an electromagnetic disruption of enormous proportions.

As expected, the biggest effect on radio communications was at shortwave frequencies, which are most dependent on "bouncing" off the D layer to travel beyond the line of sight and along the curvature of the Earth. Higher frequency radio communications, such as those used by airliners and television, were less affected this time than by the 1958 Teak and Orange shots. Federal aviation authorities had made plans to ground all civilian Pacific flights for several hours after the test, but it proved unnecessary.

Meanwhile, the 266 scientific stations that had monitored the test now scrutinized the radio and radar spectrum across half the planet, making measurements, conducting experiments, checking propagation patterns. In fact, as the *New York Times* noted, it was "probably one of the most widely observed scientific experiments in history," in notable contrast to the former "greatest experiment in history," Argus. But while a large number of those observations "specifically included those frequencies of greatest interest in anti-missile missions,"[3] a classified technical report noted that "Basic scientific studies—of the earth's magnetic field, ionosphere and radiation belts, for example—will be decidedly secondary." And while "the effects of the explosions on communications presumably were available to the world to observe and analyze," the results that might be pertinent to anti-ICBM measures would be more closely held. That was ensured by the fact that "only approximate information about the timing, altitude and energy yield of the nuclear weapons has been or will be distributed. This would be enough for most basic scientific studies but insufficient information for those not in on the tests to gain much knowledge about certain of the military experiments."[4] It was another lesson learned from Argus: revealing some, but not all, of the scientific data, straddling the line between secrecy and openness.[5]

More lasting effects on the Van Allen belts, if any, would take a little longer to confirm. Most of that data would be coming from Injun 1, TRAAC, Ariel, and perhaps less directly from other satellites—US and otherwise—that happened to be in space. One pioneering spacecraft was about to have a fateful encounter with the aftermath of Starfish Prime.

The day after the shot, another momentous event occurred: Telstar 1, the world's first dedicated communications satellite, was launched from Cape Canaveral. The first stage of its booster carrying it into orbit was a Thor rocket, nearly identical to the missile that had lofted Starfish Prime the night before. Built by Bell Labs and sponsored by ATT as part of an international effort to create a worldwide communications and television network, Telstar assumed an elliptical orbit with a closest approach to Earth of just under six hundred miles, moving out to about 3600 miles, circling the planet every two and a half hours.

It was an event of international import, especially after Telstar began relaying television broadcasts between North America and Europe on July 23. Since President Kennedy wasn't quite set to go on the air before Telstar was ready, the first live public satellite TV broadcast turned out to be part of a baseball game between the Philadelphia Phillies and the Chicago Cubs from Wrigley Field in Chicago (the Phillies won, 5–3). For perhaps the first time since Sputnik and the dawn of the space age, Telstar demonstrated to the world at large that space travel could have a definite and tangible value that transcended scientific or military purposes.

The satellite quickly became a cultural touchstone. An English guitar band, the Tornados, even scored a #1 single on the US record charts with an instrumental dubbed "Telstar." Unfortunately, although it would live long enough to secure its place in history, Telstar 1 was already doomed to an early demise. "Telstar was dying from nuclear effects while it was #1 on the Hit Parade," wrote Stimson Center co-founder Michael Krepon in a 2011 online op-ed.[6]

With each circuit it made around the planet, Telstar passed through an intense band of electrons generated by the Starfish Prime explosion, an artificial radiation belt just as had been postulated by Nicholas Christofilos and first created and observed with Argus. But the Starfish belt would soon prove to be far more intense—and persistent.

Back on the ground, Starfish Prime made itself known even to those who weren't out partying on the beaches of Honolulu under the summer skies. The electromagnetic pulse (EMP) of the detonation created a massive induced electrical surge in Hawaii's power grid, blowing fuses and instantly darkening about three hundred streetlights on the island of Oahu. Burglar alarms were set off and a telephone company microwave link on Kauai was knocked out. Initial speculations that the streetlights may simply have been automatically turned off by their photocell controls when the sky lit up with daylight intensity were soon disproved on more detailed analysis.[7]

From his own vantage point at Christmas Island, Admiral Mustin witnessed even more dramatic EMP effects. A low-frequency long-wave radio antenna, running from a ground station to a balloon, put on quite a display. "This field of electrical voltage induced on Johnston Island, as a result of that burst, was so intense that great big blue sparks were flying all over the antenna up to the balloon . . . it was a spectacle that people talked about for a long time. Even the most blasé of the scientists, I think, were seeing things that they had conjectured about, but now they knew they were real."[8]

As the excitement over Starfish Prime passed and Johnston Island crews busied themselves in preparations for the next Fishbowl shot, discussion and argument continued over the effects of Starfish Prime on the Van Allen belts. Obviously they hadn't been utterly destroyed as some had feared, nor set afire as in *Voyage to the Bottom of the Sea*, but they had definitely been strongly affected. As were the satellites now regularly passing through the new belt created by Starfish, just underneath the natural Van Allen belts. The British satellite Ariel began to suffer electrical problems beginning only four days after the shot, as its solar panels were steadily being degraded by the high electron flux. Telstar was beginning to experience similar problems. For his own part, James Van Allen told a Cleveland rocket society meeting that while the natural radiation of the Van Allen belts might pose some hazard to manned spaceflight, he doubted that the recent high-altitude nuclear tests would either add much to the danger or seriously disrupt the natural belts.[9]

The next show over Johnston Island and the Pacific would be Bluegill Prime, the second try for Bluegill. By July 24, all was ready, another Thor poised on the Johnston Island launch pad, but bad weather pushed the shot to the next day. It would have to wait until July 25, at about 11 PM.

The Thor missile ignited, but failed to rise off the pad; there was insufficient thrust because of a stuck fuel valve. Then fuel began to burn around the base of the missile and the Thor erupted into flames. To ensure that the dying missile wasn't about to haphazardly take off out of control with its live warhead, the range safety officer again hit his destruct button, and the Thor, the launch pad, and the immediate vicinity of Johnston Island immediately went up in a titanic—but safely non-nuclear—explosion.

"This time the disaster was even more horrendous," remembered Mustin, who had been watching through binoculars from a command ship offshore. "This was really an awesome occurrence." A sailor aboard one of the nearby ships remembered, "I got a real sick feeling knowing that there was a fully active A-bomb on the rocket. It gave a new meaning to 'Put your head between your legs and kiss your ass goodbye.' I monitored the countdown and opened the outside hatch (against orders, but what the hell, if it blew, no one would know) when we heard the abort code. Hell of a fireball!"[10]

Fortunately there were indeed no casualties, with the few people still remaining on the island at a safe distance from the conflagration. It was bad enough, however. Even after the fires were extinguished, radioactive plutonium from the destroyed W-50 nuclear warhead was strewn all over the area. Any further launches from Johnston Island would require extensive decontamination procedures and weeks, perhaps months, of extensive repair work to restore the launch pad and support facilities. For the moment, Operation Fishbowl was at a standstill.

For the test personnel—frazzled and overworked from the repeated failures and continuing problems—it was perhaps a welcome break. Aside from those directly engaged in decontamination and repair operations, the

Fishbowl portion of the DOMINIC task force withdrew to plan and prepare for the eventual resumption of activity. For the military, AEC, and administration, this latest fiasco posed an embarrassing problem. Fishbowl was already behind schedule, with no chance to be completed by the deadline originally set by President Kennedy—July 25. Which left only two options: cancel the remainder of the planned high-altitude tests, or extend the deadline. The first option meant the loss of valuable data eagerly awaited and desperately needed by the Pentagon and weapons scientists; the second option meant political complications for the continuing test-ban negotiations.

In the end, there was no real choice. Fishbowl would continue. "Although rumors were rampant that the President would call an end to the operation, this was really very improbable," Ogle later wrote. "On July 22, 1962, the USSR had announced their intention to begin a new series of atmospheric tests. Kennedy was still trying to pressure the Russians about a test ban. Furthermore, in the game of international power it was bad enough for the US to have such publicly miserable failures; it would be even worse to stop the tests, admitting that we could not finish the job."[11] But even as Kennedy agreed to allow Fishbowl to continue, he demanded it be completed as soon as possible.

After laying low for most of the year, the Soviets resumed their own atmospheric tests at the beginning of August, including a forty-megaton shot that recalled their even larger test of the previous year. For now, until Fishbowl could be resumed, it would be the United States that was quiescent. Ideally, the remaining Fishbowl tests would be the final US atmospheric shots before a test ban treaty put an end to them all over the world. Or so Kennedy hoped.

As the repairs and cleanup continued at Johnston Island, new plans took hold. Urraca, the high-altitude test originally planned to open the Fishbowl series but repeatedly delayed, was finally cancelled by Kennedy, "both because of its possible effect on satellites and because the President really did not wish to develop another method of testing," as Ogle described. "His objective was to prevent testing, not to help it."[12] If conducted, the Urraca test would have been at the highest altitude yet—

about five hundred miles, twice that of Starfish Prime. Instead, along with the twice-delayed Bluegill, three new high-altitude shots were added to Fishbowl, named Checkmate, Kingfish, and Tightrope.

Two of those would not make use of the troublesome Thor booster. "People were getting a little touchy about this," said Mustin. "Questions were beginning to arise: 'Where's all that 98% reliability that you Air Force guys told us had been in the record for this Thor missile?'" Aside from questions of reliability, there weren't a lot of Thor missiles remaining to be used, since it was no longer in production by its manufacturer, Douglas Aircraft. So the low-yield Checkmate and Tightrope tests would be borne by smaller boosters. Air Force officials were quick to emphasize that the recent problems shouldn't be taken to imply any lack of military readiness on the part of the United States, nor any particular flaw in the missile, since some of the failures were not related to the Thor's military capabilities.

As they continued their new tests, the Soviets couldn't resist needling the United States. "On August 11 we received word that the Soviet Union was anxious about the safety of its astronaut, Nikolayev, whose orbit around the earth was expected to last for several more days," Seaborg wrote. "They sent us diplomatic signals that were essentially appeals not to conduct any tests that might endanger the astronaut's life." The State Department assured the Russians that the US wished their cosmonaut well and would do nothing to endanger him.[13] Still, the Russian concerns certainly agreed with Van Allen's statements about possible hazards for space travelers, specifically an upcoming Mercury flight by US astronaut Walter Schirra.

For the public and other observers not directly involved, the continuing debates about dangerous outer space radiation belts were decidedly confusing. On one hand, respected scientists such as James Van Allen declared that while there could be danger, the Fishbowl tests had caused no lasting damage to the natural radiation belts. On the other hand, official statements from the AEC and Defense Department stated that Starfish Prime had created a new artificial radiation belt that had not only knocked out three satellites so far—Ariel, TRAAC, and a Navy satellite—but that the new belt was stronger than previously thought and might persist for years. Arguments that orbiting astronauts, unlike satellites, would mostly travel at altitudes below the radiation belts were not always convincing.

By October, almost three months to the day after the Bluegill Prime disaster, Fishbowl was finally ready to pick up where it had left off, with another attempt at Bluegill, now called Bluegill Double Prime. Unfortunately, the third time, launched before midnight on October 15, was decidedly not the charm. Less than three minutes after leaving the launch pad, the Thor missile began tumbling out of control, and yet again the range safety officer exercised his prerogative and sent the destruct signal.

It was hardly an auspicious way to resume Fishbowl. "The Thor crews and, for that matter, everyone else were tremendously dejected," Ogle recalled.[14] Task Force commander Starbird was more than fed up with the Thor by this point, but he had no other ready option for the remaining high-yield shots.

Meanwhile, on the other side of the world, another collection of missiles, this time of the Soviet variety, was causing major trouble in Cuba. Thanks to some timely U-2 reconnaissance photography, President Kennedy was just finding out about the Soviet medium- and intermediate-range missile sites being constructed on Cuba, and he and his advisors were secretly debating how to respond.

For the next two weeks, the world tottered on the precipice of nuclear war, as Kennedy and Khrushchev made move and countermove, struggling to resolve what had become the gravest crisis of the Cold War. American strategic forces all over the world were reshuffled and redeployed in preparation for a possible Cuban invasion, a Soviet attack on Western Europe, or, perhaps, Armageddon. Some of them came from JTF-8, with aircraft and ships called away from the Pacific to reinforce preparations elsewhere. General Starbird was reassigned to Washington to head the Defense Communications Agency, which would soon set up the "hotline" link between Washington and Moscow in the wake of the crisis. As his deputy, Admiral Mustin became acting commander of JTF-8—once again the reluctant leader of a nuclear test series.

Despite international tensions at perhaps their highest level in history, the tests went on. It was probably in part due to simple inertia: the whole DOMINIC operation was simply too complex, too far-flung, and too far along already to shut down so abruptly for an indefinite period. But the saber-rattling element was also undoubtedly a factor. What better way to demonstrate one's resolve to an adversary than to detonate nuclear weapons?

So, on October 19, five days after the humiliating failure of Bluegill Double Prime, the next shot of Fishbowl was launched. Called Checkmate, it was a more modest effort all around, using a smaller XM-33 rocket instead of the massive Thor, and with a much smaller yield: less than 5 kilotons. It detonated successfully at an altitude of just over ninety miles, creating a lovely light show, though not of Starfish Prime proportions. Ogle described "a green and blue ring with spikelike protrusions at the edge, surrounded by a blood-red auroral ring which faded in less than a minute. Auroral streamers to the north and south formed immediately. Pink streamers were still visible 30 minutes after the explosion."[15]

Meanwhile, the USSR was following suit, having resumed their own high-altitude experiments. They fired off two high-altitude tests over the ensuing week, as if to match the US in saber-rattling belligerence and also to continue research on their own missile defense concepts. Although these tests were still smaller than Starfish Prime (around 300 kilotons), and at altitudes under two hunded miles, they created massive EMP effects over Russia, by design and in keeping with the scientific intent of investigating the military utility of EMP. In the midst of it all, the Cuban Missile Crisis was rapidly building to its climax. Whether that would mean a peaceful resolution or the end of civilization remained to be seen.

One way or another, it was not going to stop yet another try for Bluegill. Just before midnight on October 25, Bluegill Triple Prime was launched from Johnston Island—the fourth attempt for this particular test. To the enormous relief of all concerned, the Thor flew straight and true, and the 400-kiloton Bluegill Triple Prime warhead detonated at a relatively low thirty miles. But it was enough. The scientific experiments and photography all went well, and all three of the instrument pods were successfully ejected and recovered from the Thor booster. Notes the Defense Nuclear Agency history, "That was a good thing, for, as Air Force Chief of

Staff General Curtis LeMay pointed out, there were no Thor missiles left in case any failed."[16]

There were, however, at least two casualties. After first being recognized as a danger in 1958, precautions against the eyeburn problem had become standard procedure for high-altitude operations. Test personnel were either issued eye protection or otherwise prevented from seeing the initial fireball, and a vast protected area was routinely established around the test location and kept clear of unauthorized civilian interlopers.

But that, of course, did not preclude accidents or simple misfortune. Two enlisted military men on Johnston Island, one Air Force and one Navy, were inadvertently caught without their protective goggles when Bluegill Triple Prime went off. Fortunately, neither was completely blinded, though both suffered eye damage.

Back in Washington and Moscow, Kennedy and Khrushchev had managed to step back from catastrophe over the Cuban crisis, partly through the auspices of their own better angels and partly through sheer luck. That did not change matters either in the Pacific or over the Soviet testing range. There were still bombs to test, experiments to be carried out.

But Fishbowl, at least, was finally approaching its long-delayed finale. On the evening of October 31, the last remaining Thor missile stood ready to launch the Kingfish device from Johnston Island. The weather and some last-minute technical problems delayed the proceedings until about 2 AM, but the launch and detonation of the 400-kiloton device at about sixty miles went off smoothly. Again, the central Pacific was treated to a light show of "a yellow-white, luminous circle with intense purple streamers."[17] Again, some EMP effects were recorded, but of very low intensity compared to Starfish Prime. Back on Johnston Island, "The rest of the night was spent in celebration."[18]

Two nights later, the ill-starred yet spectacular Fishbowl operation would draw down the curtain. Tightrope—planned as a test for the Nike-Hercules air defense missile—exploded its low-yield warhead at about thirteen miles above the earth, demonstrating the ability of the Nike-Hercules system to knock out an incoming Soviet missile, at least theoretically.

For all the long-frustrated, sorely frazzled Fishbowl personnel, their work was done. Fishbowl and DOMINIC itself were over. Some were not exactly happy at the prospect, such as dedicated Pentagon weapons scientist Frank Shelton. "After observing the success of Tightrope, Frank Shelton returned to his living quarters in a melancholy mood. 'That was the 65th atmospheric nuclear weapon burst that I have observed in the past 10 years,' he recalled saying to himself, 'and I think it is probably the last one that I will ever see conducted in the atmosphere.'"[19]

Although it wasn't at the time officially planned to hold the particular distinction, Tightrope would, in fact, be the final nuclear weapon exploded in the atmosphere by the United States, closing an era that had begun with the Trinity test on July 16, 1945. With the conclusion of DOMINIC, US nuclear testing would retreat to underground caverns and tunnels, mostly in southern Nevada.

But not without a struggle. The Pentagon and the weapons labs, perhaps sharing Shelton's gloomy feelings, pressed for new nuclear tests in 1963 and beyond, and not just underground. For the time being at least, the Pacific testing facilities were only being shuttered, not completely abolished. As far as the AEC and the military were concerned, there remained new avenues to explore, new phenomena to test and observe, and perhaps new weapons and defenses to develop. As always, there was the fear that the Soviets were pulling ahead somehow, in ominous ways that would ultimately threaten the security of the United States.

But there could be a way to counter the new threats. First Teak and Orange, and then Nicholas Christofilos and Argus had opened new frontiers of tantalizing military potential. Fishbowl and especially Starfish Prime had confirmed and expanded that potential, inspiring and firing the imaginations of the planners of war and the builders of its tools. So even as Kennedy and Khrushchev, sobered by their recent brush with oblivion and newly anxious to find some way to reduce the danger, continued to move fitfully toward some kind of lasting reconciliation, others in the Pentagon and weapons laboratories were taking a deep and thoughtful look at new possibilities. If the politicians and diplomats were still talking—striving toward concord in Geneva, striving for test bans and treaties—the generals, admirals, and weaponeers were imagining and planning for what might happen if peace failed.

CHAPTER 17
The Fire of Damocles

EVER SINCE THE FISHBOWL TESTS HAD BEEN ANNOUNCED TO A WARY WORLD still reeling from the resumption of atmospheric nuclear testing, authorities from President Kennedy on down had been reassuring everyone that not only would the Van Allen belts remain unharmed from the atomic assault, but also that any fallout from the high-altitude shots would be nonexistent or negligible at best, taking years to drift down to ground level, by which time it would have decayed to safe levels anyway. Unlike the dirty, widely contaminating shots being fired off by the Russians, went the unspoken implication.

As the Cuban Missile Crisis passed into chilly memory and test-ban negotiations continued apace, those official reassurances began to feel less than reassuring. First, at the beginning of September, the Pentagon and AEC had issued a somber joint statement that the residual Starfish Prime radiation was stronger than predicted and might last for years, having already disabled three satellites. That statement had been vehemently disputed by James Van Allen, based on the data he had been collecting from the Injun 1 satellite. But he had noted that there might be some hazards to human space travelers passing through either the natural or Starfish-created radiation belts. The President's Science Advisory Committee (PSAC) backed the more alarmist assessments, despite protests from Van Allen that the public statements had been issued before the scientific evaluation of the satellite observations had been completely analyzed.

Then, in November 1962, Telstar began to have serious problems, and finally went dark altogether. The combination of Starfish Prime, some of the other Fishbowl tests, and the recently conducted Soviet high-altitude tests proved too much for its sensitive electronics to endure. Engineers did manage to coax the satellite back into operation briefly in January 1963, but it proved only a temporary reprieve, and the world's first telecommunications satellite went out of business permanently the following month.

Van Allen continued to criticize the government's handling of the matter. Throughout the remainder of 1962 and into early 1963, speaking at various scientific conferences and meetings, he derided the administration's statements as "hasty, ill-considered" and inaccurate. Said the *Washington Post*, "There is a growing body of expert opinion which holds that the artificial Van Allen radiation belt created by the [Starfish] blast is neither as intense nor as long-lived as was officially suggested by Defense Department and Atomic Energy Commission scientists in August." Noting that such concerns had led to the substantial revision of the Fishbowl testing plans (though overlooking the various technical problems that had also played a part), the *Post* continued, "there appears to be growing evidence that those scientists who foresaw only a temporary and relatively slight enrichment of the natural belts were correct . . . whether these questions will be resolved to everyone's satisfaction is debatable. The measurement and mapping of artificial radiation has become vastly complicated."[1]

At the annual meeting of the American Association for the Advancement of Science in Philadelphia, Van Allen took his criticisms beyond the technical and into the realm of the political, directly challenging the PSAC, calling it a "vague and authoritative machine." Van Allen told his colleagues that "the PSAC meetings at which I've been present have been exceedingly intimidating sessions . . . They are essentially governmentally dominated." The PSAC, in effect, was little more than a body of "high-handed autocrats" who tended to disregard independent, non-government scientists in favor of hasty decisions and political expediency. Not only that, but "our failure as a nation to produce a substantial study of the scientific consequences of these tests long before the decision was made to conduct them and before an announcement was made that they were to be conducted, is, it seems to me, quite inexcusable." It was, said Van Allen, a "shabby" episode all around. "Van Allen Sees Science 'Clique'; Says Data on Radiation Belt Reflect Hasty Judgment By Government Insiders," read Walter Sullivan's *New York Times* headline.[2]

Such broadsides from America's most prominent space scientist in such a high-visibility forum could not go unanswered, particularly when other scientists began to speak out in agreement, both on the specifics of Starfish and on the government's scientific policies in general. Government scientists soon began to respond, claiming that instead of any nefarious intentions to "intimidate" or ignore their non-administration colleagues, the early, dire reports on Starfish Prime effects had been due to "piecemeal leaks" of initial data that considerably exaggerated the danger both to satellites and to human space travelers. More intriguing was the contention that the government's reports had also been intended to give the Soviets some second thoughts about conducting their own high-altitude tests, perhaps convincing them that there might be some tempting propaganda value to calling off or limiting their own plans. It had not dissuaded the Russians at all, of course, but it was at least a plausible explanation given the realities of Cold War politics. Administration scientists also pointed out that not everyone agreed with Van Allen's criticisms, and he had had ample opportunity to speak up publicly before the reports had been issued. Attempts to discover how he may have been actually "intimidated" yielded nothing.[3]

Obviously, it had all been a routine scientific controversy, mostly originating from the fact that Van Allen had been relying mostly on Injun 1 data while the government had trusted measurements mostly from Telstar. A few weeks later, however, the AEC, Pentagon, and NASA issued a joint report that officially revised their earlier estimates and stated that the Starfish belt would likely vanish within a few more months, or even weeks.

But the controversy was not quite laid to rest. By this time, more detailed and careful studies of the Starfish data had been conducted by all the various sources, and papers were beginning to appear in scientific journals. In March, Van Allen changed his mind, announcing that he now believed that the Starfish Prime radiation belt would persist for a least a decade, with an intensity that would substantially interfere with scientific studies of the natural belts. He explained that his earlier position had been based upon "intuitive" scientific expectations, but that the new mass of hard data now appearing from the various satellites had proven him wrong. To his immense credit as a scientist, he had followed the data, readily reversing his previously strongly held position when new facts made it necessary, with no fears of saving face or embarrassing himself. "It's the difference between intuitive expectations and actual observations," he remarked.[4]

Scientific disagreements were one thing, and of little concern to the military and defense establishment. Far more concerning to them was the fact that the Soviet Union had been conducting their own high-altitude tests—and that they also had satellites in orbit capable of observing and collecting data on the US tests. Two Kosmos satellites had been launched in the spring of 1962 and had been in excellent position to observe Starfish Prime that June. It was not lost on Pentagon officials that, just as the data collected by US satellites could be employed for both benign scientific discovery and darker military purposes, so could the observations of the Kosmos spacecraft. And if the United States was detonating nuclear weapons in space to investigate their military relevance, then the Soviet Union was undoubtedly doing the same thing.

The prospects for any resumption in atmospheric testing, much less Fishbowl-style high-altitude and outer space shots, had receded to near-impossibility as the test-ban talks proceeded and the US and USSR sought to ease tensions after the Cuban Missile Crisis. But Fishbowl, with both its successes and failures, had fired up new concepts. The goal of establishing an anti-ICBM defense system remained elusive. But a fresh arena of possible conflict had opened, a new frontier of offense and defense: satellites.

America was already operating its first attempts at a spy satellite system with the CORONA project, and undoubtedly the Soviets would soon be doing likewise. But there was another disturbing possibility: nuclear warheads not on missiles, but on orbiting satellites. Air Force intelligence experts worried that the Soviets could bypass the low accuracy and range of their existing missiles by simply lofting warheads into orbit—allowing them to be "de-orbited" and brought down at will on any target. All such a capability required were huge multimegaton warheads and the massive rocket power to put them into space, both of which the Russians had already amply demonstrated. A State Department report observed that "a thermonuclear 'sword of Damocles' would seem to hang over everyone's head in a way which, logic and military technology aside, ICBMs do not . . . in anticipation of the contingency of a Soviet weapon in space and recognizing that it may be necessary to undertake physical countermeasures, we should develop as rapidly as possible anti-satellite capabilities."[5]

Fishbowl had already demonstrated just how such a capability might work by exploding nuclear weapons at high altitudes, carried aloft by missiles. "The Starfish Prime test results showed that a high dose of radiation could provide the basis for an ASAT [anti-satellite] system," noted an Air Force historical study. Only two months after Starfish Prime, Major General Bernard Schriever, commander of the Air Force Ballistic Missile Division, proposed to Air Force Secretary Eugene Zuckert that the Thor launching facilities on Johnston Island could form the nucleus of an ASAT system. Secretary of Defense Robert McNamara approved further studies and development work on November 20. By February 1963, Program 437 would be going full speed ahead.[6]

In many ways, Program 437 was the logical culmination of Project Argus. Argus had demonstrated that Nicholas Christofilos's original concepts of a defensive shield against Russian missiles were intriguing but ultimately impractical, while suggesting tantalizing possibilities for further investigation. Fishbowl and especially Starfish Prime had shown the potential of these possibilities: not only for defense, but for offense. Slowly, steadily, the Argus idea had evolved from gathering plowshares into forging swords.

Program 437 was actually the second American ASAT system. Preceding and then overlapping it for a time was Program 505, an Army system based on its Nike-Zeus anti-ballistic missile (ABM).[7] The Nike-Zeus was the centerpiece of a bitter, complex interservice rivalry between the

Army and the Air Force over the ABM mission throughout the late 1950s and early 1960s. Program 505 was the Army's bid to beat the Air Force at its own game. A Nike-Zeus ASAT battery based on Kwajalein Atoll in the Marshall Islands seemed promising in initial 1962 tests during Fishbowl, but pesky technical limitations persisted, including tracking and guidance problems, a relatively short effective range, and the inability of Nike-Zeus to carry anything other than a fairly small warhead (low "throw-weight," in missile jargon).

Program 505 would continue to drag on for several more years, but for the ASAT job, the Thor-based Program 437 seemed a better alternative, both to Secretary of Defense McNamara and, of course, to the Air Force. By the summer of 1963, President Kennedy himself declared it to be "in the highest national priority category for research and development."[8]

But research and development didn't necessarily translate to a fully operational and deployed system. An official meeting later that year chaired by McNamara showed that some in the administration had nagging doubts about both the practicality and advisability of Program 437. Noted an official Air Force history: "Most of the civilian leadership of both the State and Defense Departments were very nervous about even having a program of research and development for something like 437, let alone the prospect of having such a system operationally ready and manned by 'blue suiters' [i.e., Air Force personnel]. Certainly the aspect of detonating a nuclear weapon in space was politically unattractive to them." Finally, journalist Edward R. Murrow, attending the meeting in his official capacity as director of the US Information Agency, calmly remarked: "If the Soviets place a bomb in orbit and threaten us and if this administration has refused to develop a capability to destroy it in orbit, you will see the first impeachment proceeding of an American President since Andrew Johnson." That caused "about two minutes of total silence . . . Finally, McNamara said testily, 'Well, it doesn't cost much, and the JCS [Joint Chiefs of Staff] want it, so let's approve 437.'"[9]

The Johnston Island launch complex that had hosted Fishbowl became the home of the newly established 10th Aerospace Defense Squadron (ADS) of the US Air Force, with a backup and support facility at Vandenberg Air Force Base in California. Beginning in 1964, tests and exercises began, all using non-nuclear-armed missiles, and the 10th ADS was declared fully operational by the middle of the year. For target practice, the crews used spent rocket stages and other space junk in orbit. Two Thor missiles would remain on twenty-four-hour alert at Johnston Island, with two kept in ready reserve at Vandenberg.

Yet it was unknown to the public at large. President Kennedy had occasionally commented on a US ASAT capability, but made no official announcements of its existence. In fall 1964, his successor, Lyndon Johnson, "during a reelection campaign trip to Sacramento, disclosed that the United States had developed an ASAT capability to intercept a satellite that might be carrying a weapon that threatened US national security." The following day, McNamara announced it officially, without giving up much in the way of details. It was unclear whether Johnson's announcement had been inadvertent or intentional, but "whatever his reasons . . . President Johnson not only put the Soviets on warning that the United States had an operational ASAT system, but he also told the electorate that he was prepared to defend the country from any possible attack, even if it came from outer space."[10] No doubt Johnson's proclamation didn't hurt his landslide election victory two months later.

It may have been comforting to both the public and the Pentagon to know that Program 437 existed, but in reality it was far from perfect. As defense funding began to be increasingly siphoned away by the steadily growing demands of the Vietnam War, the Air Force found it difficult to keep paying for the Thor missiles needed for test launches and operational proficiency maintenance for the 10th ADS crews. Also, the single location at Johnston Island didn't permit global coverage; the Soviets could conceivably avoid the Program 437 defenses altogether by choosing different launch and orbital profiles for their satellites. Another practical military consideration was that, tactically speaking, Johnston Island was hardly a stronghold, and could easily have been overwhelmed by a commando raid aimed at destroying the missiles and launch pads. Air Force commanders were quite aware that Soviet submarines routinely parked in international waters near Johnston Island to observe test launches. Any conceivable support forces against an attack were hundreds of miles away on Hawaii. Mother Nature posed another threat: "A more likely source of damage to Program 437 was from strong tropical storms that potentially could batter the island and reduce the site to rubble."[11]

Perhaps the biggest problem of all harkened back to Program 437's nuclear roots in Argus and Starfish. The effects of a nuclear explosion in space had no respect for national boundaries. Attacking another country's satellite with a nuclear weapon—even if it was an orbiting warhead and not merely an innocuous weather satellite—could quite naturally be interpreted as the opening of an all-out nuclear strike, sparking general war. Even under the best circumstances, the EMP and radiation effects of a Program 437 strike could quite likely cripple or destroy friendly satellites, as Starfish Prime had so clearly demonstrated.

The supposed threat of orbiting Soviet nukes never materialized, and as funding continued to diminish, Program 437 slowly faded into oblivion. Attempts to keep it alive by altering or enhancing its original ASAT mission proved abortive, while the Pacific Ocean took its toll. "The Thor boosters stood alert on open launch pads, unprotected from the harsh environment and strong Pacific storms or other natural disasters. Over time the rocket bodies and launch support equipment were susceptible to the corrosive effects of the heat, humidity, and salt-water spray."[12] Launch equipment began to fail. By 1970 the Air Force began to shut down operations. Then, in August 1972, a hurricane passed close to Johnston Island, severely damaging the launch pads and other facilities and speeding the program's demise, which finally became official in 1975. The notion of anti-satellite weapons persisted, however, taking different and sometimes outlandish forms, such as the use of F-15 fighter planes to launch ASATs from high altitude, a sequel to the Navy's old NOTSNIK idea.

Program 437 would not be the end of further talk of using nuclear weapons in space, however. Several years later, the grandiose schemes of Ronald Reagan's Strategic Defense Initiative, more commonly known as "Star Wars," would propose orbiting X-ray lasers powered by hydrogen bombs and other similarly apocalyptic devices as defensive countermeasures to enemy ICBMs. The electromagnetic pulse effects that had been first revealed by Teak, Orange, Starfish Prime, and even Argus were not forgotten either by SDI planners or by the military officials, scientists, and political strategists who followed them.

Some ideas, it seems, refuse to go away. As the more immediate descendants of Argus and Starfish such as Program 437 fizzled out and passed into historical obscurity in the years that followed, the original dreams of Nicholas Christofilos would continue to mutate into a dark specter, a shadow that persists into the twenty-first century and beyond.

ON MONDAY, JUNE 10, 1963, PRESIDENT JOHN F. KENNEDY DELIVERED WHAT would be one of the most influential and important speeches of his brief presidency, a commencement address at the American University in Washington, D.C. He and his speechwriter Theodore Sorensen had titled it "A Strategy of Peace," but it would soon become better known as JFK's American University speech, or more simply, his "peace speech."

With all the Cold War crises and tensions that had haunted his presidency, and the nightmarish days of the Cuban Missile Crisis still fresh in his mind, Kennedy was anxious to set out on a new course, a more hopeful path to the future than the nuclear oblivion that, so often, had seemed inevitable. He spoke of world peace, "the kind of peace that makes life on earth worth living . . . not merely peace for Americans but peace for all men and women, not merely peace in our time but peace in all time."

Too many, Kennedy said, "think it is impossible. Too many think it is unreal. But that is a dangerous, defeatist belief. It leads to the conclusion that war is inevitable, that mankind is doomed, that we are gripped by forces we cannot control. We need not accept that view. Our problems are manmade; therefore, they can be solved by man."

Kennedy went beyond such stirring rhetoric, however, to make concrete and practical proposals. Our attitudes toward the Soviet Union had to be reexamined. In the event of war, he noted, "our two countries would become the primary targets . . . all we have built, all we have worked for, would be destroyed in the first twenty-four hours."

To forestall that catastrophe, the president called for early agreement on a comprehensive nuclear test ban treaty, while also pledging that the United States "does not propose to conduct nuclear tests in the atmosphere so long as other states do not do so. We will not be the first to resume." He observed that while "such a declaration is no substitute for a formal binding treaty" or "a substitute for disarmament," he hoped it would help achieve both goals.

The speech stands as one of the most remarkable statements ever made by an American president, not only in historical hindsight but especially considering the time in which it was delivered. And it would have an immediate impact, most importantly upon Nikita Khrushchev, who found Kennedy's words profoundly inspiring and encouraging. Less than a month after the speech, Khrushchev proposed a partial nuclear test ban treaty, barring all but underground tests. Several weeks later, a formal treaty was signed by the US, USSR, and Great Britain. The Partial or Limited Test Ban Treaty, more formally designated as the Treaty Banning Nuclear Tests in the Atmosphere, in Outer Space and Under Water, was soon ratified by the US Senate and signed into law by Kennedy on October 7, 1963. It went into effect three days later.

After years of temporary moratoriums, diplomatic wrangling, military planning, successful and completely botched test operations, radioactive fallout and mushroom clouds and fireballs brighter and hotter than the sun, the days of open nuclear testing were over. At least for the United States, Soviet Union, and United Kingdom. Other nations such as China and France would soon conduct their own atmospheric tests, quite unconcerned with any agreements concluded by their more powerful international rivals.

But since the Tightrope shot that concluded Operation Fishbowl in 1962, no nuclear explosions have yet taken place in or near outer space.

There are, however, no guarantees.

CHAPTER 18
Threats and Legacies

O<small>NE DAY IN</small> J<small>UNE</small>, 1999, R<small>EPRESENTATIVE</small> R<small>OSCOE</small> B<small>ARTLETT</small> (R-M<small>ARYLAND</small>) <small>SAT</small> in a Vienna hotel room along with ten of his colleagues and some congressional staffers, facing three members of the Russian Duma and a representative of Serbian president Slobodan Milosevic. The group had been busy hammering out a framework agreement to end the bloody war in Kosovo.

Tensions were high and tempers short, with the Russians feeling slighted that they had been brought into the negotiations on an almost after-the-fact basis by the United States and NATO powers. As Bartlett later recalled, the dominant member of the Russian group, former ambassador to the US and deputy Duma chairman Vladimir Lukin, "was very angry and sat with his arms crossed looking at the ceiling for a couple of days during these discussions." Lukin was visibly offended by what he perceived as an American snub, complaining that "you spit on us, now why should we help you?"

Finally, Lukin made an offhand remark that stunned the leader of the American delegation, Curt Weldon, who spoke Russian. "Did you hear what he said?" Weldon asked Bartlett, before the translator repeated it in English.

Bartlett, who spoke no Russian, shook his head. Then the translator gave them Lukin's words: "If we really wanted to hurt you, with no fear of retaliation, we would launch an SLBM [submarine-launched ballistic missile] from the ocean, detonate a nuclear weapon high above your country, and shut down your power grid and your communications for six months or so." As if to emphasize the point, a younger member of the Russian group added, "And if one weapon wouldn't do it, we have some spares."[1]

It was a remarkable threat, chilling in its implications, plain in character, and entirely plausible. The Russians were talking about an EMP weapon—essentially a scaled-up version of Argus, Starfish Prime, or Teak, specifically designed to generate an intense electromagnetic pulse effect when detonated at high altitude.

It was a threat unlike the blustery Cold War boasts of Nikita Khrushchev—his "we will bury you," or when he pounded his fists on his desk at the United Nations. At the time, as exercised as some Western leaders and strategists allowed themselves to become in response to such statements, some fundamental understanding remained that in the end, it was all talk, all sound and fury signifying very little, if not nothing.

But this was different. This was an unguarded, ill-advised remark made by a frustrated and exhausted man who would probably have never said such a thing under better circumstances. It was certainly not an official statement of Russian policy that required a decisive US response.

Yet it was its very casualness that gave it such impact. Aside from being a congressman, Bartlett was also a scientist, specifically a physiologist, and a former director of the Space Life Sciences Group at the Applied Physics Laboratory of Johns Hopkins University, working on NASA contracts. He also served on the House Armed Services Committee and the Committee on Science, Space, and Technology. The phenomenon of EMP was certainly not new to him. But until this moment, he had never really thought through its ultimate meaning.

Soon after, the Kosovo negotiations successfully ended with an agreement adopted by the G-8 nations, and the Russian and American delegations went home. But Bartlett continued to be haunted by Lukin's words. He became a major force in calling for hearings on the EMP threat, which led to the formal establishment of the Commission to Assess the Threat to the United States from Electromagnetic Pulse (EMP) Attack.

In a 2004 report, the Commission noted that while "EMP effects from nuclear bursts are not new threats to our nation," they previously would have likely occurred as a consequences of general nuclear war, when their impact would pale in comparison to the wholesale obliteration of cities and populations. Defense against EMP meant deterring nuclear war, period. But now, the threat can come from "terrorist groups that have no state identity, have only one or a few weapons, and are motivated to attack the US without regard for their own safety."[2]

The Commission also noted that the threat didn't merely encompass an attack on obvious vital US infrastructure targets such as the power grid. Other government agencies, including the Pentagon's Defense Threat Reduction Agency, conducted their own studies and issued their own reports, pointing out that EMP can also be used as an antisatellite weapon, as Starfish Prime had demonstrated back in 1962.

Since Argus and Starfish Prime, the United States and much of the rest of the world have come to depend on a robust and extensive infrastructure of satellites and communication networks. Losing them would affect far more than our economies and cultures. Satellites are indispensable for modern military forces—particularly those of the US. They are involved in intelligence collection, strategic planning, and tactical operations of all kinds. And that indispensability has made us more vulnerable than ever before.

Even a relatively small nuclear warhead, sent aloft by a small rocket to a humble altitude of as low as sixty miles, could cripple or destroy many vital satellites. It's technology that's within the reach of many countries, including North Korea, Iran, India, Pakistan—nations not as dependent upon space resources as more advanced nations, and thus less likely to feel their loss. It's perhaps one of the most underappreciated threats we face today. Just as a band of terrorists managed to shock the world with hijacked airliners and a few box cutters, any country or group with access to nuclear weapons and 1950s-era launch technology has the potential to bring twenty-first-century Western civilization to its knees.

After a long career in Congress that began in 1982, Roscoe Bartlett finally became a private citizen after losing a reelection bid in the 2012 midterms. Aside from being one of the longest-serving members of the House, he's now famous for retreating to a distant mountain cabin in West Virginia to live completely off the grid, with no outside electricity, plumbing, or phone service. Instead of retiring to plush luxury in the usual tradition of career politicians, Bartlett lives with solar panels, wood-burning stoves, and composting toilets. Still active as a private consultant, he continues to crusade for measures to protect the US infrastructure from EMP, solar storms, and cyberattack, whether from natural origins or terrorist action. He is confident that he and his family are prepared for catastrophe. He still worries that the United States is not.

The congressional EMP commission that Bartlett helped to establish offered some words of hope: "The Nation's vulnerability to EMP that gives rise to potentially large-scale, long-term consequences can be reasonably and readily reduced below the level of a potentially catastrophic national problem by coordinated and focused effort between the private and public sectors of our country," its members wrote. "Such actions are both rational and feasible."

More than a decade after that report, however, little if anything has been done. Tucked away on a remote mountain, Roscoe Bartlett remains frustrated that despite all the talk, all the commissions and studies and congressional testimony, and long after an annoyed Russian diplomat made an offhand remark in a Vienna hotel room, no definitive steps have been taken to address what he sees as an existential threat to Western civilization.

AFTER STARFISH PRIME AND HIS INJUN 1 SATELLITE, JAMES VAN ALLEN WAS FINished dealing with nuclear weapons. Even had he desired to continue any such involvement, the Partial Nuclear Test Ban Treaty and the subsequent Outer Space Treaty in 1967 essentially ensured that the only nuclear technologies that would henceforth be used in space would be wholly peaceful in nature. With the days of exoatmospheric nuclear testing over, the only radiation in space would be generated either by natural sources or by small devices generating power for deep space probes and Mars landers.

With one notable exception. The Starfish Prime radiation belt would continue to persist at a detectable level into the 1970s, and would indeed complicate scientific observations of the natural Van Allen belts and other solar and exoatmospheric phenomena. In the end, Van Allen had been proved right in discounting his scientific intuition and trusting the hard data that his instruments provided.

He would continue his distinguished career as America's premier space scientist, extending his explorations past Earth's orbital neighborhood to the outer reaches of the Solar System and beyond into interstellar space. Based at the University of Iowa[3] for the rest of his life, Van Allen built instruments for almost all the major space probe missions of the 1960s and 1970s, including the Mariner spacecraft that went to Venus and Mars and Pioneer 10 and 11, the first probes that ventured beyond the asteroid belt to Jupiter and Saturn and ultimately left the Solar System entirely. He would teach and mentor legions of undergraduate and graduate students, many of whom, such as George Ludwig and Carl McIlwain, would go on to distinguished scientific careers and achievements in their own right. Even after stepping down in 1985 as head of the Department of Physics and Astronomy at the University of Iowa, he continued to work tirelessly as an emeritus professor, showing up bright and early every morning at the Iowa City campus building where he had spent most of his career, the building which now bore his name. He died in 2006 at the age of ninety-one.

Van Allen's place in the history of physics and space exploration is unassailable. He did, after all, make the first true scientific discovery of the space age—the first step for transforming space travel from a nationalistic stunt into a serious human endeavor. Yet some historians view his career with a somewhat jaundiced eye, questioning the close, often inextricable relationship with the military that characterized and enabled so much of his work.

Van Allen, of course, never denied or tried to hide that connection, and readily acknowledged that he had been conducting military-related research since his days as a Navy officer in World War II. But until Argus, he had never worked with nuclear weapons, a fact that entails a new level of ethical consideration. He was never directly involved in designing and building nuclear weapons, like so many of his fellow physicists. But in a real sense, he used them to conduct and benefit his own research. Where, some have asked, should he have drawn the line?

To some degree, Van Allen had no real choice. Especially during the years of the Cold War, the tools of his trade, including rockets and high-altitude balloons, were almost exclusively under the control of the military, so any scientist who needed to use them had to deal with military authorities. But some argue that perhaps Van Allen went too far. "By participating in a project to detonate bombs in outer space aimed at disrupting and militarizing the magnetosphere, he was behaving quintessentially as a product of the mid-twentieth-century cold war," wrote historian James Rodger Fleming. Referring to the effects of Starfish Prime, Fleming argues that "his actions, admittedly miscalculations, rendered the scientific study of a newly discovered planetary feature difficult if not impossible for over a decade."[4]

That seems an unfair criticism; after all, Van Allen had nothing directly to do with the planning or execution of Starfish Prime, nor of Argus or any of the other high-altitude shots. While it could be argued that he might have used his status and prestige to protest against them more vigorously, ultimately he had no power to stop such tests. But he also didn't hesitate to take advantage of them as a scientist. "He wrote about the science of it all, but he eagerly participated in the military aspects as well," Fleming said.[5]

Unlike some of his other colleagues, Van Allen could hardly be characterized as a militaristic Dr. Strangelove type. Rather, he may have been something of an innocuous opportunist. Historian Lisa Mundey cites a 1981 oral history interview with Van Allen in which he explained, "I didn't really know much about the bomb business. I thought, if they were going to make a test, [space] was a good place to make one, as far as absence of fallout goes and adverse effects."[6] Pointing out that Van Allen also fought for openness and making the results of Argus and the other tests public,

Mundey concludes that "like many scientists of the era, he bought into the Cold War competition with the Soviets and engaged in defense-related research. His behavior after the public revelation of the [Argus] experiment, however, suggests that he wanted public credit for his achievements and so supported declassification."[7]

Whether James Van Allen willingly compromised himself as a scientist by co-opting his work to the military or was merely doing whatever he had to do out of dedication to his profession is too complex a question to be ultimately resolved. As nuclear historian Alex Wellerstein points out, "Very little in good history boils down to easy ideological stances." But James Van Allen's connections with Argus and the other space nuclear tests—activities that were the first human attempts to intentionally alter the environment on a global scale—remain an inescapable part of his larger legacy. As Fleming observed, for better or worse, "his halo now has a decidedly nuclear glow."[8]

FOR NICHOLAS CHRISTOFILOS, ETHICAL OR MORAL QUESTIONS ABOUT WHETHER or not a scientist had any business being involved with the military were a non-issue, nothing more than a foolish distraction. Following Argus and the subsequent analyses of the data, he returned to his pet project: the Astron accelerator at Livermore Lab.

Some people already considered Astron outlandish enough, but that didn't stop Christofilos from continuing to generate other wild ideas, always with the same manic enthusiasm and persuasiveness. When he realized that Argus would not work as the impenetrable barrier to Russian missiles he had originally envisioned in his dreams, he refused to be discouraged. He simply moved on to other possibilities. "His ideas were grandiose and bizarre," historian Sharon Weinberger wrote, "but usually so genius that they dazzled the physicists around him. What seemed to attract scientists was that the ideas themselves were scientifically sound but required technological miracles to make them work."[9]

One of them was called Seesaw, a scheme for a massive particle beam weapon to knock down incoming Soviet ICBMs. It was just the sort of notion that would have fit in perfectly with the "Star Wars" schemes of the 1980s, except that Christofilos first proposed it in 1958. With the trademark Christofilos touch, nothing about Seesaw was modest or conservative. The weapon would have required massive amounts of energy, far more than any conceivable power source could provide. Conceivable, that is, to anyone but Christofilos. At one point, he proposed detonating hydrogen bombs to drain the Great Lakes, generating the necessary electrical power by using the resulting massive deluge of (radioactive) water. (He did at least recognize that such a measure would only be considered in an absolutely last-ditch scenario, such as when the US was already under massive attack.) Colleagues did the math and concluded that, absurd and unthinkable as it was, the idea would actually work—provided one accepted the immolation of the entire Midwest, of course. As Weinberger notes, "Christofilos's imagination was not tethered to practicality."[10] As an indication of the bizarre desperation driving the Cold War, Seesaw continued to be seriously studied and considered, if only theoretically, for decades after Christofilos first proposed it.

Not all of Christofilos's ideas were quite so apocalyptic. His Project Sanguine—a system for generating extremely low-frequency (ELF) radio waves using immense antennas buried deep underground to enable secret communication with submerged submarines all over the world—didn't involve setting off nuclear weapons. The underground basing would supposedly render the system invulnerable, ensuring that America's nuclear-armed submarine force would always be able to respond to a Soviet attack. The problem was the ELF antennas. Unlike conventional radio and TV signals, which range from millimeters to yards in wavelength, ELF waves are miles long, which means that the antennas must also be likewise. Christofilos's ideas involved even longer ELF waves that would actually be transmitted using natural ground electrical currents and the ionosphere.

But burying such a system underground would entail digging up thousands of square miles and causing extreme environmental disruption. When the Navy's plans to build a Sanguine site settled on northern Wisconsin, environmentalists and the public rebelled. "Isn't it about time that we refused to be brainwashed as to the necessity of bigger and more terrible things in the name of peace?" asked one letter to the *Chicago Tribune*.[11] Though experimental tests proved that the concept actually worked, Christofilos's original Sanguine plans, conceived with his typical grand panache, were doomed. For years, however, the Navy employed a smaller-scale ELF system for submarine communications that used some of Christofilos's ideas.

And there was always Astron. It had been his passion for particle accelerators that had first brought him to the United States and landed him his position at Livermore, and had burned continuously throughout his life. Its basic concept of using relativistic electrons to generate magnetic fields and contain plasma for fusion power had driven most of his other work, beginning with Argus.

Yet definitive success with Astron continued to elude him, despite years of experimentation, bureaucratic wrangling over funding, and controversy over the direction of the project. Christofilos achieved interesting results and intriguing insights, but never the grail of practical, controllable thermonuclear fusion. "No matter how tightly Christofilos clung to Astron's reins, he could not force the electrons, or the resistors, or the pulser, or any other part of his apparatus, to behave as he wished," observed a history of the project.[12] Yet his stubbornness impelled him to keep working, keep pushing. When Astron was dismissed as a "dark horse" in the quest for fusion power, Christofilos responded, "No, it is just a white horse, standing in the shadows."[13]

By the beginning of the 1970s, the Astron project was struggling to survive; Christofilos was under ever greater demands for concrete results while under ever stricter deadlines imposed by the AEC. Always a workaholic, Christofilos was driving himself and his assistants through twelve-hour days, punctuated only occasionally by after-hours drinking bouts at local bars.

His personal life was no source of solace either. After his messy divorce from his first wife, his second marriage also ended in divorce. His sons, one from each of his wives, lived with their mothers. Christofilos was essentially alone, with only his ideas, his work, and the elusive dream of Astron. His health deteriorated, his visions clouding over.

By the fall of September 1972, it all caught up with him. After a meeting with AEC chairman James Schlesinger at Livermore, Christofilos checked into the local Holiday Inn, a practice he'd adopted to avoid a long commute home to Berkeley on late nights. The next morning, September 25, his secretary went in search of him when he failed to appear at the lab on his usual bright and early schedule, and found him in his room, dead of a massive heart attack. He was only fifty-six years old. The Astron project joined him in oblivion the following June, officially and permanently cancelled.

The "crazy Greek" was gone, finally overwhelmed by the passion of his ideas and relentless strivings. Though some of the various press obituaries that followed mentioned Argus in passing, it was Christofilos's thermonuclear work with Astron that got the most attention, ensuring that he would be remembered as an inventive, original thinker, not as a weaponeer or military scientist.

For an individual such as Nicholas Christofilos, who lived his life and conducted his work with an unapologetic, uncompromising spirit, it was appropriate that his final legacy should be based on his strongest and most long-lasting passion. As a friend once described him: "For Nick, all pieces are written fortissimo."

But some of his darker and more apocalyptic visions—Argus and the power and fury of nuclear weapons extending from the surface of Earth into the heavens and beyond—also survive. Thus far, those visions are still only the "crazy ideas" of a uniquely imaginative scientist. We can only continue to hope that they become nothing more.

Postscript:
A Persistent Afterglow

IN THE TWENTY-FIRST CENTURY, IT SEEMS INCREDIBLE THAT SOMETHING SUCH AS Argus or Fishbowl could have ever been contemplated, much less actually carried out. Surely such an enterprise, one nation deciding to conduct experiments that could conceivably affect the entire planet in unknown and perhaps dangerous ways, without the knowledge or consent of the rest of the world, was nothing less than the height of arrogance and hubris.

From the perspective of the Cold War era, when both the US and USSR were gripped by a more or less constant state of existential dread and when almost every move by the other side seemed to herald the path to doomsday, it's perhaps somewhat more understandable. A desperate struggle for survival can make the irrational seem rational, the terrible risk worth taking, the mad scheme seem reasonable. In such a climate, far removed from the context of a humane and peaceful culture, even Dr. Strangelove becomes a paragon of rationality.

Coupled with that sort of paranoid recklessness born of fear was also a certain naive ignorance. In the 1950s and 1960s, nuclear weapons were still a relatively new technology, and much about their capabilities remained uncertain or completely unknown. The first edition of *The Effects of Atomic Weapons*, a one-volume summary of the current state of knowledge about the atomic bomb published jointly by the Atomic Energy Commission and Department of Defense in 1950, contained absolutely no mention of the electromagnetic pulse phenomenon or the effects of high-altitude detonations, simply because they had not yet been observed in the relative handful of atomic blasts that had so far occurred. It wasn't until the third edition of the book (by then retitled *The Effects of Nuclear Weapons*), published in 1977, that detailed descriptions of EMP and high-altitude and outer space nuclear weapons phenomena could be included, after Argus and Fishbowl had provided the data.

Also, any thought that human beings could seriously do anything to profoundly affect the entire Earth at a single stroke seemed absurd, the stuff of science fiction rather than science. At the time of Argus and Fishbowl, climate science was in its infancy, and the concept of the Earth as a single, unified system of interrelated parts was even more remote. James Van Allen's discovery of the radiation belts, along with other geophysical research during the IGY, had begun to hint at such a perspective, but it would be years before it became common scientific or cultural coin.

So it may be comforting to think of Argus, Fishbowl, and the various Soviet nuclear space tests as historical anomalies, relics of their peculiar era, something that could never again be an issue. Even Herbert York, who had been one of the chief architects of Argus, seemed to hold this view. Many years afterward, he remarked: "Imagine proposing such a thing today. You'd never get away with it. But in that moment, you could."[1]

But consider the historical sequence of events. Argus was hastily conceived, organized, and executed in perhaps the most absolute secrecy attainable at the time, and would have quite possibly have remained classified to this day, but for the efforts of some enterprising journalists and scientists who finally forced its revelation. Once it went public, the very idea of Argus shocked and outraged many people, even some of the fiercest Cold Warriors. Yet a mere four years later, tourists threw parties on Hawaiian beaches to watch the light show produced by weapons that were orders of magnitude more powerful than the Argus shots exploded in outer space. Some people still protested, but for most of the public, Operation Fishbowl was merely a visual extravaganza, produced by their government with their tax dollars.

By the time of Fishbowl, the idea that humans might actually possess the power to affect and alter the entire planet had become a faint glimmer in the public perception, though still far dimmer and subtler than the brilliant displays of auroral fire from Fishbowl's tests. Ironically, the example of Argus and Fishbowl were one reason for this growing perception, inspiring many to worry about disrupting or destroying the Earth's natural radiation belts, climate, or even the tilt of its axis. And the tests now provide a powerful counterargument to those who, at a time when human beings are being forced to confront the long-term effects of their civilization upon the Earth's continued habitability, still argue that our activities can't possibly affect our planetary environment.

But the transition of nuclear weapons from the surface and near-surface of the Earth to outer space, the shift of their targeting from cities and military bases to a hemispheric and global scale, was perhaps even more alarming. By simply introducing it to a completely new environment, the most physically destructive weapon ever invented was found capable of wreaking devastation in entirely new ways that its creators had never contemplated. Now, argued some strategists, space-based nuclear weapons could destroy without killing and attack an enemy's vital interests without dropping a single warhead on its territory. The EMP and antisatellite capabilities of nuclear weapons offered an enhanced military versatility that made the consideration of their use in various scenarios seem more tempting, reasonable, and even humane. And the path was cleared to a brand new potential arena of warfare that could engulf and threaten the entire planet.

Fortunately, with the Limited Test Ban Treaty and the Outer Space Treaty, the international community chose to turn away from such a dangerous potential future, no doubt partly influenced by the brief preview that Argus and Fishbowl had provided. But the dreams of nuclear-based military space dominance persist, and have only been encouraged by our ever-increasing dependence on a satellite-based infrastructure, and the challenges posed by the growing space capabilities of rival nations.

Keeping the reaches of space a completely sacrosanct civilian refuge, free of any military presence, was never a realistic possibility. "The militarization of space has proceeded steadily and inexorably since the launch of Sputnik in 1957," wrote Stimson Center co-founder Michael Krepon in a 2003 report on military space policy. But Krepon and his co-author Christopher Clary also emphasize that while a military presence in space is a fact of life, "the crucial distinction between the militarization and weaponization of space remains in place."[2]

At present, that distinction still holds, but is becoming ever more tenuous. If we allow it to dissolve whether through casual indifference or conscious intention, the sky may yet again burn with nuclear fire.

Maps

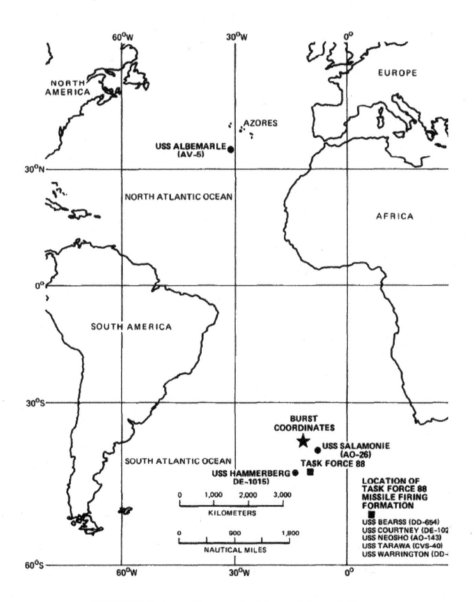

ARGUS 1, locations of ships at burst time.

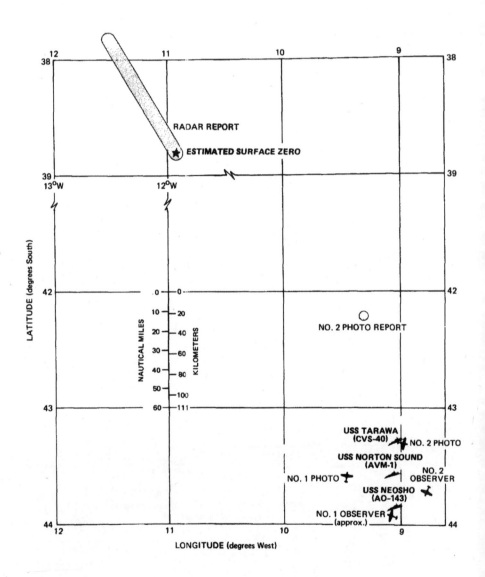

ARGUS 1, Positions of Task Force 88 units and reported bursts.

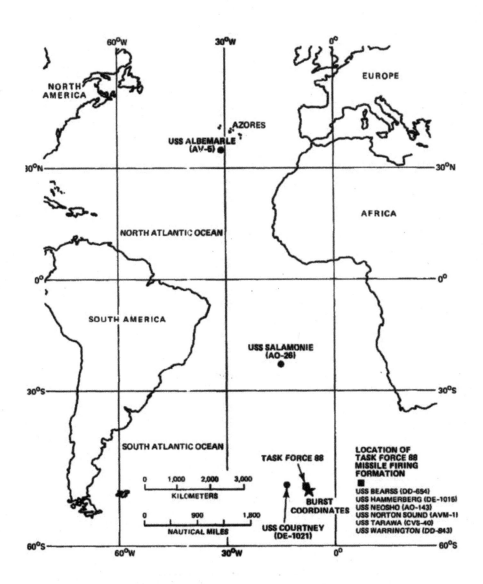

ARGUS 2, locations of ships at burst time.

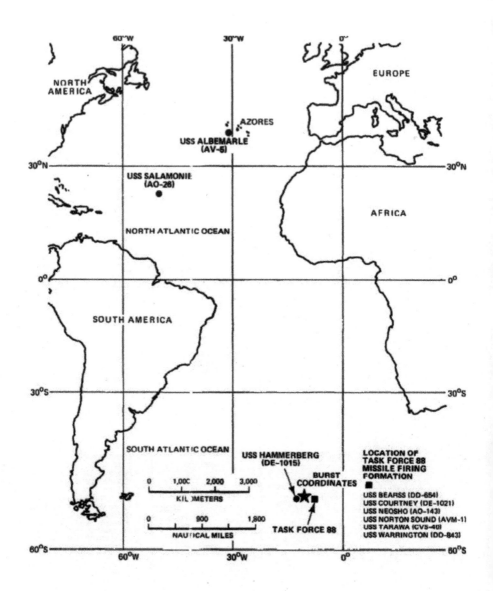

ARGUS 3, locations of ships at burst time.

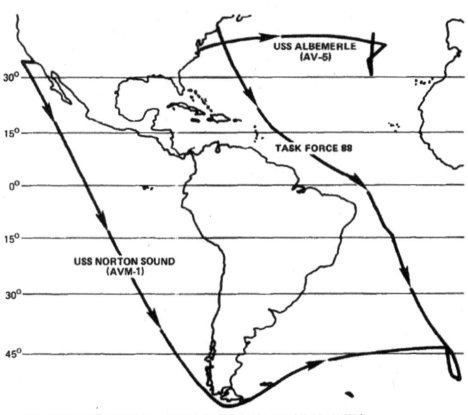

TASK FORCE 88 RETURNED TO NEWPORT, RHODE ISLAND, VIA RIO DE JANEIRO

USS ALBEMARLE (AV-5) RETURNED TO NORFOLK, VIRGINIA, DIRECTLY

USS NORTON SOUND (AVM-1) RETURNED TO PORT HUENEME, CALIFORNIA, VIA
RIO DE JANEIRO AND THE PANAMA CANAL

USS NEOSHO (AO-143) AND USS BEARSS (DD-564) RETURNED TO NORFOLK,
VIRGINIA, VIA RIO DE JANEIRO

USS SALAMONIE (AO-26) RETURNED INDEPENDENTLY TO NEWPORT, RHODE ISLAND

Task Force 88 track chart, 1 August to 6 September 1958, ARGUS

Notes

Introduction

1. Walter Sullivan, *Assault on the Unknown* (New York: McGraw Hill, 1961), 140–41; Walter Sullivan, "News of Atom Test Took 2 Years To Reach Island 60 Miles Away," *New York Times*, October 31, 1960.

Chapter 1

1. Abigail Foerstner, *James Van Allen: The First Eight Billion Miles* (Iowa City: University of Iowa Press, 2007), 144.

2. Sharon Weinberger, *The Imagineers of War: The Untold Story of DARPA, the Pentagon Agency That Changed the World* (New York: Alfred A. Knopf, 2017), 32–3.

3. Paul Dickson, *Sputnik: The Shock of the Century* (New York: Simon & Schuster, 2001), 137.

4. Herbert York, *Making Weapons, Talking Peace* (New York: Basic Books, 1987), 101.

5. Dickson, *Sputnik*, 146.

6. Quoted in Evan Thomas, *Ike's Bluff: President Eisenhower's Secret Battle to Save the World* (New York: Little, Brown, 2012), 280.

7. York, *Making Weapons*, 131.

8. U.S. Department of Energy, *Briefing to Admiral Arleigh Burke, Chief of Naval Operations, The Argus Experiment*, July 29, 1958, DOE OpenNet (https://www.osti.gov/opennet), NV0059492.

9. Frank H. Shelton, *Reflections of a Physicist: Project Argus* (Colorado Springs, CO: Shelton Enterprises, 2000) 17, slide 58.

Chapter 2

1. Elisheva R. Coleman, Samuel A. Cohen, Michael S. Mahoney, "Greek Fire: Nicholas Christofilos and the Astron Project in America's Early Fusion Program," *Journal of Fusion Energy* 30, no. 3 (April 2011), 241, https://doi.org/10.1007/s10894-011-9392-5

2. This correspondence seems to be the origin of this particular sobriquet, which would subsequently come to be inextricably linked with Christofilos, at first only in private and professional circles and then finally by the public and press at large. There is no record that Christofilos ever seemed to mind.

3. Edward Teller, Biography of Nicholas C. Christofilos, April 8, 1959, Nicholas C. Christofilos Papers, Lawrence Livermore National Laboratory Archives.

4. Somehow, the usually impeccable *Physical Review* copyeditors overlooked the misspelling of "synchrotron" in the title of the paper, though the word is correctly spelled in the text.

5. Robert P. Crease, *Making Physics: A Biography of Brookhaven National Laboratory, 1946–1972* (Chicago: University of Chicago Press, 1999), 219.

6. Quoted in Crease, 220.

7. Coleman et al., 241.

8. York, *Making Weapons*, 130.

Chapter 3

1. The capitalization styles for code names of nuclear test series and shots in the primary literature vary greatly among different agencies, departments, and time periods. For consistency's sake in this book, except for those contained in direct quotations, only the names of test series (e.g., DOMINIC) are fully capitalized, while individual shots (e.g., Starfish) are not. The one exception is Argus, which is the only US test series that did not name individual shots.

2. Defense Threat Nuclear Agency, U.S. Department of Defense, *Defense's Nuclear Agency, 1947–1997* (Washington, D.C.: U.S. Government Printing Office, 2002), 137.3. York, *Making Weapons*, 131.

3. York, *Making Weapons*, 131.

4. *Defense's Nuclear Agency*, 137.

5. James R. Killian, Jr., *Sputnik, Scientists, and Eisenhower: A Memoir of the First Special Assistant to the President for Science and Technology* (Cambridge, MA: The MIT Press, 1977), 187–88.

6. Foerstner, 193.

7. Ibid., 180.

8. George H. Ludwig, *Opening Space Research: Dreams, Technology, and Scientific Discovery* (Washington, D.C.: American Geophyiscal Union, 2011), 362.

9. James A. Van Allen, "Energetic Particles in the Earth's Magnetic Field," in *Discovery of the Magnetosphere*, ed. C. Stewart Gillmor and John R. Spreiter (Washington, D.C.: American Geophyiscal Union, 1997), 240.

10. Ludwig, Opening Space, 365.

11. Van Allen, "Energetic Particles," 243.

12. Ibid., 243.

13. Ibid., 244.

14. Foerstner, 190.

15. Ibid. 191.

Chapter 4

1. Defense Nuclear Agency, U.S. Department of Defense, United States Atmospheric Nuclear Weapons Tests, Nuclear Test Personnel Review, *Operation Argus 1958* (Washington, D.C.: U.S. Government Printing Office, 30 April 1982), DNA 6039F, 18. (Henceforth DNA report)

2. Lisa M. Mundey, "The Civilianization of a Nuclear Weapon Effects Test: Operation ARGUS," *Historical Studies in the Natural Sciences*, vol. 42, no. 4 (2012), 298.

3. Ibid., 295.

4. DNA report, 18.

5. York, *Making Weapons*, 117.

6. Dr. James R. Killian, Jr., "Report of NSC Ad Hoc Working Group On the Technical Feasibility of a Cessation of Nuclear Testing," March 27, 1958, 7, The National Security Archive, Washington, D.C.

7. York, *Making Weapons*, 149.

8. Transcript, *The Reminiscences of Vice Admiral Lloyd M. Mustin, U.S. Navy (Retired), Volume II*, interviewed by John T. Mason, Jr., August 28, 1974; September 4, 1974; October 23, 1974; October 30, 1974; December 18, 1974; January 15, 1975 (Annapolis, MD: U.S. Naval Institute, 2003), 1200.

9. Transcript, Lloyd M. Mustin interview, September 22, 1980, 15, DOE OpenNet (https://www.osti.gov/opennet), NV0068994.

10. DNA report, 25.

11. Ibid.

12. Mustin, *Reminiscences*, 1215–6.

13. Ibid., 1212.

14. Ibid.

15. Ibid., 1207.

16. Ibid., 1205.

17. Ibid.

18. Ibid., 1206–7.

Chapter 5

1. Defense Nuclear Agency, U.S. Department of Defense, United States Atmospheric Nuclear Weapons Tests, Nuclear Test Personnel Review, *Operation Hardtack I 1958* (Washington, D.C.: U.S. Government Printing Office, 1 December 1982), DNA 6038F, 259.

2. *Defense's Nuclear Agency*, 140.

3. James Rodger Fleming, "Iowa Enters the Space Age: James Van Allen, Earth's Radiation Belts, and Experiments to Disrupt Them," *The Annals of Iowa* 70 (Fall 2011), 314.

4. *Defense's Nuclear Agency*, 140.

5. *Operation Hardtack I 1958*, 257–73.

6. *Defense's Nuclear Agency*, 142–3.

7. Ludwig, 370.

8. Mustin, *Reminiscences*, 1217.

9. Ludwig, 369–70.

10. Richard S. "Dick" Culp, telephone interview with author, August 2, 2016.

11. Frank Shelton, "Reflections of a Physicist, 67.

12. Keith Mayfield, email interview with author, September 14, 2016.

13. Mustin, *Reminiscences*, 1210.

14. Mayfield, ibid.

15. Shelton, 65.

16. Mustin, *Reminiscences*, 1213.

17. McMaster email interview, September 17, 2016.

18. Culp interview.

Chapter 6

1. Mustin 1980 interview, 9.

2. Mustin, *Reminiscences*, 1218.

3. Ibid.

4. U.S. Defense Atomic Support Agency, L.M. Mustin, RADM, USN, *Operation ARGUS: Report of the Commander, Task Force 88,* March 31, 1960, DOE OpenNet (https://www.osti.gov/opennet), 23. (NV0133192)

5. Mustin, *Reminiscences,* 1217.

6. Ibid., 1220.

7. Ibid., 1209–10.

8. Ibid. 1223.

9. Ibid., 1208.

10. *Operation ARGUS: Report of the Commander, Task Force 88* (NV 0133192) 36.

11. Culp interview.

12. Mustin 1980 interview, 21.

13. Mustin, *Reminiscences,* 1221.

14. Culp interview.

Chapter 7

1. *Operation ARGUS: Report of the Commander, Task Force 88* (NV0133192)

2. DNA report, 63.

3. Martin Walt, "From Nuclear Physics to Space Physics by Way of High Altitude Nuclear Tests," in *Discovery of the Magnetosphere,* ed. C. Stewart Gillmor and John R. Spreiter (Washington, D.C.: American Geophyiscal Union, 1997), 255.

4. James A. Van Allen, Carl E. McIlwain, and George Ludwig, "Satellite Observations of Electrons Artificially Injected Into the Geomagnetic Field," *Proceedings of the National Academy of Sciences,* vol. 45, 1959, 1157, 1159.

5. DNA report, 63.

6. Mustin, Reminiscences, 1223.

7. U.S. Department of Energy, Argus Event Message Traffic (Aug.–Sept. 1958), December 31, 1958, 19, NV0069040.

8. Mustin, *Reminiscences,* 1223.

9. Ibid., 1224.

10. Ibid.

11. Walt, 256.

12. Mustin, 1224.

13. *Defense's Nuclear Agency,* 143.

14. Ludwig, 383.

15. Ibid.

16. Ibid.

17. Quoted in U.S. Library of Congress, Aerospace Technology Division, Surveys of Foreign Scientific and Technical Literature, *Modification of the Ionosphere*, (Washington, D.C: Library of Congress, 30 Deember 1968), 45–6.

18. Ludwig, 384.

19. *Modification of the Ionosphere*, 46.

20. Ludwig, 384.

21. *Modification of the Ionosphere*, 46.

Chapter 8

1. U.S. Department of Energy, *Argus Event Message Traffic (Aug.–Sept. 1958)*, December 31, 1958, NV0069040. 32.

2. Interview with author.

3. Interview with author.

4. Quoted in Philip Newman, "Optical, Electromagnetic, and Satellite Observations of High Altitude Nuclear Detonations," *Proceedings of the National Academy of Sciences*, vol. 45, 1959, 1214.

5. *Operation ARGUS: Report of the Commander, Task Force 88*, 45–53.

6. Mustin, *Reminiscences*, 1225.

7. DNA report, 103.

8. Interview with author.

9. Interview with author.

10. Mustin, *Reminiscences*, 1229.

11. Interview with author.

12. Mustin, *Reminiscences*, 1230.

13. *Operation ARGUS: Report of the Commander, Task Force 88*, 23.

14. Even *Norton Sound*'s monthly logbooks were cloaked in official secrecy. Instead of listing the vessel's origin and destination for her Argus mission travels per naval tradition, the logbooks say only that the ship was "at sea."

15. Mustin, *Reminiscences*, 1231.

16. History of AVM *Norton Sound*.

17. Ludwig, 376–7.

18. Van Allen, "Energetic Particles," 245.

19. J. R. Killian, Jr., *Memorandum for the President, Preliminary Results of the ARGUS Experiment*, November 3, 1958. Dwight D. Eisenhower Presidential Library.

20. Ibid.

Chapter 9

1. *Operation ARGUS: Report of the Commander, Task Force 88*, 22.

2. Killian, "Sputnik, Scientists, and Ike," 189.

3. George B. Kistiakowsky, *A Scientist At the White House: The Private Diary of President Eisenhower's Special Assistant for Science and Technology* (Cambridge, MA: Harvard University Press, 1976), 72.

4. Sullivan, *Assault on the Unknown*, 141.

5. Ibid.

6. James Van Allen to Texas Instruments Company, October 22, 1958, James A. Van Allen Papers, University of Iowa Archives, Iowa City, IA.

7. Texas Instruments to Van Allen, November 21, 1958, ibid.

8. Sullivan, *Assault*, 143.

9. Ibid., 146.

10. Herbert York to James Killian, January 2, 1959, Argus Experiment Collection, Department of Archives/Special Collections, M. Louis Salmon Library, University of Alabama in Huntsville, Huntsville, AL.

11. York, *Making Weapons*, 149–50.

12. Sullivan, *Assault*, 147.

13. Bradley to Killian, January 14, 1959, Argus Experiment Collection, Department of Archives/Special Collections, M. Louis Salmon Library, University of Alabama in Huntsville.

14. Karl Harr to Killian, January 20, 1959, Ibid.

15. Sullivan, *Assault*, 147–8.

16. Sullivan to Killian, February 2, 1959, Argus Experiment Collection, University of Alabama in Huntsville.

17. Sullivan, *Assault*, 148.

18. "Radiation Belt May Monitor A-Tests," *The Observer*, February 15, 1959.

19. Ludwig, 387.

20. John Jackson to Herbert York, March 4, 1959, Argus Experiment Collection, University of Alabama in Huntsville.

21. Van Allen to Killian, February 21, 1959, Van Allen papers.

22. FLORAL was an alternate code name for Argus used in some military and governmental circles.

23. PSAC minutes, March 16, 1959, Argus Experiment Collection, University of Alabama in Huntsville.

24. Sullivan, *Assault*, 149.

25. Briber memo, March 19, 1959, Argus Experiment Collection, University of Alabama in Huntsville.

26. Mundey, 309.

27. Sullivan, *Assault*, 149.

Chapter 10

1. Hanson W. Baldwin, "U.S. Atom Blasts 300 Miles Up," *New York Times*, March 19, 1959.

2. Walter Sullivan, "Called 'Greatest Experiment'," *New York Times*, March 19, 1959.

3. Goodpaster memos, March 19, 1959, Argus Experiment Collection, University of Alabama in Huntsville.

4. Sullivan, *Assault*, 149.

5. *New York Times*, "Excerpts From the Defense Department's News Conference," "Quarles Says Atom Shots Aided Weapons Research in Attack and in Defense," March 20, 1959.

6. Mundey, 311.

7. "US Seen on Right Track," *Los Angeles Times*, March 20, 1959.

8. "Scientists Draft Report on Argus," *New York Times*, March 20, 1959.

9. Sullivan, *Assault*, 149.

10. *New York Times*, ibid.

11. Marvin Miles, "Space Blast Can Stop Missiles, Expert Says," *Los Angeles Times*, March 20, 1959.

12. "Christofilos Sues for Divorce," *New York Times*, April 1, 1959.

13. "Scientist's Wife Denies Divorce Plea," *Washington Post*, April 2, 1959.

14. *Time*, "Times and the Secret," March 30, 1959, 67.

15. Robert Davies, *Baldwin of the Times: A Military Journalist's Life, 1903–1991* (Annapolis, MD: Naval Institute Press, 2011), 241.

16. Ibid, 242–43.

17. Francis P. Jennings, "To the Editor," *New York Times*, March 27, 1959.

18. Katharine B. Faulkner, "To the Editor," *New York Times*, March 30, 1959.

19. "Argus and Man's Quest," *Washington Star*, March 22, 1959.

20. Herbert B. Loper to Clinton Anderson, March 20, 1959, Argus Experiment Collection, University of Alabama in Huntsville.

21. Joint Committee on Atomic Energy, Anderson press release, March 22, 1959, DOE OpenNet (https://www.osti.gov/opennet), NV0076931.

22. A. R. Luedecke to Margaret Chase Smith, April 1, 1959, DOE OpenNet (https://www.osti.gov/opennet), NV0104103.

Chapter 11

1. Murray Snyder to General Goodpaster, March 24, 1959, Argus Experiment Collection, University of Alabama in Huntsville.

2. "Text of White House Report on the Argus Experiments," *New York Times*, March 26, 1959.

3. John W. Finney, "U.S. Gives Data on Argus Tests," *New York Times*, March 26, 1959.

4. "Argus A-Tests Reveal Ray Gaps" *Montreal Gazette*, April 1, 1959; "Polar Hatches Into Space Proved By Argus Test," *Boston Globe*, April 1, 1959.

5. Marvin Miles, "Project Argus called Failure," *Los Angeles Times*, April 5, 1959.

6. W. Selove, "Nuclear Reports Queried: Issue Taken With Conclusions in Scientific Data," Letters to Editor, *New York Times*, March 29, 1959.

7. Mundey, 312.

8. "Pentagon Studying News On Argus Test," *New York Times*, April 27, 1959.

9. "Release of Argus scientific results," March 24, 1959, Argus Experiment Collection, University of Alabama in Huntsville.

10. "Argus Atom Tests Scored in Brazil," *New York Times*, April 4, 1959.

11. Porter and Odishaw to Killian, April 20, 1959, Argus Experiment Collection, University of Alabama in Huntsville.

12. Richard W. Porter, "Chairman's Introductory Remarks," *Proceedings of the National Academy of Sciences*, vol. 45, no. 8, 1959, 1141–1144.

13. N.C. Christofilos, "The Argus Experiment," *Proceedings of the National Academy of Sciences*, vol. 45, no. 8, 1959, 1144–52.

14. James A. Van Allen, Carl E. McIlwain, and George Ludwig, "Satellite

Observations of Electrons Artificially Injected Into the Geomagnetic Field," *Proceedings of the National Academy of Sciences,* vol. 45, 1959, 1152–71,

15. Lew Allen et. al, "Project Jason Measurement of Trapped Electrons From a Nuclear Device By Sounding Rockets," *Proceedings of the National Academy of Sciences,* vol. 45, 1959, 1171–90.

16. "New Horizons in Science" radio program, United States Information Agency, May 7, 1959, National Archives and Records Administration, College Park, MD.

17. Quoted in "Project Argus Probes Outer Space," *The Magnet,* Lawrence Livermore Laboratory, May 1959, 11.

18. Edward Gamarekian, "Expert Says One Bomb Can End Satellite Life Around World," *Washington Post,* April 30, 1959.

19. U.S. Congress, House of Representatives, Committee on Science and Astronautics, *"Nuclear Explosions in Space,"* 86th Cong., 1st sess., April 10, 1959.

20. Ibid.

21. Ibid.

22. Ibid.

Chapter 12

1. "High A-Blasts 300 Mi. Away Damage Eyes," *Chicago Tribune,* June 16, 1959; John W. Finney, "Radio Was Snarled By H-Bombs in '58," *New York Times,* June 16, 1959.

2. "2 High-Altitude H-Explosions by U.S. Revealed, With Long Radio Blackout," *Washington Post,* May 4, 1959.

3. Willard Edwards, "Big 2 Capitals Vulnerable to Far Off Blasts," *Chicago Tribune,* June 21, 1959; "High Atom Blast Could Jam Radio," *New York Times,* June 21, 1959.

4. "Project Argus," FAS newsletter, April 9, 1959.

5. Foerstner, 197.

6. Ludwig, 391.

7. Quoted in Foerstner, 197.

8. Ibid., 198.

9. Jack Raymond, "Fallout of Strontium-90 Is Found Highest in US," *New York Times,* March 22, 1959.

10. Clinton P. Anderson, "'Top Secret' - But Should It Be?," *New York Times,* May 3, 1959.

11. *New York Times,* 150.

12. Richard G. Hewlett and Jack M. Holl, *Atoms for Peace and War 1953–1961* (Berkeley, CA: University of California Press, 1989), 557.

13. Quoted in *Defense's Nuclear Agency*, 154.

14. Ibid., 154–55.

15. Ibid., 155.

16. William E. Ogle, Test Ban History notes (undated), DOE OpenNet (https://www.osti.gov/opennet), NV16023063.

17. Ibid.

18. John A. Osmundsen, "Atom Tests Made 2d Energy Shell," *New York Times*, November 3, 1959.

Chapter 13

1. Terrence R. Fehner & F.G. Gosling, U.S. Department of Energy, *Atmospheric Nuclear Weapons Testing 1951–1963* (Washington, D.C., September 2006), 195, 197.

2. "Nicholas Christofilos Marries Joan Jaffray," *New York Times*, June 29, 1960.

3. Sullivan, *Assault*, 163.

4. Sullivan to Van Allen, May 18, 1960, James A. Van Allen Papers.

5. Sullivan, *Assault*, 140–41; "News of Atom Test," *New York Times*, October 31, 1960.

6. Walter Sullivan, "Soviets Detected U.S. Blasts in '58," *New York Times*, November 28, 1960.

Chapter 14

1. Quoted in William E. Ogle, *An Account of the Return to Nuclear Weapons Testing By The United States After the Test Moratorium 1958–1961* (Nevada: U.S. Department of Energy, October 1985), 336–7.

2. Ibid.

3. Ibid.

4. Glenn T. Seaborg, *Kennedy, Khrushchev and the Test Ban* (Berkeley, CA: University of California Press, 1981), 132.

5. Ibid, 138.

6. Quoted in ibid., 139.

7. Ibid., 152.

8. Mustin, *Reminiscences*, 1360–61.

9. Ibid., 1372.

10. Ibid, 1372–3.

11. Robert C. Toth, "Will New A-Test in Space Backfire? Yes! Say British - Bunk! Says U.S.," *Boston Globe*, May 8, 1962.

12. Jeremy Murray-Brown to Van Allen, June 20, 1962, James A. Van Allen Papers.

13. Wayne Thomis, "High H-Blast Test Hailed By Van Allen," *Chicago Tribune*, June 20, 1962; "Van Allen Backs H-Blast in Belt," *New York Times*, May 3, 1962.

14. Walter Sullivan, "H-Test May Erase Radiation Belt," *New York Times*, April 30, 1962.

15. "No Real Damage to Space Belt Seen From A-Tests," *Los Angeles Times*, May 4, 1962.

16. "Explosive Venture in Space," *Wall Street Journal*, May 11, 1962.

17. "Experiment in Space," *Guardian*, June 20, 1962.

18. Quoted in Seaborg, 154.

19. AEC form letter, U.S. Department of Energy (undated).

Chapter 15

1. Mustin, *Reminiscences*, 1401–2.

2. Ogle, *An Account of the Return to Nuclear Weapons Testing*, 402–3.

3. U.S. Department of Air Force, Message from *Commander, Joint Task Force Eight*, June 4, 1962, DOE OpenNet (https://www.osti.gov/opennet)

4. Mustin, *Reminiscences*, 1448–9.

5. Ogle, *An Account of the Return to Nuclear Weapons Testing*, 420.

6. Seaborg, 155.

7. Ibid., 156.

8. Mustin, *Reminiscences*, 1450.

9. "Johnston Memories-Atomic Years," http://johnstonmemories.com/wordpress/?page_id=1097

10. Ibid.

11. Mustin, *Reminiscences*, 1458.

12. *New York Times*, July 10, 1962.

13. Francis Narin and Walter A. Dumas, *A 'Quick Look' at the Technical Results of Starfish Prime*, Los Alamos Scientific Laboratory, August, 1962, 20–21.

14. *New York Times*, July 10, 1962; A Quick Look, 19.

15. John A. Osmundsen, "Blast Makes Visible Fields of Magnetism In Sky Over Samoa," *New York Times*, July 10, 1962.

16. Walter Sullivan, "Experts Foresee No Peril in Test," *New York Times*, July 10, 1962.

17. John A. Osmundsen, "Samoans Terrified By H-Blast; Some Fear Heavens May Fall," *New York Times*, July 11, 1962.

18. "Britons Protest Outside Embassy," *New York Times*, July 10, 1962.

Chapter 16

1. *Preliminary Plan for Operation Fishbowl*, Headquarters Air Force Special Weapons Center, Air Force Systems Command, Kirtland Air Force Base, New Mexico, November 1961, 1.

2. *A Quick Look*, 10.

3. Ibid.

4. "Blast Over Pacific Opens Tests of a Tenuous Anti-Missile Plan," *New York Times*, July 10, 1962.

5. One experiment kept carefully quiet was the inclusion of a small amount of cadmium-109 radioactive tracer material in the Starfish Prime device to track upper atmospheric circulation patterns.

6. "How Not to Test in Space," November 7, 2011, The Henry L. Stimson Center, https://www.stimson.org/content/how-not-test-space

7. *A Quick Look*; Charles N. Vittitoe, "Did High Altitude EMP Cause the Hawaiian Streetlight Incident?" Sandia National Laboratories, June 1989; Wilmot N. Hess, "The Effects of High Altitude Explosions," NASA Goddard Space Flight Center, September 1964 (NASA TN D-2402); Herman Hoerlin, "United States High-Altitude Test Experiences: A Review Emphasizing the Impact on the Environment," Los Alamos National Laboratory, October 1976.

8. Mustin, *Reminiscences*, 1459.

9. Harold M. Schmeck, Jr., "Van Allen Doubts Effect of Blast," *New York Times*, July 18, 1962.

10. "Johnston Memories-Atomic Years" http://johnstonmemories.com/wordpress/?page_id=1097

11. Ogle, *An Account of the Return to Nuclear Weapons Testing*, 426.

12. Ibid., 428.

13. Seaborg, 156.

14. Ogle, 430.

15. Ibid..

16. *Defense's Nuclear Agency*, 163.

17. Defense Nuclear Agency, U.S. Department of Defense, United States Atmospheric Nuclear Weapons Tests, Nuclear Test Personnel Review, *Operation Hardtack I 1958* (Washington, D.C.: U.S. Government Printing Office, 1 December 1982), DNA 6040F,. 247.

18. Ogle, pp. 431.

19. *Defense's Nuclear Agency*, 163.

Chapter 17

1. Howard Simons, "It Looks as Though Starfish May Not Sparkle Too Long," *Washington Post*, November 25, 1962.

2. Van Allen talk to AAAS, December 31, 1962, James A. Van Allen Papers; Walter Sullivan, "Van Allen Sees Science 'Clique'," *New York Times*, December 31, 1962; Howard Simons, "President's Advisers Intimidating Individual Scientist, Van Allen Says," *Washington Post*, December 31, 1962

3. Robert C. Toth, "U.S. Radiation Belt Statement Made to Deter Soviet Testing," *New York Times*, January 10, 1963; John W. Finney, "U.S. Revises View on Electron Belt," February 5, 1963.

4. Howard Simons, "Van Allen Reverses Self on Belt," *Washington Post*, March 16, 1963; James Rodger Fleming, "Iowa Enters the Space Age," 320.

5. Quoted in Curtis Peebles, *High Frontier: The U.S. Air Force and the Military Space Program* (Washington, D.C.: U.S. Government Printing Office, Air Force History and Museums Program, 1997), 61.

6. Clayton K.S. Chun, *Shooting Down a "Star": Program 437, the US Nuclear ASAT System and Present-Day Copycat Killers* (Alabama: Air University Press, Maxwell Air Force Base), 4.

7. Its Army origins explain the discrepancy in numerical designation—505 was Army, while 437 was USAF.

8. National Security Action Memorandum 258 from McGeorge Bundy, August 6, 1963, John F. Kennedy Presidential Library, https://www.jfklibrary.org/Asset-Viewer/Archives/JFKNSF-342-002.aspx.

9. Peebles, 61–2.

10. Chun. 22.

11. Ibid., 21.

12. Ibid, 29–30.

Chapter 18

1. Statement of Rep. Roscoe Bartlett (R-Maryland), Congressional Record, June 9, 2005.

2. "Report of the Commission to Assess the Threat to the United States from Electromagnetic Pulse (EMP) Attack," Vol. 1, Executive Report, 2004, 2.

3. The University's name officially changed from "State University of Iowa" to "University of Iowa" in 1964.

4. Fleming, 322.

5. Ibid., 323.

6. Quoted in Mundey, 319–20.

7. Ibid.

8. Fleming, 323.

9. Weinberger, *Imagineers of War*, 95.

10. Ibid.

11. "Against Project Sanguine," *Chicago Tribune*, November 9, 1969.

12. Coleman, et al., "Greek Fire," 255.

13. John S. Foster, T. Kenneth Fowler, Frederick E. Mills, "Nicholas C. Christofilos," *Physics Today*, January 1973, 109–15.

Postscript

1. Quoted in Michael D'Antonio, *A Ball, a Dog, and a Monkey* (New York: Simon & Schuster, 2007), 207.

2. "Space Assurance or Space Dominance? The Case Against Weaponizing Space," Michael Krepon with Christopher Clary, The Henry L. Stimson Center, 2003, 29, 32.

Selected Bibliography

The following is a partial list of the major book-length volumes and other resources that were helpful in the writing and research of this book. All other sources are listed in the Notes.

Books

Crease, Robert P. *Making Physics: A Biography of Brookhaven National Laboratory, 1946–1972*. Chicago: University of Chicago Press, 1999.

Davies, Robert B. *Baldwin of the Times: Hanson W. Baldwin, A Military Journalist's Life 1903–1991*. Annapolis, MD: Naval Institute Press, 2011.

Defense Threat Reduction Agency. *Defense's Nuclear Agency, 1947–1997*. Washington, DC: US Government Printing Office, 2002.

Dickson, Paul. *Sputnik: The Shock of the Century*. New York: Walker, 2001.

Finkbeiner, Ann K. *The Jasons: The Secret History of Science's Postwar Elite*. New York: The Penguin Group, 2006.

Foerstner, Abigail. *James Van Allen: The First Eight Billion Miles*. Iowa City: University of Iowa Press, 2007.

Gillmor, C. Stewart, and John R. Spreiter, eds. *Discovery of the Magnetosphere (History of Geophysics 7)*. Washington, DC: American Geophysical Union, 1997.

Halberstam, David. *The Fifties*. New York: Ballantine Books, 1994.

Killian, James R. Jr. *Sputnik, Scientists, & Eisenhower: A Memoir of the First Special Assistant to the President for Science and Technology*. Cambridge, MA: The MIT Press, 1977.

Kistiakowsky, George B. *A Scientist at the White House: The Private Diary of President Eisenhower's Special Assistant for Science and Technology*. Cambridge, MA: Harvard University Press, 1976.

Ledbetter, James. *Unwarranted Influence: Dwight D. Eisenhower and the Military Industrial Complex*. New Haven, CT: Yale University Press, 2011.

Ludwig, George H. *Opening Space Research: Dreams, Technology, and Scientific Discovery*. Washington, DC: American Geophysical Union, 2011.

Manno, Jack. *Arming the Heavens: The Hidden Military Agenda for Space, 1945-1995*. New York: Dodd, Mead & Company, 1984.

Mark, Hans. *The Space Station: A Personal Journey*. Durham, NC: Duke University Press, 1987.

Miller, Richard L. *Under the Cloud: The Decades of Nuclear Testing*. New York: The Free Press, 1986.

Seaborg, Glenn T. *Kennedy, Khrushchev & the Test Ban*. Berkeley, CA: University of California Press, 1981.

Shelton, Frank H. *Reflections of a Physicist: Project Argus*. Colorado Springs, CO: Shelton Enterprises, 2000.

Sullivan, Walter. *Assault on the Unknown: The International Geophysical Year*. New York: McGraw-Hill, 1961.

Thomas, Evan. *Ike's Bluff: President Eisenhower's Secret Battle to Save the World*. New York: Little, Brown and Company, 2012.

Weinberger, Sharon. *The Imagineers of War: The Untold Story of DARPA, the Pentagon Agency That Changed the World*. New York: Alfred A. Knopf, 2017.

York, Herbert F. *Making Weapons, Talking Peace: A Physicist's Odyssey from Hiroshima to Geneva*. New York: Basic Books, 1987.

Films

The atmospheric nuclear testing years of the United States were well-documented by official agencies, mostly the US Air Force's Air Photographic and Charting Service at Lookout Mountain Air Force Station in California. Lookout Mountain's dedicated and fearless corps of filmmakers developed new photographic technologies to document the unique phenomena of nuclear explosions. Most (but not all) of their work has been declassified and is readily available online at YouTube and other sources, and provides an invaluable historical record.

Armed Forces Special Weapons Project. *Report of Chief, AFSWP to ARPA, Operation Argus*. Film. United States Air Force, Lookout Mountain Air Force Station, Air Photographic and Charting Service, 1959; declassified by US Department of Energy Albuquerque Operations Office, June 1997.

Commander, Joint Task Force Eight. *Operation DOMINIC Nuclear Tests 1962.* Film. United States Air Force, Lookout Mountain Air Force Station, Air Photographic and Charting Service. Undated; declassified by US Department of Energy Albuquerque Operations Office, March 1998.

Commander, Joint Task Force Eight. *Starfish Prime Event: Interim Report.* Film. United States Air Force, Lookout Mountain Air Force Station, Air Photographic and Charting Service. Undated; declassified by US Department of Energy Albuquerque Operations Office, March 1998.

Defense Atomic Support Agency. *Operation HARDTACK: Military Effects Studies. Part Two: High Altitude Tests.* Film. United States Air Force, Lookout Mountain Air Force Station, Air Photographic and Charting Service, 1959; declassified by US Department of Energy Albuquerque Operations Office, June 1997.

Defense Atomic Support Agency. *Operation Fishbowl 1962. High Altitude Weapons Effects.* Film. United States Air Force, Lookout Mountain Air Force Station, Air Photographic and Charting Service. Undated; declassified by US Department of Energy Albuquerque Operations Office, March 1998.

Those wishing to see for themselves the ominous grandeur of nuclear detonations in the atmosphere and outer space are directed to the work of filmmaker Peter Kuran, who has meticulously restored and edited much of Lookout Mountain's original work in new documentary films.

Kuran, Peter. *Nukes in Space: The Rainbow Bombs.* DVD. Directed by Peter Kuran. Thousand Oaks, CA: Goldhil Home Media International, 2000.

Abbreviations and Acronyms

AAAS	American Association for the Advancement of Science
ABM	Anti-ballistic missile
ABMA	Army Ballistic Missile Agency
AEC	Atomic Energy Commission
AFSWP	Armed Forces Special Weapons Project
ARPA	Advanced Research Projects Agency
ASAT	Anti-Satellite (i.e., weapons)
CNO	Chief of Naval Operations
DASA	Defense Atomic Support Agency
DNA	Defense Nuclear Agency
DOD	Department of Defense
ELF	Extremely low-frequency
EMP	Electromagnetic pulse
ICBM	Intercontinental Ballistic Missile
IGY	International Geophysical Year
JCAE	Joint Committee on Atomic Energy
JPL	Jet Propulsion Laboratory
JTF	Joint Task Force
JTF-8	Joint Task Force 8
LLNL	Lawrence Livermore National Laboratory
NAS	National Academy of Sciences
NACA	National Advisory Committee for Aeronautics
NASA	National Aeronautics and Space Administration
NOTS	Naval Ordnance Test Station
PSAC	President's Science Advisory Committee
SUI	State University of Iowa
TF 88	Task Force 88
TI	Texas Instruments
UCRL	University of California Radiation Laboratory

Timeline of Outer Space/ High Altitude Nuclear Tests

The generally accepted boundary between Earth's atmosphere and "outer space" is most often demarcated by the "Kármán line" (after the Hungarian-American physicist and aeronautical engineer Theodore von Kármán), at an altitude of 100 kilometers (62 miles) above sea level. Other tests are considered merely "high altitude" or "near space."

This list does not include failed shot attempts, but only those with confirmed nuclear detonations.

Of special note is the frantic pace of tests by both the US and USSR in October and early November 1962, coinciding with the approximate period of the Cuban Missile Crisis, which although not directly related, undoubtedly helped to ratchet up the level of international tension.

Nation	Date/Time UT (Universal Time)	Test	Location	Altitude	Nuclear Yield
US	28 April 1958/ 02:40	HARDTACK Yucca	Johnston Island, Pacific	26.2 km/ 16.2 mi	1.7 kilotons
US	1 August 1958/ 10:50:05	HARDTACK Teak	Johnston Island, Pacific	76.8 km/ 47.7 mi	3.8 megatons
US	12 August 1958/ 10:30:08	HARDTACK Orange	Johnston Island, Pacific	43 km/ 26.7 mi	3.8 megatons
US	27 August 1958/ 02:28	Argus 1	South Atlantic	200 km/ 124.2 mi	1.7 kilotons
US	30 August 1958/ 03:18	Argus 2	South Atlantic	240 km/ 149.1 mi	1.7 kilotons
US	6 September 1958/ 22:13	Argus 3	South Atlantic	540 km/ 335.5 mi	1.7 kilotons

USSR	6 September 1961/ 06:00	#88 Groza ("Joe 79")	Kapustin Yar, USSR	22.7 km/ 14.1 mi	10.5 kilotons
USSR	6 October 1961/ 07:15	#115 Grom ("Joe 98")	Kapustin Yar, USSR	41.3 km/ 25.6 mi	40 kilotons
USSR	27 October 1961/ unknown	K Project #127	Kapustin Yar, USSR	150 km/ 93.2 mi	1.2 kilotons
USSR	27 October 1961/ unknown	K Project #128	Kapustin Yar, USSR	300 km/ 186.4 mi	1.2 kilotons
US	9 July 1962/ 09:00	DOMINIC/ FISHBOWL Starfish Prime	Johnston Island, Pacific	400 km/ 248.5 mi	1.4 megatons
US	20 October 1962/ 07:30	DOMINIC/ FISHBOWL Checkmate	Johnston Island, Pacific	147 km/ 91.3 mi	uncertain; approx. 7 kilotons
USSR	22 October 1962/ 03:40:45	K Project #184	Kapustin Yar, USSR	290 km/ 180.1 mi	300 kilotons
US	26 October 1962/ 08:59	DOMINIC/ FISHBOWL Bluegill Triple Prime	Johnston Island, Pacific	48.2 km/ 29.9 mi	400 kilotons
USSR	28 October 1962/ 04:41:20	K Project #187	Kapustin Yar, USSR	150 km/ 93.2 mi	300 kilotons
USSR	1 November 1962/ 09:12	K Project #195	Kapustin Yar, USSR	59 km/ 36.6 mi	300 kilotons
US	1 November 1962/ 11:10	DOMINIC/ FISHBOWL Kingfish	Johnston Island, Pacific	96.3 km/ 59.8 mi	400 kilotons
US	4 November 1962/ 06:30	DOMINIC/ FISHBOWL Tightrope	Johnston Island, Pacific	21 km/ 13 mi	uncertain; approx. 7 kilotons

Author's Note and Acknowledgments

Even if Operation Argus had actually been "the greatest scientific experiment of all time" as it was breathlessly proclaimed, such hyperbole hardly holds up sixty years later, in a world with smart phones, molecular biology, and the Large Hadron Collider. But in its time, it was certainly one of the most secretive. As they all played their various parts to bring Argus to its successful conclusion, practically none of its direct participants were aware of the full picture. One telling example is the crew scrapbook of the *Norton Sound*'s 1958 summer cruise, titled *The Horned Shellback*. It features plenty of photos of the ship, its officers and crew, the initiation of pollywogs in the "crossing the line" ceremonies, icebergs and aircraft, even liberty in Rio—but nothing at all from the mysterious doings of the *Sound* during its weeks in the South Atlantic Ocean. It's as if a whole chunk of pages has been torn out covering the time from the ship "rounding the Horn" until her arrival in Rio de Janeiro.

While the crew scrapbook wasn't an official document and hence not formally redacted by upper echelons, it's probable that the crew was under orders to avoid taking any snapshots of the highly secret Argus activities. Even official visual documentation of Task Force 88's operations in late August and early September 1958 is almost nonexistent, save for some grainy and unedited 16mm footage that survives in the National Archives and the scenes included in the official (and formerly classified) film reports. The *Norton Sound* logbooks for that period simply list her cruise as beginning from Port Hueneme and ending at a "special project firing area, south

257

Atlantic Ocean"—accompanied by a note from Captain Gralla that the commander of Task Force 88 "has directed all ship's deck logs classified as Confidential for operations conducted south of latitude 20 S."

Such missing pieces are quite familiar to researchers of previously classified history. It's necessary to become something of a detective, hunting down evidence, piecing together clues, seeking connections, and engaging in educated, if reluctant, speculation where necessary—which leads to the frustrating realization that it's virtually impossible to tell the entire story. Inevitably, those missing pieces, whether still classified or simply lost or destroyed over the years, leave some parts of the tale forever clouded, never to be fully known. As previously noted, this problem is particularly marked in the case of Argus, since the breakneck pace of the operation coupled with its intense secrecy meant that many important aspects weren't formally recorded and chronicled in the usual manner of such undertakings.

I say all this not to excuse any inadequacies on my part in telling this story, but to point out that many similar tales remain lurking in the shadows of the Cold War, waiting to be discovered. I've done my best in this book to chronicle the histories of Argus and Fishbowl, but with the full awareness that there are likely more details and more secrets yet to be revealed, not only about these projects but many others. I hope that this volume may serve as a starting point for future efforts, and look forward to learning the secrets that I wasn't able to uncover.

One fact that's not at all secret is that no author can possibly create a book such as this one without the help and support of a great many people. I must first thank my agent, Michelle Tessler, who was the first to believe in this project and relentless in her efforts to place it. I'm also deeply grateful to my colleague Sharon Weinberger, who not only offered helpful guidance on research sources but also referred me to Michelle. At The Overlook Press, Tracy Carns and Chelsea Cutchens provided stalwart editorial guidance.

As every nonfiction author knows, libraries and librarians are among our greatest national resources. My thanks to the special collections staff of the University of Iowa Libraries, the University of Alabama Library, the library of Lawrence Livermore National Laboratory, and the MIT Libraries. The archivists of the National Archives and Records Administration in College Park, Maryland, and Washington, DC, and the National Security Archive at George Washington University guided me to valuable material.

I wrote most of this book while at Massachusetts Institute of Technology on a Knight Science Journalism Fellowship from 2016–17. Aside from granting invaluable time for writing and research, the fellowship gifted me with the precious camaraderie, friendship, and guidance of Iván Carrillo, Sally Deneen, Chloé Hecketsweiler, Robert McClure, Maura O'Connor, Rosalia Omungo, Meera Subramanian, Bianca Vazquez Toness, Fabio Turone, and Lauren Whaley, along with fellowship director Deborah Blum and the rest of the Knight crew: David Corcoran, Tom Zeller, Bettina Urcuioli, and Jane Roberts. What an extraordinary group of people you all are, and how fortunate I am to have met and worked with you.

Several distinguished scholars provided valuable advice and perspectives, including Peter Galison of Harvard University; Michael D. Gordin of Princeton University; George Woodwell of Woods Hole Research Center; and David Kaiser, R. Scott Kemp, and Ted Postol of MIT.

While writers are by and large solitary creatures, most of us function best with the support and encouragement of friends and family, and I am no exception. So many thanks and undying appreciation to Cat Calhoun, Amy Chamberlain Fisher, Linda Chamberlain, Kristina Finan, Jeff Harris, Diana Kenney, Tarra Navarro, Tom Purdom, Zan Rosin, Denise Shubin, Sue Smith, and Judy Weightman.

Finally, special recognition must go to the Argus veterans who agreed to share their unique experiences with me: Malcolm Allen, Richard S. Culp, Henry R. Kizziah, Frederic P. Lamb, Keith P. Mayfield, Ken McMaster, Quintin Owens, William F. Reagan, and Bobby W. Terrell. Gentlemen, thank you all, and I hope I've done justice to your service and contributions in these pages.

Index

A

AAAS, 112, 116, 206
ABM (anti-ballistic missile), 209–10
ABMA (Army Ballistic Missile
    Agency), 11; Explorer 1, 76;
Sputnik, 12;
Adobe, 175
Advanced Research Projects Agency.
    See ARPA
AEC (Atomic Energy Commission):
    Anderson, 130; Argus, 43;
    atomic testing, 39–40; Castle
    Bravo, 52; Christofilos licensing
    fee, 36; *The Effects of Atomic
    Weapons*, 225–26; fallout, 151,
    154, 160, 199, 205, 207; Joint
    Committee on Atomic Energy,
    151; *Lucky Dragon*, 52; morato-
    rium, 164; press, 123, 133, 151;
    Project Fishbowl, 186, 198, 205,
    207; Project Rover, 157; public
    opinion, 152, 179; secrecy, 112,
    119, 133; Smith, 130; Teak and
    Orange, report of, 148
Aerojet General, 135
AICBM, 54
Air Force Special Weapons Center, 77
Allen, Irwin, 166, 167
Allen, Lew, Argus symposium, 140
alternating field gradient focusing
    principle, 33

American Association for the
    Advancement of Science
    (AAAS), 112, 116, 206
American Physical Society, 21, 44,
    111–12, 134
Anderson, Clinton P., 130, 133, 151
Argus, 22–24; Astron, 22; Brazil, 137;
    Committee on Science and
    Astronautics, 142; criticism of,
    135; documentation, 99; Eisen-
    hower, 42, 44, 105; EMP, 174;
    Explorer 4, 46, 89, 91; fallout
    concern, 150–51, 154; FLORAL,
    51; global phenomenon, 49–50;
    Gough Island, 54; government
    information release, 114–15;
    HARDTACK, 53–54; IGY, 107–8,
    133, 138; international knowl-
    edge of, 93; Iowa, 46; Irani, 135;
    Jason rockets, 140; JPL meeting,
    46; Jupiter C, 61; "magnetic
    conjugate point," 55; Midas,
    78; military considerations,
    141; NAS symposium, 137–40;
    NOTSNIK, 77; official approval,
    44; PSAC, initial presentation,
    42; public reaction, 129, 226–27;
    radiation, 104, 155; radio circuits,
    148; radiological safety, 80; re-
    sults of, 105–6; S2F, 83; scientific
    corps, 75, 133; secrecy, 49, 50, 91,
    93; Shell, 103, 155; Sputnik 3,

50; Tarawa, 74; Troitskaya, 162; Van Allen, 45, 46; *Voyage to the Bottom of the Sea*, 166; W-25, 59; Wertheim, 67; whistleblower, 109; White House report, 134; Willow-Argus, 104, 153; X-17a, 58

Argus 1, 87–89

Argus 2, 90

Argus 3, 95–98

Argus effect (Christofilos effect): Baldwin, 121; Brazilian Anomaly, 55; confirmation of, 103–4; defense application, 142; Eisenhower, 42; Explorer 4, 89; Fishbowl, 194; JPL meeting, 45; "magnetic conjugate point," 55; NAS symposium, 139; Navy's final Argus report, 108; PSAC, 42; Sullivan, 122; Willow, 154

Ariel 1, 191, 195, 196, 199

Armed Forces Special Weapons Project (AFSWP), 24, 43, 56; Christofilos, 98; Congressional hearings, 154; DASA, 154; fallout, 154; Johnston Island, 63–64; Mustin, 96; Panama Canal, 69; Parker, 96; Shelton, 67, 98, 127; Willow, 154–55

Army Ballistic Missile Agency (ABMA), 11–12, 46, 76

ARPA (Advanced Research Projects Agency), 23; Explorer 4, 61; Explorer 5, 61; Order #4: Argus, 24, 42–44, 54, press, 91, 108–10, 119, 123

"Artificial Modification of the Earth's Radiation Belt" (Singer), 112

ASAT, 209–13

Assault On the Unknown (Sullivan), 110

Astounding Science Fiction, 16

Astron, 22, 36, 139, 223–24

Atomic Energy Commission. *See* AEC

atomic testing, 39–40

B

Baldwin, Hanson, 109–15, 118–20, 121–22, 128–29

Ballistic Missile Early Warning System, (BMEWS), 193

Bartlett, Roscoe, 215–18

Bay of Pigs, 164

BBC, Operation Fishbowl protests, 177

Bennett, Charles, 167

Betatron, 29

Bikini Atoll, 52

Bluegill, 174, 183–84, 199. *See also* Bluegill Prime, Bluegill Double Prime, *and* Bluegill Triple Prime

Bluegill Double Prime, 200–1

Bluegill Prime, 197

Bluegill Triple Prime, 201–2

BMEWS (Ballistic Missile Early Warning System), 193

Brazil, Argus, 101, 137

Brazilian Anomaly, 54–55

Briber, R.M., 119

Brookhaven National Laboratory, 33–37

Bundy, McGeorge, 186

Burke Arleigh A., 102, 128–29

C

Campaign for Nuclear Disarmament, 191

Campbell, John, Jr., 16

Castle Bravo, 52, 62, 152

Catledge, Turner, 119

Checkmate, 199, 201

Chicago Tribune, 148, 223

Chief of Naval Operations (CNO), 55, 102, 128

Christmas Island, 171, 172, 175, 182, 189, 196

Christofilos, Nicholas Constantine, 21–24; AAAS meeting, 117;

American Physical Society, 111–12; Argus records, 98; Argus tests, 98; Argus, 22–23; Astron, 22, 158, 221, 223; background electrons, 41; Brookhaven, work at, 37; cab drivers, 26; childhood of, 26; "that crazy Greek," 32–33; Christofilos effect, 45, 49, 89, 99, 103–4; death of, 224; divorce, 127–28; Elly, 37; ethics, 221; Explorer measurements, 67; German occupation, 27–28; Jaffrey, 158; Kennedy committee, 178; NAS symposium, 138–39; *New York Times*, 122, 127; "On the Possibility of Establishing a Plasma Shield of Relativistic Electrons in the Exosphere of the Earth as a Defense against Ballistic Missiles," 23; Panofsky, 45; particle accelerators, 28, 29–30; piano, 43; press, 127; *Proceedings of the National Academy of Sciences*, 147; Project Sanguine, 222–23; Proposition 1, 117; PSAC, 42; Radiation Laboratory, 30–33; security clearance, 37–38; Seesaw, 221–22; Sputnik, 21; strong focusing, 31–36; submarines, 158; temperament, 26; Voice of America, 140–41; white horse, 223; Wisk Inc., 27

Christofilos effect. *See* Argus effect
Clark, George W., 150
Clary, Christopher, militarization of space, 228
CNO (Chief of Naval Operations), 55, 102, 128
Cohen, Samuel A., 32
Coleman, Elisheva R., 32, 36
Commission to Assess the Threat to the United States from Electromagnetic Pulse (EMP) Attack, 217, 218

Committee on Science and Astronautics, Argus hearing, 142–45
CORONA project, 208
Cosmic Ray Conference of the International Union of Pure and Applied Physics, 147
"Cosmotron, The," 33
Courant, Ernest D., 33, 34
"crazy Greek, that," 32
Crease, Robert P., 35
"Crossing the Line," 74
Culp, Dick, 66–69; Argus 3, 96; cancer, 81; launch, 87; missile loading, 83; Sputnik 1, 101
Cyclotron, 28–32

D

D layer, 194
Daddario, Emilio, 144
DASA (Defense Atomic Support Agency), 154–55
Davies, Robert D., Baldwin, 128–29
Day, P. A., 159–60
Day the Earth Stood Still, The, 25
Deacon sounding rockets, 82
Defense Atomic Support Agency, 154–55
Defense Nuclear Agency (DNA): Argus report, 99; Eisenhower, 152; nuclear explosions, high-altitude, 40; Operation Fishbowl, 201; and Orange, 64; Teak, 63; testing and politics, 154; Willow, 155
Defense Threat Reduction Agency, 217
Department of Defense:; Argus, 43; Argus secrecy, 50, 119, 126, 136; Christofilos, 40; *The Effects of Atomic Weapons*, 225–26; eye damage, 62–63; high-altitude nuclear explosions, 40; moratorium, 153; *New York Times*, 126, 127, 136; Porter, 138; Quarles, 124

Destroyer Flotilla Two, 55
Deterrence and Survival in the Nuclear Age, 18
Dickson, Paul, 17
DNA. *See* Defense Nuclear Agency
DOMINIC, 172–76; Adobe, 175; conclusion of, 202–3; Cuban Missile Crisis, 201; P2Vs, 182; Polaris, 175; protests, 191; safety, 186; Soviet monitoring, 181; . *See also* Operation Fishbowl
Douglas Skyray F4D-1 jet, 76
Doyle, Arthur Conan, 166
Dryfoos, Orvil E., 119
Dulles, John Foster, Argus, secrecy of, 50

E

Effects of Atomic Weapons, The, 225–26
Effects of Nuclear Weapons, The, 226
Einstein, Albert, 25–26, 91
Eisenhower, Dwight D.: Argus, 42–44, 91; Argus security breach, 121, 123, 136; arms race, 18, 53; farewell address, 162–63; Gaither report, 18–19; Killian, 17; moratorium, 95, 155; "New Look," 52; *New York Times* and Argus, 121, 123; peacemaker, 152, 161; space race, American fears during, 16–17; Vanguard, 12
electromagnetic pulse. *See* EMP
ELF (extremely low-frequency radio waves), 222–23
EMP (electromagnetic pulse), 41, 174; Bartlett, 215–18; *Effects of Atomic Weapons, The*, 225–26; *Effects of Nuclear Weapons, The*, 226; Hawaii, 196; Kingfish, 202; Program 437, 212; Soviet Union, 201, 216; Strategic Defense Initiative, 212
Eniwetok Proving Ground (EPG), 63
Ethan Allen, 175

Explorer 1 satellite, 17, 19, 20; instrument package, 20; Jupiter C missile, 17, 19, 62; lift off, 20; redstone, 62; Sputnik, 76; Van Allen belt, 44
Explorer 2, 20–21
Explorer 3, 20–21, 44
Explorer 4, 43, 46, 65, 90–91; and Teak and Orange, 70, 75; Argus 2, 90–91; Argus 3, 98; Argus effect, 89; Argus symposium, 140; end, 103; IGY and, 47, 107–8; PR, 111; press and Argus, 112, 116, 121, 122, 125, 149; radiation detectors, 104; second belt, 155; secrecy, 47, 51
Explorer 5, 70, 76, 121
eye damage, 62–63, 148, 176, 202

F

F4D-1 jet, 76
fallout controversy, 150–51
Fleming, James Rodger, 47, 63, 220–21
FLORAL, 51, 118. *See* Argus
Fluegge, Siegfried, 28
Foerstner, Abigail, 44, 46, 47, 149
Ford Foundation, 18
France, 155, 165, 214
"fratricide," 172
Frisch, Otto, 27
Frost, Robert, 19
Fulton, James, 143

G

Gaither Report, 17–19
Gaither, Rowan, 18
Geneva talks. See moratorium
Ghana, 191
Godel, William H., 110
Goodpaster, Andrew J., 123, 133
Gough island, 9, 54, 55, 75
Gralla, Arthur R.: Argus orders, 56; drills, 69, 75; launch command,

86, 96; missile training, 64–65;
Sandia Corporation, 67; Shelton,
67; W-24 warheads, 67
Green, Kenneth, 35
GREENHOUSE, 40
Grumman S2F Tracker fixed-wing air-
craft, 82–83
Guardian, 178

H

Hagerty, James, 133
HARDTACK, 41; Argus, 41, 51, 53,
54; eye damage, 62–63; first
phase, 71; HARDTACK I, 53;
HARDTACK II, 53; press, 112;
redstone missiles, 61–62; second
phase, 95, 104; test site concerns,
63; wrapping up of, 104.
See also Teak *and* Orange
"Hardtack Argus," 51
Harr, Karl G., 114–15
Harris, G. Francis, 9–10, 159–60
Hawaii: EMP, 196; Hawaii, Teak, 63,
148; Orange, 148; Starfish Prime,
189, 191
Heisenberg, Werner, 27
"horned shellbacks," 74
Hoyle, Fred, 177

I

ICBM: anti-ICBM, 54; high-altitude
bursts, 193; Seesaw, 221–22; spy
satellites, 208; "throw-weight," 15
IGY, 11, 51, 108, 147; Argus secrecy,
107–8; Argus, 51, 65, 93, 108–9,
115, 133–34; Eisenhower, 12; Explorer 4, 47, 108; National Academy of Sciences symposium,
137–38; Quarles, 124; Soviet effort, 162; Sputnik 3, 50; Sullivan,
110, 113; Van Allen, 13, 44, 46
Inaccessible Island, 9, 54

Injun 1, 191, 195, 205, 207
International Astronomical Union, 177
International Astronomical Year.
See IGY
Introduction to Nuclear Physics, An
(Fluegge), 28
ionosphere, 63, 194, 222
Irani, Joseph H., 135
Iwo Jima, 187
Izvestiya, 93

J

Jack, Max C., 78
Jacques, Philippe, 179
Jaffe, Sam, 25
Jaffrey, Joan, 158
Jastrow, Robert, 44
jet fighter, missile launch from, 76
Jet Propulsion Laboratory (JPL), 20,
45–46, 126
Jodrell Bank Observatory, 176–77
Johnson, Lyndon B., 17, 21, 211
Johnson, Roy, 109, 119, 123
Johnston Island: ASAT, 209–12;
Bluegill Prime, 197–98; Bluegill
Triple Prime, 202; Bundy, 186;
Operation Fishbowl, 175–76, ;
Soviet ship, 181; Starfish Prime,
188, 190, 196; Starfish, 185, 187;
Teak and Orange, 62–64
Joint Committee on Atomic Energy
(JCAE), 130, 151
Joint Task Force 7, 64, 153
Joint Task Force 8 (JTF-8), (Operation
Fishbowl), (DOMINIC), 173
Jupiter C missile, 17, 19, 61, 70.
See also Redstone

K

Kellogg, Paul, 9293, 116
Kennedy, John F.: address to nation
on testing, 171; ASAT, 211;

committee on radiation belts, 178; Cuban Missile Crisis, 200–2; DOMINIC/Fishbowl, 173, 178, 186, 198; Khrushchev, 165; Macmillan, 171; moratorium, 164, 165, 171; Nobel Prize reception, 176; "peacenik," 163; "peace speech," 213–14; Program 505, 210; Soviet testing, resumed, 165; Treaty Banning Nuclear Tests in the Atmosphere, in Outer Space and Under Water, 214; underground tests, 166; Van Allen belt, 179, 205

Khrushchev, Nikita: and Soviet arms production, 18; Cuban Missile Crisis, 200–2; Eisenhower, 157, 161; Kennedy, 163, 165, 200–2, 214; test moratorium, 53, 160–61, 163, 214; threats, 216; Treaty Banning Nuclear Tests in the Atmosphere, in Outer Space and Under Water, 214; Tsar Bomba, 169–70; U-2 spy plane, 160; US visit, 157

Killian, James R., 17; Argus secrecy, 109, 112, 118, 123, 138; Argus, results of, 105–6; Christofilos, 42; Eisenhower, 44, 123; Sullivan, 115–16

King, David, 144
Kingfish, 199, 202
Kistiakowsky, George, 109
Kosmos, 208
Kosovo, 215–16
Krasovskiy, V.I., 93
Krepon, Michael, 195, 228
Kwajalein Island, 189–90, 210

L

Laika, 15
Lawrence, Ernest, 28, 31
Lawrence Livermore National

Laboratory (Livermore Radiation Laboratory): Argus, 43; Christofilos, 21–22, 30, 158, 221; conference, Argus secrecy, 117; NAS symposium, 139, 141; Plowshare, 158, public opinion, 152

LeMay, Curtis, 18, 202
Libby, Willard, fallout, 151
Limited Test Ban Treaty (Partial Test Ban Treaty, Treaty Banning Nuclear Tests in the Atmosphere, in Outer Space and Under Water), 214, 218, 227
Livingston, M. Stanley, 33
Lockheed Missiles Systems Division, 64–65
Loki sounding rockets, 74
Loki/Dart missiles, 70
Loper, Herbert, 130, 151
Los Angeles Times: Irani, 135; Operation Fishbowl, 178; press conference, 126; Van Allen, 126
Lost World, The (Doyle), 166
Lovell, Bernard, 176–77
Lucky Dragon, 52
Ludwig, George, 219; Argus, 46, 65; Argus secrecy, 94, 117; Argus symposium, 139; Explorer 4, 47, 103; IGY, 65; JPL meeting, 45; Ney and Kellogg, 92; Soviets, 93, 94, 150; Van Allen, 150
Luedecke, A. R., 64, 130, 151
Lukin, Vladimir, 215–16

M

Macmillan, Harold, 171
"magnetic conjugate point," 55
Mahoney, Michael S., 32
Martin P6M SeaMaster, 57
Mattauch, Joseph, 28
Mayfield, Keith, 67, 68, 97, 100
McElroy, Neil, 13, 23

McIlwain, Carl: Argus secrecy, 46, 66; data screening, 76, 103; leak, 109; NAS symposium, 139; Van Allen, 219

McMaster, Ken, 69, 87, 102

McMillan, Edwin, 29

McNamara, Robert, 209–11

Medaris, John, 11, 12–13, 17, 20, 45

Montreal Gazette, 134

moratorium: Argus, 108; Eisenhower, 53, 95, 152, 155, 157, 161, 163; Kennedy, 163–65, 171, 198, 214; Khrushchev, 53, 157, 160, 161, 163, 214; Nevada Test Site, 158; Outer Space Treaty, 218, 227; Partial Nuclear Test Ban Treaty, 218, 227; pentagon, 152–53, 164; policing, 162; PSAC, 53; U-2 spy plane, 160; USSR, 165

Moscow Radio, and Sputnik, 12

Mundey, Lisa: Argus, secrecy of, 50; Quarles, 126; Sputnik 3, 50; *Times*, 119; Van Allen, 220–21; White House report, 136

Murrow, Edward R., 210

Mussolini, Benito, 27

Mustin, Lloyd M., 55–56; Argus 1, 87, 89; Argus 2, 90; Argus 3, 91 98; Argus secrecy, 68–69; Bluegill, 183–84; Bluegill Prime, 197; DOMINIC, Soviet monitoring, 181; EMP, 196; film badge, 81; Johnston Island evacuation, 187; JTF-8, acting commander, 200; Loki, 74; missile shot concerns, 58, 60; *Norton Sound*, 56, 75, 175; Operation Fishbowl, 173–74; P2Vs, 182; P6M, 57; Rio, 100–2; S2F, 82; schedule, 65; South Atlantic Ocean, 73; Starfish Prime, 189, 196; Thor missile, 199; USS *Tarawa*, 70, 73; weather, 75, 78–80; X-17a rockets, 59, 90

N

NAS (National Academy of Sciences): Argus symposium, 137–38, 147; *Proceedings of the National Academy of Sciences*, 147; Van Allen belt, 21, 43–44

NASA (National Aeronautics and Space Administration), 61, 76, 157, 207, 216

National Academy of Sciences. *See* NAS

National Security Council, *Deterrence and Survival in the Nuclear Age*, 18

Nature, 92, 116

Naval Ordnance Test Station (NOTS), 76

Naval Research Laboratory, 11, 44

Nelson, Harriman, 166–67

Neosho, 70, 79

"New Horizons in Science," 140

"New Look," 52

New York Times: Anderson, 151; Argus and radio, 148; Argus story, 110, 120, 121, 127; Christofilos, 122; Dryfoos, 119; Eisenhower, 123; fallout controversy, 151; Harr, 114; Hawaiians, 191; Pentagon, 113; press conference, 127; Quarles, 125, 127; radiation, 134; Samoa, 190; Starfish Prime, 189, 190, 194; Sulzberger, 119; Tristan da Cunha, 10; Troitskaya, 162; Van Allen and PSAC, 207; White House, 113. *See also* Baldwin, Hanson *and* Sullivan, Walter

Newman, Philip, Argus symposium, 140

Newsweek, Argus, 112

Ney, Edward, 92–93, 116

Nike, 188

Nike-Hercules, 202

Nike-Zeus, 193, 209–10

Nikolayev, 199

Nobel Prize reception, 176

Norway, 170
NOTSNIK, 76–77, 212
Novaya Zemlya, 169
Nuclear Physics Tables (Mattauch), 28

O

O'Neal, Patricia, 25
Observer, The, 116
Odishaw, Hugh, 137–38
Ogle, William: Bluegill, 184; Bluegill
    Double Prime, 200; Checkmate,
    201; Kennedy and Fishbowl, 198;
    moratorium, 153; Starbird and
    Russian captain, 182
On the Beach, 167
"On the Possibility of Establishing a
    Plasma Shield of Relativistic
    Electrons in the Exosphere of the
    Earth as a Defense against Ballis-
    tic Missiles" (Christofilos), 23
Operation Argus. *See* Argus
Operation Fishbowl (DOMINIC), 172–
    73; ASAT, 209; Bluegill, 183–84;
    Bluegill Double Prime, 200;
    Bluegill Prime, 197–98; Bluegill
    Triple Prime, 201; Checkmate,
    199, 201; *Effects of Nuclear
    Weapons, The*, 226; EMP, 174; end,
    202; eye damage, 176, 202; John-
    ston Island, 175, 187; JTF-8, 173;
    Kennedy, 186; Kingfish, 199, 202;
    Nike, 188; P2Vs, 182; press, 178;
    protests, 176–79, 191; public per-
    ception, 226–27; purpose of, 174,
    193–94; Starfish, 185; Starfish
    Prime, 188; Thor missile, 173,
    182; Tigerfish, 183; Tightrope,
    199, 202; Urraca, 198; Van Allen
    belt, 176–78, 205–6, 227; X-rays,
    174–75
Operation Nougat, 166
Oppenheimer, J. Robert, 25, 91, 176
Orange: Atomic Energy Commission

report, 148; detonation of, 64;
    EMP, 174; Explorer 4, 70, 75; eye
    damage, 176; Jupiter C, 62; Oper-
    ation Fishbowl, 174, 193; radio
    communications, 194; redstone,
    61; Troitskaya, 162; York, 142
Osmers, Frank, 144
Outer Space Treaty, 218, 227
Owens, Quincy, 87, 100

P

P2Vs, 176, 182
Pacific Proving Grounds, 39, 62
Panofsky, Wolfgang, 45
Papa, 78
Parker (Admiral), 63, 96
Partial Nuclear Test Ban Treaty, 214,
    218
Pauling, Linus, 176
Peterson, Allen Argus symposium,
    140
Physical Review, 28, 32–35
Pickering, William, 20, 44–46, 126
Plowshare, 158
Polaris, 58, 90, 172, 175
"pollywog," 74
Porter, Richard, 110, 137–38, 140, 177
Powers, Francis Gary, 160–61
President's Science Advisory Commit-
    tee (PSAC), 23, 42, 53, 109, 118,
    131, 205–6
*Proceedings of the National Academy of
    Sciences*, 147
Program 437, 209–13
Program 505, 209–10
Project Jason, 77; Argus 2, 90; Argus
    finale, 98; Argus symposium,
    140; Explorer 4, 91, 104–5, 138,
    140; launch, 88, 90
Project Midas, 78, 82, 104–5
Project Pilot, 76
Project Pluto, 157
Project Rover, 157

Project Sanguine, 222–23
Project Sherwood, 36
Project Willow, 153–55
Proposition 1, 117
Proposition 2, 117
protests, 176–79
PSAC. *See* President's Science
   Advisory Committee

Q

Quarles, Donald, 113, 119, 123–28

R

R-7 rocket, 21
radiation belt. *See* Van Allen radiation
   belt
"Radiation Belt May Monitor A-Tests,"
   116
Radiation Laboratory, University of
   California (UCRL), 43
RAND Corporation, 18
Range Tracker, 183
Reagan, Ronald, 212
Redstone missile, 61–62
rockoons, 13
Romeo, 78
Rosenbergs, 16
Ryle, Martin, 177

S

Sagan, Carl, 93
Samoa, Starfish Prime, 190–1
Sandia National Laboratory, X-17a
   missile, 67
"Satellite Observations of Electrons
   Artificially Injected Into the
   Geomagnetic Field" (Allen,
   McIlwain, Ludwig), 139
Schirra, Walter, 199
Schlesinger, Arthur, 171
Schriever, Bernard, 209

Scoville, Herbert, 41–42
Seaborg, Glenn, 171; antimissile mis-
   sile, 173; Nikolayev, 199; Opera-
   tion Fishbowl failures, 186
Sedov, Leonid, 150
Seesaw, 221–22
Selove, William, 135
"shellback," 74
Shelton, Frank: Argus secrecy, 91; at-
   mospheric blasts, 203; Christofi-
   los, 23, 98, 99; Committee on
   Science and Astronautics,
   142–44; congressional testimony,
   148; *New York Times*, 127; *Norton
   Sound*, 67, 69; Shelton, Frank,
   press conference, 123
Shklovskiy, I.S., 93
Simpson, John A., 150
Singer, Fred, 112
Smith, Margaret Chase, 130
Snyder, Hartland S., 33
Snyder, Murray, 133–34, 136
Sorensen, Theodore, 165, 213
South Atlantic Anomaly, 54
Soviet Union atmospheric tests, 198
Soviet Union high altitude tests, 201,
   206, 208
Space Life Sciences Group, 216
Sputnik, 11, 100; 20MHz, 12, 13;
   Christofilos, 21; Eisenhower, 17;
   Norton Sound, 101; radio signal,
   13–14; York, 16
Sputnik 2, 15, 100, 150
Sputnik 3, 50, 100, 150
Starbird, Alfred, 173; Bluegill, 183–84;
   Defense Communications
   Agency, 200; Fishbowl schedule,
   186; Russian captain, 182;
   Starfish Prime, 188; Thor, 200
Starfish, 174, 185–88
Starfish Prime, 188–89; Hawaii, 196;
   ionosphere, 194; objectives
   193–94; protests, 191; radiation,
   195, 199, 205, 207–8; Telstar, 195,

206; Van Allen belts, 196; view of, 189–90

State University of Iowa (SUI), 44; Argus leak, 109; Explorer 1, 44; Explorer, 3, 44; Explorer 4, 46, 61, 65, 75, 103; Explorer 5, 61, 65; Injun 1, 191; JPL meeting, 45; PR, 111; Soviet visit, 150; Teak and Orange, 75

Stevenson, Adlai, 53, 170

Strategic Defense Initiative, 212

Strauss, Lewis, 50, 52, 62

"strong focusing principle," 31–32

"Strong Focusing Synchrotron—A New High Energy Accelerator, The" (Courant, Livingston, Snyder), 33

submarines: Christofilos, 158, 222–223; ELF, 158, 222–223; *Ethan Allen*, 175; Johnston Island, 211; Lukin, 216; New Zealand, 190; Polaris, 172, 175; SLBM, 216; USOS *Seaview*, 166; USS *Nautilus*, 167

Sullivan, Walter: AAAS, 112; Argus story, 119, 120, 121–22; *Assault On the Unknown*, 110, 159; Baldwin, 110; Dryfoos, 119; Fishbowl, 178; Godel, 110; Killian, 115–16, 119; Porter, 110, 113; praise for, 128; Quarles, 124, 126; Starfish Prime, 190; Sulzberger, 119; Tristan Da Cunha, 10, 159–60; Troitskaya, 162; Van Allen, 159, 207; York, 112

Sulzberger, Arthur Hays, 119

synchrotron, 29, 33

T

Task Force 88 (TF 88), 56, 57; and satellite records, 108; blast observation, 98; Project Midas, 78; Rio, 100, 102; vessels of, 70; weather and, 73, 79–80

TASS, Starfish Prime, 191

Teak, 61, 62, 70; Atomic Energy Commission report, 148; blackout, 193; detonation of, 63–64; EMP, 174; eye damage, 176

TEAPOT, 41

Teller, Edward, 33, 53, 117

Telstar 1, 195–96, 206–7

Terrell, Bobby, 100–2

test ban. *See* moratorium

testing, clandestine, 161–62

Thaler, William, press conference, 123

Thiokol XM20 Sergeant, 86

Thor missile, 187, 199; Bluegill, 183Bluegill Double Prime, 200; Bluegill Prime, 197; Checkmate, 201; DOMINIC, 182; Fishbowl, 173, 174, 187; Johnston Island, 187; Kingfish, 202; Program 437, 210–12; Starfish Prime, 188; Starfish, 185–86; Telstar 1, 195

"throw-weight," 15

Tigerfish, 183

Tightrope, 199, 202, 203, 214

Time magazine, Baldwin and Sullivan, 128

Tornados, 195

TRAAC, 195, 199

Treaty Banning Nuclear Tests in the Atmosphere, in Outer Space and Under Water, 214

Trinity, 203

Tristan da Cunha, 9, 10, 55, 75, 159–60

Troitskaya, Valeria I., 162

Tsar Bomba, 169–70

TUMBLER-SNAPPER, 40

20MHz, 12

U

U-2 spy plane, 18–19, 160–61, 200

UCRL, 43. *See also* Lawrence Livermore National Laboratory

United States Atmospheric Nuclear

Weapons Tests/Nuclear Test Personnel Review, Argus report, 99
UPSHOT-KNOTHOLE, 40
Urraca, 174, 176, 198
USOS *Seaview*, 166
USS *Albemarle*, 57–58; Argus 1, 88, 89; Argus 2, 90; Argus 3, 96–97; Argus operation role, 70, 75, 78; coordination with, 82
USS *Glacier*, 13
USS *Hammerberg*, 96
USS *Nautilus*, 167
USS *Norton Sound*: Arctic operation cover, 68; Argus, 56–58, 69Argus 3, 96, 97; Crossing the Line, 74; Deacon sounding rockets, 82; DOMINIC, 176; film badges, 81; Horn, 74; launch, 85–87; nuclear warheads, 67; radiation, 81–82; Rio, 100; second launch, 90; Shelton, 67; "Snortin' Norton," 66; Sputnik 1, 101; *Tarawa*, 75; *Times*, 122; voyage of, 75; X-17a, 66, 80, 83
USS *Princeton*, 187, 188
USS *Tarawa*, 70, 73–74, 78, 80, 92, 100
USS *Warrington*, 70, 74

V

Van Allen, James: AAAS, 112, 206–7; Argus aftermath, 158; Argus effect, 89, 103; Argus planning, 46; Argus secrecy and IGY, 107–8; Argus Shell, 103; background electrons, 41; Explorer 1, 20; Explorer 4, 61, 65, 103, 111; Explorer 5, 61, 65; federal agent, 149; Injun 1, 191, 195; Jet Propulsion Laboratory meeting, 45; Kennedy committee, 178; legacy, 219–21; Livermore conference, 117–18; Mariner spacecraft, 219; military, 47; NAS symposium, 138–40;

New York Times, 122; Operation Fishbowl and radiation belt, 177–79, 199; Pioneer 10 & 11, 219; press conference, 126; PSAC, 206–7; radiation belt, 43–44; Soviet Union, 147–50; space probe missions, 219; Sputnik, 13; Starfish Prime radiation, 205–6, 208; Sullivan, 159, 207; Van Allen belt and Starfish Prime, 196–97. *See also* Van Allen radiation belts
Van Allen radiation belts, 44, 92; Argus, 139; Explorer 3, 21; Injun 1, 195; *Izvestiya*, 93; Operation Fishbowl, 177–79, 199; Ryle, 177; Starfish, 196; Starfish Prime, 196, 219; *Voyage to the Bottom of the Sea*, 166
Van de Graaff generators, 31
Vanguard, 11–15, 76–77; 108MHz, 13; launch, 17, 19
Vatican, 170
Veksler, Vladimir, 29
Vernov, Sergei, 150
Voice of America, 140
von Braun, Wernher, 11–13, 17, 20, 43–44
Voyage to the Bottom of the Sea, 166, 167, 196

W

W–25 warheads, 59, 67, 87
Wall Street Journal, 178
Walt, Martin, 88, 90, 91
Washington Post: Argus and radio, 148; atomic experiments in outer space, 141; Christofilos, 127; Starfish Prime radiation, 206
Washington Star, 129, 134
Weinberger, Sharon, 14, 221–22
Weisskopf, Victor, 134
Welch, Jasper, 140
Welch, William, 140

Weldon, Curt, 215
Wellerstein, Alex, 221
Wellington Café, 26
Wertheim, Bob, 67
West Germany, 170
Whiskey, 78
Whitaker, William, 140
white horse, 223
White House report, Argus, 134, 136
Willow-Argus, 104, 153
Winder missile. See X-17a missile, 66
Wolf, Leonard, 144

X

X-17a missile: design, 58–59, 66, 90;
    drills, 65, 69; HARDTACK sec-
    ond phase, 95; *Norton Sound*, 56,
    68; platform, 85; preparation, 83;
    test firing, 66; trajectory, 80
X-rays, 174–75, 185, 212
XM-33 rocket, 201

York, Herbert F., 16; Argus secrecy
    and IGY, 108, 117, 133, 138, 148;
    Argus, 23, 44; ARPA, 23; back-
    ground of electrons, 41;
    Christofilos, 22, 23, 36–37; cli-
    mate science, 226; Committee
    on Science and Astronautics,
    142–45, 148; Eisenhower, 53;
    Gough Island, 54; *New York Times*
    story, 123; press conference, 123,
    125; PSAC, 42; space tests as
    anomaly, 226; Sullivan, 112–13;
    Van Allen, 44; White House
    report, 133–34

Y

Yucca, 64

Z

Zuckert, Eugene, 209